D0849729

Asian and African
Systems of Slavery

Asian and African
Systems of Slavery

edited by

JAMES L. WATSON

University of California Press
Berkeley and Los Angeles

University of California Press
Berkeley and Los Angeles, California

Library of Congress Cataloguing in Publication Data
Main entry under title:
Asian and African systems of slavery.

Six of the eleven essays included were presented as
papers at a seminar held at the University of London,
School of Oriental and African Studies in 1976.
Includes index.
1. Slavery—Economic aspects—Addresses, essays,
lectures. 2. Slavery—Economic aspects—Africa—Addresses, essays, lectures. 3. Slavery—Economic
aspects—Asia—Addresses, essays, lectures. I. Watson,
James L. II. London. University. School of Oriental
and African Studies.

HT891.A74 1980   301.44′93′095   79-19728
ISBN 0-520-04031-7

Printed in Great Britain

Contents

Contents

Editor's Preface

This volume originated as an Intercollegiate Anthropology Seminar held at the University of London (School of Oriental and African Studies) in 1976. The theme of that seminar, 'The Economics of Slavery', is thus reflected in the essays that follow. The papers by Bloch, Burnham, Goody, Morris, Shepherd, and Watson were presented at the original seminar; the other contributors joined the project at a later date.

The editor wishes to thank various colleagues for the help and encouragement they offered during the preparation of the manuscript: Lionel Caplan, Igor Kopytoff, John Middleton, David Parkin, Richard Rathbone, Andrew Turton, and Rubie Watson. All have discussed problems of slavery and exploitation with me but they are not, of course, responsible in any way for the views put forth in the Introduction. I would also like to thank Kate Owen of the Contemporary China Institute, University of London, for her editorial assistance.

J. L. Watson
S.O.A.S., London

1

Introduction

Slavery as an Institution: Open and Closed Systems

JAMES L. WATSON

Until recently anthropologists have not shown a great deal of interest in slavery as an institution. This is not to say that the subject has been ignored but, in comparison to other problems of social stratification (e.g., caste hierarchies and ethnic divisions), slavery has rarely been subjected to the painstaking and exhaustive analyses for which anthropologists are justly famous. The relative neglect of this topic seems to be ending, however, as more and more anthropologists return to their field notes after having read the extremely challenging work of Stanley Elkins, Moses Finley, Eugene Genovese, and a host of others who deal with the social history of slavery. The specialist now faces a virtual tidal wave of new literature on the economics of Black slavery in the Southern United States, following the publication of Fogel and Engerman's *Time on the Cross* (1974). Their book touched off a debate that has had a profound impact on American intellectual life. At the same time anthropologists on both sides of the Atlantic have been actively involved in a movement to rescue the writings of Karl Marx from the rigid orthodoxy of state ideologies. In Britain this has taken shape as a neomarxian challenge to 'traditional' social anthropology (see e.g., Bloch 1975; Godelier 1977; and the London journal *Critique of Anthropology*, first published in 1974). One of the primary aims of the emerging neomarxian school has been the delineation and analysis of various 'modes of production', including a slave-based mode

(Hindess and Hirst 1975:125ff; Meillassoux 1975, 1978; see also Bloch's essay in this book).

The present volume arose in response to these intellectual cross-currents. All of the papers are concerned, in one way or another, with economic aspects of slavery. Many are directly inspired by the recent work on American slavery and attempt to deal with the problem of slave 'productivity': did slaves produce more than they consumed and, if not, what were the economic implications? Other essays focus on the internal organisation of the slave trade itself and on the overall market in human beings, including price structures. The organisation of slave labour and the economic effects of manumission are also discussed.

Before proceeding, I would like to stress that the essays in this volume, save one, are concerned with *indigenous* systems of slavery. The authors are, of course, careful to explore interconnections with the world-wide traffic in slaves whenever appropriate. The primary focus, however, is on the social organisation of slavery within specific Asian or African societies. The only exception is Benedict's study of slavery and indenture in the Indian Ocean; here Asians and Africans were brought together on previously uninhabited islands to labour on European-owned plantations. This essay describes the final link in a complex chain of slavery, the origin points of which can be traced to the 'indigenous' markets in Africa and Asia. Benedict's work also represents a new approach to the age-old problem of slavery and capitalism. Most studies of this type focus on the Atlantic shores and take New World plantation systems as the end products of the African slave trade. The chapters by Benedict, Bloch, and Shepherd are complementary; together they constitute a general picture of slavery in the Indian Ocean.

Definitions of Slavery

It will soon become obvious to the reader of this book that anthropologists are uncharacteristically diffident when they write about the institution of slavery. Only a few of the contributors even attempt a definition; most are content to get on with the task at hand and assume that they are writing for an audience of sensible people who know full well what slavery entails. Were this not the case the present volume, and the University of London seminar that preceded it, would have disintegrated into a dry, lifeless exercise in taxonomy. The general reluctance to define slavery is taken to an extreme in an important new book edited by Miers and Kopytoff (1977). In order to demonstrate their uneasiness about using the term slavery in an African context the word itself is set off by inverted commas whenever it appears in their long introduction. Given the difficulties involved in translating a bewildering variety of terms from a dozen or more African languages, their decision is understandable. The English term 'slave' does conjure up a range of historical associations that clearly do not apply when discussing (some) forms of servitude in Africa. But this is not in itself a valid reason for abandoning the term. The problem would be made even worse if anthropologists used only native terms whenever they wrote about exploitation and domination. To deny that slavery exists as a recognisable institution in a great many societies is, it seems to me, to treat this particular social phenomenon with a reverence that is altogether inappropriate for a discipline that has produced a whole library of comparative studies based on such concepts as 'adoption' or 'lineage'.

There seems little doubt that the special relationship of domination (i.e. slavery) described in the essays that follow can be discussed and compared cross-culturally. This does not imply that slavery as an institution has identical characteristics in all societies, nor that it only exists as an abstract ideal somehow divorced from social reality (cf., Hindess and Hirst 1975:125ff). The relationship characterised by slavery is by no means universal but it is 'special' in the sense that, wherever and whenever it appears, slavery *is* distinguishable from other forms of exploitation in the same society.

There have been several attempts to define slavery but none has gained widespread acceptance in anthropological circles. The reason, perhaps, is that most of these definitions focus on one aspect of slavery (outsider status, acquisition as property, etc.) and underplay other general features. Slavery, as I shall argue below, is a complex social institution; it cannot be defined or pigeon-holed with reference to a single attribute. What follows, then, is a general discussion of slavery as an institution. Out of this a definition, of sorts, emerges but it is offered more as a provocation than a pronouncement.

A vast literature exists on various forms of slavery, so it should not be surprising that definitions of the institution are correspondingly diverse. However, two general defining criteria emerge from these discussions: one is the *property* aspect of slavery and the other is the *marginal status* of slaves. Few who have written on this subject fail to point out that slaves are acquired as chattels either by capture or purchase and that, henceforth, they are owned by specific individuals or groups (see e.g., Davis 1966:31; Elkins 1959:50; Finley 1968:307; Hindess and Hirst 1975:110; Mendelsohn 1949:34; Nieboer 1910:5; Wilbur 1943:62—3). Perhaps the boldest expression of the equation between slaves and property is found in the work of Tuden and Plotnicov: 'We propose defining slavery as the legal institutionalization of persons as property' (1970:11—12). Others who have written on this subject are more cautious or, depending on one's view, less forthright. Nonetheless, it is the property aspect that most observers single out when they distinguish slavery from other forms of servitude, including serfdom and debt bondage (see e.g., Finley 1968:307; Lasker 1950:70; Leach 1967:13).

Recently, however, doubts have been raised about the suitability of defining slaves as property, especially in parts of Africa where 'rights-in-persons' are not easily disentangled from outright ownership. The argument is a familiar one to those who know the African literature: 'rights-in-persons' (i.e., rights over labour, sexuality, procreation, etc.) exist in all societies but in Africa these rights are explicitly recognised and defined in customary law. Furthermore they are subject to complex transactions, such as those associated with marriage payments (see e.g., Radcliffe-Brown 1952:36–48). Kopytoff and Miers argue that in many African societies the individual must be seen not only as a member of the kin group but also as part of that group's corporate property.

'African lineages "own" their members and these members constitute lineage wealth' (1977:11). They continue (1977:12):

> Neither the criterion of property nor that of salability can be useful, then, in separating 'slavery' from simple 'kinship' in African societies, in which rights in wives, children, and kin-group members are usually acquired through transactions involving material transfers and in which kin groups 'own' and may dispose of their blood members in ways that Westerners consider appropriate to 'property'.

Although their critique is forceful and convincing, Kopytoff and Miers do not themselves offer a coherent definition of slavery. Instead they fall back on another time-honoured device for dealing with the ambiguities of servile relationships—slaves are categorised as outsiders or marginal people: 'slaves [in Africa] have one thing in common: all are strangers in a new setting' (*Ibid.* 15). They then proceed to outline a 'slavery-to-kinship continuum' along which slaves pass as they are absorbed into new kinship groups (p. 24). Like so many before them, therefore, Kopytoff and Miers see African slavery as a *process* and not a status. They do not deny that slavery involves the capture and sale of human beings; nor do they underplay the exploitative dimension of slavery. But, at base, slavery is for them an institution for the incorporation of outsiders into the dominant society. For Kopytoff and Miers, African slavery has to be understood, and discussed, in the same context as marriage and adoption. Few can deny that the argument works—for most parts of Africa. However, as the essays in this volume make clear, the 'slavery-to-kinship continuum' does not apply in many Asian societies and, hence, for these systems it is not at all helpful to view slavery as a mode of incorporation. But before we consider the Asian systems, more needs to be said about attempts to define slaves as outsiders.

In any discussion of slavery as an institution the work of M. I. Finley necessarily looms large. His article in the *International Encyclopedia of the Social Sciences* is widely regarded as the definitive statement on the subject; in it he stresses that 'the property element remains essential' in

distinguishing slaves from other servile dependents such as
serfs and peons (1968:307). A close reading of Finley's work
reveals a subtle change of emphasis over time. Writing for the
Times Literary Supplement in 1976, for instance, Finley no
longer argues that the property element is primary. Although
his later article deals with many aspects of slavery (and,
incidentally, is one of the most perceptive papers in the
entire literature on servitude), Finley maintains that: 'The
slave, in sum, was always an outsider in the fullest sense of
that term, and that distinguishes slaves as a class from all
other forms of involuntary labour' (1976:819). The fact that
slaves are outside society and do not have divided loyalties
explains why, in the ancient world and in African state systems, they were often entrusted with positions of considerable power and authority (Finley 1959:147); Nadel 1942;
Smith 1960).

For some anthropologists the essential kinlessness of slaves
becomes the main defining characteristic of slavery as an
institution. Leach (1967:23—4) argues that it is precisely this
—the absence of kinship between slave and master—that
distinguishes 'chattel slavery' from other forms of servitude
(see also Davis 1966:31; Mendelsohn 1949:34; Watson 1976:
368–9). Bohannon (1963:180) goes even further: '[Servile
relationships] are not merely *non*kinship, as are relationships
based on contract or those established by rank. They are,
rather, actively antikinship in that a slave can have no kinsmen and is connected with kinship groups by nonkinship
criteria.'

Thus we come full circle. Kopytoff and Miers conceive of
slaves as, essentially, outsiders who are in the process of being
incorporated as kinsmen while Leach and Bohannon maintain that slaves, by their very nature, remain outside the
dominant kinship system. This, in a nutshell, is the main
reason why there is so much confusion in the field of comparative slavery studies. It also helps explain why many
Africanists hesitate even to use the term 'slave' in their
writing. There are, in fact, two major types—or modes
—of slavery that correspond roughly to the open or closed
nature of kinship systems. Kopytoff and Miers are talking

about one mode of slavery that happens to correspond with most indigenous African systems. Leach, on the other hand, clearly has in mind another type of slavery that one encounters more often in societies where the dominant kinship groups are exclusive rather than inclusive (e.g., India and China). I hesitate to label these two modes of slavery 'African' and 'Asian' because there are open-ended slave systems in Asia (see chapters 10 and 11 on Thailand and Sarawak) and closed systems in Africa (chapter 5 on Madagascar). Furthermore the Asian/African dichotomy loses its heuristic value when one is forced to deal with American slavery, perhaps the most closed and caste-like of any system known (Elkins 1959; Genovese 1975). Nevertheless, the open mode of slavery outlined by Kopytoff and Miers simply does not work in many parts of Asia and the closed mode discussed by Bohannon does not have any real meaning in a society such as the one described by Fortes (1949).

Definitions of slavery that put primary emphasis on the outsider status of slaves are not very useful, particularly if one's aims are comparative. One is forced to look elsewhere for more universalistic criteria. In reviewing the literature on slavery I have found myself returning, again and again, to the seminal work of H. J. Nieboer. His largely forgotten survey, *Slavery as an Industrial System: Ethnological Researches* (1910), contains what is still, in my opinion, one of the most useful definitions of the institution available anywhere: 'A slave . . . is the property of another, politically and socially [he is] at a lower level than the mass of people, and [he performs] compulsory labour' (1910:5). Nieboer's emphasis on compulsory labour, in conjunction with chattel status, avoids the pitfalls that others have encountered in defining slaves as outsiders. Save for the work of Davis (1966:31) and Finley (1976:819), this concern for coercion and forced labour is curiously absent from much of the recent literature on slavery. It stems, perhaps, from the assumption that 'coercion' automatically implies physical punishment and harassment. However, as Finley (1976) and Genovese (1975) demonstrate in their analyses of slave societies, the relationship between slave and master is far more complex than it might appear.

Physical abuse is only one form of coercion prevalent in slave-based economies; in order to ensure a reasonably contented, and productive, work force the master classes usually had to devise more subtle means of control. This often involved incentives and 'liberties', such as the freedom to travel or to contract one's own marriage, that one does not ordinarily associate with systems of slavery (see e.g., Fogel and Engerman 1974; Gutman 1976).

The argument above is particularly relevant in those societies where slaves are primary producers or, more precisely, instruments of production. Several of the essays in this book, however, deal with systems in which slaves often consumed more than they produced and were maintained largely as status symbols (see chapters 4, 7, 9 and 10). Even in these societies the relationship between slave and master—not being based on the extraction of productive labour in the first place—is nonetheless heavily weighted in favour of the owners. By supporting slaves who might be less productive than hired workers the masters are, in effect, displaying their wealth for all to see. The coercive element is no less real in this form of slavery than it is in any 'productive' system; even slaves who are little more than status symbols are expected to perform some type of service, if only to stand in hallways. The exhibition of idleness may be the slave's only real duty but this has to be extracted like any other service. More will be said about 'luxury' versus 'productive' slavery later in this essay.

Having criticised others who are bold enough to define slavery it is only fair that I should expose myself to the same treatment. I offer the following set of guidelines for a definition of the term 'slave' that can be applied cross-culturally, irrespective of local variation and historical era: 'Slaves' are acquired by purchase or capture, their labour is extracted through coercion and, as long as they remain slaves, they are never accepted into the kinship group of the master. 'Slavery' is thus the institutionalisation of these relationships between slave and owner.

Building on the work of Nieboer and Finley, I would argue that the property aspect of slavery must be accepted as primary—this is what distinguishes slavery from all other forms of dependency and involuntary labour. Similarly, the coercive dimension of slavery must never be underplayed; all slaves are, in the final analysis, subject to the will of their owners. When this control begins to break down it is doubtful that the relationship can still be described as one based on slavery. And finally it seems obvious that a true slave cannot be absorbed into the kinship group of the master, even as an inferior member, at the time of purchase. My only difference with those who accept the 'slavery-to-kinship continuum' as an adequate representation of the slave's position in society is that it obscures, rather than clarifies, the relationship between slavery and kinship. A slave stops being a slave, I would argue, precisely at the moment when he or she begins to play a role in the dominant kinship system. The continuum model assumes that all, or at least most, slaves will eventually emerge at the other end—as recognised kin.

There are, as I have noted above, two basic modes of slavery: open-ended and closed. I am not suggesting that the African systems surveyed by Kopytoff and Miers should be dismissed as 'weaker' versions of slavery by virtue of their openness. According to the guidelines outlined above, the eventual fate of the person who enters society as a slave is not relevant when one is constructing a definition of slavery as an institution. Both open and closed modes are equally to be regarded as systems of slavery, so long as they match the criteria established for the use of that term. It is less than helpful, however, to conceive of slavery as an institution for the incorporation of outsiders.

Open and Closed Modes of Slavery

In this book the essays by Caplan (Nepal), Levine (Tibetan-speaking Nyinba), and Watson (China) illustrate the closed nature of slavery that prevailed in many Asian societies. It would have been inconceivable for a slave to be accepted into the kinship systems of their owners; instead they were maintained as separate ethnic groups that reproduced themselves either by natural processes or by the constant recruitment (i.e., purchase) of new slaves from the 'free' sector of society. The barriers that kept these Asian slaves from entering, or re-entering, the dominant society were often formidable. Far from being absorbed, these dependents were kept at arm's length by virtue of the stigma attaching to the status of slave. Among the Southern Chinese and the Nyinba, for instance, slaves were thought to be polluting and so were not allowed to participate in certain activities. Caplan (chapter 7) presents an interesting variation on this theme: in India and Nepal slaves were used by the wealthy primarily as household servants and, as such, they could not be recruited from the lower, polluting castes. This meant that slaves had to be protected from some forms of labour (lest they pollute their masters) and were given special privileges. Nevertheless, the South Asian system of slavery, as Caplan describes it, was every bit as closed as the Chinese or the Nyinba systems. These servant slaves were never, under any circumstances, absorbed into their masters' kinship groups. In most parts of Asia the only way for a male slave to change his status was through manumission, but even this did not entail absorption: it was more a matter of 'up and out' rather than 'up and in' as in Africa.[1]

One does not have to delve very deeply into the African literature to find support for the open model of slavery. Tuden, for instance, found that among the Ila of Central Africa 'no clear social differentiation existed between slaves and free' (1970:31). Fortes, in his classic study of the Tallensi, describes how male slaves were given the same rights as illegitimate sons and were eventually incorporated into the lineage (1949:25–6). The essays in *Slavery in Africa* (Miers and Kopytoff 1977) provide a host of examples that illustrate the open mode of slavery. The editors of that volume explain the remarkable openness of these African systems as a logical extension of the institutionalised need for more people: 'African institutions—including households, kin groups large and small, offices, and whole societies—have been strikingly absorptive of outsiders' (1977:61). This has created 'a particular kind of consumer society—one in which social groups have a driving urge to take in new persons' (*Ibid.* 64).

There are, of course, exceptions to this general model of open systems in Africa. Slaves among the Ibo in Nigeria were never absorbed into the dominant society and the stigma of slavery has not disappeared (Tuden and Plotnicov 1970:13). And, in this volume, Bloch's essay explores two relatively closed systems of slavery in Madagascar (chapter 5). The same kind of reservations about the universal applicability of the closed model when discussing slavery in Asia might be raised as well. It is perhaps ironic that one of the most 'open' systems of slavery recorded anywhere in the literature should be found in Sarawak, among the Melanau (see chapter 11). Morris shows how captive slaves are gradually absorbed into Melanau society by a fascinating process that involves working oneself up through a system of ranks; manumission and absorption are thus built into the very fabric of that society.

Bearing in mind that African and Asian societies do not automatically correspond to the general models of open and closed slavery, it is nonetheless instructive to take the comparison one step further. The differences between the dominant modes of slavery that emerged in these two continents correspond to different concepts of property. Here I should like to acknowledge the work of Jack Goody whose *Technology, Tradition, and the State in Africa* (1971) provided the stimulus for the argument that follows. Goody shows how land, being in relatively abundant supply, was not the primary source of wealth and power in Africa. In contrast to feudal Europe, therefore, the key to power in pre-colonial Africa 'lay in control over women and slaves, and guns and horses, rather than goods and land' (1971:32). African slavery, he maintains, is closely related to warfare and raiding; captives were, in fact, the main source of booty and, not surprisingly, they were also one of the leading items of internal trade (1971:36,72; see also his essay in this book).

The political economy in most parts of pre-modern Asia was strikingly different. Land *was* the primary source of wealth in societies like China and India—a fact reflected in the dominant role that landlordism plays in the Asian literature. In contrast, the only significant form of landlordism to

emerge on the African continent (exclusive of the Mediterranean fringe) was in Ethiopia (Goody 1971:30). It is possible
to read the history of entire civilisations in Asia as a struggle
for land and, hence, control over land meant automatic
control over people. Rather than being 'absorptive', therefore, the institutions, kin groups, and communities of Asian
societies were more exclusive—the problem was to keep
people out. A comparison between the lineage systems that
emerged in Africa and in South China illustrates this fundamental difference: the classic African patrilineages, as
described by Fortes (1949) and a host of others, recruited
new members from outside the society and incorporated
slaves after suitable periods of service. The picture is so
radically different in South China that one begins to wonder if we are dealing with social institutions, namely 'patrilineages', that are even remotely comparable (but this is
another problem, best taken up elsewhere). For instance, the
only way for an outsider to be incorporated into an elite
Chinese lineage is by adoption, and this can only be arranged
for infants at great personal expense to the adopting father.
Slaves, hired hands, sons-in-law, and other non-agnates are
never accepted as full, or even partial, lineage members.
The reason, of course, is that Chinese lineages are landowning corporations and the living members are shareholders
in the ancestral estates (usually rice paddies). Not surprisingly, these shareholders do everything in their power
to restrict access to the lineage's corporate resources.

Returning to the question of slavery, it can be argued that
the open mode predominated in Africa where land was
plentiful and control over people was the main avenue to
wealth and power. The closed mode, prevalent in Asia, is
clearly a reflection of the high premium placed on land
which, in turn, affects attitudes towards outsiders. This
dichotomy between open and closed modes of slavery is, of
course, based on ideal types and I do not pretend that it fits
all known cases. Yet the argument does help to explain why
one of the most open systems of slavery emerged in Southeast
Asia while certain transformations in the local economy had
quite opposite effects along Africa's eastern shore (see chapters

5 and 11). The cases of Sarawak (where land was plentiful and labour was scarce) and Madagascar (where the emergence of the Merina state brought new relationships between land and people) thus give added support to the general model outlined above—they do not contradict it.

Markets, Prices, and Reproduction

The market factors that prevailed in open and closed systems of slavery also seem to have varied considerably. In most parts of Africa there was a supplier's market that corresponded to the intense demand for extra people. Because women were particularly desirable as reproducers of both the slave and the free population, it has been suggested that captive males were released for the trans-Atlantic trade[2] while more women were retained internally (Kopytoff and Miers 1977:72). Goody argues in chapter 2 that, in the indigenous African markets, 'the price of women slaves was almost always higher than that of men' (p. 37).

In China, a society for which we have comparable data (see chapter 9), the market was quite different from that outlined for Africa. Here the demand for slaves was dampened somewhat by the high cost of maintenance and by the fact that they were rarely used as primary producers. A buyer's market thus prevailed in most parts of China, but one with an interesting twist. Most slaves entered the market as children who were sold by destitute parents, especially during bad harvest years. Male children were less likely to be sold because sons, and not daughters, assumed the burden of support for ageing parents in pre-Revolution China. Hence there was always a glut of female children on the market and a (relative) shortage of 'healthy and whole' males. A complicating factor was that boys thus purchased could be used as slaves or as heirs. But once this decision was made by the buyer there was no possibility of change in later life—Chinese slavery was closed. In a curious reversal of the African pattern, therefore, males rather than females were more highly valued as reproducers (heirs) in the internal Chinese market. Being of more value, an infant male would usually cost three to four times as much as a healthy ten-year-old girl. Only the very wealthy could afford to buy a male child, provide for his maintenance, and *not* convert him into an heir.

The Chinese slaves mentioned above were, in the final analysis, luxuries that consumed more than they produced. There are many other cases of 'luxury slavery' on record, both in open and closed systems (see e.g., chapters 4 and 10). In the ancient world, as Hopkins notes: 'Slavery ceased to be a major method of procuring wealth, while it long survived as a method of displaying it' (1967:167). The problem here is to determine exactly what is meant by 'production' (cf. Meillassoux 1978). Few anthropologists, or classicists (Finley 1976:621), have access to the kinds of data that would satisfy economic historians, especially the new breed of cliometricians who work on American slavery. It is perhaps relevant to note that the most ambitious attempt to measure the efficiency and profitability of slavery in the Old South, namely Fogel and Engerman's *Time on the Cross* (1974), has met with a storm of criticism—primarily over interpretations of data (see e.g., David 1976; Gutman 1975; Haskell 1975; Walton 1975).

Social anthropologists, both Marxist and non-Marxist, would no doubt make the point that a slave's role in the mode of production has to be understood in the broadest possible terms. Some forms of slavery may not be 'productive' in the strict sense used by economists but, from the perspective of the owners, investments in 'luxury slaves' may be absolutely essential as a symbol of wealth and power. They are, as Turton so aptly puts it in his essay on Thai slavery (chapter 10), crucial 'for the reproduction of [the aristocratic] class, its mode of consumption and prestige production' (p. 292). Slavery of this type cannot be directly compared to the capitalist systems described by Benedict (chapter 6); in the latter case, slavery was the dominant feature of the mode of production, while in the former, slavery had little to do with the creation of surplus.

The essays that follow are offered in the spirit of inter-disciplinary exchange and debate. The contributors may all be social anthropologists but we have not written specifically for an anthropological audience. This volume would never have been possible without the stimulation offered by the historical literature on slavery. We can only hope that the historians, in turn, will find our work to be of some value in their own efforts to understand the past.

Slavery in Time and Space

JACK GOODY

Any account of slavery in a comparative, or indeed particular, setting ought to begin with the setting of some boundaries. This is not a task that I can pursue in a short paper, but I would offer two general comments. Firstly one should see slavery (and here as elsewhere I am indebted to the work of M. I. Finley) as the most servile of the set of dependent statuses, whose general features are best understood in terms of a grid that analyses the characteristics of the roles of pawn, servant, serf, client, subject, etc. Secondly we must distinguish between the label 'slave' (or its local equivalent) as a statement of origin and as a statement about present status. A slave in the full sense has a master; slavery involves a specific social relationship (often a relationship of production), whether it is 'household' or 'chattel' slavery, to use a distinction of limited utility. We can best understand the problem if we think of the same double meaning that occurs in our use of labels for nationality or classes; sometimes we refer to origin, sometimes to present position, though less confusion arises when we know the context.

In particular I will be concerned with the nature of slavery in Africa, which has recently been discussed in the context of attempts to define an African mode of production. My own view is that i. the institution of slavery has been more prevalent than is commonly supposed (and by prevalent I include considerations of numerical predominance and centrality to the socio-economic system); ii. terms like 'dominance' and 'basis' are in general too vague to distinguish 'a slave mode of

production' as such; iii. slavery as an institution cannot usefully be analysed separately from the means of production
which slaves employ, nor the 'class' system that employs
them.

This position runs counter to the theme of Althusserian
social science taken up in extreme form by Hindess and Hirst
when they proclaim the universal priority 'of the social relations of production' over the 'forces of production'. But in
rural economy slavery has different implications in the
simpler agricultural systems of Africa than in the more
advanced ones of the Eurasian continent, under industrial
than under craft production. To make such an assertion is
viewed by some Althusserians as 'technological determinism'
or 'vulgar Marxism'. However the obverse position is an
equally 'vulgar' form of 'idealism', which can be maintained
only by those who have little concern with the interplay of
'theory' and 'research' and who view 'theory' as a body of
ready-made constructs insulated from the realm of empirical
systems. Such a binary approach to social theory and research
has a long tradition in the decontextualised discussion of
philosophers. It has little relevance to the dialectical process
involved in the study of human society.

I cannot avoid referring in a cursory way to the central
distinction made by many writers on the subject between
slavery as an institution and slavery as a mode of production.

The slave 'mode of production' is said to exist when slave
labour forms 'the basis of production' (Hindess and Hirst
1975:109), or to be the dominant form. Slavery as an institution occurs much more widely, whenever there is a legal or
jural form of slave status (or property). Many writers have
held the view that true slavery in its fullest form is found only
in Greece (except Sparta), Rome, and the American South
and the adjacent lands and islands of the Caribbean; these
are the societies that M. I. Finley would distinguish as
'genuine slave states' (the equivalent of the slave mode of
production). Yet he would make a further distinction, and
speak of the early states of the Ancient Near East (including
Egypt), India and China as being 'slave-owning societies'
once again distinguishing slavery in these complex socio-

political systems (what Nieboer referred to as the 'industrial system' of slavery) from the occurrence of slavery as an institution among a much wider range of societies (1968:308).

I want briefly and broadly to review the evidence on the occurrence of slavery in time and space as well as the extent or intensity of its occurrence, and to discuss the utility and relevance of these distinctions in the comparative study of systems of production and reproduction.

References to slavery come very early indeed, right at the beginning of written history. The earliest known legal documents concern not the sale of land, houses, animals, boats, and such like, but the sale of slaves (Oppenheim 1964:282). The first written reference to slavery appears in the Ur-Nammu tablet, which is the first legal code of which we have any knowledge (Kramer 1966:47ff.); it deals with that perpetual problem of slavery, a problem that was the subject of a host of magical acts and spells among the Arabs of North Africa (Doutté 1909), of legal procedures in the South of the United States,[1] and of international understandings between the Gonja and Ashanti kingdoms of West Africa,[2] that is, the problem of the escaping slave. Again, the earliest known inventories of positions (or role categories) within a particular society, contained in those amazing lexical lists analysed by Landsberger, and employed for teaching scribes intellectually as well as technically, include the terms for both male and female slaves (1955:pt.1; 1969:4).

The situation in Mesopotamia is interesting from a number of points of view. Not only does the institution of slavery appear in very early documents, but even at this early stage it shows many of the characteristics of later slavery. The sale of slaves is known from 2300 B.C. and the most numerous references are to captive foreigners. The leaders of the enemy were not spared; it was the followers, usually of more distant enemies rather than those from adjacent city states, who were taken alive. They were kept in the prisoners' compound, let out for labour on the temple estates and provided with regular rations. They even worked for market production.

House-born slaves, i.e. second-generation slaves, had a higher status than bought slaves; indeed it is clear that there was a good deal of movement out of the slave role, even though a mobile individual might still remain within a category designating slave origin. In Babylonian times, a slave concubine should be set free after her owner's death; the children could be adopted by the master, in which case they shared in the inheritance. The children of a free woman and a slave were free and had rights to inherit (Laws of Hammurabi, paras 146–7, 170–4, see Driver and Miles 1952).

Hence, quite apart from the apparent changes in status that took place between the first and second generation, any marriage across the slave-free boundary meant a diminution in the strength of forced labour: not of the total labour force, but of those who could be utilised for tasks designated as servile. In Mesopotamia, slaves worked not only in agriculture but also as artisans, for example, as weavers and bakers, alongside free men and women. As later in Solomon's copper mines, mining was often carried out by slaves; they also engaged in construction projects and were even recruited for military service, as in the case of Joseph in Pharoanic Egypt, whose story reminds us of the heights to which such men might climb.

The point to note here is that, right at the beginning of the historical record, certain features associated with, for example, white slaves in the eighteenth-century Maghreb (Bennett 1960) or black and white slaves in nineteenth-century Egypt (Baer 1967) and Turkey, were already present. Moreover, the roles played by slaves were many. This diversity emerges in the very early documents, but it is even clearer in later texts such as those from the ancient town of Mari in northern Mesopotamia. Of the documents found in the royal archives in Mari (c. 1800 B.C.) the majority were economic; they include 'a list of nearly 1000 male and female captives from the Harran-Nahor region, engaged in manufacturing clothes for the palace' (Malamat 1971:8). Again there is the evidence of the wine lists, that is to say, daily schedules for the issue of wine to the king's household found in the Assyrian capital of Nimrud and dating from the eighth century B.C. (Kinnier Wilson 1972). Apart from large harems, which presumably consisted of slave concubines, we find court eunuchs (undoubtedly slaves), both those of the inner and those of the outer court, the former concerned with the king's private apartments, the latter with the council chamber, and who also appear as courtiers, army officers and as 'eunuch governors'. One of the functions of the eunuchs, a function so frequently handed down to those incapable of assuming the succession by those in danger from the continuity of their peers, was the protection of the king and his family (1972:47). Some indeed were involved, at a later date, in temple administration, possibly, Kinnier Wilson suggests, as spies of the king in the camp of a powerful rival (1972:48).

The proportion of slaves in Mesopotamia has been the subject of considerable dispute, partly because of the problems of identifying and translating the set of concepts centring upon servility. The Soviet historian, Struwe, regards Egypt and Mesopotamia as slave societies; 'slaves' were those on ration lists who possessed no instruments of production, a category to which some 35 per cent of the population were held to belong. Another Soviet historian, Diakonof, reckons that in the Old Akkadian period (c. 2300 B.C.) slaves formed only 13 per cent of a work force of 35,000 and became rarer towards the end of the second millennium, though they increased later on. These fluctuations depended upon changes in the economy and in other relations of production, e.g. the dominance of guilds of free artisans. Anglo-American historians tend to accept a lower level of slavery, and hence the idea of a society depending less on the production of slaves than Greece and Rome.

Whatever the proportion, the roles of slaves were many and were confined neither to household functions nor to the economy, in the narrow sense normally used by the economists of industrial societies. This range of activity is seen in the employment of not only males, but of neutered males, eunuchs, as well as in the roles of women who played a part not only in reproduction (and sex) but also in production, even in manufacturing production. Among the earliest Proto-literate tablets, the sign for 'slave girl' begins to appear before that for slave, a word deriving from the expression for a 'foreign country'. It is also significant that male slaves appear not only later but 'in far smaller numbers than do female ones' (Adams 1966:97). Adams suggests that 'possibly the means for the retention and effective employment of male captives had not yet been worked out, so that they were generally killed' (p. 97).

The suggestions seem unlikely; men would in any case be more likely to be killed or to make their escape than women, especially those burdened with children. But it seems that women were not only more plentiful but also more valued. In Syria at a later date, a reward of 500 shekels was given for the return of a male slave; double that for a fugitive female. Indeed female slaves clearly played an important part in the economy. For example, in the Bau community there were some 250 to 300 slaves out of a total of 1,200 persons, of whom the overwhelming proportion were women. One tablet lists 205 slave girls and their children, who, according to Adams, were probably employed in a centralised weaving establishment (p. 102). In spite of arguments about numbers, then, slaves appear to have been concentrated in critical sectors of the economy such as the manufacture of wool and thread, which formed the basis of the export trade (Adams 1966:103), but was one of those areas where freemen were reluctant to work.

Slavery, then, is found right at the beginning of written records, so that we may be led into thinking of it as intrinsically, even causally, connected with the great advances of the Bronze Age, with plough and irrigation agriculture, with the growth of craft activity, the rise of towns, with the very birth of 'civilisation' itself. According to that great prehistorian, Gordon Childe, who puts the position with his usual terseness, it was the advances of the Bronze Age that made it possible to employ slaves in a productive way. One result of the development of advanced agriculture was that 'it now became worthwhile to keep prisoners or slaves instead of eating, or torturing them' (1954:43). The trouble with Childe's argument (which takes up a theme in Hobhouse, Wheeler and Ginsberg 1930:254) is that firstly, torturing and even killing other human beings was certainly not incompatible with slavery, which may even have encouraged such activities. And on the other hand, eating people never seems to have been a widespread culinary choice of the human race. Indeed the whole argument displays an altogether too simplistic view of the relationship between slavery, the economy and society. We must not underestimate for one moment the economic factors behind slavery, but the thesis, like other discussions of the topic, adopts a narrow view of productive activity at the same time as totally neglecting the question of reproduction, both of the individual and of the social system, without which one cannot understand the nature of the phenomena (and I deliberately use the plural) with which we are dealing.

For information on the social statuses present in human societies, we cannot delve further back than the earliest written record. The other techniques that we can use to say something about the appearance of slavery in human society and the kind of forms it might take, are two. Firstly, there is the comparative analysis of ethnological data, such as was carried out in Nieboer's well-known study, *Slavery as an Industrial System* (1900). Secondly, there is the kind of 'logical' analysis that Marx and others have initiated in laying out a model of social development. I want to look briefly at recent contributions to both these approaches, turning to the work done since Nieboer, mainly in Holland, on comparative analysis, as well as to the recent work, especially by Marxist anthropologists and historians in France, on African slavery, with a view to trying to locate more precisely the position of these phenomena in man's history.

In his book Nieboer put forward the proposition that slavery would be found together with open resources; where a man was not forced to work for another by shortage of land, he had to be made to work by slavery. Slavery could only exist where subsistence was easy to procure without the aid of capital, that is, in agricultural societies with a high land-labour ratio. The thesis has been subject to further testing by Baks *et al.* (1966) who found that the cross-cultural evidence showed no significant correlation between the two factors. The evidence is clear enough. Most simple agricultural societies have plenty of land, especially if they are

practising hoe agriculture. Yet slavery is no more common in
that range of society than elsewhere, less so in many cases.

Take New Guinea for example. Earlier ethnographers
claimed to have found something they called slavery in the
Mount Hagen area (Vicedom and Tischner 1943–48); more
recent ethnographers have denied the claim (Strathern 1971).
Among the Waropen of West Irian, across from the Celebes,
Held (1957) reports slave raids made from large canoes
like those used in the kula expeditions of the Trobriands.
Certainly captives were taken. As among the Iatmul, where
Bateson describes how a bought victim may be used in the
naven ceremony (1958:6), captives were bought or exchanged
after a raid (p. 201), though some were ransomed by their
respective groups. Indeed, Held regards the ransom as one
of the main motives (p. 223). Note that apparently no use is
made of slave labour since they 'have few tasks which they
could leave to servants' (p. 215). Instead those who are not
ransomed are incorporated, as individuals, into the clan of
their captors as part of 'a ritual game in which the parties
maintain certain contractual barter-relations' (p. 225). As
Held sees it, these activities probably developed out of head-
hunting, and the regulated raid was possibly developing into
'a battle of gifts', a kind of potlatch (p. 226).

A modification of Nieboer's thesis has been suggested by
Domar (1970), based upon the account of Russian serfdom
provided by V. Kliuchevsky. In order to support the military
forces required to combat her neighbours, the Russian
government had, in the fifteenth century, to assign estates to
'servitors' who used peasant labour for maintenance and for
weapons; this was the classic pattern of many feudal states.
Because of a shortage of labour and an abundance of land,
the 'servitors' were unable to control the peasants as they
wished and pressed the government to restrict their movements, i.e. to introduce 'serfdom'. Note that a high land-
labour ratio is not in itself seen as sufficient; a centralised
government (and associated 'class' hierarchy) has to be engaged in the extraction of surplus, and the manner in which
it does so depends upon the technology available.

Domar's economic analysis relates mainly to serfdom

rather than slavery, and in the latter the political-military element becomes yet more significant, as Childe and others have suggested. Already in that part of New Guinea described by Held, there was contact with the states of Indonesia proper, and it is clear that slavery is very much more likely to be found with forms of stratification, of which it is frequently a part, rather than in so-called acephalous societies, which lack a centralised government and lack a division into classes, castes or estates.

This is the theoretical position examined by Baks and others (1966), using the Ethnographic Atlas (see also Köbben 1967). Let me put the hypnothesis in my own terms. As we have often been reminded, slaves are mainly acquired persons, outsiders, strangers, prisoners of war. And they are acquired by processes through which one group exercises temporary domination over another by the use of force. Typically, annual expeditions, occasional razzias, or relations of tribute feed the requirements of the dominant power by cropping the human booty in the dominated one. This dominance may be economic; but in most cases economic domination has to take a military form at some point; there has to be a victim, preferably one that can be continually exploited. It is not simply a question of demand (the demand for extra help on the farm or an additional sexual partner is widespread), but of supply. Moreover slavery involves a type of supply which stands in contrast to the armed conflict found among stateless peoples that are relatively equal in strength, characterised as it is by a more-or-less reciprocal give and take of negative acts. Of course, such conflict may produce occasional captives, potential slaves; and pawns may also be exchanged. But more general slavery involves external as well as internal inequality, an unequal balance of power between peoples. Inequality of this kind takes a number of forms, but it has been especially common where states existed side by side with zones inhabited by 'uncontrolled', stateless or tribal peoples, whom they could raid for human booty without fear of reprisals, or when mobile pastoralists lived near sedentary farmers who were unable to escape their depredations nor match their military force.

We find some confirmation of this view in the distribution of slavery geographically and 'economically'. I turn first to the geographical distribution in recent times, in an attempt to discover whether there are any correlates of slavery with other features of social organisation. Confining himself to 'savages', Nieboer points out (and more recent evidence does not substantially alter his conclusions) that slavery is unknown in Australia, a continent previously populated only by hunters; in North America it existed along the Pacific Coast from the Bering Strait to the northern boundary of California; in South and Central America we find it scattered here and there in some third of the reported cases: in Oceania it was rare, except in Tahiti and New Zealand. Rare too in Central Asia and Siberia, but occurring very frequently in the Malay archipelago, India, Arabia, the Caucasus, and especially in Africa, where it was very widely reported.

We get an idea of its distribution in different socio-economic systems if we look at the evidence from recent ethnographic studies summarised in Murdock's *Ethnographic Atlas* (1966), a resource I use, not to establish absolute statistical accuracy, but to counteract the episodic and impressionistic treatment so frequently employed by those interested in the history of human culture. Here, as one might expect (though the percentages must be taken only as rough indicators), we find that slavery is virtually absent in hunting and gathering societies, being reported in approximately 3 per cent of cases. On the other hand, it is found with 43 per cent of societies with advanced agriculture, almost the same percentage with extensive agriculture, but in only 17 per cent with 'incipient agriculture'. Within this range of societies the trend is fairly straightforward; the more complex the economy, the greater the inequality. The full implications of this correlation are not always expressed as clearly as they might be. But before we reach that point, there is another aspect of these figures to which I wish to draw attention. If we take two other types of socio-economic system, both of which are dependent upon the complementary activities of other societies, the percentages are somewhat surprising. In societies that are predominantly dependent upon fishing,

B

34 per cent have slavery, while in pastoral societies, the total reaches a remarkable 73 per cent.

I do not want to place too much emphasis on these figures. But, leaving aside once again a consideration of the role and proportion of slaves in a society (i.e. slave labour as the 'basis' of the economy), what do they suggest? Slavery is clearly compatible with all types of post-neolithic economy, and could therefore have been found long before the rise of the civilisations of the Bronze Age, with their relatively advanced technology of the plough, elaborate water control, the wheel, as well as the writing that at once begins to record the existence of the institution.

The existence of slavery, even at the most elementary level, implies incipient stratification, because it involves the presence, within the society, of a radically different type of social relationship and category of social person. The acquisition of a human being, by outright purchase or directly by capture, involves the most extreme exploitation of human potential, the height of domination, the depth of subordination.

Even among hunters and gatherers there are some exceptional instances where slavery occurs. In particular there is the case (so often commented upon since the days of Boas) of the Northwest Coast of America (Ruyle 1973). While many anthropologists, basing themselves upon recent observations, have tended to see societies such as the Kwakiutl as aiming at some sort of over-all equality of distribution by means of the potlatch, the historical picture is very far from the relatively egalitarian tribal system of most hunting and gathering systems. Jewitt offers the following comment on slavery in the area. After describing the fact that slaves often live in the homes of their masters, he goes on:

> They are compelled, however, at times, to labor severely, as not only all the menial offices are performed by them, such as bringing water, cutting wood, and a variety of others, but they are obliged to make the canoes, to assist in building and repairing the houses, to supply their masters with fish, and to attend them in war and to fight for them (1898 [1815]: 130).

In other words, they performed the basic domestic and economic processes, including reproducing their own unfreedom. It is perhaps not surprising that MacLeod could write (though he saw the case as an argument against economic determinism and perhaps as an excuse for the American past) that 'slavery ... among the natives was of nearly as much economic importance ... as was slavery to the plantation regions of the United States before the Civil War' (1928:649). To sustain the system of rank and potlatch, war and raiding were essential. 'In addition to the enslavement of captives of war, raids for the special purpose of acquiring slaves were frequent, and a highly developed inter-tribal trade sprang up, apparently with the special purpose of disposing of slaves acquired on such raids' (Siegel 1945:365). Slaves were considered chattels and destroyed in the course of potlatches, as was any other kind of property.

While the Northwest coast constitutes an important exception to the general absence of slavery among hunting and gathering peoples, it is explicable in terms of their economic dominance over other societies, derived from their abundant food resources (especially salmon), as well as of the mobility and military strength which were provided by their huge canoes, though they exercised this dominance not so much over their neighbours as over tribes further down the coast.

Among agriculturists, slavery is associated with stratification, though in areas like Africa, where states exist side by side with stateless tribes, it is in fact found in both types of social system, though of course mainly in the former. It existed, for example, among the stateless LoDagaa of Northern Ghana who were raided for slaves by neighbouring states, just as it existed in states such as Gonja, who raided uncontrolled, unprotected peoples, to provide slaves for internal use, to pay tribute to their conquerors, and to supply the external market as well (Braimah and Goody 1967:11). Among the LoDagaa, slaves were limited both in their number and in their roles; most of them seem to have come from nearby communities under conditions of famine, under a kind of protective slavery or pawnship. Some were unprotected strangers captured on the road (Goody 1956:9). Others were purchased from freebooters who had acquired a gun or a horse; and they could be used, as Fortes reports for the Tallensi, by a man who had no sons, to help him plug a demographic gap (1949:25).[3]

Slavery was very different in these two types of society, though I do not think the difference can be properly described by using the terms 'household' and 'chattel' slavery, especially if the former term implies domestic service or a peripheral role; household slaves, domestic slaves, may clearly be central to the economy where production is largely a domestic concern. But whereas people earlier thought of indigenous slavery in Africa as entirely of the former type, a shift in historiography, a revision in social analysis, has provided us with a new picture where slavery is seen to play a very much more important part in the internal structure of African states. Indeed, some Marxists, including some Africans themselves, now see certain indigenous states as marked by a 'slave mode of production' (e.g. Dieng 1974). I do not find this formulation very useful, since it neglects other significant aspects of the process of production in Africa. But the view provides a counterweight to the one that regarded African slavery either as a kind of serfdom or servanthood (Davidson 1970), or else as the result of the Atlantic trade (Rodney 1970).

I want to make three points about slavery in Africa. We have here a system of slavery which was undoubtedly ancient and not simply a product of the European trade. Secondly, the role of slaves in the economy was often extensive and directed to reproductive as well as productive ends. And thirdly, since our views are often influenced by the 'ethnic' situation in the American South, we need reminding that slave status was usually a sliding status; there were institutionalised procedures, not only under Islam but under other regimes as well, for escaping from servile bonds. Let us see see how these elements fit together.

The question of the origin of slavery in Africa has been confused by the public washing of hands over European guilt. But attitudes of this kind often make bad history and worse sociology. Even if we allow that the origin of slavery in Africa lay in the 'external' trade, such trade existed long before Western Europe had the naval technology to sail down the African coast and to cross the Atlantic. At an early date trans-Saharan Africa was a source as well as a user of slaves. Already in the second century A.D., slaves were coming across the Western Sahara (Law 1967); the Eastern route to Egypt was used much earlier. In the tenth century, Ibn Haukal reported that the Maghreb was chiefly remarkable for black slaves, the white slaves coming mainly from the quarter of Andalus. And this ancient trade continued until recent times. In a book published in 1902 Budgett Meakin describes 'slavery and servitude among the Moors', where Africans of slave origin were so numerous that Europeans still imagined the Moors, like Shakespeare's 'Othello', to be black in colour. In fact, they paid more for white slaves, and it was women, sexually attractive women, who fetched the highest prices.

In the context of Islam and the comparative history of slavery in various parts of America, it is interesting to note Meakin's comment upon the absence of race hatred and the relatively lenient treatment of slaves by their masters. Neither all freemen nor all slaves were black; even at this late stage Circassian slaves were being brought from Turkey, entering as members of their owners' families; in houses on the Bosphorous 'young children are trained for the harems by instruction in music and dancing, and even in English and French, as well as in the degrading arts by which the women of these lands endeavour to secure the favour of their lords' (1902:138). Such women fetched high prices and could achieve high rank. Meakin states that 'the mother of the present sultan was one of these women, bought from the hareem of a well-known pasha of Cairo by a friend of mine— along with two others whom he kept for himself. . .' (p. 138).

It was such women who produced the next heir to the throne. Like the children of any other slave woman by a free master, they were free; so too were the women themselves at their masters' death. Slave men, on the other hand, produced slave children who could be sold, though manumission was always a meritorious act in Islam and might be held out as a promise under a man's will. Moreover, if he prospered, an individual might buy his own freedom.

That slavery was already present in the coastal area of West Africa is shown by the role of the Portuguese when they arrived there. Primarily interested in gold, they made their major centre the Costa da Mina (the Gold Coast, or present-day Ghana). 'It was soon discovered' writes Ryder, 'that the African merchants—many of whom were attracted to these markets from the interior—preferred, or even insisted, on receiving part of the price of their gold in slaves' (1969:26). Consequently the Portuguese turned to the Bight of Benin, the slave rivers leading to the Kingdom of Benin, in order to acquire the necessary slaves from the Ijo, the Itsekiri and the Edo, who in their turn obtained them from interior markets, from their own criminals, and from the capture of outsiders. Nor was this the only call for slaves; soon they were needed as labour for the colony of young Jews, Portuguese settlers and exiles established in Sao Tome in 1493. A third demand was from the slave market in Lisbon, where they were sought mainly as domestic servants; in 1554, ten per cent of the population of Lisbon consisted of slaves, though many were of North African origin (Ryder 1969:36).

I have been arguing here for the antiquity of slavery in Africa; the trade in slaves long pre-dated the activities of Western Europeans: it was widespread under Islam, not only across the Sahara, to the Maghreb and the Nile, but also from the east, from Zanzibar to the Middle East. And even before, African slaves were transported into ancient Greece and earlier Egypt. If external trade existed over this long period, it seems likely that internal slavery was also present as well, though this notion cannot be confirmed in the absence of written records.

There are three questions that need to be asked about internal slavery in Africa and that bear upon more general questions. Firstly, was it really slavery, or was the institution more like European serfdom, with slaves being treated quite differently than under the cruel plantation owners of the American South? On this question it would be absurd to hazard a generalisation. Slaves may have been treated with more consideration in the fields and in the house; one could indeed argue that, given the ease with which they could

escape and mix with others, they had to be so treated to prevent their disappearance (though their self-inflicted brands,
their tribal marks, would often identify them); one could also
argue that after the initial trauma of capture and sale they
were usually on the way, if not to becoming free, at least to
being the parents of children who, though slaves in origin,
were no longer slaves in status. They could look forward to a
vicarious freedom, a prospect for the future, that may have
inhibited revolt, though their rulers (e.g. the Ashanti and the
Yoruba) were at times very worried about just this possibility.
But let us be clear about their condition. Quite apart from the
appalling conditions of capture and of transfer to the market
place, conditions which at times rivalled the horrors of the
Atlantic trade, they were kinless persons; their insecurity of
life was often great. In that complex and sophisticated state
of Ashanti, slaves fled the town when they heard the funeral
drums, for fear they would be slaughtered on the spot. Those
writers who look upon African slavery as a species of domestic
service are sometimes misled by the kind of retrospective
accounts recorded fifty years after emancipation and on
which recent American historians of slavery place so much
weight. The contemporary documents give a very different
picture; to regard African slavery as a kind of serfdom is to
misunderstand the socio-economic systems of both Africa
and of Europe.

This leads to the question of the role of slaves in the
economy. Let me first touch upon the extent of slavery, a
notion which can refer either to the spread within or between
societies.

Slaves were predominantly found in African states, in
societies with some centralised administration, that is to say,
societies that were stratified internally and held a superior
military or economic position in relation to the groups that
surrounded them and from whom they could obtain slaves;
all slave-holding societies required victims, only a small
number of whom ever came from within. What they needed
were victim societies, groups who consisted not of subjects
but of outsiders who could be dominated by force.

Within societies, the proportion of slaves to freemen could

be high, particularly in and around the urban centres of West Africa involved in the long-distance trade, but not only in these. We have no census data that would shed light on the problem; I would myself be unable to estimate the proportion of slaves in the pre-colonial population in any area I have studied. In the state of Gonja, north of Ashanti, the percentage of slaves seems to have been very much larger than I had earlier suspected. These high percentages receive some confirmation from the observations of early travellers, though it is difficult to imagine how they arrived at their estimates. More reliable information is available for Northern Nigeria and the Savannah belt which suggests that, from the standpoint of numbers, slavery was of great importance in these states (e.g. Last 1967; Lovejoy 1978). The production and employment of slaves was a major aspect of their social processes which inevitably had a significant influence on all the surrounding areas, since these tribal societies were the major source of human booty.[4]

But if the number of slaves was great, did slavery also play a dominant role in the economy? Here lies the second point central to discussions about slavery as a mode of production. What were the roles slaves did play? To what extent was the economy dependent on their labour?

Their importance in the gold-mining operations in Gyaman, the Akan kingdom north-west of Ashanti, has been emphasised by Terray (1974). Early in the eighteenth century, Dupuis reported that on the banks of the river Ba 'there is work there for eight to ten thousand slaves for two months' during the rainy season (Dupuis 1824: II,LVI). In West Africa as elsewhere, mining for metals and salt was often carried out by slave labour, so that intensive slavery was found where local mineral resources were in large demand, especially as the result of the external trade. According to Ibn Battuta, who visited the salt mines of Teghazza in the fourteenth century, they were worked by the slaves of Massufa (1969: iv, 137—8; Terray 1974:339). The same was true of the copper veins of Takedda, of which he wrote that 'slaves of both sexes' take it into the town to melt it down (1969:iv,441). Indeed it has been argued that during the fourteenth century the merchant economies of the Sudan 'depended in large measure on slave labour' and it was this source that was tapped by the Atlantic trade (Fage 1969a: 1969b).

So, contrary to the thesis that long-distance trade was the critical factor in state formation in the Western Sudan (a thesis recently restated by Coquéry-Vidrovitch 1969), Terray argues that the real role of such trade 'consisted in the introduction of slave-type relations of production into social formations dominated until then by the kin-based mode of production' (1974:339). Aristocracies acquired slaves through war, and put them to work in productive employment which formed the basis of the long-distance trade. So the role played by slavery in these states was not simply a matter of meeting the demands for the export of human slaves, but was closely involved with their own productive system. Yet this productive system was of course much simpler in type than that associated with ancient or American slavery, being still articulated with a kin-based mode of production, whose emphasis, Terray claims, was upon use rather than exchange value (the needs of consumption rather than of commerce), which meant that there was a less intensive exploitation of slaves than we find elsewhere.

Slaves were also required in the long-distance trade itself. The carriage of goods in Africa was always problematic, even where the difficulties of transport restricted trade to valuables. The more limited the technology, the more inhospitable the environment, the more one had to depend on human labour in the development of complex socio-economic systems. In Africa, the wheel, which played such an important part in the early Near East, was absent; even today carts are a rarity. Animals were used for transport, but they had limited carrying capacity and in any case were vulnerable to the ubiquitous tsetse fly. Transport was frequently dependent upon human beings and it was largely slaves that were recruited to ply the trade routes between Kano in Hausaland and Salaga in Gonja, as well as in many other areas. So prevalent was the use of slaves for trading caravans in the last quarter of the nineteenth century, that when the British in the 'Gold Coast' wanted to recruit soldiers for the West African Force, they dispatched officers on the long and dangerous journey to Salaga to arrive there at the time when the annual caravans came down from Northern Nigeria to seek kola. Their intention was to attract members of these caravans to join the army and they were authorised to offer a bounty for each recruit. The British saw themselves as recruiting soldiers; the locals saw them as buying slaves, or, much worse, as encouraging slaves to desert one master for another.

There is a further point to be made about the role of slaves. In Africa, craft activity was much less developed than in the Ancient Middle East. While one did not find the extensive use of slaves in manufacture that is indicated in records of the Mesopotamian weaving trade, they were certainly employed as assistants in craft enterprises; indeed they even ran certain small-scale undertakings. Significantly, they were also employed as gun men, and hence as instruments of their own oppression, presumably because, as kinless persons, they were more loyal to the king than to others and more ready to engage in martial tasks, having nothing to lose but their chains. In some states, slaves worked as traders or became advisers and administrators.

The performance by slaves of certain specialist tasks is critical to the discussion of African slavery in the major economic history of West Africa (Hopkins 1973). Recognising that slavery was 'not simply a European invention', Hopkins asks why should it have come into being at all, given his view on the general efficiency of domestic labour in the precolonial system. He argues that slavery existed mainly in states, 'where the development of domestic exchange activities created employment opportunities which could not be met by local, free labour' (1973:23). Slaves were 'usually fairly specialised workers, performing work which was usually menial, sometimes gruelling and occasionally dangerous' (1973:24).

Slavery was related then to a 'shortage of labour'. But why did not Africa use machinery? Or wage labour? Hopkins suggests that 'the use of slave rather than wage labour was a matter of deliberate choice on the part of African employers' (p. 24). The scarce factor was labour rather than land.

Hence 'hired labour would be expensive. Production costs in common activities, such as farming and craft production, would be higher for wage labour than for independent house-holds . . . Slaves were preferred because the costs of acquiring and maintaining them were less than the cost of hiring labour' (p. 25).

Hopkins recognises that this argument stands opposed to the claims of Montesquieu and Adam Smith, that the additional costs of free labour was more than justified by its greater efficiency. He calls in support the discussions concerning the efficiency of slave labour in Rome and in nineteenth-century America, suggesting that 'it seems highly unlikely that African employers would have failed, during the course of many centuries, to act in their own interests' (p. 25).

His theory depends upon the assumption, directly contrary to the notion of 'substantivist' anthropologists, that

there *was* a long established labour market in Africa. The fact that this market took the form of slave labour rather than wage labour was the result of *deliberate choice* based on an elementary, but broadly accurate, cost-benefit analysis, that is to say on principles which the substantivists regard as peripheral or non-existent in 'traditional' societies (1973:26).[5]

I have emphasised the phrase 'deliberate choice' because it seems the key to Hopkins' individualistic theories about the nature of social life. In what sense can African 'employers' be said to be exercising a choice between hired labour and slave labour? There is no evidence that hired labour was an alternative. Indeed a moment's reflection on the economic situation would indicate the reason. Where land is short, labour is the significant factor of production. But if individuals have relatively free access to land, why (as Nieboer and Domar asked) should they become hired labourers? The 'wages', security and job satisfaction must all be less. Under these conditions you can force someone to work for you as a slave but not as a hired hand. The argument from economic principles appears to neglect the location of slavery in a social system.

Despite the role of slaves in mining as well as in other unpleasant but critical areas of the economy, such as the

long-distance transport of goods, and despite all the auxiliary
activities I have mentioned, these activities do not account
for the extraordinary extent of slavery in some African kingdoms. For by far the bulk of male slaves worked in agriculture, sometimes on what can perhaps be called plantations,
but the largest part on family farms, i.e. within the sphere of
what Terray calls kin-based production and what others have
seen as the domestic sphere of production. Lacking adequate
records, it is not easy to specify who employed slaves. Terray
writes of the Abron and Ashanti as if slaves were the possessions of the aristocrats. The nature of mass dynasties in this
part of the world meant that the ruling estates were constituted by the many rather than the few, though only a few
were major office-holders at any one time. But quite apart
from the nature of the class structure, my own information
from Gonja indicates that the ownership of slaves was widely
distributed, that commoners, as well as members of the
Muslim and the ruling estates, owned slaves.

What did these slaves do? Given the prevailing system of
extensive agriculture based on the hoe, they often worked
in small-scale 'household' units (which were not therefore
purely familial), and worked closely with their masters. Technological limitations meant that their surplus product was
small. But it was large enough to relieve chiefs, merchants
and even commoners of painful labour on the farm, or at least
from part of that work, since supervision was required, and
participation often given, by the family members of the
owners. Moreover, rural slavery could be integrated into
market activities. Around trading towns, food was produced
for sale to traders and caravans, often on a considerable scale
(Binger 1892). But market activities could also be more extensive, more direct, more commercial, when they involved
'cash-crops'. In Zanzibar, plantation slavery was used in the
production of spices for export, in particular cloves, which
formed part of the spice trade that had existed on the East
African coast at least since the Roman period (Miller 1969).

Accounts of slavery in Zanzibar recall those from the New
World. The *msimamizi* was head of all the plantation slaves,
responsible only to the master. He was followed by the *nokoa*

who were reputed for their harsh treatment of their fellow slaves. Overseers (*kadamu*) of the individual slave gangs labouring on different parts of the plantation or on construction sites, saw to it that the work was done.

> The required output in threshing and harvesting was reckoned on an 'hour' basis, slaves working from eight till five. For sowing they had to be out at early dawn. But for groundwork an acreage basis was followed. . . . The responsibility for the completion of the alloted tasks by each gang of slaves rested with the . . . head slave.

Women slaves were often used to sell the produce of the master's garden in the market (Prins 1961:69). In addition, most of the crews of Swahili trading vessels engaged in the active trade up the coast to Muscat and Oman were slaves.

Although Zanzibar is an extreme example, in other regions of Africa agricultural slavery was partly directed to the market, as it certainly was in craft, transport and in mining. At one level this labour can be described as domestic slavery, since it was often performed within the family context; though not in the *domus* itself, it contributed to the *oikos*. Placed in opposition to 'chattel slavery', the term 'domestic' suggests an institution of minor importance. Yet the contribution of this type of slavery to the economy of African states was often considerable.

My brief account of the role of slaves in Africa, under conditions of production that were essentially simpler than in the Ancient Near East, omits any consideration of one central issue upon which there has been virtually no comment. In the market the price of women slaves was almost always higher than that of men. How can we explain this fact in view of the emphasis given to the role of the slave in the productive process?

We cannot make the kind of cliometric analysis of African slavery that has occupied scholars working on slavery in the New World. But there are certain facts that differentiate the Saharan trade, the northern export of slaves, from the Atlantic one. The slave trade directed to the sugar plantations had a sex ratio weighted very heavily in favour of the male; at the

beginning of the nineteenth century there were between two
and five males imported for every female (Curtin 1969:41).
A high percentage of 'African' slaves (i.e. imported slaves as
distinct from their descendants) meant a high rate of natural
decrease since, unable to find enough mates, the males were
failing to reproduce themselves. The African situation was
very different. In the slave market of Timbuctu in the
nineteenth century, Shabayni reports that the slaves on sale
were ninety per cent male, not because they were more in
demand, but because they were apparently less so. Women
captives were usually kept by their captors, so in the market
they were 'more expensive and very rare' (Shabayni 1967:47;
Bazin 1975:151). Further east in the same inland savannah
zone, a European commissioner pointed out in 1892 that in
the Abron capital of Bondoukou women were more valuable
than men. One of the most systematic price-lists for human
beings is given by the German explorer, Nachtingall, who
travelled extensively throughout the Western Sudan during
the latter part of the nineteenth century. His list for the Kuka
market in Nigeria (Fisher and Fisher 1970:164) shows the
following hierarchy:

Category	Maria Theresa dollars
Old man	4–5
Old woman	6–10
Strong adult man	12–14
Middle aged woman	10–15
Young adult man	15–18
Five span boy (10–13)	16–20
Seven span youth (15–20)	16–22
Six span boy (12–15)	20–25
Five span girl (10–13)	20–25
Young girl or woman	40–100
Boy eunuch	50–80

The table has an interesting consistency. At any given age,
women are always more valuable than men, the younger than
the older, while the neutered more valuable than all the rest.

In some respects this situation is the opposite of that obtaining in the Americas, where the main labour demands were for male plantation workers, preferably those who would reproduce themselves. Consequently, in the coastal markets of West Africa, from where the bulk of the American slaves were exported, it was males that usually fetched the highest price. Why then do we find a situation where the reproducers were in greater demand than the producers? For this price structure runs counter to theories that link the role of slaves with the production of gold, with the transport of goods, and with craft production, for all these are basically male tasks. It also casts doubts upon those arguments which have seen internal slavery as the reflex action of the American trade upon African society. The production of slaves was undoubtedly increased under the impact of European colonialism, not only because of the external trade but also because of the import of new weapons that changed the nature of raiding activities. But, as we have suggested, slaves were already present, employed for farming, for domestic service, for mining, for trade, for administration and for sacrifice.

Why did women dominate the African market in contrast to the American one? It could be suggested that since women are often the main producers in Africa, under a system of hoe agriculture, they were acquired as labourers in the fields. However, in the savannahs of West Africa, where slave raiding and slavery were particularly widespread, it is men rather than women who wield the hoe. Moreover men slaves carried out not only the usual male tasks on the farm but some of the female ones as well. For example, they collected firewood and drew water. Male slaves did women's work as well as men's. In this way, slavery not only affected the division of labour by relieving owners from irksome labour, it also broke with the sexual division of labour, anyhow as far as men were concerned. Indeed, men were sometimes turned into sexual neutrals by castration, thus negating their capacity to reproduce either themselves as individuals or the slave strata as a whole. The rape of the slave women was parallelled by the unmanning of men. As we have seen, the most valuable slaves in the Kuka market were neither men nor women, but those of neutral gender, the butt of music-hall jokes north of the Mediterranean, but a common social category on its southern shores, in the Middle East, China and indeed throughout West Africa, a category whose value in political and household affairs lay precisely in the fact that they were no longer interested in reproduction or continuity, either sexual or social.

This same ranking system of i. men made women, ii. women, iii. men, operated in the slave markets of North Africa and gave the trans-Saharan trade a different character from the Atlantic one. Of course women were found in the first, and men in the second. But the difference in emphasis relates to the uses and origins of slavery, not only in Africa but elsewhere. For example, in nineteenth-century Cairo, girls fetched a higher price than boys. Adults here were 50–100 per cent higher. But highest of all were eunuchs, who fetched two to three times the price of the adults who could reproduce themselves. We cannot explain these facts except by seeing the role of slaves as related to sex and reproduction as well as to farm and production, and in the case of eunuchs to power and its non-proliferation.

If slave women are widely used as spouses by free men, especially by the upper classes in harem situations (and their higher price is to supply the owners of slaves, not the slaves themselves, with sexual partners), the indications are twofold. Genetic differences, such as colour, will be quickly diffused throughout the population. This is clear in North Africa, where society was never divided into slave and free along colour lines. Even though colour was important, there were white slaves and black free men.

The second implication connected with the role of women is that slave status was for many, though not all, a sliding status. Muslim law is perhaps most explicit on this issue. Firstly you do not enslave fellow Muslims, nor members of protected religious communities. In other words, you don't enslave your own kind. Secondly, the emancipation of slaves was considered a worthy act, meritorious in the eyes of God, even though slavery was widespread and permitted. For slavery did present a certain kind of moral contradiction, the ambiguity of which Finley has noted in Roman Law (1973:63) and which manifested itself in various ways, one of which was to provide not for a way out but for a way up. But more important than emancipation was the fact that the child of a free male by a slave concubine was legally free; indeed the mother too became free at the death of her owner.

The result is clear, especially in societies where men could legitimately proliferate spouses. There was a constant drift of the offspring of slave women into non-slave status (even though the notion of slave origin might continue to have some political and social drawbacks). Equally, since free males required female slaves for sexual purposes much more frequently than the reverse, male slaves had less opportunity to reproduce themselves. This would have been so, even if the sex ratio of the slave population duplicated that of the free population. But it didn't.

Under these conditions, the slave population (owned slaves, not those of slave origin) was constantly diminishing, unless we assume a higher reproduction rate among female slaves. Where there is no mobility for slaves out of the slave class, the original population can be maintained without acquisition from outside. But the more liberal their treatment and the more numerous the escape routes, the more devastating the results. I mean devastating here in the literal sense of the word. Economists and others have rightly argued that there is no slavery without the slave trade. But the social consequences begin further back, because in order to supply the trade, violence has to be applied by someone, in many cases far removed from the eventual slave owner. So that the consequence of the sliding status of the slave is the continual violence required to replenish the ever-emptying pool of forced labour.

To conclude, it is unlikely that slavery emerged fully armed in the city states of the Bronze Age, but the absence of records means that we have to look at its more recent manifestations in simpler societies. We may dismiss the argument that in these societies slavery was a result of feedback from the activities of more advanced systems, anyhow in the form that it has so far been presented. Slavery could have developed out of the acquisition of strangers at a much earlier stage. In simple agricultural and in some advanced gathering societies, people can be utilised in a variety of ways depending upon the economy, especially in unpleasant or new jobs, in harder work. Hired labour is unavailable where resources are plentiful and the technology (or capital) limited. Forced labour through slavery is the solution. But the economy needs to be treated as a more complex variable than is often assumed. It is not enough simply to differentiate domestic from chattel slavery, nor general from sporadic slavery. The forces of production require more discriminating attention, for the productivity of slavery depends largely on the techniques available; the plough has very different implications from the hoe. Differences in the relations of production also demand more recognition. Slavery, then, is common in a wider range of societies than has often been supposed, but the emphasis varies. In African states based on hoe agriculture, mining, trade and craft played important parts, and these were largely male activities. But women were more valued as slaves than men. This higher valuation arose not only because they were the producers of the slave producers but more importantly because they were acquired as mates, and specifically as legitimate sexual partners, as mothers of their children, by the free population. This contrast with North America is reinforced by the escape mechanisms that existed for slaves of both sexes whereby slavery was usually a sliding status. But the very fact that it was liberal for some meant future slavery for others. Thus it offered the carrot of freedom for the offspring of present slaves at the cost of continuous replacement from outside. If we cannot say that slavery originated in warfare, the institution certainly depended upon perpetual conflict between peoples, especially between those with states and weapons on the one hand and those that had neither on the other.[6]

Raiders and Traders in Adamawa: Slavery as a Regional System

PHILIP BURNHAM

Judging from the volume of recently published literature on the subject, there has been a marked increase in interest in the study of the indigenous slave systems of Africa over the past few years (Fisher and Fisher 1970; Meillassoux 1975; Hill 1976; Miers and Kopytoff 1977). However, far from exhausting this topic, these works are just beginning to provide the data and theories necessary for an understanding of the structure of African slave systems, and the present essay is a further contribution to this dialogue.

In the case in question, that of ninteenth-century Adamawa in what is now northern Cameroon, we are dealing with slavery on a major scale. The Fulbe states in this region were engaged in the capture and export of thousands of slaves annually to the slave markets of Hausaland and Bornu. The size of the slave populations in these receiving areas was very large. Polly Hill (1976:396—397) believes that there were 'several million' slaves out of ten million total population, and other authors also estimate that the proportion was between thirty and fifty percent (Barth 1857:II:143–144; Robinson 1896:127; Meillassoux 1975:17). All authors agree that there was a constant need to replenish the stock of slaves due to substantial losses from death, escapes, manumission, and export across the Sahara. Looked at in a regional focus, one can see that this insatiable demand for slaves in Hausaland and Bornu created a centre-periphery relationship with the surrounding peoples, as an endemic pattern of slave raiding and warfare emerged on the frontiers of these large states in order to supply their requirements. Adamawa was such a peripheral area, and in the present paper, I look at the implications of slave raiding and trading for the Fulbe state of Ngaoundere and its 'pagan' neighbours, the Gbaya people.[1]

The Fulbe Conquest of Ngaoundere

The Adamawa *jihad* (religious war), an extension of Usman dan Fodio's conquest of the Hausa states of Nigeria, was undertaken by Fulbe clans which had been resident in Bornu, the upper Benoue valley, the Mandara Hills, and the Diamare region since at least the eighteenth century (Mohammadou in press; Abubakar 1972:72). One of these clans, the Wolarbe, directed its attacks toward the south and penetrated the heart of the Adamawa plateau itself in an area which had largely been beyond Fulbe influence previously. In these pioneering efforts, the Wolarbe attacked the many pagan tribes of this region and during the period 1815 to 1840, managed to establish a series of conquest states at Ngaoundere, Tibati, Kontcha, Tinyer (Tignere), and Banyo (see Strümpell 1912).

Historians of the Adamawa *jihad* agree that despite the overt religious rationale for this war, political and economic motivations were more important (Mohammadou in press; Abubakar 1972:74). To quote Eldridge Mohammadou (in press),

> The religious argument furnished only a supplementary motivation [for the Adamawa *jihad*] . . . The *jihad* [permitted the Fulbe] to systematise and organize the conquest and although the religious motive was certainly predominant for certain of the participants, for the majority the conquest of Adamawa was above all a political act. Its aim was to transform the [Fulbe] position in the area from a subordinate to a dominant one and then to engage in territorial expansion so as to consolidate their political power.

One prong of the Wolarbe conquest, led by Ardo Njobdi of

Bundang, directed its principal attacks against the several Mbum groups living at Ngaoundere and other towns nearby. Although the conquest of the Mbum and their neighbours the Duru was not completed by Njobdi himself, who died in 1839 (Mohammadou in press; Froelich 1954:14), Njobdi's successors were able to consolidate their hold on Ngaoundere over the next decade and transform it into the most important Fulbe state of southern Adamawa. The Fulbe of Ngaoundere became more sedentary during this period, setting up a complex system of territorial administration and establishing a sizeable walled capital which counted about 11,000 inhabitants in the late nineteenth century (Ponel 1896:207). In theory, throughout the nineteenth century, the rulers of Ngaoundere continued to stand in a relation of subordination to the Emir of Adamawa at Yola, owing him an annual tribute of 1,000 slaves, 1,000 cattle and 10 large elephant tusks (Abdoullaye and Mohammadou 1972; see also Lacroix 1952: 34). However, Ngaoundere was sufficiently strong and distant from Yola so that, in practice, it only paid this tribute when it suited Ngaoundere to do so.

By the 1850s, Ngaoundere's desire for territorial expansion *per se* began to dim. The Fulbe state already controlled extensive tracts of lightly populated land near to home, and its emphasis progressively shifted from territorial conquest to a less direct exploitation of its peripheries via slave raiding and trade. Hemmed in on three sides by other Fulbe powers, Ngaoundere's main attentions in this regard were aimed toward the southeast, in particular against the Gbaya and Laka peoples who lived 200 kilometres or more from Ngaoundere town in what is now the Central African Empire and Chad. This contact with peripheral 'pagan' groups by the military and commercial agents of Ngaoundere, the 'raiders and traders' of my title, forms the main subject of this paper and will be examined in detail after a brief discussion of the significance of slavery in the structure of the Ngaoundere state itself.

Slavery and the Ngaoundere State

The Adamawa *jihad* was undertaken by small groups of Fulbe who were substantially outnumbered by the auto-chthonous 'pagan' groups of the region. Ngaoundere was certainly no exception in this regard, and the rapid integration of conquered Mbum and other peoples into the Fulbe state, which transformed large numbers of former enemies into effective elements of the state political and economic apparatus, is truly remarkable.

The limited information that we possess concerning the organisation of the Wolarbe Fulbe who first penetrated the Adamawa Plateau and attacked the Mbum of Ngaoundere suggests that they were a semi-nomadic pastoral group.[2] Slaves definitely formed a part of Wolarbe society prior to the *jihad*, and it is possible that some of these slaves were settled in fixed farming villages which served as wet-season foci and political and ceremonial centres for the transhumant families of Fulbe pastoralists. At least a rudimentary system of political offices, with titles for both freemen and slaves, was in operation prior to the *jihad* and had probably been adopted by the Wolarbe during their earlier period of residence in Bornu.

On analogy between the pre-*jihad* Wolarbe and better-documented cases of similar semi-pastoral Fulbe groups composed of both free and slave elements, it is probable that the initial group of Wolarbe who took Ngaoundere did not exceed 5,000 in number, including women, children and slaves.[3] But in the course of several decades of fighting against the indigenous peoples of the Ngaoundere region, the Fulbe were able to conquer and reduce to slavery or tributary status large groups of local populations who certainly outnumbered the Fulbe conquerors by several orders of magnitude. These conquests were assisted by alliances between Ngaoundere and other Fulbe states as well as by the progressive incorporation of 'pagan' elements into the Ngaoundere army. Conquered 'pagan' village populations located near Ngaoundere town were often allowed to remain on their traditional lands. Their chiefs were awarded titles, and the whole village unit was allocated to the *tokkal* (political following) of a titled Fulbe or slave official in the Ngaoundere court, who became responsible for collecting annual taxes and raising levies of soldiers for Fulbe war expeditions. In return, the 'pagan' group's loyalty to Ngaoundere was rewarded principally by opportunities to secure booty in war, and this incentive was probably the primary factor which allowed the Fulbe to secure the allegiance of conquered groups so rapidly.

The *tokke* units (plural of *tokkal*) which formed the basis of the Ngaoundere administrative system, had their origins in the leadership patterns of mobile pastoral society and were not discrete territorial domains ruled by resident overlords. Rather, *tokke* were sets of followers, both Fulbe and members of vassal peoples, who were distributed in a scattering of different rural villages or residential quarters in town and who were allocated to individual office holders living at Ngaoundere at the whim of the Fulbe ruler (*laamiido*). Such a spatially dispersed administrative organisation lessened chances of secession by parts of the Ngaoundere state and yet was an effective means of mobilising and organising an army.

In addition to locally conquered 'pagan' peoples, the size of the servile population at Ngaoundere was further enlarged by slaves captured at distances of 200 to 500 kilometres from Ngaoundere town itself. These captives were brought back for resettlement at Ngaoundere either as domestic slaves or as farm slaves in slave villages (*ruumde*). This long-distance raiding, which was a regular occurrence from the 1850s up until the first decade of the twentieth century, was a large-scale phenomenon, and European observers at the end of the nineteenth century estimated that as many as 8,000 to 10,000 slaves might be taken on these raids annually (Coquery-Vidrovitch 1972:76, 204–205; Loefler 1907:225; Ponel 1896: 205–207). Those captives who were not settled at Ngaoundere were sold to Hausa or Kanuri traders, and Adamawa soon gained the reputation as a slave traders' Eldorado (Passarge 1895:480). By the second half of the nineteenth century,, Adamawa had become the main source of supply for the Sokoto Caliphate (Lacroix 1952:34).

Summing up the demographic situation at Ngaoundere in

the nineteenth century, we can say that at no time following the establishment of the Fulbe state did the proportion of slaves and vassals to freemen ever fall below a one-to-one ratio and that for most of the period, the ratio was probably more like two-to-one. Modern census figures, although they can be applied retrospectively with only the greatest of caution, tend to support this interpretation, Thus, in 1950, there were approximately 23,000 Fulbe living in the Ngaoundere state as compared with 35,000 non-Fulbe who were still identifiable as ex-slaves, vassals or servants of the Fulbe (Froelich 1954:25). It goes without saying that in modern conditions, when all legal disabilities and constraints on movement have been removed, the proportion of servile to free would be expected to drop. But nonetheless, as late as 1950, we still encounter almost a three-to-two ratio.

Whatever the exact number and proportion of slaves in the pre-colonial period, they were not all of uniform social or legal status, and it is instructive to attempt a classification of the various forms of servitude in practice in nineteenth-century Ngaoundere. The Fulbe language makes a distinction between *dimo* and *maccudo*, meaning respectively 'freeman' and 'slave', a discrimination paralleling the basic one made in Koranic law. Membership in the legally free category was attainable through birth to two free parents, through birth to a slave concubine having relations with a freeman, or through manumission. A slave concubine herself, having borne a free child, would also become free on the death of her child's father. Free offspring of slave concubines were not jurally disadvantaged and as the decades passed after the conquest, many of the Ngaoundere aristocracy and even several of the rulers had such parentage.

Manumitted slaves were known as *dimdinaado*, a term formed on the same verbal root as *dimo* but with the addition of causative and passive infixes which literally means 'one who has been freed'. Although a freedman suffered no subsequent legal disabilities, his low birth could be socially disadvantageous, particularly when it came to contracting marriage.

The term *maccudo*, or slave, when used in its broadest

non-technical sense, referred to all subject 'pagans' (or *haabe*) regardless of their exact legal or social situation. Jurally speaking, there was a clear distinction made, for taxation and other purposes, between conquered tribute-paying groups who were permitted to live on their traditional lands under the control of their traditional chiefs, and captive individuals or groups who were brought back to Ngaoundere and re-settled. Vassal groups including various Mbum and Duru populations living near Ngaoundere were required to pay annually the Koranic *jizya* tribute to the state, consisting minimally of a large basket of millet of about 20 kg. per household (Froelich 1954:48). Slaves, on the other hand, were not taxed, since in principle all their produce belonged to their masters who in turn fed and clothed them and provided their other basic needs. However, despite the distinctions which existed between the slave and vassal categories in Koranic law, it would be an error to draw an overly sharp line between the two groups. In practice, the Fulbe clearly viewed the vassal populations as functionally similar to slaves and did not hesitate to demand extra produce or labour from them as required. Many concubines were also procured from vassal groups, and the status of these women often differed little from that of concubines of slave status. In the last analysis, the most important point with regard to vassal groups at Ngaoundere was that the Fulbe still regarded these people as potential reservoirs of slaves and if these groups and their leaders did not submit to Fulbe demands, they would be raided and reduced to total slavery (Passarge 1895:297).

Even among the slave population at Ngaoundere itself, there were marked variations in status. Slaves could be owned by private owners or by the state. In the case of private ownership, slaves normally performed farming or herding work or could serve as domestic slaves in the master's household. The state owned substantial numbers of farm slaves as well, but there was also a category of court slaves (a few of whom were eunuchs) linked to the office of ruler, *laamiido* (Passarge 1895:490–491). Many of the latter performed domestic tasks in the ruler's compound while others served as officers in the government or military. For example, the offices of *sarki lifida,* the head of the heavy cavalry, and *sarki bindiga,* the leader of the corps of musketeers, were both slave titles (Passarge 1895:267, 494; Froelich 1954:79). Farm slaves settled in slave villages known as *ruumde* had the hardest life, while the court slaves in certain cases could wield substantial power and live a life of ease, supported by state funds and owning their own slaves (Passarge 1895: 489, 490).

One problematic issue with regard to the Fulbe system of slavery at Ngaoundere is the question of the increasing rights enjoyed by at least some of the slaves who had been born in captivity (*diimaajo,* pl. *riimaibe*).[4] Some form of progressive modification of slave status was only logical in a situation where slaves might hold important public offices and where, in theory at least, masters were under the obligation to convert their slaves to Islam. Although the full details of the practice are not clear, it appears that in the case of household and court slaves who had been raised as Muslims in their masters' households, their owners were morally, although perhaps not legally, barred from selling them.[5] On the other hand, farm slaves in Ngaoundere were subject to a more severe regime, and they and their children were sold at their masters' will.

At first glance, the presence of numerous slave villages around Ngaoundere might lead one to the conclusion that the principal economic dynamic of the society was based on the extraction of an agricultural surplus from the servile population by the Fulbe state and private slave-owners for sale on the market. More careful consideration of the case, however, leads to the rejection of this conventional 'slave mode of production' interpretation. Ngaoundere's reputation during the nineteenth century was built on the importance of its trade, and yet agricultural commodities as well as the output of Ngaoundere's rudimentary craft production played virtually no role in this commerce (Lacroix 1952:32–33). The transport of bulky foodstuffs for long distances by human or donkey porterage was uneconomical, and the lightly populated Fulbe states of southern Adamawa had few difficulties in feeding their populations in any case. The agricultural produce of the slave settlements was used to support the ruler's court and the related administrative and warfare apparatus, and the growth in the number of slave settlements around Ngaoundere during the nineteenth century was principally linked with a political and demographic strategy of increasing the manpower available to the state.

On the other hand, Ngaoundere maintained an important pastoral component in its ecology throughout the nineteenth century and slave herdsmen were often used in this activity (Passarge 1895:261). Cattle did serve as an important form of tribute and general means of exchange between the states of Adamawa as well as between Ngaoundere and its 'pagan' peripheries where cattle were exchanged for slaves.[6] But cattle production at Ngaoundere did not require large inputs of labour and consequently cannot constitute an adequate explanation for the voracious appetite for slaves of the Ngaoundere state.

The slave-raiding activities of Ngaoundere had their own inbuilt and self-perpetuating rationale. The majority of the slaves taken in raids were traded to other Fulbe states, and it was more as means of exchange than as means of production that slaves constituted the principal source of Ngaoundere's wealth. Captives who were resettled in slave villages at Ngaoundere primarily served to strengthen the slave-raiding machinery, by producing food to feed more warriors and/or by serving as warriors themselves. The continued existence of the Ngaoundere state in its nineteenth century form clearly depended on its slave raiding and trading, activities which implied a continuing integral relationship within a regional system between Ngaoundere and its 'pagan' peripheries. It is this relationship which I shall concentrate upon in the remainder of the paper—in particular the impact of Ngaoundere's activities on the Gbaya, a people among whom I carried out field research.

The Fulbe and the Gbaya

Dropping back to pick up the thread of our history of Ngaoundere, the 1830s and 1840s were spent by Njobdi and his successor, Lawan Haman, in establishing and consolidating their control over Ngaoundere and its immediate environs. By the 1850s, however, sufficient local control had been established around Ngaoundere so that the Fulbe could turn their attentions further afield. Until major Fulbe raiding parties began to range the western Gbaya region at this time, infrequent long-distance trade carried out by daring individuals appears to have provided the only significant link between the Gbaya and the Muslim world, and we have no evidence of substantial Muslim penetration beyond the few trading centres on the western margins of Gbaya territory (Flegel 1885:15). This trade, which was in the hands of traders from Hausaland and Bornu, was very perilous and focused on low-volume, high-profit items, particularly ivory (Flegel 1885:15, 21; Lacroix 1952:34–36). But when sizeable Fulbe military expeditions began to be launched against the Gbaya by Ardo Issa, who reigned from 1854 to 1878, we start to get evidence of significant political and religious accommodations on the part of the Gbaya to the Fulbe presence, and the volume and complexity of trade, especially in slaves, increased markedly (Flegel 1885:15–21; Mohammadou in press; Charreau 1905:74–76; Froelich 1954:14).

Most Fulbe expeditions against the Gbaya took place during the dry season and normally lasted for several months, although in some cases they stretched over several years (Passarge 1895:275; Charreau 1905:78–79; Strümpell 1912:84). A sizeable proportion of Ngaoundere would participate in these major raids and one French traveller reported that when he visited the town in 1893, 3,000 out of the total town population of 11,000 were absent for such a purpose (Cholet 1896:207). Once the war party, complete with women and domestic slaves to look after the warriors' needs, had travelled to within striking range of the enemy, a fortified military camp (*sangyeere*) was established to serve as a safe base (Ponel 1896:205). The *sangyeere* also served as a slave market after captives had been taken. The ruler of Ngaoundere profited heavily from these raids, since he claimed a minimum of fifty percent of the slaves taken. When the ruler's titled slaves commanded such a slaving expedition, he had first choice from the whole take, although he of course would reward his officers well. The bulk of the slaves taken were sold by the successful warriors to Hausa traders who visited the *sangyeere* for this purpose, and these captives were then exported for resale in the large slave markets of Hausaland and Bornu.

In the second half of the nineteenth century, several Gbaya towns on the western margins of Gbaya territory, in particular Kounde, Baboua, and Gaza, which were conquered early in the Fulbe attacks on the Gbaya, began to serve as regular bases for Fulbe military forces and entrepôts for Hausa traders (Charreau 1905:12, 24, 76–77, 139; Strümpell 1912: 83–84; Froelich 1954:14; Burnham in press).

During the half-century of Fulbe contact with the Gbaya prior to the European arrival in 1892, the political situation ebbed and flowed, depending mainly upon the extent of Fulbe military presence among the Gbaya at the moment. When a full-scale Fulbe raiding party, complete with the mailed horsemen on which Fulbe military superiority was based, actually travelled the two hundred or more kilometres from Ngaoundere to the western Gbaya area, they were more or less assured of military success (Passarge 1895:484). Some Gbaya clans and their leaders submitted with little or no fighting, accepting to pay tribute, to conduct slave raids on behalf of Ngaoundere, and to allow Muslim traders free access to their territory (Charreau 1905:10–30; Mizon 1895: 365; Brussaux 1908:82–83). Other Gbaya fled in the face of the Fulbe, scattered in the bush, and thus evaded Fulbe control (Mizon 1895:365).[7] Still others, particularly those with strong leadership, offered a stout resistance and were sometimes sufficiently successful to escape Fulbe conquest (Charreau 1905:77, Tessmann 1937:165). In any case, once the Fulbe forces returned home, even the subjugated groups were apt not to live up to their pledges of tribute (Charreau 1905:77; Ponel 1896:193, 202; Anon. 1893; Anon. 1895:134–135).[8] And on various occasions, Ngaoundere was prevented from sending a new military force against such recalcitrant Gbaya for several years due to more pressing military requirements nearer home.

Ngaoundere never succeeded in directly administering most of the Gbaya territories it raided, since the several hundred kilometres separating Ngaoundere from the Gbaya rendered continuous effective Fulbe control very difficult.[9] It must be remembered that the Adamawa *jihad* had been accomplished by quite a small number of Fulbe and despite the remarkable incorporative tendencies of the Fulbe state system, which had managed to transform enemy groups like the Mbum of Ngaoundere into vassal allies in less than a generation, it was too much to expect that a state with the logistic and manpower limitations of Ngaoundere could effectively administer the tens of thousands of square kilometres of thinly populated Gbaya territory. True, the Fulbe were able to establish one of their Mbum vassals at the important Gbaya village of Kounde, probably during the late 1870s (Charreau 1905:74–76; Burnham in press), but there is no indication that the Mbum of Kounde ever treated the Gbaya region as anything more than a frontier area ripe for slave raiding. The Gbaya at Kounde were never incorporated into the internal administrative and fiscal system of the Ngaoundere state. In fact, the Hausa and other Muslims living as traders in the Gbaya region were governed separately by their own leaders appointed by Ngaoundere and paid tax to the Fulbe state, while the sources speak only of tribute, not tax, being levied on conquered Gbaya groups (Charreau 1905:21, 28; Mizon 1895:358–359; Burnham in press).

As already explained, it is by no means certain that the Fulbe of Ngaoundere really wished fully to incorporate the Gbaya into their state as they had done with the Mbum. The vast unconquered lands to the east of the Adamawa states interested the Fulbe more as a source of valued commodities such as ivory and kola nuts and as a reservoir of slaves than as a potential increment to their territory. The Ngaoundere state already controlled large tracts of very lightly populated territory nearer home on which slaves captured on its eastern frontiers could be settled in slave villages (*ruumde*) to increase agricultural production and animal husbandry.

It was in conjunction with this strategy of indirect exploitation of the Gbaya region that the rulers of Ngaoundere supported the establishment and maintenance of permanent colonies of Muslim traders among the Gbaya (Mizon 1895: 358–359; Flegel 1885; Passarge 1895:275).[10] The activities of these colonies of traders under the leadership of former caravan leaders entitled *madugu*, served to funnel the lucrative trade of the Gbaya region toward Ngaoundere and bolstered the effectiveness of the uncertain tribute relations with various Gbaya groups (Burnham in press). As a result, several Gbaya villages including Kounde, Baboua (Doka), and Gaza grew in size and importance, their leaders expanded their power, and these centres served as foci of Fulbe political influence and Muslim conversion (Tessmann 1937: 175–176).

Looking at a map, the political situation in the Gbaya region by 1890 can be summarised as follows. The villages of Kounde, Baboua, and Gaza on the extreme western margins of the Gbaya region were quite firmly submitted to Fulbe influence, but Gbaya groups only a few hours' march to the east were much less sure (Tessmann 1937:169). Nonetheless, beyond the immediate environs of these three centres, it is possible to trace, in a fairly rough fashion, a zone of relatively strong Fulbe influence which stretched from the headwaters of the Lom and Nana rivers in the north, to the Nana and Mambere river valleys in the east, and down to the level of Gaza in the south (Charreau 1905:10–30; Mizon 1895:360–365; Tessmann 1937: 174). In this zone, the Fulbe presence was visible in a number of areas of Gbaya life including warfare technology, the adoption of Islam by some, familiarity with the Fulfulde language, styles of dress, and various other elements of material culture and economy (Brussaux 1908: 82–83; Harttman 1927). This was an area of heavy Fulbe military activity in the second half of the nineteenth century, and many of these Gbaya groups had entered into tribute and trade relations with the Fulbe. Warfare continued to be prevalent in this area in the 1890s, but conditions were usually stable enough for Hausa traders to operate there with some regularity, although they still travelled in armed caravans (Charreau 1905:10–12; Ponel 1896:204).

Beyond the Nana and Mambere rivers to the east and north

and in the area south of Gaza, Fulbe military forces penetrated only infrequently and when they did, they encountered
considerable resistance from a number of Gbaya groups as
well as from peoples like the Kare, the Yangere, and the
Kaka. Right up to the early colonial period, these continued
to be dangerous frontier areas which were frequently raided
for slaves (Loefler 1907:225 *et seq.*; Charreau 1905:12, 22,
74 *et seq.*).[11]

These gradations in Ngaoundere's influence on neighbouring Gbaya groups map out in a synchronic fashion the centre-
periphery relationship that I have already mentioned. But in
reality, this was a dynamic process spanning more than a half
century, through which certain Gbaya groups were mobilised
as agents for the Fulbe designs in the area. In addition, as we
shall now see, the Fulbe influence had a marked centralising
effect on many Gbaya groups, both those collaborating with
the Fulbe and those who contested Fulbe penetration.

Gbaya Political Structures in the Mid-Nineteenth Century

When first contacted by the Fulbe in the mid-nineteenth
century, the Gbaya were organised in clan territory group-
ings, which consisted of a number of small hamlets scattered
over five to ten square kilometres of wooded savanna and
surrounded by much larger expanses of uninhabited hunting
grounds. These clan territories normally housed populations
of several hundred people. A clan territory had a leader,
usually termed '*chef*' in French sources. Clan territories had
recognised boundaries and were defended by their inhabitants
against encroachments by other similar groups (Tessmann
1937:143, 161). Clan territories occasionally entered into short-
term military alliances but were usually the largest units of
collective political action.

Ideally speaking, the Gbaya thought of the membership of
such a clan territory as being composed solely of men drawn
from a single patriclan (*zu duk*) along with their wives and
children (Tessmann 1937:120–124). However, this ideal of
clan homogeneity was rarely achieved in practice and
although many of the inhabitants of such a territory were

members of one dominant clan, the rest of the adult male population would be drawn from several other clans. When a number of clans inhabited one territory in this way, Gbaya cultural idiom held that the politically dominant clan was the founding clan of the territory and on this basis had the right to provide the 'chief' of the group as well as to practise various rituals associated with the control of the territory.

Men from subordinate clans were willing to ally themselves with a dominant clan for a number of reasons, the principal one being that unless a Gbaya hamlet formed a part of a clan territory large enough to defend itself from its neighbours, it was at grave risk of attack and enslavement (Tessmann 1937:120). Consequently, a clan which had lost membership through war or an epidemic had to seek an alliance with a dominant clan. Likewise, if a segment of a clan quarrelled with its fellow agnates, it could leave its home clan territory and join another. Thus, although a clan territory grouping acted as a more-or-less cohesive unit in external political affairs, at least on the shorter term, the dispersed settlement pattern within the territory as well as a substantial rate of residential mobility betrayed tendencies toward individualism and competitiveness in local level politics over the longer term.

Gbaya geographical mobility also had important implications in the sphere of political leadership. When a small collection of clansmen moved away from their fellows to found a new hamlet, the senior man of the new hamlet was recognised by his co-residents as hamlet headman (Tessmann 1934:88–89, 1937:125). This easy multiplication of leadership roles at the hamlet level was another index of fluidity in the Gbaya political system.

The role of clan territory leader among the Gbaya prior to Fulbe contact was not formalised into a corporate office but was a position of considerable uncertainty that was largely reliant on continued military success. As just mentioned, such a war leader's influence could wane and his followers would tend to reallocate their allegiances. The clan-leader role was not characterised by a well-defined rule of succession—any

C

adult male member of the locally dominant clan being eligible to assume the position.

Although Gbaya might well recognise the existence of a powerful leader in their clan territory, they would give him support only to the extent that it suited them. If the disadvantages, in the form of reduced local group autonomy, degree of success in warfare, and access to booty from raiding or to external trade, appeared to outweigh the advantages of continued support, a subordinate group could 'vote with its feet' and relocate its hamlet further away from the hamlet of the clan leader. Depending on the degree to which such dissidents wished to withdraw from a 'chief's' sphere of influence, they could either simply move their hamlet to a site further from his settlement but still within the same clan territory or they could secede altogether by going to live on the territory of another clan. A strong leader sometimes opposed such secessions with force, using warriors drawn from his own clan plus other dependents such as slaves to attempt to impose his will upon the dissenters (Tessmann 1937:122–128). We do not have extensive data on the leader's probability of success in such an undertaking, but the general tone of our sources seems to indicate that in most cases it would not be high.

Gbaya 'chiefs', in addition to their duties as war leaders, also arranged inter-clan trading expeditions, which were organised in much the same manner as war parties (Tessmann 1937:109, 110). In addition to trade, marriages would also be arranged on these visits. Omaha-type rules of exogamy, combined with shallow genealogies and fluid local group composition, precluded regular patterns of marriage exchange and forced many men to look for wives outside their own clan territory. As a result, Gbaya frequently 'married their enemies', marrying women from clans with whom they had only tenuous relations (Tessmann 1937:162–163).

Although such external marriage links had their dangers, they also could provide potential avenues of political attraction and readjustment through residential relocation of clan segments, since the mother's brother's village was considered to be the next-best choice of residence if residence with one's own clan became impossible or unwise. It was therefore structurally feasible for leaders of strong clan territories to build up larger followings on the basis of marriage alliances. In this connection, clan leaders were usually polygamists, making use of the extra wives to create such alliances as well as to provide a larger domestic and agricultural labour supply (Charreau 1905:95, 149; Tessmann 1934: 53).

However, such a political expansionist strategy also contained the seeds of its own destruction, since the larger a clan territory got, the greater the possibility for the group to subdivide into two viable military units. In addition, ramifying external marriage alliances did not necessarily work in favour of a unified clan territory since they might just as well provide avenues for the secession of the various subordinate clans from the unit. A Gbaya clan leader appears to have had no effective means at his disposal to control the patterns of marriage alliance of the members of his clan territory group, since marriages were contracted between the two partners and their immediate senior kin co-resident in the same hamlets and were not subject to corporate regulation by the clan as a whole or by the clan territory grouping.

Tendencies toward Political Centralisation in Gbaya Society

Prior to the impact of the Fulbe, then, Gbaya political structures and leadership patterns were quite fluid. But throughout the latter half of the nineteenth century, the political organisation of those Gbaya groups in contact with the Fulbe began to firm up, and the roles of certain important Gbaya war leaders took on more of the attributes of corporate political office. The progressive centralisation of Gbaya political structure was intimately linked with the increasing demand for slaves from Ngaoundere and the Hausa-Fulani states beyond, and this process had as its essential pre-condition the threat or fact of large-scale Fulbe raids.

As already noted, this continual military activity by the Ngaoundere state against the Gbaya owed little to a desire for further territorial conquests *per se* and was rather an expression of the commercial and demographic expansionism which was the principal dynamic of this political system.

After 1850, Ngaoundere's main problem was to ensure a regular flow from its peripheries of slaves, ivory, and other desired commodities such as kola nuts, without having to completely dominate and incorporate distant groups like the Gbaya. Effective exploitation of politically acephalous peoples like the Gbaya in the absence of total military control posed particular problems for Ngaoundere and, in response, the Fulbe adopted a policy of support for selected Gbaya war leaders. According to de Brazza who commented on the situation in 1892, Gbaya clans that submitted to the Fulbe without a fight were respected and 'their chiefs go to Ngaoundere, receiving there the investiture in the name of Abbo (the ruler of Ngaoundere), who sends them back to their country'. On the other hand, 'populations that put up resistance are raided (for slaves) and the sons of chiefs and other important young men are taken to Ngaoundere and brought up in contact with the Fulbe and Hausa. Then, after several years, they are sent back to their homeland where they rule the country in the name of Abbo'.[12]

The primary obligations of a Gbaya leader whose clan territory had submitted to the Fulbe was to assure the security of Hausa traders working in his area and to pay regular tribute to the ruler of Ngaoundere. We have no record of the exact amount of tribute levied on Gbaya clan territories annually, but this does not appear to have been too burdensome. For example, Charreau (1905:28) reports that the village of Bingue near Baboua paid an annual tribute to the ruler of Ngaoundere consisting of slaves, salt, mats, and ivory, but received a return gift of cattle from the ruler which was often of equal local value to the tribute. From the Fulbe point of view, of course, tribute received from the Gbaya was still an important source of wealth even when the Fulbe returned cattle to the Gbaya, because of the very high prices that commodities such as ivory and slaves would bring when traded westwards to Hausaland (Flegel 1885).

Ngaoundere's insistence that Hausa traders be protected reflected the fact that much of the trade in slaves and ivory, the two most important commodities, passed through the hands of these men. A method used by the Fulbe to deal with subjugated Gbaya groups was the settlement of Hausa traders in important Gbaya villages to act as resident representatives of Fulbe interests (Tessmann 1937:175; Charreau 1905:11–13, Mizon 1895:358–359; Burnham in press).[13] These Hausa served a number of functions including overseeing Gbaya leaders to try to ensure that tribute payments continued to flow to the ruler, collecting caravan taxes on all long-distance traders passing through the area, welcoming strangers and emissaries, disseminating Islam, and acting as leader of the local non-Gbaya Muslim community. The resident leader of such a colony of traders held the title *madugu*, the Hausa term for the leader of a long-distance caravan, and Mizon (1895:358–359) explains that this title was a holdover from the earlier careers of these men who had formerly served as caravan leaders (see also Flegel 1885). These *madugai* (plural of *madugu*) along with the many other Hausa and Kanuri traders in the Gbaya regions, also traded for their private benefit and would buy slaves and ivory from Gbaya warriors for cloth, cattle (for butchering), cowries, horses, military equipment, natron, salt, beads, soap, tobacco, leather goods, and silver thalers. Hausa traders also purchased mats, locust bean cake, kola, African pepper (*Xylopia aethiopica*), and parrot feathers from the Gbaya (Burnham in press). Firearms did not form a part of this trade, since the Hausa traders in this region had no source of supply prior to direct European contact in the 1890s (*cf.* Charreau 1905:140; Mizon 1895:367).

Not only was the flow of trade and tribute between the Gbaya region and Ngaoundere significant to the Fulbe but it was also of great importance to Gbaya leaders interested in consolidating their positions in their own clan territories. It is difficult to determine just how important the redistributive role of Gbaya clan leaders had been prior to Fulbe contact. Although wealth does not appear to have been a necessary prerequisite for selection as clan leader even in protocolonial times, the assumption of this role implied that the incumbent would take an active part in the patterns of wealth accumulation and exchange in his group and would probably grow relatively wealthy in the process (Charreau

1905:92, 152; Harttmann 1927:45–47). The organisation of collective hunts within the clan territory was another of the responsibilities of a clan leader, and he had the right to a share of the meat of any large animals killed by his men. In return, the leader would organise feasts, providing the manioc porridge and possibly beer for consumption with the meat (Charreau 1905:95; Harttmann 1927:31, 47). As already mentioned, clan leaders normally became polygamists so as to have sufficient wives to cultivate larger fields and to undertake extra cooking duties in connection with this feasting (Charreau 1905:144; Tessmann 1934:53).

The redistributive aspect of the war-leader role must have been enhanced through contact with the Fulbe/Hausa tribute and trade network. By the late nineteenth century, at least some Gbaya war leaders around Kounde and Baboua claimed a right to a portion of the slaves captured by individual Gbaya warriors during a raid, despite the fact that Gbaya custom normally gave an individual the right to any booty he personally captured (Charreau 1905:138). When a Gbaya leader sent such slaves to Ngaoundere, or traded them to Hausa traders, he gained access to a superior military technology including horses, horse equipment, chain mail, and swords as well as to high-prestige trade goods such as cattle and cloth (Harttmann 1927:46; Tessmann 1937:168–172; Charreau 1905; 20, 28).[14] When a Gbaya clan territory stood in a tributary relation with the Fulbe, this tribute was also funnelled through the clan leader who might take it personally to Ngaoundere and who received gifts from the ruler in return. Judicious distribution and control of such wealth and warfare objects could then be used to enhance the clan leader's position in his own group. As long as a clan leader continued to enjoy success in warfare and/or could maintain advantageous relations with the Fulbe, these patterns of exchange combined and mutually reinforced one another to shore up his power and give added cohesiveness and stability to his clan territory and his own leadership role (Tessmann 1937:175). As a result, his position as leader became less dependent on fleeting charismatic qualities. By the beginning of the colonial period, such succesful Gbaya leaders could mount miniature court displays in the

Fulbe style to impress visiting Europeans, complete with a few cavalry and a well-equipped escort of retainers and musicians (Tessmann 1937:168–170, 174–178; Harttmann 1927:20, 46). Harttmann (1927:47) mentions as well that in some areas of strong Fulbe influence, 'chiefs' were able to require their followers to build houses and cultivate fields on their behalf—obligations which Tessmann (1937:125) considered to be uncharacteristic of most Gbaya groups.

These major Gbaya 'chiefs' relied heavily on slave raiding to sustain their position of power. So common was this large-scale raiding in the northwestern margins of the Gbaya country that a special trail was opened to convey the slaves directly to Ngaoundere. Ponel, one of de Brazza's lieutenants who travelled to Ngaoundere in 1893 along this route, called it the 'Laka road' and mentioned that he regularly saw 'human debris' along it—the remains of slaves who were too feeble to reach Ngaoundere.[15] Raiding provided slaves, and trade or tribute in slaves gave access to wealth and superior armament (Charreau 1905:22, 182; Tessmann 1937:126–128; Harttmann 1927:48).[16] Success thus bred success, and the several more important Gbaya leaders of the late nineteenth century were occasionally able to bring about short-lived but extensive inter-clan alliances that, according to contemporary accounts, could field as many as one thousand warriors, at least some of whom were mounted.[17] On the other hand, the various Gbaya groups that offered a sustained opposition to the Fulbe and their Mbum and Gbaya tributaries also had to field large forces, and certain well-known Gbaya leaders emerged in this context (Tessmann 1927:165; Anon. 1895: 134–135; Ponel 1896:193; Mizon 1895:360; Charreau 1905: 77).[18] In other words, tribute relations with the Fulbe were not the only means by which political cohesiveness was enhanced in Gbaya society.

Although the bulk of the slaves taken in Gbaya raids were sold to Hausa traders for cattle, cowries, cloth, and other trade goods, when Gbaya captured other Gbaya, the captives were sometimes ransomed by their relatives (Charreau 1905: 139, 167).[19] Tessmann (1937:127) quotes ransom rates of ten goats for young people and twenty goats for adults. As another alternative, slaves could be kept by their captor, eventually to be incorporated into his clan. A female slave would be taken as a wife. Young male captives served as agricultural workers and when they had matured, they would be given a wife by their master and would enjoy more freedom. They could normally be expected to serve their master throughout their lives and were valuable supporters in local political struggles. But Gbaya slavery never developed beyond this domestic form, with slaves enjoying a pseudo-kinship or clientage relation with their masters, which led to the progressive incorporation of their descendants into the master's clan (Tessmann 1957:126–128; Harttmann 1927:48). This contrasted with the practice of the Muslim traders at Kounde and Gaza and the Mbum vassal chief at Kounde, who owned substantial numbers of slaves whom they settled in separate slave settlements and used both as agricultural labourers and as a corps of trusted warriors.[20]

The Traders' Role in the Regional System

Thus far, this paper has focused primarily on the 'raiders', and the political implications of Ngaoundere's military activities and tribute collection among the Gbaya groups on its periphery. I now want to turn to the other part of my title and consider in more detail the activities of the long-distance traders in this regional system.

As we have already seen, long-distance traders began to operate in the Gbaya regions in earnest in the second half of the nineteenth century, after the advent of large-scale Fulbe raiding had provided the conditions of military control necessary for effective trading. From the accounts of Barth (1857: II:613–621; see also Burnham in press) and Mai Gashin Baki (Flegel 1885), it seems that a few Hausa traders had made contact with the westernmost Gbaya groups at least a decade before 1850, but this commerce was limited only to those daring enough to take great risks in order to secure the potentially high profits that were available.

After 1850, large caravans of 200 to 300 traders accompanied by their wives and slaves visited the western Gbaya groups on a regular basis. The traders did their trading on an individual basis but travelled in armed caravans for mutual protection. Some of the traders were mounted on horseback and wore chain mail. But the actual transport of merchandise appears to have been accomplished primarily by head carrying, although donkeys were also sometimes used. These caravans were led by a *madugu* (caravan leader) and operated according to a well-defined set of customary rules. The caravan leader and his lieutenants (*ubandawaki* and *jangaba*) regulated conflicts internal to the caravan and represented the caravan's interests in negotiations with local chiefs. The caravan leader paid tolls and tribute on behalf of the whole group and then would recoup these outlays from the caravan members according to the number of loads of merchandise each trader was transporting (Flegel 1885:15—17).

The relatively safe trading entrepôts which developed among the Gbaya, particularly at the towns of Kounde, Baboua, and Gaza, attracted some of these traders to settle on a more permanent basis and act as bulk makers. These men accumulated stocks of kola nuts, ivory and other commodities through regular trade with the Gbaya, and these stocks were later exported when caravans visited the towns. As already mentioned, although these resident traders did not explicitly form a part of the administrative system of the Ngaoundere state, their presence in the Gbaya region did contribute to the effectiveness of the Fulbe economic exploitation of their 'pagan' peripheries. In addition, these communities of Muslim traders also constituted an important source of Islamic influence (Tessmann 1937:175, 176), since some of their leaders and other prominent traders had made the pilgrimage to Mecca, were literate in Arabic, and gave instruction in the Koran. This influence mainly made itself felt on Gbaya leaders who, as Tessmann (1937:174–175) and others note (Mizon 1895:358–359), saw in Islam a new road to power.[21] The mass of the Gbaya people remained unconverted and little influenced by Islam.

These long-distance and locally resident traders were not natives of Ngaoundere and although they are often referred to in the literature as 'Hausa' traders and used the Hausa

language in their trading, they were not necessarily Hausa
either. Their ethnic origins were diverse and included Kanuri,
Jukun, Nupe, Wangarawa, Mandara, and Choa Arab as well
as Hausa. These traders displayed weak political allegiances
and constituted a floating population which circulated widely
throughout the Muslim societies of West Africa. They would
trade wherever it seemed most profitable, and the great concentration of these men in Ngaoundere and the Gbaya
regions in the latter half of the nineteenth century is good
evidence for the high profitability of the trading opportunities
available in this area at that time. Indeed, one of the principal
economic correlates of the centre-periphery relations in a
regional system of slavery is the relatively low cost of slaves
procured on the periphery in comparison with the selling
price of slaves in the centre. Even with little trading capital,
the long-distance trader who was willing to assume the risks
of trading among the Gbaya in the nineteenth century stood
the chance of amassing a fortune after only a few visits
(Flegel 1885:9).

The presence of large numbers of long-distance traders was
very advantageous for the finances of the Ngaoundere state.
The state treasury collected taxes from each caravan in the
form of gate taxes, river-crossing taxes, and taxes levied
on all traders seeking the right to trade in Ngaoundere's
dominions. In this way, revenues accrued to Ngaoundere
from its peripheries without the necessity of establishing
complete domination over the Gbaya borderlands. Yet despite Ngaoundere's vital interest in these revenues and the fact
that traders of various ethnic groups including the Hausa and
Kanuri had titled representatives at the ruler's court to
defend their interests, this trade never became a full-fledged
state trade. In most cases, the profits from the export of slaves,
ivory, and other commodities from Ngaoundere accrued to
the traders as private individuals. On the other hand, particularly in the case of slaves taken by Gbaya groups which had
submitted to Ngaoundere, the ruler expected that all of these
captives would be given to him for sale to the traders or for
other form of disposal, and failure to follow this practice was
taken as a sign of revolt.

Conclusion

The structure of the system of slavery in Adamawa in the nineteenth century was determined primarily by military and commercial factors. The involvement of slaves in production activities in Adamawa, while undoubtedly the source of much of the food on which the Fulbe states subsisted, was of relatively minor structural importance. In this regard, the Adamawa case is hardly unique in Africa and bears close comparison with several of the studies presented in the recent symposium *L'Esclavage en Afrique Précoloniale* (Meillassoux 1975:17). Such cases, as Meillassoux (1975:21) notes in his introduction, do not lend themselves to an analysis based on the classic Marxist concept of slave mode of production and rather 'lead one to reject the slapping on of prefabricated modes of production, summarily borrowed from a few remarks or writings of Marx and Engels.'

A good example of the Marxist dogmatism that Meillassoux probably has in mind is provided by Büttner's study of slavery in nineteenth-century Adamawa which analyses Fulbe state structures as being based on the extraction by the ruling class of an agricultural surplus produced by a servile population. At first glance, the presence of substantial numbers of slave agricultural settlements in Adamawa would appear to support Büttner's case, but she (1967:57) is forced to admit that craft production, commerce, and transport were not sufficiently developed in Adamawa to permit the Fulbe rulers directly to convert any agricultural 'surplus' which might accrue into other forms of wealth (*cf*. Terray 1975:429). On the contrary, a military and demographic strategy was pursued in which slave capture and slave production of foodstuffs were used to create and support larger and larger armies (composed mainly of slaves) to permit the further expansion of raiding activities (*cf*. Büttner 1967:53). The cattle production of slave villages, to the extent that it entered into commercial circulation rather than being used for household dairy production, bridewealth or other ceremonial exchanges, could only be exploited by using the cattle as a quasi-monetary means of exchange to reward the 'pagan' vassals of the Fulbe for securing slaves, ivory or other commodities. In the last analysis, therefore, I would argue that the slave systems of the Adamawa states were primarily oriented toward the production of more slaves, who were easily traded to the states of the Sokoto Caliphate and Bornu in return for luxury goods. Faced with the fact that Adamawa states were not primarily oriented toward slave agricultural production, Büttner (1967:48, 53) is ultimately forced to put forward the grossly teleological argument that the Fulbe polities would inevitably evolve in this direction.

Other Marxist writers, although not as wedded to the classical schema as Büttner, still attempt to preserve the primary analytical importance of the production concept with equally poor results. Coquery-Vidrovitch, for example, in her writings on the 'African' mode of production, engages in a ridiculous metaphorical extension of the term 'production' in order to include in this category the 'production' of slaves by military activities (see also Goody 1971:36). Thus she writes (Coquery-Vidrovitch 1975:54),

> We should not be criticized here for emphasising too strongly the mode of circulation of goods over the mode of production; the basic problem was not that of transporting goods but indeed getting hold of them, in some way to 'produce' them. The activity in question was obviously a bastardised form of production, one both immediate and apparent, but in fact contradictory and predatory; because in the long term it laid waste the countryside rather than enriching it. There were two avenues open: war (in the form of slave raiding) or peaceful exchange with neighbouring peoples . . .; an external circulation which can be reduced to a form of production in contrast to the internal circulation within a given society.

Only a nervous Marxist with her eyes on the ancestors rather than on the data could have concocted such a tortuous argument.

Althusserian Marxist formulations (Althusser and Balibar 1970), which attempt to preserve the primary role of the production concept as 'determinant-in-the-last-instance' while allowing for temporary 'dominance' of other institutional 'instances' such as politics, religion, or kinship cannot adequately deal with cases of the Adamawa type either. Demonstrably, it was the military and distributional structures themselves, and not any hidden influence of the forces and relations of production or any of the other elements of the Althusserian *combinatoire* (Althusser and Balibar 1970:215, 311), which effected the transformations toward greater political centralisation both in the Ngaoundere state itself and among its Gbaya tributaries. In broader terms, the Althusserian concept of 'determination-in-the-last-instance' must be seen for what it is: a definitional trick of the same order as Coquery-Vidrovitch's metaphorical extension of the production concept which has no real analytical value.

Another unfortunate effect of the Marxist preoccupation with the internal dynamics of the production process is that it tends to obscure the regional nature of these systems. In contrast with the more orthodox Marxist position, writers such as Meillassoux (1975:22–24), Friedman (1976:9–10) and Kopytoff and Miers (1977:65) have argued for the value of a regional focus on the grounds that the structural requisites for the persistence ('reproduction' in Marxist terminology) of these systems are inter-societal in character. The necessity of such regional interlinkage in Adamawa is evident: the dominant slave-holding society needed continually to replenish its stock of slaves, given that the rate of reproduction of already captured slaves was not sufficient to replace losses from escape, export, manumission, and death. The term 'necessity' in the preceding sentence is to be understood in a logical or structural manner, rather than in a functionalist one, in the sense that the resupply of slaves from the peripheries was, by definition, requisite for the persistence of the regional system in an unchanged form.

The structural zoning effect produced by this replenishment process, which I have referred to as a centre-periphery relation, is primarily a function of political and military factors which determine who will be the raider and who will be the raided. At the centre is the militarily secure, dominant group with its demands for slaves. On the peripheries are the groups being raided at the effective limit of the centre's direct or indirect military influence. In between these two extremes are to be found various forms of intermediary structure, including groups ensuring the continued flow of slaves toward the centre via trading, tribute collection and payment, and raiding activities. In Adamawa, both Ngaoundere and the western Gbaya groups around Kounde, Baboua, and Gaza functioned in such an intermediary capacity, funnelling slaves from Gbaya and Laka groups on the extreme margins of the system in toward the states of the Sokoto Caliphate and Bornu at the centre. The multi-ethnic corps of traders functioned in such an intermediary capacity as well, being attracted to points of supply and demand within the system with little regard for societal boundaries or allegiances.

In the light of the Adamawa case, I cannot agree with Kopytoff and Miers' (1977:64) contention that, 'in the larger societies and the larger regional economic systems, trafficking in people must always have been but a minor part of the total entrepreneurial activity.' These authors seem to believe that the middleman role in a regional system of slavery would inevitably be the occupation of individuals or small groups of traders who engaged in slave trading almost as a side-line, rather than a function of the military hegemonies of state structures themselves as in the Adamawa region. As we have seen, the Fulbe states of Adamawa placed primary emphasis on the development and maintenance of a strong slave-raiding force, recruited through slave raiding itself or mobilisation of vassal groups. As Terray (1975:446–448) has noted in his discussion of Abron slavery, states that depend in this way on the military services of their subject peoples tend to minimise the level of tribute demanded from these same people. Ngaoundere was similar to the Abron in this regard, extracting small agricultural tributes from subject groups and offering the chance of substantial rewards of booty to slave officers and warriors and to subject 'pagan' groups who participated in Ngaoundere raids. On the other hand, the Ngaoundere state was strict in its insistence that the great bulk of slaves taken during these raids be passed through official state channels, a further indication of the central importance of the slave trade for Ngaoundere's fortunes.

At the same time, Meillassoux's (1971:24) portrayal of such systems in terms of an alien military class progressively dominating and exploiting an indigenous 'peasantry' is misleading because it overdraws the division between rulers and ruled. Moreover, Meillassoux does not give sufficient recognition to the fact that the stability and remarkable incorporative tendencies of states like Ngaoundere, whose population was composed in the majority by vassals and slaves, were based on the possibility for the subject peoples to participate in and profit from slave raiding themselves.

In a like manner, Ngaoundere's relatively open attitude to foreign traders can also be understood as a function of their overall strategy of wealth extraction from the peripheral regions. It was not in Ngaoundere's interest to impose too rigid a system of state controls on the activities of these long-distance traders, who collected valuable commodities such as ivory and kola from the Gbaya and other groups without the necessity of a formal state trading apparatus. As long as the trading conditions were reasonably safe and highly profitable, Ngaoundere could be assured of a large influx of these traders and a satisfactory profit would accrue to the state via moderate market taxes, gifts and tolls.

The military and commercial strategy of the Ngaoundere state resulted in a progressive development and extension of Fulbe political and economic structures toward the peripheries. This extension, however, did not necessarily involve the conquest and total incorporation of neighbouring 'pagan' groups. Many Fulbe cultural and social influences penetrated ahead of the expanding frontiers of the Ngaoundere state via contacts with Hausa traders and the efforts of Gbaya war leaders, who wished to enhance their control over their followers by channelling desired trade goods and Fulbe military equipment through their own hands. Only at a later date might the Fulbe succeed in establishing more direct control and begin to reorganise peripheral groups. This was the case of the Mbum and Gbaya villages of Mboula and Kounde which were at least partially incorporated into Ngaoundere's *tokkal* form of administrative structure by the late nineteenth century. At the same period, slave villages (*ruumde*) housing the Laka retainers of the Mbum vassal chief were established at Kounde. These diffused effects are best understood as structural entailments of the 'inflationery' demand for slaves at the centre of the regional system, a dynamic that was only checked by the advent of colonial rule.

The Comorians and the East African Slave Trade

GILL SHEPHERD

This paper has two aims. Firstly, it traces the long-standing but small-scale involvement of the Comoro Islands with slave owning and slave trading to the period in the nineteenth century when Western Indian Ocean trade was transformed by a vastly increased demand for slaves. Secondly, it examines the effects of new wealth and the incorporation of larger numbers of slaves into their islands on Comorians, who were geographically admirably situated to benefit from the boom period.

The Comoro Islands to the End of the Eighteenth Century

Trade has been vital to Comorians since the islands were first settled over a thousand years ago. Arab trading posts down the East African coast were early extended to Madagascar; and the Comoros were a convenient stop-over point for the vessels exchanging Indian cotton in Madagascar for food-stuffs, especially rice, needed at Kilwa and Malindi on the East African coast (Vérin 1972:76).[1] Comorians certainly took part in this local trade and some travelled more widely as sailors, pilots and interpreters (Grandidier 1903:312; Coupland 1938:170–171).

Like the Swahili on the mainland coast, Comorians have mixed Arab-African origins and have regularly incorporated new immigrants from Arabia. Until the beginning of French

colonial rule in the nineteenth century, they were grouped
into about a dozen sultanates ruled by *sherifs*—descendants
of the Prophet. They seem to have had domestic slaves
(probably acquired at Arab trading ports in North West
Madagascar) for as far back as there are records (Grandidier
1903:15; Vérin 1972:93).

In the late sixteenth and early seventeenth centuries the
Comorians appeared prosperous. Dutch sailors in 1598 encountered a richly clothed 'king' and his court, and trade
with the Portuguese at Mozambique was well established
(Grandidier 1903:256). Comorians exchanged foodstuffs for
cotton, and sold the Portuguese Malagasy slaves at ten times
their original purchase price (Grandidier 1904:83–85). On the
islands, the Comorian revictualling trade had been aug-
mented to cater to the increasing volume of European shipping *en route* for the East Indies. Contemporary European
writings all note the abundant availability of livestock,
poultry and fruit, and on the eagerness of islanders to exchange their produce for commodities like cloth, paper and
swordblades (Grandidier 1904:99, 400–401). Fierce rivalry
between sultanates for trade with European ships was one
result of this period, and the large number of slaves reported
in the islands in 1614 was probably related to the importance
of increasing the production of food for sale (Grandidier
1904:93; *Ibid.* 1905:559).

For the next century and a half there was little change.
Comorian trading with the Portuguese continued and extended north as far as Pate (Freeman-Grenville 1965:104).
Anjouan monopolised the revictualling of European shipping,
but all four islands seem .to have prospered (Freeman-
Grenville 1965:110–113). The ruins of fine buildings and
tombs date from this period and the islands apparently
attracted well-born settlers from other East African coast
towns (Viallard 1971:169–184).

Sakalave Slave-raids on the Comoro Islands

This tranquil era ended abruptly in 1785 when the Sakalave
of North West Madagascar launched the first of a series of

slave-raiding expeditions against the Comoros. Several hundred thirty-man outrigger canoes would set sail every three or four years with the northerly monsoon and would ravage the islands for three months, until the onset of the southern monsoon enabled the raiders to make an easy return home (Vérin 1972:153, 157–163). Expeditions were planned by the Sakalave but piloted by local 'Arabs' or Swahilised Malagasy (Boteler 1835:119). Slave labour was vainly employed in coastal Comorian towns for the construction of walls, look-out forts and defences: the Sakalave successfully carried off slaves, freemen and cattle, while the burning of villages and crops completed the utter disruption of the Comorian economy (Coupland 1938:173). One group of freeborn women committed mass suicide rather than be enslaved (Faurec 1941:18) and a few well-born individuals were subsequently ransomed (Harries 1977:53), but generally there was little the islanders could do to escape the Sakalave. They sent messages for help to the Portuguese, and to British Governors in Bombay, Cape Town and Mauritius (Coupland 1938:170, 200–201; Vérin 1972:162), but had little respite until 1823 when Merina expansion from Madagascar's central plateau finally paralysed the Sakalave.

Changes in the Economy of the Western Indian Ocean: the Growth of the Slave Trade

To understand Comorian prosperity in the nineteenth century, despite the earlier Sakalave raids, we need to understand why demand for slaves began to rise dramatically.

The crucial factor was France's need for labour in Mauritius and Réunion, islands devoid of indigenous populations where coffee and sugar were being planted. Demand, from the mid-eighteenth century onwards, was met partly by slave imports from Madagascar—which provided about forty-five per cent of the estimated 80,000 acquired between 1769 and 1793—and partly by purchases of Mozambique slaves brought to Madagascar by local Arabs (Vérin 1972:151).

The Sakalave had long been the only Malagasy slave suppliers. The guns (among other commodities) which they obtained from Arabs on the North West Madagascar coast had given them unique advantages (Vérin 1972:153). But when, late in the eighteenth century, the Merina first got guns from the French in Mauritius, they could challenge the Sakalave and begin selling slaves to the French directly.[2] The Sakalave then turned outside Madagascar for the slaves which underpinned their economy and began raiding first the Comoros and then mainland East Africa (Boteler 1835:59, Nicholls 1971:130).

Eventually, Madagascar became too unreliable a source for slave supplies. French shipping began to frequent the East African coast, buying from the Portuguese in Mozambique, from Swahili traders operating illegally within Portuguese dominions (Boteler 1835:60–61, 64; Hafkin 1973:26, 93, 224) and from Arabs on Pate in the north (Beachey 1976:25). Those who put in at East African ports in the early nineteenth century found that many local inhabitants spoke some French (Coupland 1938:168, 421).

France lost Mauritius to Britain after the Napoleonic Wars, and thereafter the island was supplied with Indian indentured labour. But Réunion still lacked labourers, and slave imports in the 1820s stood at 2,000 slaves a *month*, coming mostly from Mozambique and Quelimane (Beachey 1976:32).

Pressure on France to abandon slave labour was increasing, but she had added Nossi-Bé (off North West Madagascar) to her colonial possessions in 1840 and Mayotte (in the Comoros) in 1843 and the need for labour was greater than ever. Since the British denied her access to Indian indentured labour, the so-called 'free labour' or *engagé* system was started in the 1840s.

Slaves newly brought to the coast in Kilwa, Zanzibar and later Mozambique and other Portuguese towns, were offered to French agents as indentured labourers. The procedure may have satisfied French sensibilities, but for the traders and Africans involved, no real difference between *engagés* and slaves was perceived; evidence that such labourers ever had the chance to return home is scanty (Beachey 1976:34, 269 n. 81).

Swahili traders quickly adapted to the new situation. In

spots away from the surveillance of the British Anti-Slavery Patrol, such as the Comoro Islands and some of the towns near Mozambique, slaves were held until they could be transferred elsewhere as *engagés* (Alpers 1975:214). The *engagé* system was officially abolished in 1864 but the subterfuges it had stimulated made possible the illegal transfer of labour long after this date (Coupland 1938:435; Hafkin 1973:vi, 52, 308). For well over a century, French labour demands provided new opportunities for wealth. Comorians, like others who took part in the slave/*engagé* trade, stood to make profits of quite a new order.

As European interest in the area grew, so in turn Oman, under whose suzerainty the central and northern mainland coast lay, committed itself there more fully. During the rule of Sayyid Said, from 1806 to 1856, the Omani court was transferred to Zanzibar and the island speedily became the commercial hub of the whole coast (Alpers 1967:5).

Zanzibar was an ivory and slave trading centre before the Omanis came to settle (Coupland 1938:76; Beachey 1976: 38–39). But during the period of Sayyid Said's reign Zanzibar more than doubled the value of its exports and brought most of the coastal towns under its financial control (Nicholls 1971: 376–378). By the 1860s slave exports approached 30,000 a year (Beachey 1976:260) and an efficient machine, backed by Indian capital, had been created to funnel slaves into the island from all over East Africa.

Cloves, introduced from Mauritius and Réunion in the 1820s, gradually became Zanzibar's third export after ivory and slaves, and the plantations absorbed so much labour that by the 1850s an estimated two thirds of the population of the islands of Zanzibar and Pemba were slaves (Nicholls 1971: 82–83, 287).

French demand for slaves was probably the catalyst for Zanzibar's economic take-off but it quickly acquired its own impetus as the island became the main slave emporium of the region as well as turning to plantation agriculture in its own right.

Comorian Involvement in the
Nineteenth-Century Slave Trade

In the 1820s the Comoros' 'dilapidated towns and deserted villages' as the Sultan of Anjouan described them (Coupland 1938:201), bore witness to the Sakalave raids upon them. Yet within a decade they had begun a new involvement with slave trading which continued until virtually the end of the century and brought great changes to Comorian society.

The local carrying trade had remained in local hands despite the presence of so much European shipping, mainly because dhows employed slave labour and offered cheaper freight rates than Europeans could (Nicholls 1971:352–354). Slaving, in the 1820s still only a sideline in this trade, called for little adaptation when it grew profitable enough to become the main business.

Throughout the century a series of treaties and decrees progressively limited the field in which slaving could operate. The British made treaties with Zanzibar in 1822, 1839, 1845 and 1873; slave trading was nominally illegal for the Portuguese after 1836; a French Decree of 1849 declared the emancipation of slaves throughout French dominions (Beachey 1976:32) and a Ministerial Despatch to the Governor of Réunion in 1859 forbade recruitment of *engagés* in Madagascar or on the East African coast (Decary 1960:144). At each check, loopholes in the new situation were quickly perceived and exploited by traders. Numbers of slaves shipped remained fairly steady seemingly, though conditions on board dhows deteriorated as the need for secrecy increased.

Opportunities still open were used to the full. Comorians were in close contact with mainland Swahili such as the Sheikh of Quitangonha and the Sultan of Angoche, both under Portuguese control in name only and exporting Makua slaves in large numbers long after 1836 (Hafkin 1973:53, 149, 224).[3] Slaves from Kilwa could only legally be transferred within the territories of the Sultan of Zanzibar after 1845, but were frequently run southwards to the Comoros or Madagascar with papers for a northern voyage (Beachey 1976:59). Comorians were conversant enough with French rulings to understand that their own islands were still a legitimate source for *engagés*—and kept themselves well-stocked with East African slaves. 'Comorian' *engagés* were supposed to have lived in the Comoros for at least a year, but this was easily circumvented (Decary 1960:144–145). The British Anti-Slavery Patrol (which in any case consisted usually of only three ships) remained barely conscious of this southerly end of the slave trade until the 1860s, concentrating its efforts as it did on the trade to Arabia and the Gulf. Finally, because the French consistently refused the British right of search in vessels flying the French flag, Arabs and Comorians endeavoured to obtain French registration for their dhows—not difficult at Nossi-Bé or Mayotte—and sailed their slave cargoes unmolested (Beachey 1976:118, 232–235).

Slave prices indicate something of the profits to be made by Comorians. The French had long complained that they had to pay more for slaves on the East African coast than did non-Europeans (Nicholls 1971:201–202), and this continued to be true of negotiations for *engagés*. In the 1850s the total paid for an *engagé* by a Frenchman was 35 dollars on the East African coast and 30 to 40 dollars in the Comoros. Since *Comorians* could obtain slaves from the Portuguese coast in this period for 8 to 10 dollars each, it was greatly in their interest to encourage the French to trade with them: a journey of under two hundred miles each way yielded a 300 per cent profit. Similar trips to Madagascar were also profitable. In 1868 slaves bought on the African side of the Mozambique channel for 7 to 20 dollars could be sold in Madagascar for 28 to 30 dollars (Beachey 1976:33–38).[4] To make comparable profits on northern routes it was necessary to run more risks and travel much further: a male slave bought at 5 to 10 dollars in Zanzibar in 1850 fetched only 25 dollars in Muscat and 40 dollars in Basra, three thousand miles away (Beachey 1976:54).

Comorians were able to profit from the slave trade in a variety of ways. Most obviously, of course, dhow owners had the advantage. While no estimates of the numbers of dhows owned by Comorians exist to my knowledge for this period, it is clear that the shipping of slaves was a pursuit in which large numbers of people were involved. There are the statements of Gevrey (1870: ch. 2 passim) that, when he was writing, slave trading was the sole commercial activity of the populations of the islands of Ngazija, Anjouan and Mohéli. Robineau, citing a Comorian source, indicates that dhows were owned and used on commercial ventures not merely by the elite, but by middle-level artisans and the offspring of concubines belonging to wealthy men (1966:47). It is clear too that dhows were often hired out by their owners to those wishing to make slaving trips(Gevrey 1870:50–51).

Dhow crews were usually a mixture of slaves and freemen, if Comorians followed Arab and Swahili usage in this, and might be entirely manned by slaves (Cooper 1977:32–33, 188). The normal system of payment on dhows was to divide the profits of the trip between owner, captain and crew in a series of shares (Villiers 1940:343; Morton 1976:81) and this too would have spread slave profits more widely through the population. Hired slaves received wages which were split between them and their owners.

It is estimated that by the mid-1860s, at least 40 per cent of the Comorian population of 65,000 were slaves (Gevrey 1870: 38). Each of the walled coastal towns had a slave quarter, adjacent to that of fishermen and free artisans as a rule, and there were also slave villages on the hillsides where agricultural slaves lived. Artisans such as masons and carpenters were much in demand to build fine stone houses with carved doors for urban freemen who had done well financially, and they would take on slaves as apprentices. Considering that the Comoros had no plantations, the proportion of slaves in the population was very high; slaves in Zanzibar and Pemba were 66 per cent of the population, and on the Kenya coast about 25 per cent of the population (Morton 1976:44). Both were areas of plantation agriculture, among other activities.

The Effects of the Slave Trade within the Comoro Islands

The following sections deal with the effects of slave trading and the consequent opportunities for slave ownership on the

free Comorian population. It is prefaced, however, with a
sketch of conditions for slaves themselves, based on the
observations of Alfred Gevrey, Juge Imperial in Mayotte
from 1866 to 1868, who visited all the Comoro Islands during
that time. His comments on first- and second-generation
slaves are corroborated by the statements of informants made
over a hundred years later.

Newly arrived slaves in the Comoros, as opposed to the
locally born, the *wazalia*, were easily visible, with their filed
teeth and tattoos. But they quickly took on a Comorian
appearance by wearing local clothing and, in the case of
women, piercing ears and a nostril and putting local ornaments in them. Most quickly adopted Islam and a variety of
Arab customs, though burial practices seemed to mix Muslim
and Makua custom and black stones were set up in isolated
spots around slave villages, apparently for religious reasons
(Gevrey 1870:40–41).

Newly acquired male slaves were generally given agricultural tasks. Women were more likely to be taken into the
household but some, too, were put on the lands of their
owners. Here slaves worked a portion of the week—usually
five days—on their owners' land and were free for the rest of
the time to cultivate their own crops on plots allotted to
them. Comorian subsistence crops are not especially labour
intensive and, except when planting or harvesting, slaves
would not have been fully occupied in either portion of the
week.

Urban slaves lived either in their own quarter or in their
masters' houses. These slaves, who had a more intimate
relationship with their masters, had usually been born or
reared from childhood in the household. In addition, concubines were of course expressly acquired for the household
and their children would be born free. Gevrey visited the
house of a wealthy Anjouani in the company of some other
French people, including a woman who was invited into the
women's quarters:

She stumbled through two or three very dimly lit rooms
where she saw, seated upon carpets and matting, the four

legitimate wives of the householder and five or six concubines, their servants; . . . the wives were better dressed but
less pretty than the concubines, and both the women's
clothes and the furnishings of the harem were of the utmost
simplicity.

Throughout our visit, about twenty dirty malodorous
slaves—men, women and children—kept coming and going
and walking freely around the room, while the heads of a
dozen others kept appearing at the doors. Epidemics must
indeed have a devastating effect in these dirty, badly
ventilated houses, where forty or fifty people live packed
together . . . (Gevrey 1870:91).

While slaves in the Comoros had all been through humilia-
ting processes of capture and sale, their lot in the islands
seems not to have been hard. *Wazalia* (the locally born),
especially, had rights in that they had to be provided for, and
could not be sold. Slave children were not sold away from
their parents and concubines were often better loved than
wives.

Agricultural slaves were worse off than their urban counterparts, undoubtedly. However, it happens that comparison
can be made between the working conditions of Comorians'
agricultural slaves and those of the *engagés* of French
planters in Mayotte. In 1847 the emancipation of all slaves in
French territories, including Mayotte, was announced. In the
case of Mayotte, it was decreed that all freed slaves were to
render five years' service as *engagés* to the Government. At
this, most slaves declared that they preferred to remain the
slaves of their Comorian masters, rather than become the
slaves of the Christians. A look at the working conditions of
engagés explains why. Officially, *engagés* worked for eight
hours a day with Sundays and public holidays off; in fact
they worked a thirteen-hour day with neither rest nor food,
and when they stopped at seven, they were given their un-
varying day's ration in unhusked rice, which had to be
husked, winnowed and cooked before they could eat. Sundays
were working days and pay was stopped for the slightest
offence. *Engagés* often ran away for a while, as much on
account of the monotony of the food as the conditions of

work, and were glad to be sent to gaol for doing so, since life there was so much easier than on the plantations (Gevrey 1870:154–155).

Slaves and Production

In what ways did Comorian involvement with slave trading affect the local economy? Why were slaves not used to establish plantations, as had happened in Zanzibar, for instance?

While French planters in Mayotte and Mohéli began to grow sugar with *engagé* labour, and the British consul in Anjouan worked a sugar plantation with slave labour hired from local residents (Livingstone 1865:427–428), Comorians themselves were slow to follow suit. The Sultan of Anjouan was eager to imitate the consul's success, but he was not typical (Gevrey 1870:96). The answer is probably that the particular slave-trading niche which Comorians occupied in the nineteenth century was so profitable to them, and so easy to maintain, that they had no incentive to pursue unfamiliar ways of investing money. Trading by boat had always been a primary activity for Comorians and, as circumstances changed, all they had to do was concentrate their efforts upon a single cargo—slaves—instead of several. When, finally, slave trading was brought to an end, there was a serious slump before Comorians turned to the cultivation of cash crops. During the period under discussion, the existence of large numbers of slaves in the islands seems to have made very little difference to their productive output. Gevrey, for instance, noted that the inhabitants of Ngazija had become 'relatively wealthy' from the proceeds of the slave trade but still exported almost nothing but a few cattle and woven mats, while importing rice, and a wide range of luxuries from Zanzibar and Bombay (Gevrey 1870:70–71).

The Sultan of Anjouan is perhaps worth citing as an exception. He not only experimented with the growing of sugar using slave labour, but also allowed his slaves to be hired by Europeans, taking a portion of their pay himself. On these terms he allowed some of his own slaves to go as *engagés* to

Mayotte, but he insisted on their return after two years, retained their wives and children as hostages and, complained Gevrey, sent only sickly or weak men for whom he had no use himself (1870:153).

Finally, as an indirect result of the slave-trading boom, the mid-nineteenth century saw the establishment of a pattern whereby freeborn Comorian artisans, fishermen and other workers would migrate to Zanzibar town for some years. There were about 4000 Comorians in Zanzibar town in 1860 (Russell 1935:328). Their labour commanded good wages, which they invested in the purchase of slaves. An English visitor in 1876 noted:

> The Omani Arabs ... frequently hire, as head servants or stewards, poorer Arabs or Comoro men. ... [Comorians] are careful about their slaves as they constitute their entire fortune, and some of them are considerable slave holders. They seek employment for their slaves also, as underservants in European houses, or in light remunerative work, and they and their slaves almost invariably occupy the same hut (Christie 1876:329, 333).[5]

All freemen in Zanzibar owned slaves; indeed skilled urban slaves were likely to own three or four themselves (Beachey 1976:64). For poorer Comorians, the opportunity to accumulate both money and slaves was greater in Zanzibar than at home, and a stay there enabled them to retire to the Comoros with considerably enhanced wealth and social standing, the result of first their own, and then their slaves' productive labour.

Slaves and Consumption

The evidence is that slaves were valued more as items of consumption than for their productive capacities; or to put it another way, it was their ability to produce non-tangible wealth for their masters which gave them their primary value. Arabs, Swahilis and Comorians concurred in finding a man who did no manual work (because he could afford slaves) superior to a man who did. What is more, the ideal was apparently to own so many slaves that they were idle much of the time too. One of the important ways of rating a man was to observe how many dependents—kin, clients or slaves—he could afford to support, and a large train was taken as a sign of generosity.

Straightforward profits from slave trading might be invested in further trading, or the purchase of land, but seem to have gone very largely on consumption of various kinds. In addition to slaves, money was spent on hospitality, on religious observances such as making the pilgrimage to Mecca and on consumer items of Arab and European origin. Popular possessions were Arab clothing, weapons and perfume as well as European clocks, four-poster beds with mosquito nets, wardrobes, fine mirrors, artificial flowers under glass domes and carved chairs. Interest in these latter items was probably not, as might be supposed, imitated directly from Europeans, but from the Omanis in Zanzibar. Rigby commented in 1860 on the Omani taste 'for foreign luxuries such as handsome furniture and dress, costly mirrors, china, etc. . . .' (Russell 1935:332). Possibly in imitation of the Portuguese in Mozambique, well-to-do Comorians had themselves carried about on palanquins (*mantshira*) by their slaves (Hafkin 1973:70), though perhaps these were locally made. The one offered to Sulivan, at any rate, does not sound like an imported article (Sulivan 1873:125). The sultans invested their slave-trading profits in escalated warfare as well as in conspicuous consumption. For ordinary Comorians, marriage was the competitive arena in which money was used to outdo rivals. These uses of slave-trading profits are examined in separate sections below.

The value of slaves was, in the first instance, that they existed as part of their masters' property, whether in the household or in the fields. Their numbers, and their respectful behaviour to their masters, were admired and desired. Slave greetings, for instance, stressed rank differences thus. Slave: *kwezi, mwinyi!* (that you have power, Lord). Master: *bona!* (that you have life) (Fischer 1949:63). Slave behaviour enhanced the day-to-day importance of the owner. Household slaves lowered their eyes before their masters, walked behind, not in front of, the chairs on which the freeborn were seated, ate the leavings of their owners' food and wore their cast-off clothing. Concubines were the most desired type of slave for conspicuous consumption, followed by personal servants who performed a variety of tasks ranging from acting as secretaries and messengers to washing their masters' feet and massaging their bodies. Slaves were consumption items when they were given as presents by one freeman to another: such presents were slaves with a skill, or with beauty or strength.

Behind the scenes, the labour of slaves in domestic and agricultural work, or in more specialised urban employment, provided entirely for their masters' needs and made possible the conspicuous consumption of time in public. Gevrey's description of a Comorian household makes this very vivid (1870:46):

> [The reception room] opens onto a closed courtyard where during the day stay the women, children and slaves busy husking rice, cooking, making loin-cloths and mats and chewing betel. The men sit on mats on the outer verandah all day long, smoking hashish, chatting and playing draughts or cards.

Swahili-Comorian cuisine, at its best, demands enormous amounts of labour and the most delicious dishes are now only cooked during Ramadhan when the day-long fasting and gathering together of kin make larger amounts of time and labour available than usual. Comorian slave-owners could afford to give generous invitations to guests, and to acquire a reputation for hospitality, when they had at their disposal enough labour to grate coconuts, grind rice flour on millstones, knead dough lengthily and pound raw materials in pestles in addition to gathering foodstuffs, firewood and water. They consumed the time of their slaves and wives— quite literally.

Comorians also consumed the leisure-time which an abundance of slaves brought them in pursuit of the good Muslim life. By older men, in particular, this was regarded as the only moral use of free time and one which yielded spiritual profit in the eyes of the community. Such men attended all five prayer-times at the mosque, starting at dawn; read a portion of the Kor'an every day; joined sufic prayer circles; and sat in the company of other like-minded men between prayer times on the stone benches outside the mosques. Dressed in clean clothes and in a state of ritual purity, men who could spend part of each day in this way quickly acquired a reputation for piety. Among local Comorians some of these men were regarded with respect amounting to fear: their curses as well as their prayers were efficacious. Some held religious office but others used their powers to make amulets and cast horoscopes.

Internationally, the Comoros acquired something of a reputation for their Muslim teachers and law experts in the nineteenth century, which can only be attributed to their relative wealth and leisure. The sons of Muslim chiefs and traders in Mozambique were sent to study in the Comoros (Hafkin 1973:48, 57) while Comorian religious experts were of significance as kadhis and preachers in Zanzibar (Mkelle 1930; Martin 1971) and Lamu (Lienhardt 1959). Such was the career of Ahmed bin Sumeyt, a *sherif* of Itsandra on Ngazija. His father owned seven dhows, trading to Madagascar, Mozambique, East Africa and Arabia and both combined commercial acumen with a serious commitment to Islamic studies, which led each in turn to be offered posts as kadhis in Zanzibar. Ahmed bin Sumeyt became the greatest East African Muslim intellectual of his time, respected for his judgements as far away as the Hijaz and Cairo, a prolific author and the reviver of the 'Alawi sufic order in the area (Martin 1971: 541–544). Similarly, *sherif* Mohammed Ma'ruf of Moroni, on the same island, established a local branch of the Shadhiliya sufic order in the Comoros which he spread to the Muslims of North West Madagascar, Zanzibar and Pemba. His followers carried it to Mozambique and Tanganyika (Martin 1976: ch. 6 *passim*; Hafkin 1973:43). Membership of these Muslim brotherhoods became wildly popular in the Comoros. Their chief activity involved weekly attendance at *dhikri*, prayer meetings at which chanting, controlled breathing and rhythmic bodily movements led to trance.

Slavery and Becoming an Arab

For East African Afro-Arabs, Shirazi, Swahili or Comorian, being an Arab was a confused mixture of the genealogical and the social—a result of their merely colonial relationship to the Arab heartlands. Ideally, it entailed having irrefutable patrilineal links to Arabia or Oman, conditions which only *sherifs* or recent immigrants and their immediate descendants could meet. More generally it meant behaving like an Arab and being treated like an Árab: being rich, powerful, generous, learned and pious made one admired and respected. This mixture of economic and moral qualities was of specifically local relevance, but perhaps ordinary people genuinely believed that Arabia was full of such people. The confusion seems to be a product of colonial situations. 'If you are white you are rich/if you are rich you are white' was strikingly true in nineteenth-century Mozambique, for instance, where the wealthiest Christian classes were regarded as Portuguese regardless of colour (Hafkin 1973).

If being Arab is defined in this way, it is obvious that Comorians 'became' more Arab in the nineteenth century. They modelled themselves upon metropolitan Arabs more closely, as they had the means to do so, and their example was Omani Zanzibar; what they imitated from there had in turn been taken from Oman, the Hadhramawt, Mecca and Cairo. More Comorians had direct experience of Arabia, too, as increased wealth made it possible to make the pilgrimage to Mecca. And, at the same time, Arabs from Oman and South Arabia were emigrating and settling in East Africa and the Comoros, attracted by the new trading opportunities and unwittingly providing examples of Arab life-styles.

Some of the changes made direct use of the presence of slaves, others did not. Some Comorians began to wear Omani Arab clothing, for instance, and men in particular began to use more Arab names. Genealogies of Ngazija sultans (Harries 1977) show Bantu names and Bantu versions of Muslim names until the mid-nineteenth century, names such as Bamba Oma, Ju Mamba and Fum Bavu, and thereafter change abruptly to Arab names such as Hashim, Abdallah,

Ahmed, Hamza and Mohammed. The change is made earlier on Anjouan (Faurec 1941) which was the wealthier island.

The presence of slaves undoubtedly had a great effect on the Arabness of Comorians. The time-honoured way of using slaves was incorporating them as feudal retainers, swelling the ranks of the loyal followers of their owner. This, of course, was as much a tactic of African chiefs as Arab ones, and the power it bestowed was not specific to any one culture. However, the system in which Comorians competed for power and prestige had its apex in the Arab Sultan of Zanzibar while it rested upon a broad base of African slaves. It is hardly surprising that those of Arab-African origin viewed rising within this system, away from slave-like dependence on others and towards wealth and power, as a move away from Africanness towards Arabness. Nevertheless, the racial aspects of the situation should not be overemphasised. When a Comorian acquired slaves, he incorporated them into his following, as their patron, and thereafter—especially once they had Islamised—referred to them as 'his people' along with kin and free dependents. Masters and slaves were ideally united in opposition to other groups of masters and slaves and such groups were internally differentiated by rank, not race. In a society thus composed of vertically integrated groups, the occasional arming of slaves—a practice which astonished European observers in Zanzibar—was perfectly possible (Cooper 1977:190–195). That slaves were on the whole treated reasonably by their owners can be understood as an expression of their symbiotic relationship. Comorians, like Muslim East Africans, tell semi-fictional stories of loyal slaves rewarded by God, and noble Arabs hastening to help slaves in distress, which capture the spirit of the relationship in idealised form. But generosity to slaves had its self-interested side, needless to say, as well as being an admired Muslim quality.

In largely matrilineal Ngazija, a move towards stress on being Arab was liable to create a move in the direction of increased importance for patrifiliation, if not patriliny. Here concubines had a uniquely important role. As women with no local matrilineal affiliation of their own, they were able to

D

provide their master with children who were his alone, in descent terms, owing no loyalty to maternal kin and swelling the ranks of his dependants. Such children were born free, of course, and were members by birth of their father's patri-lineage, if he had one. This was the case only for *sherifs* and wellborn individuals with recent ancestry in an Arab country.

What Comorian men actually did with their children born of concubines was to graft them onto their own matrilineages. In this way children could offer their fathers support in a wider range of contexts than was possible for those with duties to fathers' *and* mothers' brothers. A legal institution resembling *waqf* (an inalienable endowment) was evolved apparently to cope with this situation. Known as *manyahuli*, its provisions followed matrilineal custom, rather than the *sharia* which assumes patrilineality. *Manyahuli* provided for land—which was normally inherited matrilineally and ad-ministered by women—to be purchased and given to a set of siblings by their own father. Thereafter it was inherited according to normal matrilineal rules (Fort n.d.; Harries 1977: 63). Such children joined their father's matrilineage without making demands on its land, and the land they brought with them was equally theirs in perpetuity. Since individual men gained power and had the chance to exercise it within the framework of the matrilineage and the matrilineal sultanate of which it was a building block, their children by concubines gave them the opportunity of becoming more Arab in local terms, and of raising politically at the same time. As Meillas-soux points out (1978:325–6) slave fertility can be used to speed up growth and accumulation—in this case lineage growth and the accumulation of dependent kin—in ways not normally demographically possible. The finite number of childbearing women is always a bottleneck on the growth of matrilineages, slowing the appearance of factional splits led by potential new leaders. However, slaves made it possible to to bend the rules a little. Men with concubine wives could establish their own villages, rather than living uxorilocally, for instance. How common a practice this was I have no idea: there is certainly one aged prince still alive, a son of the last Sultan of Ngazija, who lives in a village entirely peopled with his own offspring by concubines, and their children and grandchildren. Similar patterns occurred among the matrilineal Yao of Tanzania and Mozambique when they became slave traders and slave owners (Alpers 1969:409–413).

Slavery and Hierarchy

Just as slaves and wealth from slave trading gave new access to what had been scarce forms of prestige for most Comorians, so apparently did they exaggerate distinctions and ranking in the social order. The ranks themselves were not new. Swahilis and Comorians had for centuries shared the Arabian model for a division of society into rulers, commoners and slaves: locally, rulers were Arab *sherifs*, commoners Afro-Arabs, slaves Africans. What changed in the nineteenth century were the relative sizes of the categories, and their character. Slaves were in the majority in Zanzibar and Pemba, and composed almost half of the Comorian population. A much wider range of the free population than before could own slaves, extending as far as peasants in Anjouan (Robineau 1966:58). Plantation slaves, where they existed, performed a new economic function and occupied a more anonymous and lowly position than slaves had done in the region before. Simultaneously, in the highest rank, the Omani court in Zanzibar was presenting a more glittering local example of what it could mean to be an Arab than had been seen since the days of medieval Kilwa.

The majority of Comorians, like the East African coast Swahili, belonged to the middle category, where status achievement was all-important since the boundary with slaves was so close. Freeborn commoners aimed at the life-style of *sherifs*, if they could afford to, and if they could not, tried to avoid all manual labour, or at least those types of manual labour most associated with slavery. In the Comoros, at least, skilled manual work and clean work were less shaming for a freeborn man than unskilled work like farm labouring or porterage, or dirty or smelly work like fishing, cattle-herding, leather tanning, which were regarded as slave tasks *par excellence*. Freeborn men associated urban living, rightly, with Arabness and despised their rural counterparts.

Among slaves, as we might expect in such a milieu, ranking was important along similar lines. Locally-born, fully-Islamised and culturally-integrated slaves, the *wazalia*, despised the *wamakwa*, the Makua tribesmen newly arrived from Mozambique. These were the only slaves for whom the blunt term 'slave' was used—*mrumwa* (pl. *warumwa*)—with its literal meaning of 'used person'. Slaves partaking of urban life and living in the slave quarter of a town felt themselves superior to slaves in agricultural villages who rarely mixed with freeborn men, and slaves who lived in the houses of their masters, the concubines (*suria*) above all, ranked highest. Slaves had a term, *mjoli*, meaning 'fellow-slave' which they would use only to other slaves whom they considered their status equals.

As concepts of rank grew ever more elaborate in the nineteenth century, Comorian commoners became drawn into a ruinous marriage game in which competitors struggled to stay equal. Islam's injunction that women might only marry their equals or betters was the touchstone; while it was easy for men to make marriages with inferiors, and they frequently did so, 'marriage with an equal' measured exactly where a particular man stood in the social hierarchy, for it measured the highest point at which a woman would be made available to him.

Comorians had an age-grade system which, though it was given Muslim colour, was a long-standing Bantu institution closely resembling that of Muslim and non-Muslim mainland peoples.[6] Men passed through the grades by making payments to members of senior grades, and gained in return the right to exercise political and ritual power as they grew older. In the case of the Comorians, the penultimate grade could only be entered by making a marriage with the daughter of a man already in it. Such a marriage was deemed marriage with an equal, and may have originally been simply this; but as wealth grew in Comorian society a situation developed in which wellborn women were in effect married off hypogamously, in return for weighty payments to age-grade members, brides and their parents (Shepherd 1977). The age-grades had too general a political importance to be ignored, even by *sherifs*, and so a costly scramble for rank began between individuals and ultimately whole matrilineages.

Groups strove to force patterns of sister-exchange upon one another, as the best way of staying equal, or, failing that, encouraged their members to marry their patrilateral cross cousins, if they felt they were being turned into inferior wife-givers. The tendency for women to flow up the hierarchy could be checked, but only at a price.

Slavery and the Sultanates

In Ngazija, the only island in the Comoro archaepelago to have more than one sultanate by the nineteenth century, inter-sultanate rivalry for paramountcy was endemic. A European visitor in 1620 noted.

> there are fourteen or fifteen kings or kinglets in this island, the most powerful and best-connected being the one who holds the anchorage. They make war upon one another with the aim of capturing slaves to sell to the Portuguese and other nations. They fight only with stones and fire-hardened sticks and by throwing sand into one anothers' eyes. Few of them have firearms except the king and he is not well-equipped (Grandidier 1904:365).

Competition may have been for rights over 'the anchorage' and the control of imports and exports through it. Various authors (e.g. Harries 1977) suggest that matrilineal succession rules for the handing-on of the office of Sultan were constantly challenged, as well, so that sons were fighting sisters' sons. In any case, the ruling families of all the sultanates were closely related and intermarried. The island is only forty miles long and ten miles wide, and the localised matrilineages which formed the core of the sultanates were grouped, at the highest level, into only three major named matriclans. There were plainly rules about competition for the paramountcy (*utibe*) of the island, though it is not now easy to establish what they were. It seems that the *utibe* usually alternated between two major matriclans, for instance, with the third as the arbitrator. At any rate, centuries of 'fighting' seem to have left the political structure intact until 1820.[7] During the next fifty years, a period described in a chronicle written by one of the principles involved (Harries 1977), rivalry escalated until it was completely out of control, and all tacit rules broken. The period of increased competition coincides exactly with increased profits from the slave trade and increased numbers of slaves on the island.

A contender for the title of paramount sultan had first to establish ascendancy within his own matrilineage by a combination of charisma and the use of wealth to assure political rights and create a following. He might then be offered a position as sultan of a small sultanate in the gift of the paramount sultan. If he could attract supporters, he would be put at the head of more and more important sultanates until he was sultan of one of the two largest. (There were eleven in the nineteenth century). Moves up to this point took place within the confines of one or other of the matriclans which provided the *tibe* (paramount sultan) and did not normally involve fighting. But the final move, the ousting of the reigning *tibe*, seems always to have taken place by physical attack upon his retainers. If he could be routed from his residence and his followers pursuaded that it was no longer worth defending his claims to be *tibe*, his challenger could take the title and re-allot several of the smaller sultanates newly under control to his own close supporters—sons, sisters' sons and the husbands of daughters. The ousted *tibe* was not killed, and at times retook his title later.

At the beginning of the period starting in 1820, there seemed to be tacit rules for limiting bloodshed. Firearms were not used, and fights took place using sticks, shields and old swords. Successions may even, at times, have taken place without a fight: there were rules for doing so. Thereafter competition intensified, however. The *utibe* changed hands on average once every three years, from 1820 to 1850, and challengers increasingly drew in support from outside the island. Sultans in the other islands were induced to send supplementary fighting men. In 1848 a deposed *tibe* and his allies bought guns and gunpowder from Mayotte and Madagascar, and hired men there to train a specially purchased corps of slaves in their use. In the 1860s a French plantation owner in Mohéli was asked to persuade the French to bring a gunboat. By 1870 the two largest clans, Bambao and Itsandra, with their allies, were virtually engaged in civil war, and Bambao enlisted the intervention of the French, while Itsandra obtained help from the Sultan of Zanzibar. Itsandra's sultan was strangled and the sultan of Bambao had only a brief reign before he was himself deposed by France and the institution abolished for good.

The key to understanding this escalation in rivalries lies in the fact that tribute was paid at every level of the system, and positions of power in the gift of important men could virtually be purchased. As more money entered the island, competition for posts where inflowing tribute could be expected became more intense, and so did tribute demands. Said Bakari the chronicler describes how a bad sultan would openly threaten and rob rich men, using the size of his retinue to intimidate them. Money obtained in this way was used for slave trading, and for attempting to defend the position of power staked out.

While it no doubt suited the purposes of outside forces such as France to be drawn into Ngazija affairs eventually, the change of scale was initiated by Comorian sultans themselves, greedy for power, and helped in no small measure by the abundance of their slaves, who filled the ranks of the small standing armies they created, or grew crops to feed them.

The Aftermath of Slavery

Sayyid Barghash, Sultan of Zanzibar, signed a treaty in 1873 abolishing slave markets and slave transportation within his dominions. By the end of the century, European powers had decisively entered the area and were attempting to abolish the very status of slavery. It formally came to an end in the Comoros in 1904.

Seventy-five years later, there has been surprisingly little change.[8] The coastal towns are still the places where Arabs mostly live, and these same people own most of the land

which did not pass into the hands of French-owned plantation companies. Some poor freemen and slave descendants
live on the hillsides, while the character of town quarters has
shown great continuity, *sherifs,* commoners and slave descendants still living where their fathers and grandfathers lived.
Slave descendants in their own villages nowadays pursue
personal subsistence on land they have come to regard as
their own, both land and labour having passed out of the
control of their onetime owners. In the towns, at least, the
freeborn continue to support such elderly slaves as they still
have dependent upon them; they are politely referred to as
'grandfathers' and 'grandmothers' though their clothing and
behaviour make it clear that this is not literally what they
are. Slaves were not freed, in Comorian eyes, by European
emancipation decrees but only by the individual action of
their masters. There are thus still Comorians today, descended
in the male line from a slave who was never given his freedom, who are technically slaves. Few of these younger 'slaves'
are economically dependent on their masters' families (though
they have the right to be) and their ancestry is only of formal
importance upon marriage, when they will not be allowed to
marry a freeborn woman. They usually go abroad as migrant
labourers. Throughout the colonial period, the presence of
the French meant that in fact such people could choose
whether or not to be slaves.

While status, in Meillassoux's sense (1975:14), *has* on the
whole changed, the living conditions of slave descendants
may scarcely have done so. Unless they leave or have an
urban skill, slave descendants must work land as squatters or
sharecroppers for subsistence needs, and work as agricultural
labourers for cash. They constitute a reserve labour force for
the landed, are paid appallingly badly, and have no guarantee
of regular work. In some ways they are worse off than slaves,
since no one is responsible any longer for their welfare.

Freeborn Comorians still marry two different kinds of
wives, equals and inferiors, in a lifetime. While the latter
need not be slave descendants, there are clear echoes of the
old distinction between wellborn wives and concubines here.
Wives who are equals are known as *wana zidakani,* 'daughters

of the wall-niches' and until recently might only go out at night, veiled and accompanied. They were married in lavish customary style. Wives who are inferiors are *wandruruma*, 'women for use', and they are married simply. They behave boldly in public and can come and go as they like (Fontoynont and Raomandahy 1937:40).

Attitudes to rank have remained very rigid, and not just where marriage is concerned. Fishermen of the town of Itsandra, for instance, habitually give a portion of their catch to the town's *sherifs* and freemen. In the case of a single large fish like a tunny, the symbolism is striking: the fish is cut in three and the head is given to *sherifs*, the middle to freemen and the tail kept by the fisherman. Ordinary men kiss the hands of *sherifs*; freed slaves work in the houses of their old masters during Ramadhan, helping with the cooking, and are rewarded with a gift at the end.

While dependants cannot nowadays be accumulated in great numbers, it is not uncommon to find wealthier households gladly incorporating additional personnel. In one known to me there are, in addition to kin, the following: an elderly female slave; a senile old man, who works in the garden in return for his keep and clothes; an 'adopted' child of twelve or so, who does a variety of jobs in return for his keep and schoolfees; a young woman, with several children whose husband lives with his *zidakani* wife and does not support her. She comes during the day to help with the cooking, and is given food to take home.

Those slave descendants who have gone as migrants to Madagascar, East Africa or France have been able to escape from dependency, and their relationships with freeborn Comorians in these contexts have been founded on common island or sultanate of origin, rather than common rank, in all matters except marriage. Marriages between freeborn women and slave men have only occasionally occurred, and have always caused scandals. Male slaves who return to the Comoros having made money usually buy land suitable for cash crops if they can. They also emulate the expensive customary marriages of the freeborn, increasing their social 'Arabness' in the process, though not marrying out of their rank.

The explanation for the long continuation of the structure and attitudes established in the nineteenth century lies in French policies in the Comoros. Though the sultanates were abolished, France ruled through the families from which the sultans had been drawn, filling civil-service posts with *sherifs*. So striking was the continuity that even in the 1960s the two chief political parties were recruited from the respective supporters of the old contenders for the paramountcy—the sultanates of Bambao and Itsandra. French inputs of money and education barely reached outside the capital of each island, while village chiefs were selected from among those who had attained the highest age-and-marriage grades. Without being in the least aware of what they were doing, the French could hardly have preserved—and even reinforced—the system more carefully. The result is a society which gives some picture of what a slave-owning Muslim people, suddenly made rich, might have looked like.

Conclusion

It is perhaps a truism to say that the uses to which slaves are put teach us a good deal about what is most valuable in a particular society at a particular time. While probably occupied in domestic production most of the time, Comorian slaves could, as we have seen, be set to increasing the output of agricultural produce for sale to foreigners; or to building fortifications against the Sakalave raiders; or to establishing their owner in a position of political power. They made it possible for an owner to become a fulltime specialist as a craftsman, trader or religious expert, secure in the knowledge that his day-to-day needs would be provided by slaves.

The nineteenth century saw new uses of slaves, however. The French and then the Omani demand for slaves made it possible for the first time to live exclusively from slave trading. Comorians moved away from a cash economy based on food production and transportation and turned enthusiastically to the new alternative on their doorsteps. If this is correct, then demand for slaves as agricultural labourers must have been slackening at the very moment when they were becoming easier to own. Suddenly there was a surplus of slaves relative to needs as they had hitherto been expressed. As we have seen, some took on the nature of luxury items or were instrumental in creating a more prestigious lifestyle for their owners.

The move from slaves for production to slaves for consumption purposes was only a tendency, of course. Domestic production was always their responsibility. And some of the uses they were put to can be described either way. Were slaves fighting for a would-be-sultan productively engaged? Their owner would certainly think so, but the staging of the battle itself could be viewed as a piece of unnecessary display. Finally the distinction is artificial. Slaves were wanted first and foremost simply as people—property with a wide range of potential uses. Out of slaves, soldiers, kinsmen, workmen and retainers could be fashioned; indirectly they might be able to provide their owners with honour and high office. In such situations, where slaves were desired for a great range of reasons, they were of value before any specific use had been thought of, and their long-term availability was as potentially valuable as that of kin.

All free urban Comorians must have benefitted from slaves and the slave trade in the nineteenth century. The elite improved their position both relatively and absolutely. They grew wealthier than ever before, and did so more quickly than other Comorians. More important in the long run, they improved their position against other similar groups of Afro-Arabs outside the Comoros. Comorian *sherifs* seem to have been in a stronger economic position than their counterparts from Madagascar to Lamu. Among non-Europeans, only Omanis and Indians were more successful. With wealth accumulating independently of slave labour, the surplus energy which slaves represented was deftly directed not at economic targets, but at the building of politico-religious eminence for their owners, in the ways which have been outlined. A Comorian proverb sums up the superiority of political to economic strength succinctly. *Mali mlingo; hezi sharia*: 'wealth is a ladder, but power is law'.

5

Modes of Production and Slavery in Madagascar: Two Case Studies

MAURICE BLOCH

There is no problem so familiar yet so unavoidable in comparative sociology as what terms to use. When we use a term such as slavery to understand a system of exploitation, we are in fact using a word, or translating a word that was used to regulate and reproduce this exploitation, not to analyse it. It is not a problem easily avoided by using a culture-free 'scientific term' since in so doing we only slip back in translating, more or less systematically, the more common word into a neologism which has no greater accuracy and which is not as useful for preliminary understanding.

The problem is less a purely linguistic matter than it might at first appear; the difficulty is rather a symptom of what happens when we try to do two things at once. The first is understanding the role of certain relations of production in one or a number of modes of production. The other is understanding the classificatory system used in a society to operate these relations of production, whether for exploitation or for the reproduction of these relations by legitimising them ideologically as part of a legal or quasi-legal system.

To understand slavery, therefore, we need, at first, to separate two tasks which must both be done concurrently. On the one hand we must understand the system of exploitation of which the relations of production, however labelled, form a part; on the other hand we must look at the evolution of the terminological and legal system which produces the labels in relation to the exploitation which it services.

The relation between these two problems is no simple thing. I shall outline it historically for the Merina kingdom of Madagascar and for another small group of people, the Zafimaniry of Madagascar. From these examples we shall see that it is possible at some stages for the system of exploitation and the relations of production to transform themselves radically while the same legal and terminological system remains in use. For example, when the Merina kingdom expanded dramatically in the nineteenth century, bringing in large numbers of captives, the socio-economic significance of servile labour for the social formation changed completely but the same words and laws continued to regulate the status. The obverse of this can also exist. When the legal status of slave was abolished by the French the relation of exploitation it had denoted did not necessarily disappear.

All this, however, is not to say that there is no systematic relation between the classificatory-ideological system and the system of exploitation; a relation exists, but it is complex and the present paper is an attempt to discover it. To do this in such a short space requires that the evidence of the multiple inter-relations which concern us can only be sketched briefly and probably unsatisfactorily. This is an inevitable result of presenting the problem in such a multifaceted manner, but it is a price worth paying in that I believe it is the only way out of the many difficulties which the question of comparative slavery have presented to the historian, sociologist and anthropologist. In order to restrict myself somewhat I shall concentrate primarily on the effect of the abolition of the legal status which has generally been translated as 'slavery', since it offers a particularly illuminating instance for the analysis of the relationship on two levels.

I shall look at two cases of the effect of the abolition of the status of slave in Madagascar, firstly among the Merina, probably the most well-known group of people in Madagascar who by the nineteenth century had conquered nearly the whole island, and secondly at the Zafimaniry, one of the smallest groups in Madagascar, representing a totally different form of society. These two groups, therefore, offer an interesting contrast.

Background to Merina Slavery

All the nineteenth century missionary books in English on slavery begin with a statement that it was an institution present in Madagascar 'from time immemorial'. The missionaries had good reason to stress that point since the London Missionary Society, the missionary arm of the Congregationalist Church to which these writers belonged, became intimately involved in the growth of the Merina state during the nineteenth century, a state which contained a high proportion of slaves. This involvement of the missionaries was particularly awkward, since the Congregationalists were foremost in the abolitionalist movement in Britain. They therefore resented inevitable accusations that their actions in Madagascar encouraged slavery and even that some London Missionary Society's missionaries were actually slave owners; accusations made mainly by their rival missionaries. Perhaps the greatest irony of their attitude to slavery is its link with the way they justified their presence in Madagascar by an edifying story which I quote from a popular book about the founder of the Mission to Madagascar, David Jones:

> The Welsh tutor sighed as he folded up the news-sheet and reached out for his well-worn Bible. As he turned over its pages his thoughts were far away. He had been reading of the slave raids in Madagascar, at that time an almost unknown island off the East Coast of Africa. It so happened that he turned to the 16th chapter of Acts for his evening reading. Little wonder, then, that in his dreams that night Paul's vision at Troas became linked with the needs of slave-stricken Madagascar and he dreamed that the men of Madagascar stood on its shore, beckoning to him and crying: 'Come over and help us.'
>
> Next morning as he walked down the street of the little village of Neuaddlwyd to his school for preachers, his thoughts were still of Madagascar...yet so real did his dream appear that the plaintive cry still rang in his ears: 'Come over into Madagascar and help us.'
>
> It soon became plain to his students that morning that Dr. Thomas Phillips had something on his mind, and before long he found himself telling them the story of his dream.

Then, with that eloquence that had made him famous as a preacher, he described to these young men, training for the Ministry, the superstition and ignorance of the people of Madagascar, and the cruelties of the slave-trade there ... Dr. Phillips again described his vision and repeated the call that had come to him in the night and added: 'Who will go out as a missionary to Madagascar?'

There was a moment's pause; then from one of the desks at the back of the room, David Jones sprang to his feet. 'I will go!' he said in a ringing voice that showed clearly that he meant it. (Hayes 1923:9–10)

The Madagascar to which he and his companion went had become of crucial interest to the British as the result of the fall of Mauritius and Réunion during the Napoleonic wars and this explains the prominence of the story in the newspaper which so arrested the imagination of Dr Phillips. As a result of this war Mauritius ultimately became British, though this did not happen until after a protracted and complex diplomatic process. The connection of Madagascar on the one hand, and Mauritius and Réunion on the other, lay in in the fact that the East Coast of the great island was sometimes inhabited by small pirate colonies and sometimes by traders and adventurers who supplied the Mascarenes with rice and cattle but also, increasingly, with slaves to be used on the plantations of these islands (Filliot 1974:113–127). Up to 1770 the trading links between Madagascar, Mauritius and Réunion had been relatively small-scale and fluctuating over time. They had, however, been extremely significant in Madagascar in that they had supplied petty rulers with European weapons for their aggrandizement and slave raiding (Filliot 1974:205–208). Towards the end of the eighteenth century, however, the small but growing central state that was to become Imerina, profiting from the disarray of the Betsimisaraka League, captured most of this trade both canalising its network and reducing rivals. The trader Dumaine wrote in 1790 that Imerina 'is the part of Madagascar which supplies most of the slaves for our islands' (Mauritius and Réunion). This process was truly momentous in the history of Madagascar because in return for slaves the

Merina obtained armaments of high quality in much greater quantities than had been available to anybody else before, since they were lucky in reaching the coast precisely at the time when the demand for slaves in the Mascarenes had boomed and the prices soared (Curtin 1969:266–269; Filliot 1974:62–65, 216).

The war materials that they obtained were probably the major cause of the continuing expansion of the Merina and their ultimate domination of the islands. This expansion, however, was itself in part necessitated by the need to supply slaves in ever greater numbers in order to obtain the armaments necessary for conquest (Bloch 1977:314). By engaging in this sort of trade in order to acquire political power the Merina were following a long tradition which had dominated the political process of Madagascar perhaps since as far back as the sixteenth century. We know this pattern well in the eighteenth century when the Sakalava and the Betsimisaraka managed to dominate large areas of the island by exporting slaves to various European or Arab traders in return for armaments which enabled them to conquer their neighbours and obtain more slaves. The process in the case of the Merina, however, was even more dramatic. The reason was that they captured the trade at a time when the Mascarene economies were booming and so was the demand for slaves.

Once the Merina kingdom had really become established through this process, the pattern began to change in a way which was particularly significant for the history of slavery. In 1814 Mauritius, as it was renamed, became British and, in taking over Mauritius, the British had also gained vague but promising rights over Madagascar. Farquhar, the Governor of Mauritius, therefore encouraged the trade between his island and Madagascar since he saw the expansion of a kingdom dependent on supplies from Britain as a first step towards conquest, a policy we are familiar with in other parts of Africa. This policy was not without difficulty as it was taking place at a time when public opinion in Britain was moving strongly against the slave trade and slavery. Farquhar at first resisted pressure for the abolition of the slave trade, arguing that, in the first place, it would ruin the economy of Mauritius and make his unruly subjects even more difficult to control and, in the second place, it would end the promising connection with the Merina which he intended to use for ultimate conquest.

By 1817, however, the pressure from Britain had so increased that he had to give way, although by then the two stumbling blocks to ending the slave trade with Madagascar had vanished. The economy of Mauritius had been moving away from its dependence on the importation of slaves.[1] Secondly Farquhar had discovered a way whereby he could keep his Merina contact. He signed with Radama a treaty which in return for the abolition of the slave trade would guarantee Radama a yearly supply of armaments, as well as military assistance. By this treaty the British hoped to continue their influence in Madagascar and to ensure the ever-important supply of rice and cattle to Mauritius. This treaty had its ups and downs and for a significant period was abrogated altogether, but it remained the major template for British Merina relations during the nineteenth century. It also ensured that whenever it was in operation the Merina would be dependent on the British. For the Merina the advantage of this treaty is also obvious. Radama, the Merina King, still retained a steady supply of British armaments but gained as well, and this is probably the most significant point, a *monopoly* of European weapons in Madagascar, a monopoly which many tried to break but never with complete success. When the treaty was in operation British frigates patrolled Madagascar to stop any signs of the slave trade. In doing so they were stopping any potential rivals of Radama from obtaining arms with which to resist him. They were, so to speak, putting Madagascar in a vacuum in which only one group had access to modern weapons. Under such circumstances it is hardly surprising that nobody could offer any significant resistance to the Merina during their greatest period of expansion.

The implications of this process for the social significance of slavery among the Merina is equally dramatic. There is no doubt, as the missionaries stressed, that an institution which Europeans and Arabic writers before them had no hesitation

in calling 'slavery' had existed in Madagascar since the time
of our earliest records. This is very clear from the sixteenth
century onwards and indeed one of the most famous accounts
of Madagascar was the so-called diary of Robert Drury, a
sailor who claimed to have been captured as a slave in
Western Madagascar and whose account was romanticised
by Defoe. The earliest mention of this institution, for the
Merina, goes back to 1777 but there are several references
which give us a relatively clear idea what type of institution
had been referred to as slavery among the Merina before
the dramatic expansion of their kingdom in the nineteenth
century.

For our early period certain facts stand out. First of all
slaves were acquired in two contrasting ways. They were
obtained either by warfare and raiding of enemies, or through
legal processes which disgraced individuals and their families,
or even, in some cases, whole descent groups. The relative
importance of these differing methods of slave acquisition
seems to have changed for the period under examination and
there is no doubt that from the beginning of the nineteenth
century most slaves were captives, obtained either in wars,
slave-raiding or simply by kidnapping.

The people obtained in these traditional ways were classed
under the general term *andevo* but could be distinguished by
more specific words which indicated somewhat different
legal status. One of the most important differences seems to
have been that the process of manumission for descendants of
disgraced Merina was much simpler than it was for captives.

In this early period the uses to which the slaves were put
varied widely. Some slaves were captured for export and
these are the ones with which we have been concerned so far.
Secondly, slaves might be used for domestic purposes; until
the nineteenth century, slaves seem to have been used for a
whole range of productive tasks in a way which does not very
much differ from junior members of families. They were often
used for particularly arduous tasks such as mining and
smelting and above all for transporting wood from the forests
of Imerina. Slaves were also used as agricultural labourers as
well as household servants and as concubines. This type of

domestic slavery seems very similar to that which has been described for many African societies (Meillassoux 1975: passim).

Finally there were two small groups of slaves specifically associated with the monarch. These ranged from personal servants to quite high-ranking state officials whose positions were obviously highly privileged. This is a situation with which we are familiar from West Africa and other places. These slaves formed a trusted body of followers who, unlike the free subjects of the King, had no other allegiances. The other group of royal slaves were concerned with looking after royal cattle in remote areas, and in fact lived quite independent lives.

It is difficult to know exactly what sort of treatment the slaves might receive. There are some reports of acute ill-treatment but also many accounts of leniency; other writers stress the fact that some slaves were treated very much as family members of junior status (Ellis 1858:146–149). Legally, however, they were totally at the disposal of their masters except that they could not be killed without royal permission. Whether the slaves formed familial bonds or not was according to the whim of their masters, and similarly whatever advantages they received were only favours, whether these masters were themselves subjects or rulers.

There is, however, a striking difference between Merina, or indeed Malagasy, slavery and that found in other parts of Africa, and this difference seems to be directly due to the nature of Malagasy kinship systems. Most writers on African slavery stress the fact that after a few generations slaves became incorporated into the free population and in all cases children of free men by slave women were free. This is the main point made by Kopytoff and Miers (1977) in their typification of African slavery. Again the point is made by Terray for a much more specific West African case (Terray 1975:437–448). This integration takes place in all cases through adoption and marriage. These two possibilities would run against the fundamental emphasis on endogamy in Merina kinship.

The Merina are divided into small, endogamous descent

groups carefully ranked. Normally, to be a member of such a group one had to have both parents from the group. If both parents did not come from the same group then the offspring always belonged to the lower group. This meant that marriage was unlikely to occur between free and slave persons and that in any case the children would belong to the lower group, that is, they would be slaves. This contrasts with the general African pattern where descent groups are never truly endogamous and nearly always strictly exogamous and where status is derived from one parent only, the status of the other parent being largely irrelevant. Such a system facilitates the merging of children of slaves in the free population, while the Malagasy system hinders it. Thus Merina slavery was transmitted unaltered from generation to generation; the children of slaves were slaves as were their children and so on. Similarly, although slave women were fair game for free men, in theory at least no offspring of such unions could be considered free or were indeed thought of as related by kinship to their fathers. This characteristic of Merina slavery which marks it out so clearly from other African systems is directly attributable to the representation of society as an agglomeration of self-reproducing endogamous groups linked to each other by their rank in a kingdom, not, as in the case of most parts of Africa, as a system of inter-marrying groups. Among the Malagasy the only legitimate union was one involving two parents of equal status and the group was visualised as reproducing itself endlessly from its own stock. In such circumstances the boundary between kinsmen and outsiders is drawn extremely sharply (Bloch 1975:216) and so the halfway-house model devised by such writers as Kopytoff and Miers for Africa is inapplicable. One was either a freeman, and if a freeman a member of a descent group, or not. Another way in which this sharp break is represented can be seen in the critical relationships of tombs, territory and kinship in Imerina (Bloch 1971a). Imerina is completely divided into the territories of descent groups, where the association of people and land is symbolised by stone tombs of a permanent nature. Free Merina are thereby tied to a segment of their valued territory by a symbol of permanence. Unless such a tie can be established, one is outside society and this is precisely the position of slaves. They had no tombs to which they had a right. They were either buried in temporary graves or they were allowed to build tombs of mud, where the symbolical difference between the impermanence of earth and the permanence of stone was used to demonstrate their fundamentally different relationship to the land. (Slaves could also be buried as juniors in their masters' tombs but there the point to notice is that it was not because of themselves that they were buried there but because of their masters, and the fact that they were buried there did not give their children the right to be buried with their fathers.)

In this light we can understand the position of slaves in traditional Merina society. They were junior members of families, who though normally well treated, could be badly abused with impunity and could never become full members of society because they had no ancestral territory. Their progeny were condemned to the same fate. They were outside the social system in its ideological representation, rather than an inferior part of it, as was the case in other societies. Nothing illustrates this better than the fact that they could not be the recipient of the new year blessing of fertility and filiation which was given at the ceremony of the bath, when the sovereign sprinkled holy water on his subjects as though they were his children. The elders of every descent group then blessed their offspring in a similar fashion (Bloch 1977). If by accident slaves were touched by this water they were automatically freed.

The position of the slaves outlined above is one which may have existed for a long time but it is quite clear that the growth of the Merina state in the nineteenth century implied the appearance of what was really a very different type of slavery, although it was covered by the same terms and, with minor changes, by the same religio-legal notions. The growth of the Merina kingdom was parallelled by the development of large hydraulic works, at the end of the eighteenth century, involving the draining of the large marshes which surround Tananarive. Transformed into rice fields by immense dykes, these new lands were to supply food for the administration

and the army. At first the labour for the massive works was
largely supplied by *corvée* labour, but the unpopularity of
corvée, taken together with the ever-increasing need for
soldiers and administrators from among the free Merina,
meant that the public works required more and more labour,
which could only be supplied by slaves (de Copalle 1970:54).
We therefore find that at the beginning of the nineteenth
century the demand for servile labour was increasing from
three different causes. First of all the increase in military
service for the ordinary Merina meant that the families back
home depended more and more on slave labour to replace
those who were at the wars or in garrisons far away. Secondly
the state needed more and more labour for public works,
because on the one hand these were expanding and on the
other hand it could draw less and less on *corvée* labour.
Thirdly slaves were needed in ever greater numbers for the
slave trade in order to obtain the weapons on which the
Merina state was dependent. It is in the light of these con-
flicting demands that we can well understand why Radama
was so willing to agree to the end of the external slave trade,
so long as he could carry on obtaining his weapons. As a
consequence, the end of the external slave trade led to a
tremendous growth in the number of slaves in Imerina. This
was because the supply of slaves through conquest was continuing unabated and indeed increased, while the drain on
slaves, the export sales, stopped. By the end of the nineteenth
century probably considerably more than half the population
were of *andevo* status.

By the mid-nineteenth century the great increase in the
number of slaves implies a great change in the position of
people of such status in the Merina kingdom. By then most
Merina had slaves, and most of the productive work was done
by them for the benefit of their masters, who were preoccupied by the administrative and military needs of the
kingdom. Apart from these privately owned slaves, there also
existed an equally large group of royal slaves carrying out
public works for the Monarch, working the royal fields in
gangs and living in barracks under the eye of either slave or
free foremen. During the nineteenth century then, the whole

state had become dependent on the exploitation of slave labour and the dominant relation of production was that between slave and freeman. Thus, although the legal and terminological status of slaves had hardly changed, between the eighteenth and nineteenth centuries the significance of their presence for the political economy of the Merina had become totally different. Consequently the nature of the free sector of the population also had changed. While before the nineteenth century freemen had been primary agricultural producers, by the mid-nineteenth century they had become an administrative and military class, even in some cases a trading class, removed from the primary processes of production.

Yet this total change in the nature of the Merina state, and of the relations of production on which it relied, had taken place within the framework of ideas, laws and beliefs which had previously operated a totally different system of social production. However, before we are led by this observation to dismiss ideas and beliefs about status as irrelevant for the evolution of the social formation, we should turn to the way these ideas and beliefs affected the subsequent history of the Merina.

Social Implications of Freedom for Imerina

The situation outlined above was that found by the French at the time of their invasion of Madagascar in 1895. This invasion ultimately resulted in the Declaration of the Abolition of Slavery throughout Madagascar in 1897, a Declaration as much motivated by humanitarian motives as for the need to undermine Merina domination in the island. The effect of this measure on Imerina was inevitably dramatic, when we bear in mind the central place which the different types of slavery had achieved for Merina social organisation. However, the effect of manumission would have been much greater and of a totally different nature were it not for the fact that although it gave slaves access to their labour it did not, at the same time, give them access to land through which their labour might have directly led to freedom. The slaves were freed but no thought was given to what might happen to them after that, or how they might make a living. This forced on the slaves one of three different solutions which I shall discuss briefly in turn.

The first solution was for slaves to return to the areas from which they had been captured. This possibility, of course, could only have been open to those slaves who had been recently taken and who were likely to find relatives back home. There is no doubt that some slaves went back, but it seems that for reasons which are not clear, only a few did so.

The second solution for freed Merina slaves was to stay put in the villages where they had worked as slaves. To do this they had to get the agreement of their masters so that they could have access to land in order to survive. This arrangement is the most critical element in understanding the present-day position of the slaves who stayed in the Merina homeland (Dez 1965:76–83). It took the form of share-cropping arrangements, which still characterised the relationship of ex-slaves to ex-masters at the time of my last fieldwork in Madagascar in 1971. The share-cropping arrangement is of itself not particularly extortionate. The owner of the land received a quarter of the crop if he had contributed the seed grain. The reason for this mild arrangement was that quite simply in the areas of central Madagascar where the free Merina had always had ancestral land, the land was so unproductive without the massive input of forced labour that it gained with the system of slavery, that it would have been very difficult to get more. Also by then the free Merina were obtaining income from other and more significant sources. The exploitative aspect of the situation, however, lies not so much in the actual share-cropping arrangement as in the type of obligation which continued to exist between ex-masters and ex-slaves. During the nineteenth century, but especially after the coming of the French, most Merina of free descent left their ancestral villages, taking advantage of their better education, to become petty administrators, traders and teachers throughout Madagascar and in Tananarive, or to become farmers in newly opened lands and plantations where a higher income could be obtained. None-theless they kept their ancestral lands. This was for ideo-logical rather than economic reasons, and it was one aspect of the way the free Merina maintained their link with their ancestral villages by means of ancestral property, houses, churches and, above all, tombs.

The most important tie of the free Merina is to the an-cestral village where his tomb is found, even though he may never have lived there. This means that the descendants of free Merina need caretakers in these ancestral villages for their houses, churches, and tombs, in order to maintain their ideological status. It is to these duties that the slaves were made to answer. Significantly, these descendants of the slaves usually do not actually reside in the old villages but outside the moat which marks their boundaries, in nearby hamlets called *tananboa*, 'new village'. Here they live in much poorer houses than the largely empty dwellings of their ex-masters. The ex-slaves were given land, therefore, less in return for the rent that they might supply than for the services they would offer. A phrase used by the Merina of free descent describes these descendants of slaves who have remained in their ancestral villages as: *valala miandry fasana*, 'the grasshoppers who guard the tombs' (Razafindratovo 1971:162). When the descendants of free men whose ancestors came from such a village return for a visit, they still expect the descendants of slaves to do jobs reminiscent of their previous duties. J. Razafindratovo describes these visits with brilliant subtlety for the village of Ilafy, from which she originally came. People of free descent also expect the ex-slaves to supply them with servants, usually children, who will work in their houses for minimal or nil wages, wherever these houses happen to be: in Tananarive, in new lands, or in distant parts of Madagascar. This is probably a more economically sig-nificant form of exploitation than the tasks back home. Naturally such work is greatly resented and ex-slaves bitterly refer to it by the term for forced labour, *famanpoana*, while their employers prefer to use the less loaded term for work, *asa* (Razafindratovo 1971:127).

It seems to me, furthermore, that another element of a

more purely ideological nature is involved with this relationship. By maintaining people in quasi-slave status, even though in many cases no direct benefit may be obtained, an ideological picture of a previous domination is reproduced which is seen as the potential legitimation of future domination. In other words by still having 'slaves' the former masters demonstrate that they are members of the true ruling elite in Madagascar. The ex-slaves in the old villages are not, in my experience, unaware of this use of their position. But, in any case, their resentment could not be easily transformed into action. They know that in the end they can be pushed out of their lands, due to the share-cropping arrangement on which they depend. Some ex-slaves even say that they feel their present situation is more oppressive than when they were actually slaves and that the behaviour of their masters is even more arrogant, as well as hypocritical, since the descendants of free men shy away from recognising this relationship for what it is. An old man whose parents were slaves pointed out to Razafindratovo that, while her own grandparents (free people) would willingly share the same plate with him, her present-day relatives would not do so. They argue that his house is dirty, that he has bad eating habits and that they might catch diseases from him. A new element in the old relationship is therefore creeping in. The fact that the ex-slaves are usually poor countrymen while the descendants of the free are richer, more urban, and more sophisticated in their knowledge of the outside world is being used as a new and further justification for the continuation of an old exploitation.

Finally let us turn to the third response of the slaves to manumission in 1897. What many of the slaves of Imerina did at that point was neither to go back to their largely forgotten families, or to stay put as share-croppers, but to move into the new empty lands north and west of Imerina. There they started a new life by cultivation and the building of rice terraces. In this they were doing the same as many descendants of freemen who found that they could no longer live on their ancestral lands and could not get administrative or trading jobs or land concessions in other parts of Madagascar.

These people decided, like the slaves, to turn to the more profitable open lands. By and large this region was either empty or thinly populated, thus allowing the ex-slaves and the descendants of the free to form separate villages. Both therefore started on an equal footing, yet the subsequent history of their villages and their differential development is to be explained partly in terms of the pre-existing social structure which the ex-slaves and the free carried with them to these new lands. This is especially so in the case of kinship.

As noted above, the fundamental aspect of free Merina kinship is a division of society into groups with a high degree of endogamy. The marriage rules of the descendants of free men are contradictory. On the one hand they have an idea of incest which says that one should not marry any close relative and yet, on the other hand, they place a high value on the re-grouping of property within the family which dictates that one should marry as close a relative as possible. This leads in the case of freemen to an uncomfortable balance where one marries as close as one dares. The slaves of the Merina, in contrast, accepted this ideology without the freemen's problem. The reason is that since ex-slaves had no property the second rule about re-grouping property did not apply and they also had no concern about maintaining descent groups. What this means, and meant, is that ex-slaves now marry anybody so long as they are not closely related, while descendants of the free marry close relatives within their descent group (Bloch 1971b). The free men in the new lands, therefore, married back along the old alliance patterns of their groups; they chose relatives with whom they share a common origin. Yet these marriage partners, however close, often lead a totally different style of life, perhaps as administrators or teachers in Tananarive, perhaps as plantation owners or traders in other parts of Madagascar. They do not and can not marry their neighbours, since these most probably belong to other descent groups, and are therefore ruled out, or worse, are of slave descent.

The descendants of slaves, by contrast, have no such problems. They marry whoever they fall in love with and who is willing to have them. This means that the descendants of slaves rapidly form supportive kinship networks with their neighbours of slave descent irrespective of origin. Furthermore, when there are non-Merina nearby the former slaves will also intermarry with them. Kinship in ex-slave society becomes a continuous web, spread throughout Imerina and beyond. However, this web rapidly becomes localised in the neighbourhood as neighbours intermarry amongst themselves. Ex-slaves in new lands are therefore able to form kinship networks very much more quickly than the descendants of free men who remain isolated by their marriage rules. Ex-slaves can, as a result, organise themselves for agricultural and political co-operation much more easily. Because of this it can be argued that the ex-slaves in new lands have an initial advantage. They have the ability to quickly forge powerful new links. This initial advantage soon however disappears and subsequently turns into a disadvantage.

The reason is linked with the changing nature of Malagasy society. While at first it is an advantage for a peasant to have a strong local base it is also important for him to have, if he can, links with administrators for his relations with the government, links with traders and people living in other parts of the island for commerce, and with school-teachers, or at least with people who live near relatively good schools where his children can board. The strengthening of local networks by descendants of slaves is accompanied by a correlated lack of contact with people living different types of lives in different places, precisely the kind of people needed for contact with the administration or the educational system. Some of the old relatives of slaves from their village of origin may have gone to Tananarive and may even have become administrators. But, because the ex-slaves in new lands do not marry back into the families of these relatives, the ties fade and are eventually forgotten. This is so at present, when these contacts with towns, administration, and schools are becoming greater sources of power and wealth than subsistence or cash-cropping activities.

The descendants of free men, by contrast, marry back into their original descent groups. Because of their marriage rules, the members of these descent groups, although originating from one place, are now dispersed both throughout Madagascar and throughout the classes existing in Madagascar. Hence their traditional marriage rules maintain these links, links which for a rural peasant are becoming more and more significant. Their relationship to other people who originate from the same village do not fade and since people have gone from these ancestral villages in many directions they are, in fact, maintaining links with a diverse and differentiated network of kin. Thus the descendants of free men can inter-trade by using their kinship networks throughout Madagascar. They can obtain administrative and legal support when this is necessary (and this is increasingly necessary) by tracing kinship to administrators whether in Tananarive or elsewhere, and, perhaps most significant of all, they can gain access to education, partly through their contacts with schoolteachers and partly through the fact that they always have relatives in urban centres where they can board their children. As a consequence, the descendants of free men settled in new lands are again drawing ahead of the descendants of slaves. The latter are becoming more and more isolated in the countryside even though this was an area where it might have been thought the two groups had equal opportunities.

When we look at the effects of the abolition of slavery for the Merina we find, therefore, that the significance of slave descent does not disappear. Nor in many cases does the basis for the exploitation of slaves, the lack of access to the means of production (i.e. land), disappear either. Are we, therefore, again facing a set of historical events in which the ideology of the relations of production is irrelevant to the nature of the exploitation, as at first sight might seem to have been the case for the transformation which took place between the eighteenth and nineteenth centuries in Merina? During this period the legal ideological system did not change significantly. In this case we would be seeing the obverse although with the same implications, a situation in which the legal arrangement changed but the exploitation remained. However, although this might be justifiably argued for the descendants of slaves who stayed on the lands of their old masters, it certainly does not fit the case of former slaves who moved to new lands. Indeed for those in the pioneer areas the opposite might be true in that the old status of slave and its accompanying ideological complement seems to mould the pattern of the future, even though the material basis of exploitation has been removed. This is the critical problem. In my conclusion I want to show that both these views are limited. However, before we have enough material to resolve this apparent puzzle we must turn to another example to complete our picture, that of the Zafimaniry.

The Zafimaniry

When we turn from the Merina to the Zafimaniry the contrast could not be greater. We turn from a group of over a million who dominated Madagascar for almost two centuries, who evolved one of the largest states in Africa south of the Sahara, to a group of around 15,000 people living by shifting cultivation in a particularly inaccessible part of the Island. Nonetheless, the Zafimaniry undoubtedly share a common origin with the Merina and there are good reasons to believe that the Merina evolved from very similar groups. Perhaps the most famous peculiarity of the Zafimaniry in the part of Madagascar where they live is that rice is not the basis of their diet. This is due to their highly specific emplacement. They live below the central plateau in highly mountainous country where areas available for irrigation are restricted. At the same time the climate is too cold for the dry rice cultivation lower down the escarpment. They therefore depend mainly on maize, taro and beans, supplemented with various forest products, the two most important being honey and crayfish.

One may well ask what a group like this is doing with slaves. The answer is not altogether clear to me but the first point to note is that by contrast to the Merina the 'slaves', to use the word by which the Malagasy *andevo* is usually translated, only form (and presumably formed) somewhat less than ten per cent of the population. Furthermore these 'slaves' were not spread as a servile body throughout the population but grouped in two separate villages, closely associated with the two Zafimaniry political foci of the country. It seems that a traditional feature of the cultures to which the Zafimaniry belong is the presence of mediators (*mpifehy*, lit: 'binders') who had a kind of court (*lapa*) and settled disputes. It is with the seat of these mediators that the slaves are associated. Probably towards the end of the eighteenth century the Zafimaniry came under the rather nominal jurisdiction of rulers to the east who used these mediators as their administrators and gave them more authority. This system of delegation was taken over by the Merina in the mid-nineteenth century when they conquered the Kingdom of Ambohimanga Atsimo. The slaves continued to be closely associated with these administrative centres and were not, as far as I can judge, owned individually. They were in origin disgraced Zafimaniry, foreigners and captives. At the time of the French conquest they probably numbered less than 300 people over the age of fifteen.

It is not easy to know the task of these slaves. The only clear indication is that they had various duties such as fetching salt from the coast (Coulaud 1973:91n), collecting certain trees, carrying timber back to the village, and supplying cattle for sacrifices at key moments. They themselves may even have been used in sacrifices. The comparison of their situation with that of, on the one hand, the types of African slavery discussed in the books edited by Meillassoux (1975) and Kopytoff and Miers (1977) and on the other Merina slavery, as outlined above, is instructive. We are clearly dealing with a form of slavery which was not a major factor in the overall pattern of relations of production, and it seems that there was no great difference between the day-to-day life of slaves and that of freemen. For example, houses in slave villages and free villages antedating manumission are very much alike. We seem, therefore, to be dealing with a pattern very similar to that reported in many other parts of Africa.

In one respect, however, the same contrast that we saw between the Merina and the African cases also exists between the Zafimaniry and these as well. Among the Zafimaniry the slaves and the free did not, and do not, intermarry and produce mixed free/slave offspring who represent a halfway-house between the two statuses. The reason again is that the free marry according to relatively fixed patterns which are reproduced from generation to generation. In the case of the Zafimaniry, by contrast to the Merina, the origin of these repeated alliances is partly political and partly a consequence of the need to secure access to new virgin forest (Bloch 1975: passim). Nonetheless, as with the Merina, the result is that the alliance pattern of the free is not a continually changing one as is the case so often in other parts of Africa where the repetition of alliance is almost always forbidden by incest and exogamy rules. Furthermore, when the free Zafimaniry do marry unrelated people, which they do more easily than the Merina, it is in order to form political alliances with other powerful groups. These alliances in turn will become semi-permanent. This type of arrangement between groups is something which could not be achieved by marriage with slaves. As with the Merina, therefore, legitimate unions between free and slaves did not exist and consequently there remains little blurring of the divide between them.

The main difference between the Merina and the Zafi-maniry lies in the overall organisation of society in the two cases. The Merina were, as we saw, organised in a state whose territory was entirely divided into the 'homelands' of the various descent groups. Without an ancestral homeland one was a non-person. The Zafimaniry, by contrast, had no such systematic organisation either ideologically or geographically. Although the slaves were not members of the main alliance groups they were not by this fact outside society as they would have been among the Merina. Nothing illustrates this difference better than the ways the Merina and the Zafimaniry site their tombs. For the Merina the tomb is the ultimate symbol of social groups and territory; hence the slaves were not allowed to have permanent tombs of their own anywhere. For the Zafimaniry no such problem exists. Tombs are placed anywhere in the forest and the slaves have always been able to build their own tombs in similar locations and in similar fashions to those chosen by freemen.

This overall difference is, as we shall see, crucial to the understanding of Zafimaniry history. It is closely linked to access to land and the technology the Zafimaniry use to exploit it. Unlike their counterparts among the Merina, Zafimaniry slaves did have access to land but only through a series of temporary permissions given to them by free villagers. These permissions are a traditional part of the Zafimaniry land tenure system, and are often given to free-men as a preliminary to acceptance within the in-marrying groups. This is not so when such permission was given to a slave since there was no possibility of transforming him into an affine or kinsman through marriage. This difference is reflected in the type of land that slaves were given permission to cultivate. The Zafimaniry, as noted above, are shifting cultivators. Not only do they change swiddens when these are exhausted but also, like other shifting cultivators, the whole population is slowly moving to new areas, partly as a result of overswiddening which took place in the past and more recently because of the dramatic growth in population. This movement has been roughly from west to east, which means that Zafimaniry villages have to their east better lands and virgin forest, while to the west the land is more or less exhausted, most of it only suitable for sweet potatoes (the last crop planted on a swidden) or even beyond use for swidden, when the forest land degenerates completely into thin grass-land (Coulaud 1973:168–179). Naturally the land given for cultivation to the slaves tended to be much more of this latter type, and the siting of the traditional slave villages was sig-nificantly to the east of the two largest villages, in these semi-exhausted lands.

Zafimaniry slavery appears until the coming of the French a relatively stable system. In terms of the relations of pro-duction it was a peripheral institution but with a greater degree of ideological elaboration.

The Effects of Manumission for the Zafimaniry

Nominally slavery was abolished among the Zafimaniry at the same time as it was in the rest of Madagascar, but this had little effect until the mid-1930s when the local admin-istrator enforced manumission in the region. Previously

E

Zafimaniry slaves who wanted to benefit from the abolition of slavery had to leave their home area. A few in fact did so. However, in the 1930s the local administrator decreed that all traditional tasks of slaves should end and, in contrast to what had happened in Imerina, he insisted that free Zafimaniry grant them land. The areas thus granted were very largely those semi-exhausted lands which the free Zafimaniry had allowed slaves to cultivate before, as well as some more favoured lands near the colonial administrative posts where some ex-slaves had moved.

At the same time an equally important change took place which was directly concerned with slavery. The Zafimaniry area became intensely missionised by Jesuits. From the end of the nineteenth century, representatives of the London Missionary Society had occasionally crossed Zafimaniry country and while some villages of free men had become more or less Protestant, others had retained the Zafimaniry religion. The Jesuits, when they came, converted some of these 'pagan' free men but their greatest success was among the descendants of slaves. People in the latter category were largely excluded from the traditional religion as well as from Protestantism and thus Catholicism came to symbolise their opposition to those of free descent. While the descendants of the free may be 'pagan', Protestants or Catholics, all ex-slaves are now Catholics. Conversion to Catholicism, however, meant something different from conversion to Protestantism. In true Jesuit fashion, conversion was followed up by the wholesale construction of churches and above all primary schools. This action gave a clear educational advantage to Catholic villages, an advantage which has never been lost but which, as we shall see, has been particularly significant for the ex-slaves.

The granting of land to the ex-slaves was accompanied by a period of increasing economic difficulty for the Zafimaniry. First, it was the time when the government began to extract taxes from the Zafimaniry. This forced them to acquire cash somehow. Secondly, it was a period when land shortages began to be felt. The eastward movement had more or less reached its end as the Zafimaniry were coming close to the

escarpment which marked the edge of their traditional ecological zone. In any case there were people of other groups
living in this area (although a few Zafimaniry have settled
there). Secondly, the government withdrew permission for
the Zafimaniry to use large tracts of forests and converted
these into forestry reserves. Government officials also tried to
stop swiddening, banning it at least twice but only succeed-
ing in making nuisances of themselves as they offered at first
no alternative mode of livelihood and when they did, tried to
encourage irrigated rice which was not really viable (Coulaud
1973:329–338). Thirdly, this was a period of massive population growth throughout Madagascar, but especially in Zafimaniry territory. Coulaud calculates that for the period in
question the annual increase in population was approximately
2.5 per cent, or in other words, a doubling of the population
in 28 years.

All these factors have forced the Zafimaniry to seek a
number of alternatives. The first has been the temporary
wage migration of a large part of the male population as
woodsmen to other parts of the island. In this respect there
is, as far as I know, no difference between the descendants of
slaves and of free men. Another alternative has been trade.
This has taken two forms. The first has been the selling of
roughly prepared timber. It might seem that the descendants
of the free would have an advantage over the ex-slaves in this,
since their village lands are those with the most forest. However, the Zafimaniry have no notion of ownership, in the
Western sense of the term, as regards forest and so anybody
can cut down trees anywhere. Nonetheless, the freemen have
a better knowledge of the forest in which they make swiddens
and this has probably been to their benefit as they seem to
dominate here. Their preoccupation with timber preparation
may, however, also be due to the fact that non-Catholic free
men have had much less opportunity to engage in the newer
and far more profitable trade in wood carvings for tourists
which has developed in recent years.

There is no doubt that Zafimaniry are master carvers; their
houses are famous for their low relief carvings. The sale of
carvings (windows, honeypots, snuff boxes, etc.) was first

organised by the local Jesuits principally from Catholic villages and, as a consequence, this soon became a monopoly of the ex-slaves. The Catholic Church has channelled some of the considerable profits thus obtained into a building programme so that every Catholic Zafimaniry village of 100 or more has a massive cathedral-like structure of concrete and stone, as well as a school.

This sale of carvings has, however, proved too lucrative a source of income for the missionaries to be able to maintain their monopoly, and several Zafimaniry, not only Catholics, soon found other outlets for their wares. By 1971 a great mass of products were being sold, bringing in very large sums of money by Zafimaniry standards. Nonetheless, the fact remains that this highly significant source of income is still very largely in the hands of the Catholic ex-slaves. This is to be explained by two facts—one is the range and the nature of the contacts of the ex-slaves outside Zafimaniry country, which is discussed below, and another is the small-scale but significant growth of tourism. This tourism, of up to 400 people a year, is to be explained by the desire to buy Zafimaniry artifacts cheaply and to see the famous villages of the Zafimaniry, photographs of which appeared in the Malagasy press in 1970 and 1971. David Coulaud has estimated that in 1971 each tourist spent 5000 FM, approximately £10. Most of this money has been spent in the largest slave village, Antetezandrotra, the reason being that the tourist guides are usually from this village.

The third economic response to the worsening situation of the Zafimaniry has been perhaps even more fundamental, the turning to irrigated rice agriculture in some areas. The colonial government and even before them, the Merina, tried to stop swidden and in the end tried to suggest that irrigated rice cultivation would be an alternative which they therefore encouraged. By and large, however, for reasons tellingly discussed by Coulaud, this has been unsuccessful, not because of Zafimaniry contrariness as the French believed (an administrator in the 1950s suggested that they all be put in a concentration camp until they learned better manners), but because irrigated rice cultivation involves a dramatic fall in the productivity of labour as opposed to swidden and because the mountainous terrain of Zafimaniry country made irrigation extraordinarily difficult and highly inefficient by comparison to the plateau area. Nonetheless, in some areas, apart from the show rice fields the administration insisted on, terraced ricefields have begun to be economic. These are found, either in the few exceptional areas where the country is suitable or where the villages were running out of forest for swiddens in a disastrous way. Of the latter the first and most affected settlements in this position have been the villages of ex-slaves, since as noted above, these people were given land in the last stages of exhaustion. One of the features of irrigated rice agriculture is a high initial capital investment, so if it is going to be done at all an early start is an advantage. This is especially true in Zafimaniry territory because the basically inappropriate nature of the country means that irrigation is peculiarly complex. So complex, indeed, that the Zafimaniry have not been able to make rice terraces themselves and have had to employ outside experts, mainly Betsileo wage earners. Characteristically when Coulaud asked people in the largest Zafimaniry slave villages what they would do if they had £500, all who answered said that they would spend it on the construction of rice-fields and irrigation channels. This in fact is what the spare cash obtained by ex-slaves has gone into.

This has meant that the ex-slave villages have been the first to turn to irrigation. Subsequently other villages of freemen which have run out of land for swidden have also had to do the same. In these circumstances the ex-slave villages have had an advantage over those latecomers and they are therefore better off. They are, however, still worse off than those Zafimaniry villages which still have adequate access to forest for swiddens and they are certainly worse off in terms of the amount of time they have to devote to agriculture.

Finally, let us turn to the significance of the effect of manumission and conversion for the kinship system. Manumission left the Merina slave in a social limbo since they had no place in society and were actually excluded from it by the symbolical system of tombs and territories. This absence of location in the social system itself was a source of fundamental inferiority. The situation of the Zafimaniry slaves was very different since, as we have seen, there was no comprehensive social system containing a defined and limited number of groups. Freedom for the Zafimaniry slaves enabled them to become simply another group among the many inmarrying groups. They were not trying to squeeze into an already fully formed and complete order, as there was no such order. They did not intermarry with the groups of freemen but this did not matter because they did not have to merge into these groups to join society. The Zafimaniry slaves became just another Zafimaniry group of which there is no fixed number.

The marriage pattern of the ex-slaves among the Zafimaniry has also been significant for their history. As we saw, the Zafimaniry slaves formed an endogamous group, not because of any particular marriage rules they had, but simply because no freemen or descendants of freemen are normally willing to marry them.

However, on their annual wage migration or simply their journeying, their lack of positive marriage rules means that they are often likely to settle down and marry foreigners (usually ex-slaves of other groups). The descendants of freemen, by contrast, are caught up in long-standing alliances which require that they marry back in the complex network of Zafimaniry kinship. They therefore must return home after their migration or marry Zafimaniry girls and consequently they form no kinship links outside Zafimaniry country. No such system of alliance recalls the ex-slave migrant worker, he breaks no long-standing ties by marrying a girl he meets on his travels, and young men commonly do so. The ex-slaves, therefore, do form marriage and then kinship links well beyond the confine of their territories.

This process started at the time of manumission throughout Madagascar when the Zafimaniry slaves could obtain their freedom only by going away to more effectively administered parts of Madagascar and settling down there. The pattern, however, has carried on since. As a result, while Zafimaniry freemen have practically no affines or kinsmen outside

Zafimaniry country, the Zafimaniry ex-slaves have relatives in several of the towns outside Zafimaniry country, especially Ambositra, the nearest town of any size, and this has had significance in a number of ways. It has not given them access to the ruling classes, as geographically-dispersed ties do for the Merina of free descent, since the people they meet are not close to the sources of economic-political power. It has however given them contact with people who have some knowledge of towns, roads, post offices, etc. and even of dealings with the lowest level of the administration. This sort of knowledge is not a problem for *any* Merina but it is for many Zafimaniry and so the ex-slaves are, in this sphere, advantaged over their ex-masters. The fact that the descendants of Zafimaniry slaves have relatives outside Zafimaniry country is most important in the sphere of education, since it means that their children can board with these relatives in town when they need to go on to school in Ambositra. Young Catholic Zafimaniry are often well able to do that, due to the high standard of many of the Catholic schools in the Zafimaniry country. But it is only those children (usually of ex-slave descent) who have relatives with whom to stay in town who can take up these opportunities. It is significant that the few modern professional successes among the Zafimaniry have all, with one exception, been school-teachers and have all been descendants of slaves.

The higher number of educated men among the descendants of ex-slaves and their more widespread geographical contacts has yet a further implication. It explains why the guides for free-spending tourists are recruited from ex-slave ranks; these educated men speak French and can be contacted in Ambositra. It is not surprising either that the guides take the tourists in the first place to ex-slave villages to buy carvings, thereby enriching these communities still further.

The ex-slaves, or at least some of them, have therefore been more successful in the wider society than their former masters. The question remains, however, whether with time these successful individuals will move to towns and sever their links with their country relatives by not marrying back, thus following the same pattern as the Merina ex-slaves.

This is highly probable unless, of course, brokerage in carvings and tourism should develop into an ever more profitable business. The prospects, however, are not very good.

It is interesting to contrast this case with that of the Merina. Among the Merina it is the descendants of freemen who have the more widespread kinship networks and who have therefore benefited from access to the wider Malagasy society. This has been brought about by their marrying back within their descent groups which are in fact dispersed, while the descendants of slaves have narrowed their networks by marrying their neighbours. Among the Zafimaniry the descendants of freemen, by marrying along traditional alliance lines, have kept their networks small and localised. Their kinship groups are in one place, and therefore they do not benefit from wider contacts. The ex-slaves, by marrying during their migrations, have widened the geographical spread of these contacts and have gained in a way similar, though more modest, to that of descendants of Merina freemen.

Conclusion

Perhaps our first reaction to the evidence outlined above might well be bewilderment concerning the connection between the role of the relations of production we have looked at and the legal-ideological classification which accompanied them. One preliminary point, however, emerges: to look to either type of data exclusively as the basis for comparison is misleading. If with such writers as Kopytoff and Miers we concentrate on the legal-ideological side, we would find that we had to treat Zafimaniry and Merina slavery as identical since there is little difference in terms of the classification and representation of the status in the two societies. Similarly, we would have to treat Merina slavery during the eighteenth and nineteenth century as a single phenomenon. Even more damaging, we would have to conclude that, with the manumission of slaves, the phenomenon ended, while we have seen that its implications continued. Such a theoretical position, therefore, is critically weak and is little more than a rephrasing of ideologies. In other words, it represents a classification of some of the mechanisms of exploitation, in their own terms, as though they were what they pretend to be, a description of a social system.

The other alternative is to use as our criteria of comparison what Marxists have called the Mode of Production. Although there are numerous disagreements as to what this means there is also general agreement that it is the specific combination of the means and techniques of production and the dominant relations of production, the latter being the most significant aspect. Thus the capitalist mode of production is ultimately characterised by the relation of capitalist to proletariat whether this relationship is recognised and institutionalised or not. This perspective would sharply distinguish such systems as the Zafimaniry, the eighteenth-century Merina system, and the nineteenth-century Merina system, since these are based on radically different relations of production, while it might group together the nineteenth-century Merina situation and the twentieth century situation in the old Merina lands in spite of manumission. This approach seems to be much more satisfactory than the legal-ideological one but it requires certain discussion and elaboration.

The first point is that the mode of production approach in the broad sense is often closely associated with the attempts made by Marx, and modified by others, to establish a definite and limited list of modes of production of which the 'slave mode of production' is one. In this perspective it could indeed be argued that none of the cases discussed here correspond to the 'slave mode of production' as understood by Marx. My objection to this type of classification is more fundamental and applies to the very nature of such listings. Classifications in the social sciences lead to sterile discussions about marginal cases and in any case are, by definition, arbitrary. Classifications only have use in terms of the tasks to which they are put and I feel we should all retain the right to construct as many or as few modes of production as we like for the purposes at hand. The value of the concept of mode of production does not lie in the fact that it offers yet another list of types of systems but rather that it focuses on a set of systematic and analytically revealing interconnections. These are, as we have seen, the interrelations between the means and techniques of production and relations of production. But it also includes the relation of these to the ideology which is understood as one of the mechanisms of reproduction (Terray 1977). Using the concept of mode of production we try to understand the 'slaves' not in isolation but as part of a total system which, as far as the relations of production are concerned, includes the free. Indeed one of the striking facts which comes out of the examples we have looked at and to which we shall return is that it is as much what happens to the free or their descendants which determines the destiny of the slaves and their descendants as what happens to themselves personally.

The other characteristic of the mode of production approach is, as we have noted, that it incorporates ideological elements as part of its functioning, since they form one of the reproductive mechanisms of the mode of production. (Of course, there are non-ideological mechanisms for the reproduction of a mode of production, for example, in the case of slavery the organisation ensuring a continuing supply.) In this perspective the means and relations of production are linked indirectly to the ideological and political structures since these assure their functioning. We therefore again put together these two levels, which at the beginning of this paper I suggested we must separate for a preliminary understanding; now, however, we must put them together in an organic relation. In this case we see the ideological-legal system concerned with slavery as a mechanism for the reproduction of types of exploitation and try to understand it as such. In doing this we therefore not only link our two levels but incorporate them in the wider whole: the mode of production.

Here, however, if we tried to understand slavery for itself rather than trying to understand the mode of production, we would be faced with something of a difficulty. It is simply that there seems little or no ideological representation of slavery in any of the cases we are dealing with except for the existence of the status itself. Slavery, with the exception of royal slavery which I do not consider here, is not a status but the absence of a status, a point well understood by Kopytoff and Miers (1977). The few Merina laws dealing with slavery were introduced very late at the insistence of the missionaries. The reproduction of slaves as a category was almost entirely non-ideological but simply the result of unadorned force. Indeed it might well be because this is so often the case that anthropologists have shied away from discussing the topic. 'Unthought' by the society which uses slaves, anthropologists have lacked the tools for 'thinking' the relation for themselves, used as they are to borrowing their social theory from those whom they study. The methodological problem can be overcome, however, if we look at the relations of production as a whole. In the Merina case the outcaste nature of slaves is a by-product of the highly elaborate devices for the ideological reproduction of the free society with its in-marrying kinship groups and their mystical association with land and tombs. Their very representation produces and reproduces the non-status of slaves in that, as we have seen, it literally leaves no room for them.

In this light and with the holistic approach outlined above we can again examine our first puzzle: the fact that although the Merina economy changed drastically between the eighteenth and nineteenth centuries the ideological-legal status of the slaves did not. There simply was no slave status to change since this was a by-product of the free society and had no independence of its own. However, what did change under the impact of the dramatic influx of slaves during the nineteenth century and the consequent changes in the relations of production was the ideological representation of the free society. The free men were transformed by the massive presence of slaves from groups of farmers into groups of rulers and soldiers. The Merina therefore changed their ideological representation of their relation to production. They represented the reproduction not as the product of agricultural labour any more but as the result of an ever more mystical and abstract relation to their ancestral lands. This relationship was adapted to the military and administrative requirements of the growing and increasingly bureaucratic Merina state, and to the developing commerce (partly in

slaves) which accompanied its expansion. The free turned
enthusiastically to education and literacy. In other words,
what changed was the ideological representation of free
society. There is nothing surprising in this, however, in that
the changes in the relations of production were not limited
to the slaves but also included the free, although we may find
it difficult to think of both free and slave as part of one
system because of the very nature of the ideology which, by
forgetting the slaves, ensured their ideological subordination.

Once we have understood this process we can turn to the
other problem concerning the effects of manumission. Here,
however, we must distinguish the two different cases: that of
the slaves who remained in the old Merina heartlands and
who did not dispose of land, and those who went to empty
new lands. For the former, manumission meant very little
since their subordination to the free remained almost complete. This, however, is not difficult to understand; what is
much more difficult to comprehend is why manumission did
not end the implications of slavery for those who went to
new lands and so gained access to the means of production.
The reason why the descendants of slaves remained in an
inferior position is again due to the nature of the organisation
of the free Merina. They had before manumission assured
their position firstly by having acquired skills suitable to a
complex society and secondly by maintaining the unity of
their descent groups irrespective of their economic functions
so as not to dispense with their social advantages or at least
those which the French allowed them to keep. In ensuring
their reproduction they were excluding the descendants of
slaves and there was no reason for this to stop with manumission. It is as though manumission gave the Merina slaves
permission to enter a house with no doors. This was done,
firstly, by leaving the land in the old villages in the hands of
the descendants of the free. And, even in the new lands, the
free were allowed their exclusive monopoly over the new and
historically developing means of production: education, trade
links and administrative access by means of their ideological
practices centred on tombs and ancestral villages. For manumission to have been effective in wiping out exploitation it

would not only have had to give the ex-slaves land, and thereby avoid the situation in the old Merina villages, but it would also have had to change radically not the slaves but the free. This would have forestalled the situation which developed in the new lands where the descendants of slaves did have land but were excluded from other sources of production. So profound a change in the nature of society would have been unthinkable from a state which itself was based on a different type of exploitation—colonialism. The ideological reproductive mechanisms of the free Merina, therefore, ensured the reproduction of the non-status of slave descendants after manumission who, as a result, have remained, by comparison with the descendants of the free, disorganised and disadvantaged, scattered in a society whose most powerful centres exclude them.

When we turn to the Zafimaniry case we see the same process with different results. There too slavery was an absence of an ideological status produced by the mechanisms of reproduction of the free kinship system. Manumission in this case ended the physical exploitation of the slaves since force could not be replaced by land deprivation because of the nature of the technology; however, it did not then give the slaves a place in free Zafimaniry society since this continued in its old cycles of reproduction. The slaves remained outside the lines of alliance. For that they suffered continuing peripherality in their own land. However, this is at a time when the central concerns of the Zafimaniry are becoming themselves peripheral to Madagascar as a whole. The mechanisms of reproduction of free Zafimaniry society, therefore, serve only to isolate the free even more, while the descendants of slaves excluded from these concerns are willy-nilly thrust into contact with the wider Malagasy world to which they have accommodated more readily and earlier than the free.

The analysis outlined above can inevitably only be indicative but it overcomes, I believe, some of the difficulties raised by the topic of slavery and manumission in a few simple steps. First it does not treat the slave/master relation in isolation but as part of the total system of relations of production thereby characterising the totality, not the social relation. It sees this system in the practical setting of the technical and environmental requirements of the mode of production. Secondly it incorporates the ideological legal system again as a totality viewed in terms of its function: reproduction, for the system of production. In other words our task has been to construct one of several modes of production: that system of interlinked components which in a historical setting accounts for the dynamics of the situation.

6

Slavery and Indenture in Mauritius and Seychelles

BURTON BENEDICT

All of the nearly one million inhabitants of Mauritius and Seychelles are the descendants of immigrants who reached these islands in the western Indian Ocean between the mid-eighteenth and early twentieth centuries.[1] The vast majority came as slaves or indentured labourers. Most of those from Africa came as slaves, though indentured African labourers were brought to Seychelles in the nineteenth century. Most of those from India came as indentured labourers, though Indian slaves were imported into Mauritius in the eighteenth century. Today there are very few identifiable African cultural traits among Mauritians and Seychellois of African ancestry. There are, however, many identifiable Indian cultural traits among Mauritians and Seychellois of Indian ancestry.

Why have African cultural traits largely disappeared while many Indian cultural traits have tended to persist? There is no simple answer to this question. A multi-factoral analysis is required. Some of the factors involved are the systems of production in the islands, the conditions under which labourers were imported, the difference between slavery and indenture, the provenance of the immigrants, the conditions under which slaves and indentured labourers lived, the types of marriage and family structure which they brought with them and how these were adapted to conditions in the islands, their languages, their religions and the political structure which they left and into which they were incorporated.

Such factors in general militated against the preservation of African cultural traits, but permitted many Indian cultural traits to persist in modified forms.

The Islands

Mauritius is a volcanic island of some 720 square miles located about 500 miles east of Madagascar and 20 degrees south of the equator. Seychelles is an archipelago of more than 90 islands with a total area of 107 square miles about 1000 miles east of Mombassa and 4 degrees north of the equator. Mauritius includes the dependency of Rodrigues and a few outlying islands. Seychelles comprises two sorts of islands: a compact granitic group with a continental base and a widely scattered coralline group consisting of atolls, reefs and sand cays. The granitic group has 80 per cent of the land area and 99 per cent of the population. The largest island, Mahé, is 56 square miles in area and has 86 per cent of the population. Neither Mauritius nor Seychelles had any indigenous inhabitants when they were first discovered by the Portuguese in the sixteenth century. They were not effectively colonised until the French took possession in the eighteenth century. Britain seized the islands in 1810 and they became British colonies in 1814. Today Mauritius has a population of 900,000, of which about two thirds is of Indian descent comprising both Hindus and Muslims from five linguistic stocks. Another 28 per cent is known as Creole and is of mixed African and European ancestry. About 3 per cent is Chinese and a further 2 per cent is European, mostly of French ancestry. Virtually all of the 62,000 inhabitants of Seychelles are Creoles, though there are a few Indian and Chinese merchants and a small number of Europeans, again mostly of French descent. The economy of Mauritius is based almost entirely on the production of cane sugar while that of Seychelles rests precariously on copra and tourism. Both Mauritius and Seychelles have recently become independent nations within the Commonwealth: the former in 1968 and the latter in 1976.

Slavery

From their inception Mauritius and Seychelles were slave societies. The first colonisers of Mauritius were the Dutch who landed in 1598. They made two attempts to settle the island bringing in slaves from Madagascar to cut down the forests of ebony. They also introduced sugar cane, cotton, tobacco, cattle and deer, but they never imported a labour force sufficient to establish plantations. In over a century of sporadic occupation it is doubtful if there were ever more than about 300 settlers. The Dutch finally abandoned Mauritius in 1710. Five years later the French claimed the island. In 1722 the French East India Company brought colonists from the neighbouring island of Bourbon (now Réunion) which the French had occupied since 1674. Settlers were given tracts of land and slaves, and the plantation economy became well established by 1735. The emphasis was on cash crops beginning with coffee and followed by sugar cane, cotton, indigo, cloves and other spices. Sugar cane best resisted the terrible cyclones which periodically strike Mauritius and became the principal crop by the early nineteenth century.

The islands of Seychelles were colonised from Mauritius in the mid-eighteenth century. They remained dependencies of Mauritius until 1903 when they were constituted a separate colony. A similar system of land grants and slaves was provided to early settlers when cotton and spices and some food crops were grown.

The economy of the islands rested on slave labour. By 1735 slaves constituted 77 per cent of the population, and the percentage remained between 75 and 85 until emancipation in 1835 (Barnwell and Toussaint 1949:225).

Provenance and Prices

The origin of the slaves is difficult to determine. Slaves passed through many hands, tribal and place names were confused and variously spelled and accurate records were not kept. Filliot (1974) estimates that 160,000 slaves were imported into the Mascarene islands (Mauritius, Réunion, Rodrigues, Seychelles and dependencies) between 1670 and 1810 (p. 51). He estimates that about 45 per cent came from Madagascar, 40 per cent from East Africa especially Mozambique, 13 per cent from India especially Pondicherry and 2 per cent from West Africa (1974: 113–186). Between 1810 and 1820 approximately 20,000 slaves were imported into Mauritius (*Report of the Slave Trade* 1829: 10, 20) though the British were supposed to be engaged in the abolition of the slave trade at this period. A report made at Mauritius in 1755 states that most slaves came 'from Goree, an island off the coast of Guinea belonging to the East India Company, Madagascar, the East coast of Africa and Bengal' (Noble 1793:113). D'Unienville (1838: Vol. I: 276–279) states that there were 67,619 slaves in Mauritius on January 1, 1830, about a third of whom were Creoles (i.e. born in the colony), a seventeenth were Indians (Telegus, Malabars and Bengalis), a fifth were Malagasis (Hovas, Betsileos, Antateimes and Sakalavas), two fifths were from Mozambique from the following tribes: Makua, Monjavoa, Sena, Mashona, Shengwe, Ngido, Maravi, Makonde and Nyamwezi. The provenance of these tribes covers a very wide area from present day Tanzania in the north to Inhambane, Mozambique in the south and westwards as far as Lake Malawi (Nyasa) and Rhodesia (v. also Royal Society of Mauritius 1932).

This wide range of origins meant that the languages, customs, religious practices and general culture of the slaves were very diverse. On their arrival in Mauritius male slaves were separated from females and children for purchase by planters. In 1768 the prices ranged from a barrel of gunpowder or a few muskets to fifty crowns (£7 10s) (Grant 1801:75). By the early 1820s the price was £40 to 50. In 1825 the duty on colonial sugar was removed by Britain leading to boom conditions in Mauritius. In October 1827 slaves cost £80 to 90 and by July of 1828 the price had risen to £120 (Howell 1950:18). By 1830 the over-production of sugar led to a decline in prices, but a new boom began in 1833, and a boom-bust cycle characterised the Mauritian sugar industry until 1847 when attempts were made to regulate the market. The methods of selling slaves in Mauritius frequently separated families, kinsmen and friends leading to a further atomisation of their social life.

Living Conditions

Baron Grant, a French planter, who resided in Mauritius from 1740 to 1758 gives the following account of the social condition of slaves:

> Their manner of life is as follows: at day-break, the smacking of a whip is the signal that calls them to their work: and they then proceed to the plantation, where they labour in a state of almost entire nakedness, and in the heat of the sun. Their nourishment is ground maize boiled in water, or loaves of the manioc; and a small piece of cloth is their only covering. For the least act of negligence, they are tied hand and foot to a ladder, when the overseer gives them a certain number of strokes on their back with a long whip; and with a three-pointed collar clasped round their necks, they are brought back to their work. It is not necessary to describe the severity with which these punishments are sometimes inflicted. On their return to their habitations in the evening, they are compelled to pray to God for the prosperity of their masters.
>
> There is a law subsisting in favour of slaves, called the *Code Noir*; which ordains that they shall receive no more than thirty strokes at each chastisement; that they shall not work on Sundays; that meat shall be given them every week, and shirts every year: but this law is not observed.
>
> The Negroes are naturally of a lively disposition, but their state of slavery soon renders them melancholy. Love alone seems to allay their pain: they exert themselves to the utmost in order to obtain a wife; and, if they can choose for themselves, they always prefer those who are advanced into a state of womanhood, who, they say, make the best soup. They immediately give them all they possess; and if their wives live in another plantation, they will undertake the most difficult and dangerous journies to see them. On such occasions they fear neither fatigue nor punishment. Parties of them sometimes meet in the middle of the night, when they dance beneath the shelter of a rock, to the mournful sound of a gourd filled with peas. (Grant 1801: 76–77.)

The census figures show that male slaves outnumbered females by about two to one from 1785 to 1826 (Kuczynski 1949: 760, 768). Thereafter the proportion of females began to increase, but it did not approach parity until 1891 when the figures include both whites and those of African or mixed descent (*Ibid.* 779). There was apparently a high rate of abortion among slave women, and an edict was put into force in 1778 inflicting the death penalty on women who concealed their pregnancies (*Ibid.* 869). A report of 1834 complains that slaves from Madagascar were particularly prone to the practice of birth control and abortion (*Ibid.*).

Slaves were apparently very eager for wives. What exchange of rights and duties took place at marriage is not clear. If Grant's account (1801:76–77) is reliable it indicates that the women were expected to do the cooking and that the men gave them whatever possessions they might have. Slaves had to have their masters' permission to marry, but judging from accounts of early planters, they often co-habited with women to whom they were not married. Some were married according to Christian rites. Many ran away:

> You already know that the Council had granted me six slaves; but the strongest of these has already quitted me to join a party of runaway Negroes, who live on the fruits of nocturnal rapine. We consider them as obnoxious animals, and hunt them down in the same manner. My fugitive has accordingly suffered on one of his marauding expeditions, when he was shot. This Black cost me three hundred livres ... (Grant [1743] 1886:38.)

Conditions for hiding and living off the land must have been much more difficult on the small islands of Seychelles than at Mauritius. Seychelles runaways were more likely to take to the sea.

Owen, writing in 1825 about Seychelles, noted that although the 'attempt to escape from slavery is regarded as a capital offence, desertions are constantly taking place' (1833: Vol. II: 161). One of his ships picked up five slaves in a canoe made from a single tree trunk and with an old cotton sheet as a sail. They had been 17 days at sea and had sailed

750 miles in an attempt to reach the African coast (1833: Vol. I: 376–379). They had escaped from one of the Amirante islands where they had been left to cultivate the land by their owner.

> It is extraordinary that the proprietors of the slaves, now that they are so difficult to obtain, should pursue the same line of policy respecting their moral conduct as when they were both numerous and cheap—it not being at all uncommon for twenty men to be placed on an island for its cultivation, with not more than two or three women as their companions. (Owen 1833: Vol. II: 161–162.)

Even in 1829 slaves could not marry or own property without their masters' consent (Howell 1950:37–40). 'In Mauritius only free men had the right to wear shoes; to give slaves shoes, the colonists said, was tantamount to proclaiming their emancipation' (*Ibid.* 50).

The competition for slave women was not confined to male slaves. Many white men had slave concubines. They often manumitted these women and their children. Between 1785 and 1834 the number of 'free coloured' females outnumbered males by more than two to one. During this same period males outnumbered females in both the white and slave populations (Kuczynski 1949: 760, 770, 772). For a female slave, becoming the concubine of a white man must have seemed a favourable option in a situation of few options.

Abolition

Slavery was abolished throughout the British Empire on 1 February, 1835, but the ex-slaves were hardly free. A system of 'apprenticeship' was introduced whereby all ex-slaves over the age of six were to work as apprentices for their former masters for a period of six years to train them and provide them with wages. Mauritian planters had resisted the abolition of slavery more fiercely than those of any other colony; moreover they completely controlled the judiciary so that ex-slaves had little recourse to the courts for their rights. Vagrancy laws were established to force apprentices to remain on estates and apprentices were flogged by order of the courts for infractions of the law. Only one quarter of their time was allowed off to work for wages. Even so many managed to save to purchase their freedom (Howell 1950:99).

The apprentice system became so notorious that it was finally abolished by law on 31 March, 1839. This was followed by a mass desertion of the ex-slaves from field labour. In 1840 there were perhaps 20,000 blacks still on the estates of Mauritius (Howell 1950:174). By 1844 the number had dropped to 3,725 and by 1851 there were practically none (*Ibid.* 222f). The blacks fled to the towns and to remote un-cultivated areas. They became market gardeners, charcoal burners, small traders, artisans, and fishermen. They avoided working for wages. By the 1850's the pressure on them had diminished as the planters turned to Indian labour.

The situation in Seychelles was different. The smallness of the territory in terms of its total population, the size of the plantations, the number of slaves held by any one planter and the small size and isolation of the islands themselves probably threw blacks and whites into closer contact than was the case in Mauritius. Another factor hastened this mixing. Seychelles' chief cash crop in the eighteenth and early nineteenth century was cotton. By 1826 American competition had pretty well ruined this trade and those Seychellois who could afford it began to leave for Mauritius with their slaves (Toussaint 1972:173–174). Many of those who remained could no longer afford to keep their slaves. They let them cultivate the land on a share-cropping basis (Webb 1966:49).

Nevertheless abolition was resisted as strongly in Seychelles as it was in Mauritius. Sir Edward Belcher, who visited Mahé in 1842, wrote:

> The old French residents complain bitterly of the emancipa-tion, and their estates are fast falling into decay. Indeed the Blacks, lazy at all times, cannot be persuaded to work volun-tarily, and I very strongly suspect that the change from slavery to freedom, or rather the entire destruction of any control over their persons, rendering it necessary to hold out allurements, or adequate wages, is nearer the real cause. They either have not the means of paying or they cannot make up their minds to swallow the bitter pill of paying those

to whose services they still maintain they are entitled. (quoted in Webb 1966:52.)

By 1850 the Civil Commissioner, R. W. Keate, reported to the Governor of Mauritius:

> With the exception of those estates on which rum and arrack and a small quantity of sugar are produced, and a few others on which coconut palms have been planted and already furnish a considerable quantity of oil, with a promise of future abundance, and certain small unimportant plantations of cacao, coffee, cloves, rice and tobacco, scarcely any of the numerous 'habitations,' as they are called, can be said to be under cultivation, or to furnish anything either for exportation or home consumption. (quoted in Webb 1966:50.)

The planters blamed emancipation for their plight, but the economic decline of Seychelles antedated emancipation and slaves 'had already before their final Emancipation become a burden upon, and not an assistance to the estates to which they were attached' (Webb 1966:49). The planters had little choice but to permit the ex-slaves to remain on their estates on some sort of share-cropping basis. The ex-slaves had no choice but to remain there.

In Mauritius emancipation had been followed by the importation of large numbers of indentured labourers from India. But Mauritius had a flourishing sugar industry in which production continued to mount after emancipation. Seychelles had none. When Seychellois planters petitioned the British government for permission to import Indian labourers, they were refused.

Liberated Africans

Yet a new form of cheap labour did appear in Seychelles, the 'liberated' African. British efforts to put down the slave trade in the Indian Ocean resulted in the capture of numerous Arab dhows. The captured slaves were put ashore at the nearest convenient point and this was often Seychelles (Graham 1967:143) where they were indentured to planters or the government. Accurate records do not exist, but it seems likely that between 1860 and 1890 between 2,000 and 3,000 Africans were landed at Seychelles.

> I have the honour to report for the information of His Excellency the Governor that HMS Columbine arrived here on the 5th instant having on board two hundred & six liberated African Slaves who were landed on the following day by my direction on Long Island.
>
> The original number captured from the Slave Vessels amounted to two hundred & forty six out of which number forty died during the passage of 16 days from the Coast; many of those remaining were in a dreadful state of emaciation having been previous to their capture over four days without food & water on board the Slave Vessels.
>
> I am happy to say that owing to the unremitting attention of the Gov't Medical Officer, Mr. Underwood, corporal of the police in charge and their being supplied with proper & nourishing food only four of these unfortunate creatures have since died, and that the remainder are fast recovering strength.
>
> 135 have been allotted to Proprietors & other responsible persons who made immediate applications for them; the whole ready for allotment would at once have been applied for had not the number of women exceeded so much that of men, but I hope in a few days that the balance including those ready to be discharged from Hospital will be provided for. (Seychelles Archives Vol. B 33:54.)

There were continual reports by government inspectors of failure to pay wages, provide sufficient food and medical care. Harsh punishments were inflicted for trivial offences. 'Liberated' Africans were indentured for a period of five years. Not surprisingly few re-engaged at the end of this period. In 1864 the Civil Commissioner urged that no more Africans be released in Seychelles and reported that: 'Many of these men are anxious to return to Zanzibar preferring Arab to Creole masters' (Reports 1863 Pt. I:126).

A report of the Inspector of Immigrants in 1881 gives some idea of the condition of the women:

> I was much struck in the course of my inspections to find so few women employed, especially as there is work connected

with the making of coconut oil, which is so light that women could very well perform it; and this remark applies even more forceably to the collection and preparation of vanilla, and the collection and cultivation of coffee and cacao.

There seems on the part of the African women a strong dislike to perform work of any description for others, and I am afraid this aversion to regular employment, leaves them open to the temptation to indulge in a vicious course of life, and certainly materially interferes with their welfare. It is however difficult to find a remedy for it. Laws compelling women to work would be scarcely expedient, and nothing short of this would make them work, so I fear the evil must be left to cure itself. One bright feature in this matter however is that when the men work on what is called the 'moitie' system, the wives or the women they live with, give them considerable help in cultivating their land, bringing the produce to the market and disposing of it. (Report on Liberated Africans in the Seychelles Islands: 1035.)

The report suggests that women were motivated to invest their time and energy in work which would help the family unit. This was a better choice for them than working for the pittance they were offered on estates. The *moitié* system refers to the expedient which planters were forced to employ because they could not or would not pay or maintain their labourers. *Moitié* contracts:

were derived for the settlement on the lands of the liberated slaves who were landed in Seychelles in large numbers up to 1880. There was no scheme for the settlement of these men on the land, nearly the whole of which has been held in private hands since the final issue of land concessions by the French Government prior to the English occupation in 1815. The proprietors were then poor in cash but tenacious of their land: so a system was adopted whereby the Africans received house room and an allotment of land for gardens or for manioc cultivation and placed their labour at the disposal of the proprietors under the various methods of profit sharing which are enumerated in the Seychelles Regulation No. 3 of 1888. (Seychelles Archives Vol. C/AM/16.)

The following types of *moitié* are listed under Ordinance

No. 3 of 1911: 1. Workman agrees to cultivate a portion of land and share produce with owner. 2. Workman cultivates a portion of land for self and another portion for owner. 3. Workman cultivates a portion of land for self and works for owner without receiving wages. For both men and women the *moitié* system must have seemed the best choice of the limited options open to them. Reports from inspectors in the 1870s and 1880s continually stress the poor medical facilities available to labourers on estates and the fact that their wages were in arrears. As may be imagined planters had difficulty getting labourers to work for no wages and there were no effective means of getting them off the land. Instead planters tended to enter into more *moitié* arrangements in the hope of getting some return. A market first for coconut oil and later for copra developed. Coconuts were much less labour intensive than cotton, and some planters began to prosper.

The 'vicious course of life' mentioned in the Inspector's report probably refers to concubinage. The conditions of extreme poverty under which the liberated Africans and their predecessors, the ex-slaves, lived fostered concubinage. Men lacked the resources to support a woman and her children and this threw a burden upon the women to try to make their own arrangements for support. They did this by seeking men who would help support them, changing partners when necessary. They tended to seek men with some resources, and these were men who were squatting on the land or cultivating it on the *moitié* system. This offered more security than the meagre wages offered by employers. Their other resource was their own children, who, as they matured, could help their mothers. A woman turned to her mother, her siblings and her neighbours for help. Kinship networks were important assets without which a woman was hard pressed to exist. A similar pattern has been found in the West Indies and among poor Blacks in the United States (Gutman 1976, Stack 1975). It has little to do with African origins but much to do with the labourers' position in the system of production. This is a point which needs emphasis. R. T. Smith in his study of *The Negro Family in British Guiana* (1956) noted the similarity in living patterns between Blacks in British Guiana and low-income families in a Scottish mining community (Smith 1956:247–251). Smith cites an unpublished study by Shirley Wilson in which she shows that there is a high rate of divorce and illegitimacy among low income Scottish families. The women in such families were far more dependent on their mothers and other kinsmen than in higher-status families. Low-income couples tended to have civil marriages rather than church weddings. Civil marriage in itself was considered a mark of low status and may be regarded as the functional equivalent of concubinage.

The Indians

Indian slaves were brought to Mauritius by the French at a very early date, but the conditions of their servitude are not clear. They were imported from the French colony of Pondicherry in south India. In 1728 the Governor of Mauritius (then called Ile de France) went to Pondicherry where he procured 180 slaves of 8 to 18 years and 95 workers (Kuczynski 1949:793n). This would seem to indicate that there was a distinction between slaves and workers. Perhaps only minors were enslaved. The great developer of the island, Mahé de Labourdonnais (Governor 1735–1746), imported skilled slave labourers from Malabar at his own expense (Billiard 1822:266). Grant, writing in this period, speaks of 'blacks' from Pondicherry who 'let themselves out for a certain number of years' (1801:75) which would seem to indicate some form of indenture rather than slavery. Milbert, on the other hand, writing some 50 years later in 1801 speaks of Indian slaves coming from three principal areas: the Talinga (Telegus), Malabares (Tamils) and Bengal (Vol. II: p. 169f). He also mentions free Indians living with their wives (*Ibid.* 172). Tinker (1974:44) writes that Indian slaves were regularly sold to French planters in Mauritius and Réunion during the second half of the eighteenth century and cites a report of 1792 of ships anchored at Calicut each with a cargo of 300 slaves. It is not certain how many Indian slaves there were in Mauritius. An estimate of 1767 mentions 1,000 (Kuczynski 1949:793). A census of 1806 lists 6,162 (Milbert

1812 Vol. II:233*bis*), but in 1826 there were only 2,590 (including 239 Malays) (Kuczynski 1949:771). However, the number of 'free' Indian immigrants increased from 587 in 1767 to 7,366 in 1808 (Kuczynski 1949:176). In Seychelles there were only 38 Indian slaves registered in 1826 (*Ibid.* 905).

Unlike the Africans the Indians do not seem to have been brought to Mauritius as field labourers. 'On préfère les Indiens commes domestiques,' writes Milbert (Vol. II: 170) and he speaks of Indians letting themselves out ('se louent') as domestics (*Ibid.* 171), again seeming to indicate some form of indenture. Many, he writes, are craftsmen, masons or cabinet makers. Others are clerks and messengers in both government offices and commercial establishments. They live not with their employers, but in a special quarter of the capital (*Ibid.* 173). In both 1748 and 1810 a regiment of Indians was formed to defend the island against the British (*Ibid.* 170). According to Milbert many free Indians lived with their wives and he describes their clothes and jewellery in some detail. Figures for the sex ratio among free Indians are not available as they are lumped with the free coloured population. In 1826, however, Indian male slaves outnumbered females by 1,459 to 892 (Kuczynski 1949:771).

The scanty evidence available seems to indicate that there were considerable differences in African and Indian slavery. Many fewer Indian than African slaves were imported. Many Indians either came as indentured labourers or were given this option after reaching Mauritius. There were free Indians from early times. Indians tended to be employed as artisans or in clerical jobs rather than as field labourers. They maintained traditional patterns of dress, and there was an Indian quarter in the town in which many lived. Many were married. Today it does not seem possible to trace the descendants of these earliest Indian immigrants. Hazareesingh (1950:6) maintains that they lost all trace of the Indian way of life, becoming Christians and merging into the coloured population. He offers no evidence and cites no sources for these allegations. Some may have done so, but the new waves of immigration which occurred in the nineteenth century provided opportunity for the maintenance of Indian cultural traits.

A new form of Indian labour arrived with the British conquest of Mauritius. Indian convicts reached the island in 1815 and were put to work on roads and government buildings. In 1836 Charles Darwin, homeward bound on H.M.S. Beagle, noted that there were about 800 Indian convicts and observed that they adhered to the 'faithful observance of their strange religious enactments' (1933:402). In 1837 transportation to Mauritius was abolished and all convicts over the age of 65 were set free (Tinker 1974:46).

The importation into Mauritius of regular Indian indentured labour began in 1835 and continued off and on with varying degrees of government control until 1907. A few additional Indians arrived in 1922–23. During this period nearly 450,000 Indian labourers were imported. They were engaged in India on five-year contracts, but only about 160,000 were returned to India. The influx of Indians brought a rapid and radical change in the composition of the population of Mauritius. In 1835 Indians comprised only a minute proportion of the population. By 1845 one third of the population was Indian and by 1861 two thirds were Indian, a proportion maintained to the present.

Indenture

Indian indenture has been described as 'a new system of slavery' (Tinker 1974), and, indeed, imported Indian labourers were treated like slaves by the planters of Mauritius who had so recently lost their African slaves. Indians were beaten, forbidden to wear shoes and could receive no justice from the magistrates who were for the most part the agents of the planters. Laws were passed which were specifically designed to keep Indians bound to the estates on which they worked. In 1847 a 'double cut' law was passed which provided that no month in which an engaged labourer was absent for more than six days should be reckoned as part of his service. Immigrants were defined as 'old' (i.e. having completed one period of indenture) or 'new' (still under first indenture). All new immigrants had to carry tickets and were subject to arrest as vagrants if found without them or if found in a district of the island in which they were not employed. In 1867 the pass system was introduced for old immigrants as well in an effort to compel them to re-engage. This was coupled with drastic police control and mass arrests. 'In one year over 12,000 coolies were imprisoned for desertion or illegal absence out of an Indian population of about 250,000, while from 9,000 to 10,000 more were convicted and punished for the technical offence of "vagrancy" ' (Gordon 1894 Vol. I: 126).

Despite repeated exposés of the condition of Indian labourers in Mauritius and condemnation of the system in India and Britain (Tinker 1974:288–333), indenture persisted in Mauritius, and it was not until 1922 that labourers were really free to engage where they wished.

Yet the conditions of indenture were not the same as slavery. The Indians were not chattels. They were engaged under contract, though the conditions of the contract were often violated. They were entitled to a wage, though wages were often many months in arrears or eaten up by the double cut system. They had some protection under law, though the laws were manipulated to deny them their rights and the magistrates were often creatures of the planters.

Provenance[2]

Indentured Indian labourers were shipped to Mauritius from the ports of Calcutta, Madras and Bombay. Some 60 per cent embarked from Calcutta, 33 per cent from Madras and 7 per cent from Bombay during the 70 years of migration. The Indians embarking from Calcutta came mostly from the present-day states of Bihar, Orissa, Uttar Pradesh and West Bengal, but some were also culled from the destitute of Calcutta. The earliest were the Dhangars or Hill coolies from Chota Nagpur. They were tribal peoples, Santals, Oroans and Mundas, outside the Hindu caste system (Tinker 1974: 48f). Later villagers from a great variety of castes were recruited. Muslims were also engaged. Efforts were made to recruit gangs of labourers from the same village under a sirdar (headman) who knew and was known by his men. Sirdars became agents of communication between recruiters and migrants and later in Mauritius between planters and their labourers. This fostered the preservation of Indian languages and cultural traits in a way which had not occurred among Africans. Most of the recruits from northern India spoke a dialect of Hindi, especially Bhojpuri which is still spoken in Mauritius today.

Emigrants embarking from Madras came from both Tamil- and Telegu-speaking areas. Most seem to have come from the untouchable castes (Tinker 1974:54f), chiefly from the districts of Tanjore and Trinchinipoly (Beyts 1861:13). Those embarking from Bombay were probably Marathi speakers and came chiefly from the Deccan and Concan districts (*Ibid.*). A small random sample of 1392 arriving immigrants which I took from the immigration records in Port Louis lists 289 places of origin. Thus there was a great diversity of origin of immigrants, not only from three major areas of the sub-continent but also within each area. Yet some Indians did engage in groups and later in families and, in contrast to the Africans, there were common cultural traits which all shared to some degree such as religion and an understanding of the caste system.

Caste

In the 1950s it was often asserted by non-Indians in Mauritius that Indian immigrants all came from the lowest castes and indeed as early as 1840 the Governor of Mauritius wrote, 'These people from India have been the outpouring of the lowest caste of the population of each presidency who are deplorably disorderly and dissolute' (quoted in Tinker 1974: 55f). This was decidedly not the case, at least for the immigrants from northern India. An analysis of 1200 emigrants from northern Bihar in 1883 showed 264 (22 per cent) Muslims, 231 (19 per cent) high caste Hindus (Brahman, Rajput, Chettri), 434 (36 per cent) from the clean castes and only 277 (23 per cent) from the lowest castes. Of the 7695 Hindus embarking from Calcutta in that same year 26 per cent were high caste, 32 per cent were from agricultural castes, 6 per cent were from artisan castes and 36 per cent were from the lowest castes (*Ibid.*). My own sampling of the immigration records confirms the wide range of castes from which immigrants came (Benedict 1967:24–28). This range of castes is important not because it meant that caste was preserved in Mauritius in its original form (it was not), but because it did provide the bases for the continuation of both Hindu and Muslim ritual and endogamy, though again both these features have altered over time.

Living Conditions

The first immigrants to Mauritius were virtually all male. Between 1834 and 1842 only a little over 1 per cent were women (Hugon: para 108). Disorders arose on estates over competition for women, and gradually more women began to be imported. Between 1853 and 1865 a bounty was paid out of government funds to planters importing married immigrants with their wives, and between 1857 and 1884 the percentage of female to male immigrants arriving in Mauritius ranged between 40 per cent and 53 per cent (Précis 1905: Appx. III–IV). Marriage contracted in India was not recognised under Mauritian law unless the parties swore to their union before the Protector of Immigrants. The non-recognition of Indian marriage had legal and social effects extending into the 1950s (Benedict 1961:92ff.). Those who declared their marriages before the Protector were handed certificates of which there are perhaps 32,000 duplicates in the Mauritius Archives. Some idea of the percentage of those who arrived in Mauritius married can be gained by comparing the total number of immigrants with the number of marriage certificates and the number of immigrants under ten years of age where this is listed. On this basis it appears that about 65 per cent of the women and 20 per cent of the men arrived with spouses. These percentages must be regarded as minimal because of the numbers who did not declare their marriages before the Protector. A sample of 305

marriage certificates dating from 1851 to 1903 which I took
showed the following relationships:

Husbands	305	
Wives	312	(seven cases of polygyny)
Sons	170	accompanying both parents
Daughters	131	accompanying both parents
Grandsons	3	accompanying both parents and both grand-parents
Granddaughter	1	accompanying both parents and both grand-parents
Son-in-law	5	accompanying both parents, wife and her parents
Daughter-in-law	4	accompanying husband and his parents
Mother	1	accompanying son, his wife and children

Thus there was immigration by families, even by three-
generation families on a scale which was greater than was the
case for African slaves. Though in early years of immigration
there were reports of widespread concubinage (Tinker 1974:
202), marriage according to Indian rites soon became the
norm, again in contrast to the situation among Africans.
European males do not seem to have taken Indian mistresses,
though casual sexual relations with Indian women were reported in the estate camps (Tinker 197:221f). This was
probably due to the more balanced sex ratio among whites
and the availability of black women. A contributing factor
was the acceptance of concubinage arrangements by Creoles
and their rejection by Indians. An Indian woman who lived
with a non-Indian was condemned and avoided by other
Indians whereas concubinage arrangements bore little stigma
for a Creole woman whether her paramour were a Creole or
a European. Creoles and whites by this time also shared a
common language, religion and many cultural traits.

Indian immigrants were housed in the former slave lines
where they lived in thatched houses, often under conditions
of extreme overcrowding. They took their orders from sirdars
who could speak to them in their own language. They formed
associations (*baitkas*) to settle disputes and help with life
crises (Benedict 1961: 130 passim). These *baitkas* served to

F

insulate the Indian from the host society where he could so rarely obtain justice. Religious ceremonies were performed in them which helped preserve Hinduism. Muslims formed similar associations called *jammat*. The associations also furnished some education for children in the vernaculars. Temples and mosques were built in which religious ceremonies were held, and Hindu and Muslim festivals were celebrated on an island-wide basis (Benedict 1961:120–142). In sum, considerable social distance was maintained between Indians and other ethnic groups in Mauritian society.

Africans and Indians Compared

The foregoing brief historical summary has indicated a number of ways in which African and Indian experience in Mauritius and Seychelles differed. Now an attempt will be made to list factors which in general militated against the preservation of African cultural traits while permitting Indian cultural traits to survive in modified forms.

1. *Origins*   As noted above, the African slaves who reached Mauritius and Seychelles came from a wide range of tribes, from Madagascar, East and Central Africa and even from West Africa. This also seems to be true for the liberated Africans who were taken from Arab dhows operating out of Zanzibar, a slave market which received Africans from many parts of the continent. Africans landing at Mauritius and Seychelles lacked a common culture.

Indentured Indians too came from a wide range of areas, from the northeast, the south and the west of the subcontinent, but in comparison with Africans they shared many cultural traits. India had been a more or less unified country both under the Mughals and the British. The wide diversity of cultural groups within it lived in close contact under a pervasive political and economic system.

2. *Conditions of recruitment*   African slaves were, for the most part, unwilling recruits. They were captured and passed through many hands before reaching Mauritius and

Seychelles. Such agents might include their original African captors, other African slave traders, one or more Arab slave traders, one or more slave markets and one or more European slave traders. This resulted in the further breakup of Africans from the same tribe or area, the dissolution of friendships and consequent isolation of individuals.

Though some isolated Indians were recruited or even captured as slaves in the seventeenth and early eighteenth centuries, efforts were made to recruit Indians from the same village, caste or tribe. Though Indians were deceived as to the location of Mauritius and the working conditions to which they would be subjected, they engaged themselves. The conditions of their passage to the sugar islands were hardly less terrible than those of African slaves (Tinker 1974: 116–176), but they were voluntary emigrants not captives. They could look forward to the end of their indenture. They were recruited by men of their own culture and did not pass through as many different hands as did the Africans. Thus there was more likelihood of Indians from the same area remaining together.

3. *The breakup of families*   For African slaves this resulted from the conditions of capture, from being passed through the hands of a series of traders and from the high death rate, especially at sea. Those slaves who did manage to arrive as families at their final destination were liable to be alloted to different plantations.

In the early years of migration some Indians left their wives in India (Tinker 1974:202). Later when Indians were engaged as families, they were usually assigned to an estate as a family unit. Though conditions were hard, and Indian marriages was not always recognised by Mauritian courts, Indians were able to preserve family life to a greater extent than Africans.

4. *Youth*   Many of the slaves and liberated Africans were mere children. On the African mainland the kidnapping of children to be sold as slaves was common practice (Alpers 1975:240). The one remaining register of liberated Africans

in the Seychelles Archives shows a large proportion of children under the age of 10 landed between 1861 and 1872 (Vol. B 85). The Civil Commissioner of Seychelles in 1864 reported: 'For boys and girls there are plenty of applications, but hardly anyone will accept a full grown man, and nobody will have anything to do with the women.' (Reports 1863: 126.) There were sporadic and not very effective efforts by missionaries to provide some schooling for these children. Though they received little formal education, what they learned was the variant of French culture extant in Mauritius and Seychelles. The conditions for preserving and perpetuating the African cultures from which they came simply were not present in Mauritius and Seychelles.

Indians were engaged as adults. The demand was for field labour, and five-year contracts meant that this was only economical if the able-bodied were recruited. Most immigrants were young adults. My sample of 305 marriage certificates shows that 164 couples were childless, a further 50 had one child, 38 had two children and 44 had three or more (Benedict 1961:20). What little education children received tended to be in vernacular schools run by the Indians themselves. Thus for many years Indian children were not amalgamated into the host society through the educational system. Instead Indian customs and values were perpetuated through family life and vernacular education.

5. *Language*   Coming from many different language groups and encountering traders who spoke Swahili, Arabic, possibly an Indian language, Portuguese, French or English, the slaves and liberated Africans were under pressure to learn these languages. Early reports occasionally mention missionaries or doctors who can speak to the Africans in their own language, but this always turns out to mean Swahili, the *lingua franca* of East Africa. It is very probable that many of them knew this language. Once landed at Mauritius or Seychelles there was considerable pressure on them to learn Creole, the French patois which is still the major language of Mauritius and Seychelles. Grant in a letter of 1749 quotes a Malagasy slave in what he describes as 'corrupted French': ' ca blanc la li

beaucoup malin; li couri beaucoup dans la mer la hout; mais Magascar li la' (1801: 297). [Translation: 'That white man there, he is very clever; he runs very fast over the sea in that direction, but Madagascar is over there.'] This shows that blacks had already acquired the Creole language in a form which appears to be very similar to that spoken today. Creole derives basically from French, though today it contains a few words from English, Malagasy and Indian languages (Baker 1972:63–68). Africans seem quickly to have adopted a modified form of the French language spoken by their masters. This may have begun as a kind of pidgin, but it quickly became a true Creole, i.e. the major language learned from childhood. Today it remains the native tongue of Creoles in both Mauritius and Seychelles. It is also the *lingua franca* of these islands.

The Indians derived from three major language groups, Hindi (mostly the Bhojpuri dialect), Tamil and Telegu. There were also Marathi and possibly Malayalam speakers. The social isolation of the Indian community helped preserve these languages. They dealt with their employers through bilingual sirdars. Indian languages were spoken in the home and children were instructed in them in the vernacular schools. Later the men learned Creole, but even in the 1950s many women spoke only an Indian language (Benedict 1958). Even in the census of 1962 more than 60 per cent of the population listed an Indian language as its mother tongue and nearly 45 per cent declared an Indian language to be the one most often spoken in the home (Baker 1972:13). Recent censuses show a decline in the use of Indian languages in favour of Creole, but it was and is the case that the preservation of Indian languages was and is a major factor in preserving Indian cultural traditions.

6. *Naming* In Seychelles slave registers and the Register of Liberated Africans show that Africans were given European names. These were Christian names in either French or English. The Register of Liberated Africans lists 'name' and 'father's name.' The former is almost always a European Christian name such as Adele or Jacob; the latter may be a

tribal name, or the name of a district. Sometimes these names become anglicised. Thus the father's name of a man, no. 362 on the register, is given as Malbrookee. A few entries below a woman is listed as the wife of Malbrook, no. 362. Elsewhere the names Maboorookee and Magoolookee are given. Today Malbrook is a fairly common name in Seychelles. Some other African surnames such as Barrack (also listed as Barakee) and Saffalana (now usually Sofola) survive, but most African surnames have disappeared to be replaced by French or English surnames. Sometimes these are the names of the proprietors (Savy, Mondon); sometimes they are geographical (Cambridge, Bristol); sometimes they are derogatory jokes (Savon, Moustache, Cadeau, Mauvaisoeil). It seems clear, however, that the naming itself served further to separate the Africans and their descendants from their African heritage.

Indians retained their Indian names. These names were registered in the immigration office on arrival. They sometimes suffered orthographical distortions to conform to French or English pronunciation, but their form remained Indian. Likewise Indian children, born in Mauritius were given Indian names. Most Indians use nicknames or kinship terms to address intimates, but these too are Indian. Only in the case of conversion to Christianity would European names be adopted (Benedict 1961:39). If it be granted that naming conveys an important sense of identity, the Africans through their names became identified with Christianity and European culture whereas the Indians retained an Indian identity.

7. *Religion* The religion of the dominant section of the population in both Mauritius and Seychelles was Roman Catholicism. A special edict of 1723 proclaimed the Code Noir (1685) under which all slaves were to be instructed and baptised into the Catholic religion, but it does not appear that this was very vigorously enforced, especially after the French Revolution (Milbert 1812 Vol. II:174f; d'Unienville 1838 Vol. I: 292f.). There was a shortage of priests, and, as related above, slave marriages were rarely celebrated in church. In Seychelles during the whole period of French

occupation there was no resident priest. Births and marriages were legally registered for whites, but there were no facilities for celebrating these events religiously. Apparently no provision was made for the marriage, baptism or religious instruction of slaves.

In Mauritius religious proselytisation among blacks took hold with the arrival of Jacques-Desiré Laval (1803–1864) in 1841. With three other priests and the support of the apostolic vicar of Mauritius he began an intensive campaign among the recently freed slaves. By the end of his mission some 50 chapels had been constructed and 67,000 blacks had been converted (Delaplace and Pivault 1932). Somewhat earlier in 1818 Jean Joseph Lebrun (1789–1865) of the London Missionary Society had attempted the conversion of the blacks to the Church of England and had founded religious schools, but he was less successful (Barnwell 1942).

When the Reverend Langrishe Banks, a civil chaplain of Mauritius, visited Seychelles in 1840, hundreds flocked to his improvised chapel despite the fact that he was a Church of England clergyman and they were Roman Catholics. During his five week stay he 'published banns for thirty marriages, and baptised five hundred and forty-two children: on one day no less than eighty-seven received that rite at my hands, and on another, ninety-two' (1840:2). During the 1840s and 1850s the British made an attempt to Protestantise and anglicise Seychelles, refusing permission for Father Léon de Avanchers, who arrived in 1851, to remain in the islands. During his brief stay Father de Avanchers baptised 200 people a day (Webb 1966:38; Lionnet 1972:120f.). It seems clear that the Africans adopted the religion of their masters from an early date, even when religious facilities were lacking.

Though there are passing references to African religious practices in the early accounts of Mauritius, no specific rites or beliefs are described. It is often said in both Mauritius and Seychelles that Africans brought beliefs in witchcraft with them to these islands, yet beliefs in witchcraft were also imported by Europeans in the eighteenth century. The basic beliefs in witches or sorcerers who can harm others by supernatural means is found in both European and African forms of witchcraft. Divination is also an aspect of magical beliefs in both continents. Some of the paraphernalia used for divination in Seychelles are clearly European such as packs of playing cards. The forms that witchcraft take today seem to be as much European as African. Many European priests in the islands do not deny the existence of witchcraft or its efficacy. They condemn it as the work of the devil. Many Mauritians and Seychellois of both African and European descent see no incompatibility between believing in witchcraft and being Christians.

Considering the diversity of their origins and the ways in which families and tribal groups were broken up by the slave trade and slavery, it is hardly surprising that African traditional religions did not survive. One can conjecture another important reason: much African religion is tied to lineage, to place and to the agricultural cycle. These bases were missing in Mauritius and Seychelles. Africans were torn from their lineages and their lineage ancestors and from the localities over which their deities had influence. The agricultural cycle was controlled by the planters, not subject to traditional rites and beliefs. African traditional religions were aspects of their kinship systems which carried political and economic functions in societies which were relatively unstratified. As slaves none of this obtained. They were the bottom stratum of a plantation society over which they had virtually no control. Their traditional religious systems simply did not apply.

The religions of the Indians, Hinduism and Islam, had long adapted themselves to highly stratified, complex societies. Moreover the whites in Mauritius made little attempt to convert Indians to Christianity. Indians were on contract. Planters had no legal or moral obligations for the saving of their souls. As related above, both the conditions of recruitment and the conditions of work placed considerable social distance between the Indians and the other ethnic groups in Mauritius. Among the Indian immigrants were Brahmans and low caste priests and religious assistants, such as barbers, who were able to perform religious rites. There were also religious experts among the Muslims, but Islam was given additional impetus by the arrival in Mauritius of Muslim

traders from the Gujerati-speaking areas of west India (Benedict 1965:20). They maintained contact with India where
they often returned to marry. They established mosques and
Muslim religious associations throughout Mauritius. There
were also some Hindu traders, notably from the Vellas caste
of south India. As related above, Hindu temples were constructed in many parts of the island and Hindu and Muslim
religious associations appeared in every settlement with an
Indian population. Both Hindu and Muslim festivals were
and are celebrated throughout the island (Benedict 1961:120–
142). Some Christian Indians were imported into Mauritius,
mostly from south India and some Indians did convert to
Christianity, often it appears for reasons of social mobility.
By and large these Indians merged with the Creole population, but they represented only a very small proportion of the
Indian population.

In terms of religious organisation a striking contrast exists
between Indians and Africans. The Indians maintained control of their religion. They formed their own religious organisations which they ran themselves. The Africans, on the other
hand, belonged to churches which they did not run. Catholic
and Protestant priests and missionaries were Europeans
(Benedict 1970:62–65). The Africans were not only subjected
to an alien religion; it was also a religion run by aliens.

8. *Other customs*   In 1871 Governor Gordon of Mauritius
saw what he described as an elephant dance when he visited
Seychelles:

> It was a very curious sight. It was an opera rather than a
> dance, for the whole hunt was sung and acted as well as
> danced. A fire was lighted in the middle of a shed: three
> naked little black boys crouched and squatted near the blaze
> beating biscuit tins for tom-toms, with short sticks, the women
> stood on one side, the men on the other. They sang in-
> cessantly, dancing slightly. Then one man danced out into
> the dark, returning in great excitement to announce that he
> had seen the elephant's foot-marks. Then another goes out
> alone, and comes back frightened; two go out together, one
> alone again, and finally two two's, who return having slain the

elephant, and there is much jubilation. When the two go out
on their quest, one has a bow and arrow, the other an
assegaye and they boast what they will do. It was a curious
bit of savagery brought into civilisation (Vol. I: 231.)

the following year Gordon witnessed a war dance:

> They divided into two parties, one of which went out into the
> dark under the trees, whilst the other remained sitting and
> singing round the fire in the camp. Presently two of the party
> who had gone out stole round in the dark, and suddenly
> appearing by the fire, ran off with a boy as prisoner. There
> was a great hubbub, and the camp party rushed out, and
> there was all the appearance of a regular battle (1894 Vol. II:
> 18.)

This dance may have dramatised a slave raid. It is noteworthy that both these dances were performed by liberated
Africans who could not have been in Seychelles for more than
a few years. I witnessed no narrative dances of these types in
either Mauritius between 1955–57 or in Seychelles in 1960
or 1975. In Mauritius the most popular dance was the *sega*,
sung in Creole and similar to the Calypso of the West Indies.
In Seychelles in 1960 the *moutia* was a dance which people
maintained was of African origin. It was held in the open air
to the accompaniment of singing and the beat of large
tambourine-like drums which are periodically heated over a
fire to make them taut. Men and women, facing each other
but never touching, dance with a shuffling gait and move
their hips and torsos. By 1975 it had largely disappeared,
being replaced by the *sega*, imported from Mauritius. The
dancing and drumming are similar to the *moutia*, but the
tunes sound more European and the Creole lyrics are about
love or topical events. In 1960 I heard about a dance called
Sokwe in which the principal dancer is Sokwe and, as my
informant told me, 'not himself'. He answers questions from
the crowd and makes humorous asides. Most people were
certain the dance had African origins. I found no knowledge
of it in 1975. The Seychelles Peoples United Party was
making efforts to revive the *moutia* in 1975 as part of its
campaign for Seychellois nationalism, but the *sega* and

American style dancing are more popular. Thus the music and dancing of the descendants of Africans has become entirely secular. It probably contains African elements but the setting and context are no longer African.

Indian music is closely tied to religion. The chanting of verses of the Ramayana to the accompaniment of small cymbals (djal) is a traditional form still practiced by Hindus. Drumming and the blowing of horns accompanies many Hindu ceremonies and the Muslim festival of the Ghoons (Benedict 1961:129–134). In recent years Indian film music has become ubiquitous. Though young Indians attend Western type dances and entertainments, the Indian element remains strong in the recreational patterns of Indo-Mauritians. Its link to religion reinforces it.

Among Creoles, customs surrounding rites of passage such as birth, marriage and death seem to be overwhelmingly European. There are no puberty ceremonies apart from First Communion and the holidays celebrated are those of the Catholic calendar. Although they have undergone modification over the years, both Hindus and Muslims have retained Indian forms of ritual for rites of passage (Benedict 1961: 110–119). The major festivals celebrated are those of the Hindu and Muslim calendars.

9. *Overseas connections* The African slave in Mauritius and Seychelles was completely cut off from contact with Africa. When the slave trade was finally suppressed, there were no further avenues for the perpetuation or renewal of African cultural traits. Later when the descendants of the slaves went overseas for training, it was to Europe, particularly to France and the United Kingdom. Not until the twentieth century did some Creoles go to Africa to work, but they went not as returning Africans, but as Mauritians and Seychellois.

Indian indentured labourers were also cut off from India, but not as completely as Africans. In the first place more than a third of those indentured returned to India. Secondly, the Indian Government was concerned about the fate of Indians overseas. Investigative commissions were sent to Mauritius, and Indian politicians in India agitated for the abolition of indenture (Tinker 1974:236–333). Thirdly, Hindu and Muslim missionaries and holy men visited Mauritius to preach. Finally Indian traders, particularly Muslims, were in regular contact with India. Later, though many Indians went to Europe, particularly Britain for training and further education, others went to India. The Indian connection was kept alive in ways which had no analogues for Africa.

10. *The economic base* A major reason for the rapid disappearance of African cultural traits in Mauritius and Seychelles was the drastic shift in the mode of production which imported Africans suffered. In Madagascar and on the African mainland, most Africans were probably engaged in subsistence horticulture, perhaps supplemented with hunting and gathering. Their societies were organised along kinship lines. The kinship unit tended to be the unit of production and the unit of consumption. The political system was also kin based. In Mauritius and Seychelles these conditions did not apply. The unit of production was the plantation. The Africans constituted the unpaid or, later, the low-paid labour force of this unit. The produce itself consisted of cash crops grown for a market and marketed by the owners of the production units. The consumption unit was the individual, sometimes with a dependent wife and children, but in the case of women often only with dependent children. What they consumed was not what they produced but what they were paid in either rations or wages with which to buy rations. (Reports about the time of emancipation mention the reluctance of Africans to accept money wages. They preferred to be paid in goods whose value they understood, though, of course, they quickly learned how to handle money.) Kinship was no longer the organising principle in the economic and political spheres. The work gang replaced the kinship unit and political authority was in the hands of the white master class. In these ways the whole basis of African culture was destroyed or made irrelevant. Africans did not abandon kin ties. They used them for mutual help and social and emotional satisfaction. But kinship and the ritual and customs surrounding it were no longer the basis of society. The plantation economy was. It was not poverty

per se which led to the abandonment of African customs. Indians and Chinese were just as poor in their own lands. It was the change in their relation to the means of production.

The case was different for the Indians. They came from a complex and highly stratified society. In villages there was a complex division of labour based on the occupational specialisation of various castes. Rights and duties between castes were governed by the *jajmani* system (Beidelman 1959; Epstein 1967). There were traditionally two types of economic relationships: those between the landowning caste(s) and their labouring and service castes which were hereditary and highly prescribed, and those between the landowners and various artisan castes which were more contractual (Epstein 1967:233f). Each servicing caste received a certain proportion of the harvest, while other portions were set aside to pay landlords and taxes. Thus unlike Africa but more like Mauritius the units of production and consumption were separate. The unit of consumption was the family but the unit of production involved many castes in complex traditional relationships. Also many Indians had worked for wages, and indeed it was the wages which attracted them to indenture. The Indian system was reinforced by the ritual and religious relations obtaining between castes, a feature which was lacking in Mauritius. Also in Mauritius castes ceased to be corporate groups (Benedict 1967). In Indian villages political relationships were also based on castes. There were village councils (*panchayats*) at which representatives of various castes met to regulate village affairs. There were also caste panchayats at which members of the same caste from various villages met to regulate caste affairs. There was some attempt to replicate these in Mauritius by the formation of *baitkas*, but by and large political affairs were in the hands of Europeans. Nevertheless the plantation economy did not represent so radical a departure for Indians as it did for Africans.

11. *Endogamy* Goody (1976) has made a useful distinction concerning marriage and property between African and

Eurasian societies which bears on the different adaptations of Africans and Indians to Mauritius and Seychelles. Though Indians and Europeans differed widely in culture, they shared certain common structural features about marriage and property. In both societies marriages were largely about property. In both societies dowries were provided by the wife's kin group. In both societies there was a marked tendency for in-group marriage (among Indians, caste endogamy remained the most important survival of the caste system in the 1950s). This endogamy served to keep Indians separated from other ethnic groups. As Goody points out, the situation was quite different in Africa:

> As distinct from Eurasian societies, most African states do not discourage marriage between status groups. On the contrary, they encourage such arrangements. The consequences are clear: groups tend to merge culturally. . . . (1976:104f.)

Furthermore in traditional African societies marriages were not alliances between property holders. They were not accompanied by dowry but by bridewealth. Chiefs could and did marry commoners. Wealth, power and prestige were in terms of control over persons rather than over property.

Though it is impossible to prove, these structural features might have meant that it was in some sense easier for Africans to form marital or quasi-marital alliances with Europeans than it was for Indians. The status and property considerations which militated against Indo-European alliances might not have appeared as barriers to Africans, though they did to Europeans, who rarely legally married Africans. The system of values concerning marriage, property and stratification which the Africans may have brought with them to Mauritius and Seychelles differed fundamentally from those which Indians brought with them. Paradoxically it seems that the similarity in outlook concerning marriage, property and stratification between Indians and Europeans kept them apart, while the fundamental differences in these matters permitted Africans to accept close relations with Europeans.

Conclusions

'Should anthropologists be historians?' Isaac Schapera asked in his presidential address to the Royal Anthropological Institute in 1962. He answered that most already were, and since that time more and more historical problems have attracted anthropologists as they have moved from the study of simple societies with little or no recorded history to complex societies where historical data are available. The question asked in this paper, why have Indians retained so much more of their cultures of origin than Africans, is an historical question, but it was a question which derived from anthropological fieldwork. Moreover Mauritius and Seychelles are 'historical' societies. We know to a certain extent who came, when, from where and in what numbers. In these circumstances explanations in terms of simple a-historical functionalism are simply intellectually unsatisfying. The anthropologist of Mauritius, Seychelles and similar societies may not aspire to be an historian, but he has history thrust upon him.

This essay is only a beginning in the attempt to answer the question posed. It has shown that there was a concatenation of factors which militated against the retention of African cultural traits (or conversely which fostered the adaptation of European cultural traits) and that these factors did not operate in the same fashion for Indians. There are other important factors which bear upon the question which have not been treated. Among these are:

1. Demographic factors. Though some attention has been paid to the sex ratio, little has been said about the overall numbers of Africans and Indians in Mauritian and Seychellois societies and the effect that relative numbers had on adaptation to the host society. The Africans were an original component of the population of the islands, but the Indians came later. Jamaica presents an instructive contrast. There, relatively few Indians were imported and Indian patterns seemed to have largely disappeared (Ehrlich 1971).

2. Ecological factors. The distribution of African and Indian populations in the islands has not been treated. The dispersal or concentration of ethnic groups must have played

an important role in cultural adaptation as did the kind of work each ethnic category was engaged in at various periods (v. Benedict 1965:23–26).

3. Time factors. By and large Africans were in residence in the islands 100 years longer than Indians. This must have had an effect on cultural adaptation. Studies from Trinidad (Nevadomsky 1977) and Guyana (Jayawardena 1968; Smith 1962:136–143) seem to show that Indians are becoming more 'Europeanised.' Recent conversations with Mauritians seem to indicate a similar process.

4. Political factors. These have only been treated by implication. A detailed analysis of the place in the political structure of Africans and Indians at various periods is required.

5. Stratification. Especially in the light of Goody's hypothesis, a detailed comparison between the systems of stratification in India and Africa with those found in Mauritius and Seychelles should be made.

6. Comparative factors. Other societies have received both Africans and Indians, notably Trinidad, Guyana, Surinam, Réunion and Jamaica. African societies have also received Indians, notably Kenya, Uganda, Rhodesia, Zambia, Tanzania and South Africa. Indian indentured labourers were also sent in large numbers to Fiji, Malaya, Burma and Sri Lanka. This provides a rich field for comparison against which the generalisations I have made could be checked. I hope anthropologist-historians will take up the challenge.

Power and Status in South Asian Slavery

LIONEL CAPLAN

While recent discussions of slavery abound in controversy over the economic significance of the institution in particular social systems, the problem of the slave's place in the status order appears to have attracted relatively little comment.[1] The reason is fairly obvious, indeed, can be located in the common 'definition' of slavery itself. Notwithstanding the recent attempt by Miers and Kopytoff (1977) to question the wisdom of applying cross-culturally a notion of slavery derived from specific American and European experience, slaves, as Watson has noted, are almost uniformly defined as chattels owned by masters (whether these be individuals or corporate bodies), and can be bought and sold (Watson 1976: 368).

Thus, in as much as they are regarded and treated as a form of property, slaves are legally non-persons (Finley 1968:308), 'not fully human beings', as Leach observes (1967:23–4). And according to accounts we have of numerous societies in which slaves were found, it would appear that their legal or, more generally, political disadvantages determined and were reflected in their social status. Therefore slaves commonly constituted both a political and a social category below all others (see, for example, Nieboer 1900; Watson 1976; Elkins 1967). In some social systems, moreover, this low status attached even to ex-slaves long after their political disabilities had been removed, i.e., following personal manumission or the total abolition of the institution (Hopkins 1967:167; P. Caplan 1975:3, 85). For most observers, then, the status of slaves is simply a matter for ethnographic report, and not for analysis.

The position of slave in a society which assigns to the 'untouchable' the lowest place in the status hierarchy presents an intriguing problem for the student of social inequality. Passin, in a brief reference to two similar (but by no means analogous) stations in Korea, points out how slaves and 'pariahs' were carefully distinguished both in law and through endogamous marriage practices. His explanation is that such a separation obtained because slavery 'was a condition the individual entered into . . . and could be bought out of', whereas being a pariah was an hereditary condition (1967:22–3). In South Asia, both untouchability and slavery were heritable, but the distinction was there maintained (by the people, if not always by outsiders) because, among other things, the status of slave-owners depended on it. Domestic slavery, the kind found principally on the sub-continent, could exist only if the slaves were of sufficiently high status, i.e., caste rank to perform the duties required of them in the household. Thus, to employ Dumont's terms (1966), a dichotomy between power (the legal or political dimension) and status (the ritual or caste dimension) was crucial to the structure of South Asian slavery.[2]

Of course, ritual rank no more constitutes the full measure of a person's status than does being 'free' or 'enslaved' signify the totality of one's legal or political condition, i.e., power. But both are important enough components to allow us to isolate them heuristically, and consider their relationship. In the discussion which follows I shall examine slavery first in the Kingdom of Nepal and then in India during British rule. The final section of the paper will attempt to identify the principal common characteristics of the institution in South Asia, and place these in a wider comparative context.

In view of the extreme paucity of data on modern slavery in the sub-continent, I feel compelled to stress that this discussion is tentative and preliminary. Indeed, it raises many more questions than it answers. Nevertheless, it is offered in the hope that others will be encouraged to explore the subject more thoroughly both in its historical and anthropological dimensions.

Slavery in Nepal: Background

References to slavery in Nepal are exceedingly rare, and several of the most informative accounts of the country's history and culture make little or no mention of the institution (see Kirkpatrick 1811; Cavenagh 1851: Lévi 1905). Much of the general public in the West apparently became aware of its existence only at the time of its abolition in 1925. The main source for students of Nepalese slavery remains the speech made by the nation's Prime Minister, Chandra Shumshere Rana, in November, 1924, appealing for an end to the practice (Rana 1925).

The origin and growth of slavery in that part of the Himalayas which now contains the Kingdom of Nepal remains to this day very much a mystery. While several authors speak of its existence since 'time immemorial' (Kennion 1925: 381; Simon 1929:124), it is perhaps more reasonable to speculate, as do some historians, that slavery goes as far back as the medieval period (Jain 1972:195). It is, moreover, likely that the institution was brought to these mountain regions by Hindu immigrants fleeing the Muslim invasions of North India. Their interaction with the tribal groups previously settled in the area probably gave slavery here the particular form it developed in the course of the next few centuries.[3] But this is only speculation. What is certain is that by the time of the creation of the Nepalese state during the latter part of the eighteenth century, slavery was already an established custom.

The Nepali word *kamara* (fem. *kamari*) is generally translated as 'slave' (Turner 1931:75), and with justification in as much as such a person was regarded as a chattel. In the country's first comprehensive Legal Code, issued in 1853, slaves were not uncommonly bracketed with grain, gold and silver, and utensils (Jain 1972:195–6). A slave's time was wholly his or her master's (Rana 1925:9) and the latter had the 'same claim over (them) as over animals ...' (*Ibid.* 28).

Slaves were inherited along with land and other property, given as merit-earning gifts to domestic priests (*purohit*) at the time of a death in the family, and freely bought and sold. Furthermore, a master's rights were protected throughout the extent of the Kingdom, so that a slave who absconded could be reclaimed from anywhere within its borders, and indeed, it was the legal duty of citizens to inform the owner of a runaway in their midst (Jain 1972:196).

There was, until the beginning of the nineteenth century, a flourishing trade in the export of slaves to both India and Tibet. In Nepal, royal proclamations were issued as early as 1808 threatening severe punishment for those who engaged in these practices (Regmi 1969:44). The British eventually prohibited the importation of slaves into India in 1833, although the Nepalese traffic apparently continued for some time afterwards (Banaji 1933:55, 76).

Quite apart from instances of kidnapping and sale to professional dealers, people became slaves in a variety of 'customary' ways. Most frequently, children were sold by their parents to meet debts or simply because they could no longer provide for them. Often, it would appear, impoverished adults sold themselves into slavery (Buchanan 1819:235; Landon 1928:164). Landon draws attention to the fact that a law forbidding free persons from selling themselves into slavery or parents from disposing of their children was enacted in the middle of the nineteenth century. Neither ruling, he notes, 'was of much use' (*Ibid.*).

The Nepalese state also played an important role in the enslavement of its citizens, although it is not clear if it acted as slave owner as well. Thus the wives and children of tax-defaulters were sometimes condemned to slavery, as were the immediate families of those found guilty of murdering 'men of property', a *guru* or an elder brother (Regmi 1971:118; Hodgson n.d.:127). Enslavement could also be a punishment for fomenting rebellion, for 'incest' (including the union of descendants of ritual kinsmen), for adultery between certain categories of persons, and even for procuring an abortion. The slaughter of cows by Bhotia—descendants of Tibetan 'immigrants' settled along the northern borders of the country—or by members of tribal populations might also result in reduction to slavery (Regmi 1971:118–19; Landon 1928:245; Adhikari 1976:108–111). The children of all such persons were, of course, born into slavery, and did not possess the means themselves to alter their condition.

It is impossible to gauge the size of the slave population in the early years of the state, although it probably declined over time as the traffic into India was brought to a halt (see above), the Kingdom's control over Garhwal and Kumaon to the west ended (see Regmi 1971:120; Sanwal 1976:177), and legislation progressively reduced the categories of people who could be enslaved as well as the range of offences punishable in this way. By the end of the nineteenth century it was virtually impossible for a free person to be legally enslaved, while in the early part of this century laws were enacted to encourage the liberation of existing slaves. During the regime of Chandra Shumshere Rana (1901–1928) all slaves coming into the possession of the state by course of law were ordered to be set free; so, for example, where a person's entire property, including slaves, was confiscated by the courts, the latter would be granted their liberty (Landon 1928:165). Further, a master who wished to sell a slave had to give the relatives or other 'interested parties' (including the government) first refusal to purchase the slave's freedom (Rana 1925:27). Slaves were also offered the opportunity to become free settlers in certain parts of the country which the authorities were anxious to colonise (*Ibid.* 43). Although the Prime Minister in his abolition speech acknowledged that 'the effect of the laws is not much in evidence' (*Ibid.*) the cumulative result of these enactments was probably to stabilise if not actually reduce the numbers of slaves in the country. By the time the practice was finally done away with, there were about 51,000 slaves and 16,000 slave owners—together totalling barely one per cent of the population (*Ibid.* 35).

Domestic Slavery in Nepal

Nepalese slavery was primarily domestic in character, at least since the establishment of the Kingdom. The considerable labour services required by the state in the course of its military and administrative activities—porterage of supplies, production of munitions, construction and repair of roads, forts and bridges, even postal arrangements—were acquired by means of forced, unpaid labour (*jhara*) extracted from the peasantry. Moreover, various local officials, such as village tax-collectors (who were chosen mainly from the large land-owners) were entitled to similar exactions from the cultivator households whose taxes they collected. Thus virtually the entire adult population was obliged to provide its labour power, without return, to both the administration and the 'nobility'. Slaves were therefore not utilised for government projects or on a large scale in agricultural activities, although of course household slaves might represent their owners' domestic groups when the latter were obliged to provide *jhara* contributions (see Regmi 1971:101–17).

The slaves' relations with free members of the household obviously depended on a wide variety of personal factors which make generalisation about their position difficult. They were not entitled to own land (before 1921), nor to receive remuneration for their labour. I have already alluded to the fact that they were chattels to be disposed of by gift or sale at the will of their owners. Indeed, it appears that there were few legal constraints on the master's treatment of his slaves; certainly beatings were not prohibited (Jain 1972:196). Brian Hodgson, who was at the British Residency in Kathmandu from 1820 to 1848, relates how a domestic slave had his ear cut off for causing the young heads of the family to quarrel (L. Adam 1949–50:167). Almost a century later, slaves still had to endure hardships, if not of the same order of cruelty. In his abolition address the Prime Minister referred to 'some bad treatment at the masters' hands . . . enough to make (slaves) leave the land of their birth' (Rana 1925:29). He pointed out that the institution of slavery was a 'fruitful source' of population exodus (*Ibid.* 32); 'They go to escape persecution . . .' (*Ibid.* 34). Although by this time the courts regarded any offence which would be a crime against a free person as a crime if committed against a slave, the familiar problem of enforcement mitigated the hoped-for reforms.

By the turn of this century the numbers of escaped slaves residing in India was sufficient to cause concern in Kathmandu. A law was thereby promulgated to enable those who had resided out of Nepal for three years to purchase their liberty, and for those who had been away for ten years to claim their freedom without any payment whatsoever (*Ibid.* 32).

Against these reports of severe treatment there is evidence of other kinds which presents a contrary picture of Nepalese slavery. Some slaves were clearly very much integrated in the life of the owner's family. Thus, Chandra Shumshere Rana refers to slave children growing up alongside those of the master, mixing with them, and 'sharing their joys' (*Ibid.* 6). He notes how in some households old and respected slaves virtually ran affairs, especially during the minority of the master, and how in others they were left in charge when owners were away (*Ibid.* 8) Indeed, he adds, 'there are households where but for certain limitations the distinction between master and slave is practically abolished' (*Ibid.* 9).

In general, slaves were fed—or allotted plots of land to cultivate and thus feed themselves—clothed, and cared for in illness by their masters. Moreover, in childhood and old age they were regarded as the responsibility of their masters, however inconsequential their productivity (*Ibid.* 11, 15, 18, 19).[4] The owner was also expected to take the initiative in finding a spouse for his slave, and provide the wedding costs (*Ibid.* 7, 24).

The Rationale of Nepalese Slavery

Such 'humane' treatment of slaves by their owners, while no doubt the result of personal affection and trust resulting from long years of close association, was also encouraged by considerations of economic benefit and/or individual or family reputation. Slaves obviously constituted a considerable investment. As such, they had to be cared for: 'You cannot starve him, because his physical weakness will be your loss'; while if he dies or deserts 'his value will have to be written off as a loss' (*Ibid.* 11).

Females of child-bearing age represented the greatest investment. Buchanan, referring to the early part of the nineteenth century, quotes the price of a male slave as Rs 15, and of a female as Rs 20 (1819:235). In the middle of the century their prices were statutorily fixed by the Legal Code, although buyers and sellers could agree their own price. (For a young adult the price was fixed at Rs 100 for a male and Rs 120 for a female). By the latter part of the century the price of a female was Rs 150–200, i.e., one and a half times to twice that of a male (Wright 1877:45). The reproductive potential of females was adamantly guarded. A male slave who enticed a female slave to run off with him from their master's house would, if caught, have his nose cut off (L. Adam 1949–50:165). Widowed slave women were expressly banned from committing *sati,* even when the practice of widow immolation on the husband's funeral pyre was widespread (Jain 1972:188).

It is not clear if the children of a slave woman were invariably the property of her master, or if her husband's owner had some claim as well. The problem would of course not arise if both spouses were owned by the same master. Slave women were apparently also occasionally married to free men, and by the time of Chandra Shumshere Rana, this would entitle the husband to purchase the children's freedom (although not his wife's). But such marriages, it appears, were arranged mainly with impoverished freemen who in any case could not afford the official purchase price, with the result that the children remained the master's property (Rana 1925: 22).

While slaves represented not inconsiderable capital for their masters, it is unlikely that, save for people who traded in them as commodities, they were in crude economic terms a very good investment. A substantial proportion of the Prime Minister's abolition speech was devoted to a detailed 'cost benefit' assessment of slave ownership. After comparing the expenses of slave and 'free' labour, as well as their productive capacity (in agricultural activities) he concluded that a free labourer produced twice the amount of a slave for only 50 per cent more cost (*Ibid:* 17). Free labour, he suggested, was 'economically superior to, and in every way more desirable than, slave labour' (*Ibid.* 18).

The ownership of slaves, whether or not a profitable undertaking, was certainly a badge of esteem for the country's large landowners, symbolic of their dominant place in Nepalese society. Rana makes explicit reference to those who own slaves 'to uphold the honour of the household' (*Ibid.* 40), and notes that even to discharge superfluous slaves would 'tell against their prestige' (*Ibid.* 23).

The Status of Nepalese Slaves

Although slaves were politically the most debased section of Nepalese society, their status was, paradoxically, unaffected. Indeed, in order to perform the various duties imposed on domestic servants, to be permitted to cross the threshold of an owner's dwelling, it was imperative for the slave to enjoy a degree of ritual purity conferred only by membership in certain castes. To make the point more clearly it is necessary to say a word about Nepal's caste system.

Castes are grouped into three principal, ranked categories which, over the years, have become stabilised by enshrinement in the Kingdom's legal codes. At the top of the hierarchy are the *tagadhari jat*, the 'twice-born' castes who wear the sacred thread of Hinduism and to which, incidentally, the wealthiest and most influential families of the Kingdom belong (see P. Caplan 1972). The next category, ranked below the twice-born, includes the 'drinking' castes (*matwali jat*), many of whom are in fact previously independent tribal groups which were incorporated into the state in the course of its establishment by the forefathers of the present monarch (see L. Caplan 1970). These 'drinking' castes do not wear the sacred thread, but are regarded as pure, in so far as certain foods or foods prepared in certain ways by members of these groups may be eaten by those belonging to the twice-born category. More importantly, the latter accept water from their hands.

Below the drinking castes are the untouchables, from whom the taking of any cooked food or water is considered polluting and, in the case of certain of these groups, whose very touch requires purification by those in the higher categories. Hence they are labelled 'castes whose water cannot be taken' (*pani na calne jat*). Persons belonging to such groups have restricted intercourse with and are not allowed to enter the homes of those belonging to the superior, 'pure' castes.

While virtually all slave-owners enjoyed twice-born status, the slaves—unless they were employed exclusively in agricultural activities—could not be drawn from the untouchable groups. Domestic slaves were, in fact, utilised mainly to fetch firewood, draw water, wash cooking utensils, clean dwellings and perform a variety of other household duties which required them to be ritually pure (Buchanan 1819:236; Wright 1877:45).[5]

Until the beginning of the nineteenth century it was apparently possible for Brahmins and Rajputs—the two highest groups in the twice-born category—to be enslaved, but this practice (which probably occurred only rarely) was abolished in 1803 (Regmi 1971:121). Subsequent legislation prohibited the reduction to slavery of all twice-born groups, and even of certain drinking castes (L. Adam 1949–50:159; Sharma 1977:283). Nepalese legal codes distinguished between those groups which could not be enslaved (*na masinya jat*) and those which could (*masinya jat*). None of the larger untouchable groups (leatherworkers, tailors, metalworkers) found throughout the mid-montane regions of the country is included either in Sharma's (*Ibid.*) or Macdonald's list of non-enslavable castes (1975:292). However, a recent paper by Adhikari specifically notes that untouchables 'were reduced to slavery for incest with the wife of an elder brother' (1976: 111).

In general, then, the legal-political order, at the base of which were the slaves, did not, could not, because of the ritual purity required for domestic duties, reflect or duplicate the caste hierarchy. The household slave, while the absolute property of a master, was of superior status to even the wealthiest member of a 'free', but untouchable caste (Fürer-Haimendorf 1966:24).

Moreover, the purity of slaves had to be protected.

Buchanan points out how 'the caste of the slave is respected and no duty is imposed on him by which that would be injured'. He also notes how the Brahmin 'slaves' of important Rajput families who were employed as cooks or priests in private chapels were not degraded by the name *keta* (child) normally used to address slaves (1819:234). While it is possible that Buchanan mistook the traditional services performed by members of the priestly caste for slavery, it is equally likely that his remarks signify that Brahmins, even when slaves, were still respected for their high ritual position.

In general, ritual rank was not fundamentally affected by whether the individual was a slave or not. The acknowledgement of ritual parity allowed for the marriage of free and unfree, as already noted, although of course unions with slaves would only be contemplated by the poorest families. Then again, the issue of a slave woman by her master would not only be free, but would enjoy the same caste rank as the child of a free woman by a man of similar caste (Turner 1931: 75). Buchanan tells us that if a Nepalese ruler wished to degrade a prominent family totally, he would not merely reduce its members to slavery, but give them to an untouchable household, and in that way deprive them of their caste purity as well (1819:235).

The dissociation of power and status also enabled slaves to be easily integrated into free society. Ex-slaves were known by a variety of terms—the most common being *gharti*—and found a recognised place in the caste system below the twice-born groups, but within the ranks of the pure. I have been unable to discover precisely when the caste category of *gharti* was established, or when individuals actually became *gharti*. Regarding the second question, Sharma (1977:295) implies that the term referred only to a freed slave, although Fürer-Haimendorf (1966:25) suggests that it was applied at the time of enslavement, and not of manumission. But this would imply that slaves were not only severed from their natal caste, but that during the period when members of twice-born groups could be enslaved, the latter would have, in effect, suffered a reduction in ritual rank. Such a suggestion is belied by the early sources (see Buchanan, above) which stress the importance of maintaining a slave's inherited ritual position intact. We are led to speculate that the introduction of the category *gharti* probably occurred after it was no longer possible to enslave members of twice-born groups. There also remains the question of whether, in those (presumably rare) instances of untouchables becoming slaves (see above), they too assumed the title and status of *gharti*. One would have thought this most unlikely. Clearly, these issues are of fundamental importance for this discussion, but for the moment must remain open.

In practice, the precise location of ex-slaves in the contemporary caste hierarchy depends on local circumstances (Fürer-Haimendorf 1966:23; Borgström 1976:28, 41; L. Caplan 1975:148). Although the government invested substantial sums of money to purchase the liberation of slaves in 1925, they were in fact given nothing but their freedom: the economic disadvantages brought by generations of servitude were in no way compensated. The result is that most ex-slaves in Nepal are still landless and impoverished, and many continue to serve their former masters (Prindle 1974:58; Borgström 1976: 42–43). Occasionally, however, individual ex-slaves succeed in rising out of their former poverty and for such persons social mobility (in both economic and status terms) becomes a real possibility. For example, in the area of western Nepal with which I am familiar there are a number of relatively well-to-do *gharti* domestic groups from which some women have married into 'pure' Chetri, i.e. twice-born families. For the women, at least, the stigma of slavery has all but disappeared.

Slavery, as already suggested, probably entered the Nepalese Himalayas from India, and developed its special form partly because of the Hindu ideology at the foundation of the Kingdom's social system. It is therefore of more than passing interest to inquire to what extent it resembled practices found in the rest of the sub-continent, in particular, India.

Slavery in India: Background

Slavery in India has a long and complex history (Chanana 1960), which I am not competent to survey, even if this were the appropriate place to do so. What follows is only an attempt to identify certain significant features of the institution during the period of British rule, and especially during the first half of the nineteenth century, immediately prior to its abolition, which will enable us to set Nepalese slavery in a broader South Asian context. For comparative purposes the focus here is on slavery among Hindus: Muslims in India were subject to different norms, though the area of overlap was substantial. Even within such limited parameters the difficulty of generalising about Indian slavery can be appreciated when it is remembered that a wide diversity of local practice had grown up over the centuries on the foundations of an ancient, complex and at times contradictory legal code.[6] Moreover, the East India Company decreed that Hindu slaves were to be governed in accordance with the principles of Hindu law, and subsequent British authorities relied mainly on indigenous officials to explain these regulations to them. There was thus not only a plethora of custom but an equally great range of interpretation. In the opinion of one observer, the Hindu law on slavery was applied (by the British) without proper concern for changed circumstances or the 'higher ideals of justice', and too much reliance was placed on (no doubt, high caste, conservative) 'pundits' (Banaji 1933:219–25).

The agitation for the abolition of slavery in British India led to several official investigations and the production of numerous documents which, however inadequate in themselves (see Hjejle 1967:97–98), indicate that slavery was widespread in the nineteenth century. Sir Bartle Frere estimated that there were in 1841 eight or nine million slaves—and possibly sixteen millions if non-British territories and British-protected states were included (Banaji 1933:202–3).

A significant proportion of these were 'predial' or agrestic slaves, i.e., those attached to the soil and liable to be transferred with it. Although it is arguable that their condition was more akin to that of feudal serfs (see Leach 1967:11–12), the fact that they were alienated apart from the land suggests that 'slave' is not an inappropriate label. Hjejle, for example, employs the term because such a person could be sold, mortgaged or rented out, and because 'the master had an absolute right to whatever labour the man or woman was capable of performing' (1967:93). And despite W. Adam's claim (1840: 183) that the custom of selling agrestic slaves independently of the land began with the assumption of power by the East India Company, subsequent research indicates that the practice was not uncommon in the fourteenth- to seventeenth-century Vijayanagara Empire (Saletore 1934:115).

Agrestic slavery was found mainly in South India, although it also existed in many parts of Bengal Presidency and in Kumaon, where the agrestic slaves were owned not by individuals but by the village as a corporate group (Sanwal 1976: 62). But with the possible exception of the south, even in these areas, as in most other parts of India, slaves were employed largely or predominantly in the domestic sphere.

The manner of enslavement differed as between agrestic and household slaves. Whereas the former were initially subjugated as communities, and thereafter inherited their condition by virtue of belonging to these groups, the latter were individually recruited. The distinction was underlined in Kumaon by the fact that an agrestic slave was permitted to find a substitute for himself, whereas a domestic slave was not (Sanwal 1976:59). Individuals entered domestic slavery in a number of ways, voluntary and otherwise. As in Nepal, certain sexual offences might result in a loss of freedom; thus hypogamous unions, incest, intimate relations within prohibited degrees and, in certain instances, adultery by a woman of standing could be punished in this way (Indian Law Commissioners (henceforth ILC) 1841:158, 168, 170). By the nineteenth century, and probably throughout the British period, self-sale and the sale or 'gift' of children by their parents were the most common methods by which free persons entered the population of domestic slaves. These practices, moreover, were sanctioned by ancient Hindu law-givers such as Manu (VIII, 415) and Narada (V, 26–29). The underlying motivation for these transactions was dire poverty (ILC 1841:158, 192; W. Adam 1840:248; Banaji 1933:67). Chattopadhyay, writing of the Bengal Presidency, points out how the famine of 1770 and the agricultural distress in its wake led great numbers of starving people to sell themselves and their dependants into slavery 'as the only way to preserve their lives' (1977:14).

While slaves were brought into the country overland from Nepal (see above), and by sea from Africa, the numbers imported from abroad before the ban imposed by the British in 1833 were comparatively few (see W. Adam 1840:250–52). A much greater volume of slave traffic flowed across internal boundaries of Presidency, state and district (ILC 1841:16–20). But even then, the slave population of India was, on the whole, an indigenous one. As a contemporary author wrote: 'They are not of foreign birth and of strange aspect. They do not speak a different language and profess a different religion, or practice different customs from the rest of the inhabitants' (W. Adam 1840:132).

As regards the legal position of slaves, they were deemed the chattels of their owners, who could sell them, pledge them against loans, stake them at play, or give them away as dowry or as ritual gifts to domestic priests (ILC 1841:35, 164–65). Slaves could not own property in their own right, save by the sufferance of their owners, and where this was allowed, the property usually reverted to the latter on the death of the former (*Ibid.* 25, 166–67, 171). These disabilities were deemed to originate and find their justification in the ancient legal texts (see Manu VIII, 66, 416–17; Narada I, 29).

Generally, domestic slaves were regarded as subordinate members of the household, and one witness giving evidence to the Law Commissioners, noted that a respectable master treated them as children (ILC 1841:232). Owners provided for slaves during their working lives, whether ill or in good health, afforded them protection in old age, and even saw to their proper funerary rites when they died (*Ibid.* 171). Kumar remarks how no other category of labourer enjoyed such a measure of security (1965:48).

Slave Marriages

Owners in India took as great an interest in the marriages of their slaves as did those in Nepal, and for the same reasons.

Masters were considered to be under a moral obligation to provide suitable partners and defray the marriage expenses (ILC 1841:39; see also Harper 1968:38). Here, too, preference was for the marriage of slaves belonging to the same master, and a slave spouse might be bought from another owner if none was available in the household. A wife or husband might also be sought in a free family, and it was known for free persons—usually in impoverished circumstances—to sell themselves or their children into slavery for the purpose (ILC 1841. 40, 249). Marriages of slaves and free persons were thus countenanced in India as in Nepal, the principal condition being that the spouses were of the same or equivalent caste rank.

Where the slaves of different masters were married, practices concerning residence, the services of the slaves, and ownership of the offspring varied from place to place, although even local custom could readily be superseded by a special agreement between the owners at the time of arranging the union (*Ibid.* 41). In some regions the woman resided with her husband, in others the reverse occurred, while in others still the spouses remained with their respective masters, and were allowed only visiting rights. Where 'virilocality' obtained, the woman obviously gave her services mainly to the husband's master, and vice versa where 'uxorilocality' prevailed, although compensatory payments might be due to the owner who incurred the loss.

As to the allocation of children, these were sometimes the property of the woman's owner, at others of the man's, while the custom in certain places was for a division between the owners. Unfortunately, the evidence on ownership of offspring in the Law Commisioners' Report is not correlated with the nature of descent systems among the various groups in the regions surveyed, so it is impossible to know if these variations reflect descent norms or other local rules related specifically to slave ownership. I suspect the latter is more likely the case.

In areas of the country where female slaves far outnumbered their male counterparts, several women might be married to the same man (*Ibid.* 288). This is to be distinguished from practices found in certain regions such as

Bengal, also due in part to demographic imbalances, where masters arranged for the espousal of their female slaves to *byakara*, men who acted as 'visiting husbands' to a number of women (it is not clear if *byakara* were themselves slaves). The man did not reside permanently with any wife, and the children each bore were the sole property of her master (*Ibid.* 39–42; Banaji 1933:10).

The Rationale of Indian Slavery

Turning now to the economics of slavery, while the evidence is by no means conclusive, most writers on the subject seem satisfied that the institution did not have any major significance in the productive process. Basham (1963:153) is convinced that India was never economically dependent on slavery. Chanana (1960), who has examined its development over six centuries in ancient times, and shown that during certain periods (e.g. of the Buddhist oligarchs) slaves were employed mainly in productive work, still denies any homology with societies where they formed the predominant sector of the labour corps in agriculture, mining, etc.

During the years of British rule, and presumably for some time before this, a substantial amount of agricultural labour in South India and the Bengal Presidency was performed by agrestic slaves. While precise figures of their proportion in the work force are not available, in one region, Malabar, where slavery is reported to have been more in evidence than in most other parts, slaves are estimated to have comprised approximately fifteen per cent of the population (Hjejle 1967:89). In Bengal, after 1770, for a generation or more, there were lands lying waste because of insufficient labour to cultivate them and slaves 'provided the only certain labour force entirely at the disposal of the landholder' (Chattopadhyay 1977:67). It thus appears that slavery was of significance in the agricultural economy, if not uniformly so throughout the British period or in all the Indian territories.

Nevertheless, the main burden of the evidence gathered by the Law Commisisoners was that slavery in India existed chiefly for considerations of prestige. In testimony given by

G

a number of indigenous officials, many of whom were themselves slave owners, it was stressed how the respectability of
a family was measured by the number of its dependants.
Further, even the dismissal or sale of these dependants could
bring disgrace (ILC 1841:35, 171, 247). The Commissioners
concluded that in the greater part of the country 'it is not
production which induces men of property to acquire and
retain a troop of slaves. [They do so] because they like to
have hereditary domestics and dependants . . . a mark of
affluence and station in society . . .' (*Ibid.* 189). Indeed, they
felt compelled to warn the British government of the dangers
occasioned by the presence of European capitalists in India
who, if permitted to hold slaves and use them for profit,
would transform the Indian system into one akin to that in
the West Indies and the United States (*Ibid.* 193).

The Status of Indian Slaves

The crucial separation between the power and status of slave
becomes evident if we consider the duties attached to the
principal forms of the institution—agrestic and household—
and the groups associated with each. The former were, of
course, engaged mainly in agricultural labour, although the
government also utilised them in various public works, such
as the repair of roads, and to porter the baggage and supplies
of civil and military personnel (W. Adam 1840:174).

Although no ritual logic demanded it, virtually all agrestic
slaves in South India, the Bengal Presidency and regions like
Kumaon were drawn from the impure castes. In the latter
territory, it was the Doms, ritually debased by activities such
as the removal of dead animals, and regarded as 'dangerous'
to members of pure castes, who were held in agrestic servitude (Srivastava 1966:513; Sanwal 1976:65). In the Malnad
area of Mysore State all the slaves were untouchable Holerus
(Harper 1968). In Malabar, Cheruman, the name of one of the
largest of the impure castes, became a term synonymous
with slave (Hjejle 1967:89). Indeed, the distinction between
agrestic slaves and untouchables was occasionally lost to even
the most astute outsiders. Buchanan, for example, on the

basis of observations made during a journey in South India, remarks that slaves were so impure in the eyes of their fellow men that they were kept well away from the houses of their masters and were compelled to cry out warnings of their approach (1807:380). Such restrictions were, of course, not imposed because of their position as slaves, but because of their status as untouchables, even 'unapproachables'.

In a remark not confirmed by any other source, W. Adam suggests that certain castes in South India were so 'degraded' as to be unworthy to perform 'even the most menial offices of slavery', and were consequently exempted from 'liability to that state' (1840:14). It is possible that he mistook the fact that certain untouchable groups had simply not been en- slaved for 'unworthiness' to be so reduced. Alternatively, he could have meant that certain castes were ritually too defiled even to work alongside other untouchable groups who were placed above them in the caste order, or to be in contact with the heavy chariots containing Hindu deities which agrestic slaves were on certain occasions made to drag and push around the temples and villages (*Ibid.* 172). Generally, how- ever, no caste was too low to be enslaved, and certainly no ritual prohibitions prevented a member of any but a Brahmin group from engaging in agricultural activities.

By contrast, domestic slaves in India, as in Nepal, could only belong to pure castes since their duties included drawing water and performing services around the house (ILC 1841: 26; Chattopadhyay 1977:35). Thus, where both agrestic and household slavery co-existed in the same area, as in the south, their personnel were drawn from completely separate ritual categories. In Kumaon, the Khasi-Jimdar castes, ranked between the untouchable Doms and the highest ritual groups, provided the household slaves (Sanwal 1976:54). But while such ritual distinctions were carefully maintained, the legal or political disabilities shared by both categories of slave were symbolised by their having to live in grass huts and wear ornaments made from a particular kind of base alloy (*Ibid.* 64–5).

The significance of caste was reflected in the prices fetched by different slave categories. Not only were females more costly than males—for their reproductive potential and undoubtedly because of their importance as concubines—but men and women of pure caste were more highly valued because they could be employed inside as well as outside the house (ILC 1841: 36, 37, 169; Chattopadhyay 1977:47).

While the ancient prohibition on the enslavement of Brahmins was still observed in the nineteenth century, the ban was apparently not everywhere extended to Kshatriyas and Vaishyas, although in practice few were reduced to this condition (ILC 1841:249). The ancient texts are not of like mind concerning the enslavement of non-Brahmin, twice-born groups. Manu (VIII, 411–412) does not recognise slavery for the Kshatriya and Vaishya; Narada (V, 39), however, forbids it only in the inverse order of the *varna*, i.e., a Kshatriya may become the slave of a Brahmin, and a Vaishya of a Kshatriya or a Brahmin, but not the other way round. In Bengal during the British period 'Hindus of the highest castes could not be owned as slaves by Hindus of the lowest castes' (Chattopadhyay 1977:36), and most slaves were of the 'lower' castes (*Ibid.* 2). In India generally, domestic slaves seem to have been drawn mainly from lower Sudra groups (ILC 1841: 21).

A concern to maintain the ritual integrity of domestic slaves, and *mutatis mutandis*, that of their masters, explains the fact that slaves were married and mourned according to the same rites as were observed for free persons of the same castes. In Bengal, and probably elsewhere, a female slave, like any Hindu girl of pure caste, would be regarded as defiled if she remained single after first menstruation, so that her marriage was arranged before or upon her reaching the age of puberty (*Ibid.* 39). It also enables us to understand a master's reluctance to compel a domestic slave to perform any service unsuitable or derogatory to the latter's caste (*Ibid.* 26), although normal duties occasionally underlined the ritual distance between them. This distance was symbolised by the widespread custom requiring slaves to eat the food leavings of their masters (*Ibid.* 231; Sanwal 1976:59). But since masters were generally the ritual superiors of their slaves, such a practice did no violation to the latters' status, but only confirmed their inferiority since it is acceptable to eat the food remains of one who is ritually more exalted (see Khare 1976:39). Again, during a master's illness, a slave could be called upon to perform the 'lowest offices' for him (ILC 1841:244), which would presumably place the slave in a condition of temporary pollution, but would not result in a permanent debasement of his or her rank. Only where an individual of superior caste came into the service of a master belonging to an inferior group would the former be reduced in status irrevocably, assuming the slave was compelled to accept food from the master's table. In such circumstances manumission would not be accompanied by re-entry into the natal caste. But generally, the data gathered by the Law Commissioners gives the impression that insofar as caste was concerned, enslavement in itself did not constitute and was not regarded as a degradation (*Ibid.* 39). And, as was pointed out for Nepal, the retention of their ritual position enabled slaves, on manumission, to resume their place in free society with relative ease.[7]

Slavery in South Asia: Summation and Conclusion

The foregoing outline of modern slavery in Nepal and India, while all too brief and, of necessity, sparse in detail, nevertheless suggests that there is a wide enough area of similarity between the two systems to enable us to identify a single pattern. To conclude this essay, I want to suggest what I regard as its principal characteristics, and to do so in a comparative context, with particular reference to Finley's general discussion of slavery in the *International Encyclopedia of the Social Sciences* (1968).

The first feature which must be noted is that slavery in South Asia was primarily domestic. Although sporadically in the distant past and in certain parts of India during more recent times (but probably not at all in Nepal) slaves were employed on a large scale in productive enterprise, historians and other observers, virtually without exception, have concluded that the greatest proportion were in household service. In as much as the economic and political elites did not depend principally on slave labour for 'basic production', neither India nor Nepal were 'slave societies', although in Finley's terms, they were clearly 'slave-owning' societies (1968:308, 310).

What might also be stressed is that these servants were no less chattels for being attached to households. That they were a species of property—according to Finley, the 'essential' element in any definition of 'slave' (*Ibid.* 307)—is left in no doubt when it is recalled that masters could sell or otherwise dispose of them without their consent. This seems to raise doubts about the wider applicability of Siegel's distinction between 'chattel' and 'household' slavery among North American Indians (1945).

A second point which needs to be made about South Asian slavery is that it had significance in both economic and prestige terms: as Cooper suggests, 'dependence and labour' are everywhere the dual benefits of ownership (1977:2). There is little doubt that considerable honour accrued to those who had the wherewithal to possess large numbers of slave dependants. The latter were an important currency of power, and their acquisition by the agrarian 'nobility' may be regarded, to echo Watson about a not dissimilar situation in South China, as an 'ostentatious display of wealth' (1976:373).

But to grant that slave ownership conferred honour and reflected power is not to deny its advantages in the productive process. The observation that free labour was less costly than slave labour (see above, Rana 1925) is not necessarily an argument against the economic advantages of the latter. With particular regard to household slaves, since they performed a variety of essential tasks without recompense beyond their basic upkeep, it is difficult to agree with Finley that 'profitability does not enter into an evaluation of domestic slaves . . .' (1968:310). While it has been suggested that household slavery may be 'financed' by the use of other, more efficient methods of labour exploitation in the 'primary productive sphere' (Miers and Kopytoff 1977:58), it could equally be argued that household slavery (like the domestic labour of married women) contributes to the perpetuation of the primary productive sphere (see Bujra 1978).

Thirdly, slavery in South Asia was an indigenous system. It is generally agreed that Indian slavery originated in the conquest by Aryan invaders of the aboriginal populations, and the subsequent enslavement of the latter (Basham 1963; Sarup 1921). But well before the beginning of the Buddhist epoch (circa sixth century B.C.) distinctions of Aryan and conquered people had completely disappeared (Chanana 1960: 23). Thereafter, with some relatively minor exceptions (noted above) slaves were recruited internally and the slave population did not rely for its replenishment on warfare or any other form of organised violence, which Finley suggests characterises most systems of slavery (1968:309). It is his contention that only the enslavement of 'outsiders' makes possible their 'uprooting' and reduction to property (*Ibid.* 308). While he does not specify what constitutes an 'outsider', it is fairly clear from the discussion that he means persons belonging to quite separate and distinct local-cum-ethnic communities, i.e., aliens.[8] The South Asian example, as in the Chinese case examined by Watson (1976:361), seems not to support his hypothesis: certainly during the period under consideration the vast majority of slaves, no less than free persons, were 'children of the soil' (W. Adam 1840:132). Indeed, the need to maintain the purity of status of slave owners precluded (at least ideally) the purchase of 'outside' domestic servants about whose ritual credentials nothing would be known (ILC 1841:245).[9]

This aspect of the institution also raises doubts about the extent to which Finley's argument, that the slave, as uprooted outsider, could have no 'essential human ties of kin and community', can be applied to the South Asian context (1968: 309). This particular point is made the focus of Leach's definition of a slave as one 'who has no recognized kin outside his owner's family' (1967:14). While the evidence is insufficient to enable us to say to what extent South Asian slaves were part of a kinship network in their own right, and what role it played in their lives, the crucial point is that slave marriages—again to do with the status of both owner and owned—were required to be performed in accordance with acceptable ritual procedures. Therefore the question of slave marriages having no recognised standing does not arise. In this respect the South Asian situation is not unique. Elkins has noted that slaves in Latin America were married, and that, moreover, the Catholic Church insisted on the 'inviolability' of the marriage bond (1967:200). 'The Spanish had no difficulty in accepting the idea of slave marriage, whereas the British and then the Americans had great difficulty with this' (*Ibid.* 212).

Finally, a fourth characteristic of the institution in India and Nepal which should be noted is the distinction maintained between the power and status of slaves. On the one hand their legal condition rendered them totally powerless, as indicated by their treatment as chattels (Finley 1968:307). Accordingly, they were ranked at the very bottom of the political order. On the other hand, while agrestic slaves might and usually did belong to a stratum at the base of the ritual hierarchy, those in the domestic sphere, in order to safeguard the owners' purity (and therefore the latters' status) were compelled to be chosen from castes ranked above the line of pollution. The slave-owning elites were themselves from the highest castes, and prohibited or limited the enslavement of members of their own groups. Historically, therefore, domestic slaves tended to be recruited principally from the lower strata within the ranks of the ritually pure. Thus as between owner and owned the system itself was 'involute'.

Leach has noted that in the 'overall hierarchy' the slave is 'not necessarily at the bottom', illustrating the point by reference to the Ottoman Empire where administrative officers were often legally slaves (1967:14). Hopkins also draws attention to the fact that the actual position of slaves in classical antiquity often belied their legal condition. In Roman law, slaves were 'not humans but things'. Yet some occupied a range of important positions in the public services, the professions, and business. They were bureaucrats, skilled craftsmen, naval captains, secretaries, scribes, managing agents, bankers and doctors (1967:173). Similarly, slaves were high officials in the Nupe Empire and in other African societies (see Nadel 1942; Miers and Kopytoff 1977).

Fallers seeks to explain this apparent anomaly by suggesting that it is only in European cultures, and fairly recently, that 'degrees of freedom correlated directly with "social worth", and [where] over the centuries personal freedom became a common goal of personal ambition and of social movements' (1973:104). There are two separate issues here raised by Fallers, as by others who have noted the obvious discrepancy between the legalistic position of slaves and their actual condition. The first concerns the difficult problem of the 'power' of these slave officials. This is of peripheral importance to the main concerns of this paper, and I do not intend to do more than refer to Cooper's interesting observation that slaves could be placed in positions of trust 'precisely because their subordination to their masters was . . . so extreme' (1977:6). Thus the notion of a 'powerful slave' appears at first glance a contradiction in terms, and clearly this question needs more discussion and clarification.

The second issue bears on the relation between the 'power' of these slaves and their 'social worth'. Unfortunately, it is not always made sufficiently clear by the ethnographers of societies where slaves did hold positions of great responsibility and influence the extent to which this conferred on them a high place in the status hierarchy. This, then, is another problem needing further amplification and comparison with the situation in South Asia. There, as I have suggested, the power and status orders were largely insulated from one another. To be sure, there was a modicum of overlap or 'feedback'. Thus, for one thing, certain violations of ritual propriety could have repercussions in the political order, i.e., lead to enslavement. For another, an individual held in slavery not only stood lower in the political order than a free person of the same caste, but this inequality would also probably be reflected in status differences, so that a ban on ritual exchanges (e.g., commensality) might be imposed by the superior. But on the whole, as evidenced in the possibility of marriages between free and unfree, the similarity of their wedding and funerary rites, the purity of caste required for domestic duty and the comparative ease with which ex-slaves were integrated into free society, enslavement, while a reduction to total political subordination, was not and could not be regarded as a corresponding degradation of status.

Elkins has suggested that the shape of Latin-American slavery can be accounted for in large measure by Catholic doctrines and values as interpreted by the Church (1976: 223ff.). While Elkins's generalisation may be too broad (see Lane 1971), he does point to an interesting problem area— the link between slavery and ideology. While it would be inappropriate to argue that the kind of slave system which existed in Nepal prior to 1925, and during the period of British rule in India before 1843, can only be understood in terms of a pervading Hinduism, it does seem clear that unless its tenets and practices are taken into account, we can make little sense of the structure and rationale of South Asian slavery.

8

Opposition and Interdependence: Demographic and Economic Perspectives on Nyinba Slavery

NANCY E. LEVINE

The Nyinba might seem to an outsider to be an ethnic group undivided by any form of social stratification and largely un-marked by economic differentiation.[1] Their community gives an impression of almost uniform prosperity and appears to be characterised by an overall stress on the equality of its mem-bers. However, closer investigation reveals that like many other Tibetan-speaking Nepalese groups, the Nyinba are in-ternally sub-divided into hierarchically ranked social strata.[2] Unlike these other populations, the Nyinba ranking system rests on a radical division between former slaveholders and their ex-slaves.

It is not surprising that the system of social ranking is not readily apparent. For one thing, the slaves were emancipated over half a century ago. In addition, for a number of cogent reasons, the Nyinba are not eager to draw attention to facts of social inequality in their society. The national government has supported the full integration of ex-slaves into the com-munity and it is not only impolite but also impolitic to call attention publicly to the slave ancestry of fellow villagers.

In the past, the distinction between master and slave was a fact of major importance in social relations. Even today, though less openly acknowledged, the distinction between former masters, former slaves, and their respective descen-dants is highly significant in community social life. The

Nyinba identify individuals as being either *dagpo*, that is, slaveholders and their descendants, or as *yogpo*, slaves and their freedmen descendants. A person's status as either *dagpo* or *yogpo* is a primary determinant of all other social statuses open to him or her. The former hold full rights of citizenship in their community, the latter are at best little more than second-class citizens.

This paper will be directed toward an examination of slavery in the past and the system of social ranking in the present day. Thus it will cover a period of more than fifty years and refer to oral historical data on the past and to observable conditions today. It will also attempt to bring together diverse ethnographic materials on Nyinba household organisation and demography and on aspects of the economic and political system. Such a wide-ranging inquiry is necessary to examine *yogpo-dagpo* relations and to reveal the consequences of slavery for the society as a whole.

The system of slavery can no more be understood without reference to the total field of social structure than Nyinba society can be discussed without reference to past slavery and modern inequality. And, in particular, one cannot provide a thorough description of the economic system without mention of landowners' reliance on slave labour in the past and on auxiliary wage labour today.

The following section begins with a brief account of Nyinba's economic adaptation. I shall then summarise relevant aspects of social structure, focusing on characteristic forms of domestic organisation. This will provide the necessary background for a contextual analysis of the system of slavery.

The Nyinba: Economy and Society

The Nyinba region comprises a series of sheltered valleys near Simikot, the district capital of Humla. Humla, one of the most sparsely populated and poorest of Nepal's districts, is located in northwestern Nepal. The majority of Humla villages are inhabited by Nepali speakers who follow Hindu religious traditions and are ranked according to Hindu caste principles. Less than a fifth are recognised as Bhotias, that is,

Tibetan speakers who reside in Nepal's mountainous northern
borderlands. Bhotias are Tibetan Buddhists (the word derives
from *Bodpa*, meaning Tibetan) and are culturally closer to
their northern Tibetan neighbours. Although assigned a place
in the Nepalese caste system, their communities manifest
internal systems of social stratification based on criteria
dissimilar from those of Hindu caste ranking.

Humla is occupied by five distinct, settled Bhotia communities and serves as summer pasture for a sixth, migratory
group. Each community occupies a separate territory or series
of territories, is normatively endogamous, readily identified
by peculiarities of dress and dialect, and each fosters a sense
of unique ethnic identity. The Nyinba are one of Humla's
southernmost Bhotia communities and their nearest neighbours are Nepali speakers of high and low castes. They maintain contact with other, more distantly located Bhotia groups
through the annual cycle of herding and trade.

Topographically, the Nyinba region is rocky and mountainous, ranging from narrow river valleys to Himalayan
peaks. The land is typical of many areas in far western Nepal:
it is arid in sections, water sources are few and far between,
and annual rainfalls are relatively low. Although there is a
light cover of vegetation, trees are sparse due to the progressive effects of deforestation.

Despite these difficult conditions and the striking poverty
of the larger region, the Nyinba are among the wealthiest
people in Humla. Their villages present an overwhelming
impression of comfort and prosperity. The houses are large
and solidly built, the village lanes are broad and well-made,
passing by tidy kitchen gardens. Their fields are terraced,
neatly laid out, well-tilled, and evidently productive. When
the Nyinba are asked to account for their level of prosperity,
they invariably emphasise their large landholdings and call
attention to the amount of effort expended in agriculture.
Some individuals also mention trade, but as a contributing
rather than a determining factor. Since features of economic
organisation are central to an understanding of slave labour
in a given society, a brief summary of Nyinba land use and
modes of production is in order here.

Economic Adaptation

Nyinba villages are located at altitudes of approximately 10,000 to 11,000 feet. The villagers make use of lands above and below their homesteads, at altitudes ranging from 8,800 to 12,000 feet. Individual landholdings consist of numerous small plots at various locations and different altitudes. This enables households to utilise land in different ecozones and minimises the possibilities of overwhelming losses from localised crop failures (cf. Netting 1972:134–135; Rhoades and Thompson 1975:543). However, it also increases the workload by necessitating frequent travel between distant plots. Landowning households have varying amounts of both lowland and highland fields. The former can be double cropped, but the latter produce only one crop per year. A variety of grains are cultivated: *Eleusine* and *Panicum* millet, barley, wheat, sweet buckwheat, oats, and bitter buckwheat are the staple crops. The Nyinba also produce limited amounts of amaranth, *dal*, kidney beans, potatoes, turnips, peas, radishes, and various types of squash.

Women provide the bulk of the labour necessary for the annual agricultural output. Although men plough and sow the seed, these activities require relatively brief periods of work. Men may also participate in harvest activities, reaping grain, threshing buckwheat in the fields with the women, and carrying crops home. All else is regarded as women's work. Women manure the fields, involve themselves in the backbreaking task of weeding for weeks at a time, and also thresh and winnow the grains. No man would expose himself to ridicule by undertaking women's agricultural tasks. And only in the most unusual circumstances do women take on that labour that is properly the province of men.

Herding is much less important to the Nyinba economy than agriculture, although it serves to add a much-needed source of protein to the diet. Elderly men or adolescents of either sex can readily cope with the needs of the cattle: several households may combine their herds under the care of a single individual.

Trade is another matter entirely. It is important ideologically and significant economically as well. Trading is the full-time occupation of at least one man from each of the wealthier Nyinba households, and a part-time occupation for poorer men. The cycle of trade takes the men into Tibet each spring and summer, through southwestern Nepal in the fall and to the Indian border in winter. It is centred around the exchange of Tibetan salt for grains produced in the Nepalese lowlands. Despite declining profits in recent years (Fürer-Haimendorf 1974, 1975), the income from trade provides a valued supplement to the Nyinba economy. Households with adept traders are said to prosper; those without any traders usually have a standard of living well below the local average.

Social Structure

The Nyinba community included approximately twelve hundred individuals in 1974. Community members are organised into four separate village-districts (or *yultshan*). Each village-district is territorially distinct and residentially discrete. It also has rights over a distinct set of agricultural lands, a pasture area, exclusive use of particular water sources, and access to forest preserves. Village-districts are centred around one major village, some also including subsidiary settlements or hamlets located nearby. The village district may succinctly be described as a corporate unit with political, economic, and ritual prerogatives.

The key unit of social structure within the village district is the landholding household or *trongba*, a term most adequately translated as estate household. The household is the primary societal unit involved in processes of production and consumption. It is also the constituent political unit in Nyinba society. Political offices traditionally devolve on households, not on individuals and are assumed by the current household head or his designated representative. Nyinba citizens, by definition, belong to one named estate household. Non-citizens are all recognised to be affiliated with one such household or another.

Household properties (known as *düsang*) including land,

cattle, jewellery, and so on are passed down intact as a jointly
held estate from fathers to sons. The brothers of each generation marry polyandrously, so as to avoid household partition.
If men lack sons, they are entitled to choose a son-in-law to
be their successor. In this case one daughter remains in her
natal home; her spouse resides uxorilocally and takes super-
visory control over her property. But the vast majority of
marriages (93 per cent in 1974) are followed by virilocal residence. Another characteristic feature of landholding households is their unusually high sex ratio. In a census of fifty
estate households in 1974, I counted 223 males and 153
females—a sex ratio of 146. This may be attributed to the
indirect effects of the practice of fraternal polyandry and also
to what appears to be the result of female infant neglect.

The domestic arrangements described above are representative of Nyinba citizens, i.e., individuals of non-slave ancestry. Such arrangements were not manifested by slaves
in the past, nor are they characteristic of the majority of
freedmen today. Rather, traditional slave households differed
from, yet were systematically related to, the patrilocal, polyandrous households of their masters.

The descendants of the slaves make up only 12 per cent of
the Nyinba population today. Nonetheless their presence has
had a profound effect on Nyinba society. Masters and slaves
did not—and their respective descendants do not now—live
separately from one another. They were closely associated in
day-to-day activities and, despite the facts of social inequality, they played important parts in one another's lives.
The asymmetry of their relationship and their interdependence are revealed most clearly in their domestic arrangements—separate yet complementary parts of a single social
unit.

The Nyinba System of Slavery

The Nyinba believe that slavery has existed amongst them
since the very beginning of their society. Some Nyinba told
me that the ancestors of the landholding citizens brought
their slaves or servants with them when they first settled the

region. However, most citizens state that the *yogpo*, or population of former slaves, are the descendants of the first settlers in the Nyinba region. These people are said to have become indebted to some of the later settlers, the ancestors of the present-day *dagpo* or citizens. They lost their lands through mortgage and sale to the newcomers. Unable to pay back further loans, they became bond slaves and their descendants have remained in slavery up to the present day.[3] These beliefs about the origin of slavery serve as a rationale and charter for certain attitudes held by citizens towards slaves and their descendants. The discussion of this issue will be reintroduced at a later point.

All the slaves in Nepal were emancipated over fifty years ago. Thus it is impossible to directly observe the conditions and circumstances of Nyinba slavery. There are no published accounts of the slavery system, nor of any aspect of Nyinba history. The only possible source of information about the latter lies in the oral historical narratives of informants. The Nyinba community does include a number of individuals, citizens and freedmen, who were youths or adults during the era of emancipation and witnessed the system of slavery prior to its end. Not surprisingly, former slaves proved to be extremely reticent in discussing the facts of their prior conditions of life. Consequently I had primary recourse to aged citizens who were candid and reliable, but who viewed the slavery system from the slaveholder's perspective. There are problems inherent in the use of such sources, inasmuch as the description of the lives of the slaves is bound to be biased. I have attempted to conpensate for this fact and have tried to balance the former owners' accounts of slavery with the limited material I have on the slaves' view of their own system. Another set of problems, partially independent of the source of information, seems inevitable in reconstructions of this kind. It is not unlikely that informants may choose to suppress or have conveniently 'forgotten' some features of a practice as controversial as slavery. It is also likely that other aspects of past conditions have been reordered or reconstructed to fit better with present-day realities. However, it should be noted that the various informants—all consulted

separately—agreed on major details. Moreover, informants'
accounts, when compared with available information on the
legal circumstances of slaves and events of emancipation
elsewhere in Nepal, were found to accord with the historical
record. I have used these sources selectively, and based my
judgments on my general knowledge of Nyinba culture and
on general standards for the interpretation of such material
(see, especially, Vansina 1965).

The Status of Slaves

Nyinba slaves were, in a legal sense, a form of chattel.[4] The
fact that they were viewed as the property of other people
was the basic determinant of their position in society, and
accounts for the social disabilities they suffered. The precise
nature of their disabilities can only be understood in relation
to the advantages accruing to holders of citizen status. The
definitive attributes of both citizens and slaves in Nyinba
society will now be discussed: the former phrased in the
ethnographic present; and the latter in the past tense.

All Nyinba citizens are members of a named patriclan.
Membership in one of the small number of recognised clans
is viewed, in fact, as proof of free birth and as a prerequisite
of citizenship. All citizens also are necessarily members of a
named *trongba*, the landholding or estate household. Estate
household members as a group are entitled to equal political
representation in the community; individual members are
thereby permitted to hold particular offices. Household members maintain rights in the hereditary estate (*düsang*) which
consists of land, animals, house, slaves, jewellery, ritual items,
and the like. Citizens hold certain notable 'freedoms', rights
of self-determination (*rang'ang*) as culturally defined. Among
these freedoms are the right to trade, to marry according to
their own wishes and to leave the society either temporarily
or permanently.

The Nyinba community is unified by the belief that all of its
citizens are related through ties of kinship. These ties can be
matrilateral or patrilateral, distant or near; it does not matter.
What does matter is the fact that any citizen can (with help,

if necessary) trace a series of links, affinal and/or consanguineal, to any other citizen. The nature of the tie determines
the terms of address used between the two. Adult Nyinba
citizens may not be addressed and should not be referred to
by their personal names. Rather, they are referred to by the
kin term that describes their relationship to the speaker, and
their identity may be more precisely specified by use of their
household name in conjunction with the kinship term.

Slaves could never be citizens and correspondingly lacked
all of the freedoms mentioned above. To begin with, slaves
had no affiliation with any patriclan. They were seen as
people without any recognised antecedents, without links to
persons of good descent within or outside the society. Slaves
were not entitled to hold any property. Thus they did not
own houses, cattle, or land. They were also denied the rights
of direct political participation in the village. It is said that
slaves were utterly without '*ang.*' That is to say, they were
totally powerless.

The slave's membership in the society depended on his or
her affiliation to one or more estate households. That affiliation was based on the slave's status as chattel, i.e., as part of
the household property (*düsang*). Affiliation was based on this
asymmetrical economic relationship to the household. There
was an expectation of service for support, the type of service
and level of support depending on the master's wishes. Slaves
had little control over their personal lives. They could not
select their spouses and were unable to choose their own
place of residence. This lack of self-determination was most
clearly manifested in the fact that they, their siblings or their
children could be sold according to the master's whims.

Slaves were distinguished by their lack of kin ties to the
free community. Strict rules of status-group endogamy prevented intermarriage between citizen and slave. Liaisons
between male citizens and slave women are said to have
occurred, but any offspring of such unions were regarded as
illegitimate and were not permitted to call attention publicly
to the connection with their putative genitor. Thus slaves
were denied the possibility of recognised affinal or agnatic
connections with holders of full citizenship. This fact is one

of many used to support citizen's claims that freedmen are of
a different ethnic group than themselves. The slaves had
different origins from the citizens, they were separated from
citizens by rules of endogamy and were never assimilated into
the kinship network of the rest of the Nyinba society.

Slaves had rights and obligations in the politico-jural and
economic spheres primarily to people who were non-kin and
who, moreover, were associated with them on an unequal
basis. Their primary relationships were circumscribed by the
households of their owners; they held no countervailing
rights in any other group. Although the slaves were thus
closely tied—economically, legally, and also morally—to their
master's households, they were definitely not members of
those households. Household membership presumes a recognised kin relationship to the head and accords certain dis-
cretionary rights—gained by birth or marriage—in household
property. Slaves were attached to their masters' households in
an inferior capacity, a status based on their identification as
essentially chattel. It is important to make note of the fact, as
it will be referred to again in a later discussion, that the
Nyinba system of slavery utilised a mode of domestic
arrangement in which non-household members—slaves—
were attached for purely economic and political purposes.
Whereas Nyinba households were otherwise held together by
ties of kinship, the slave's affiliation to the household had no
comparable intrinsic value.

Conditions of Slavery

The obligations of slaves to their masters' households were
clearly specified in customary law. All adults and capable
adolescents were expected to devote their full efforts to the
service of their masters every three days out of four, eleven
months out of the year. The major part of their work is said to
have been agricultural. They were sent to work alone in their
masters' fields or, if the work demanded it, their masters
would join them there. Time-wise, the majority of this agricultural work devolved on females, though slaves of either
sex might assist in or take responsibility for the chores of

herding. Females were also kept busy at general household tasks: cooking, cleaning, washing, and so on. Male slaves might be expected to accompany their masters on some or all of the annual trading journeys. Occasionally they could even be asked to substitute for their masters on short trips or when otherwise necessary. However, there seem to have been strong reservations about relying on slaves for assistance in trading activities. In certain cases, still remembered to this day, slaves were suspected of dishonest dealings. More important, slaves were deemed not to have the qualities necessary for successful trading. They were seen as lacking self-assurance and bargaining skills. One of the most unpleasant of slave duties involved the performance of ritually dangerous and polluting tasks on behalf of their masters. They had to dispose of certain items used in ritual; they also had to wash the clothes of any deceased household members.

Just as the masters held explicit rights in the labour of their slaves, so did the slaves have undisputed moral rights with regard to their masters. All slaves were acknowledged to deserve food, clothing, and shelter. If particular slaves were judged lazy or recalcitrant, their portions might be diminished or even withheld, so as to compel more desirable behaviour. In the most extreme situations, the slave-owning household might decide to cut off all support. The case of Kunga illustrates the consequences of such a decision:

> Kunga, a slave of Barkhang village-district, had a long-standing dispute with his masters. Their conflicts intensified and his masters began to hold back his food supplies. They even went to the extent of repossessing his supply of winter firewood. Kunga responded to this harassment by fleeing and seeking sanctuary in the temple of a local deity in a neighbouring village district. The villagers there fed and protected him. In this way they upheld the right of a slave to leave a bad master. Kunga never returned to Barkhang: his descendants still live in the village which protected him and are still seen as the 'wards' of the local temple and its deity.

The ever-present threat of escape may have served to enforce equitable behaviour on the part of slaveholders. In addition, the local deities were thought to have an essentially protective attitude toward the slaves, stemming from their universal compassion and interest in social justice, and perhaps because the slaves were believed to be autochthons. Most Nyinba mediums were slaves, who could thereby indirectly exercise limited power within the community. Furthermore, mystical sanctions could be brought to bear against cruel masters, in addition to the more usual effects of gossip and other local forms of social control.

Nyinba citizens state that they treated their slaves leniently. They make no mention of any recourse to beatings or other forms of physical punishment to make the slaves work harder or behave more in accordance with their wishes. In general, all Nyinba disapprove of fighting or any abusive physical contact. Men occasionally may strike their wives and parents their children, but such occurrences are uncommon. It is not unlikely my informants would have preferred to gloss over any such aspects of slavery. Due to the lack of available evidence, one cannot even hazard a guess as to this aspect of slave treatment.

Slaves were transferred from one master to another by sale, grant, or through women's dowries. Shortly before and at the time of emancipation, slave prices ranged from forty rupees for a child or the infirm to more than one hundred and twenty rupees for a healthy young man. At that time twenty rupees was the asking price of a yak-cow crossbreed calf. The same animal cost one thousand rupees (approximately £42) in 1974. Thus slaves may be said to have been an exceedingly valuable form of property.

Former slaveholders with whom I spoke stressed that slave sales were not conducted 'crassly', in the offhand manner one might sell a goat or a cow. Rather, a prospective buyer would bring an offering of beer and humbly request the privilege of purchasing a particular slave. The agreement would be reached after deliberation on the part of the owner, and excessive bargaining was not allowed.[5]

Extremely wealthy families might choose to include an excess slave in their daughters' dowries. This practice does not seem to have been common, but some slave genealogies show evidence of ancestors' transfers to new homes in this way. Outright grants of slaves are said to have taken place when slaveholders gave their excess male slaves to the masters of unmarried female slaves. The male would marry the woman: he and all progeny of the union were considered property of the woman's master. This account of free grant of slaves in marital transfers was offered by all informants surveyed and was reaffirmed in the face of repeated questioning. The practice is particularly surprising, since the Nyinba are not known to part lightly with any form of property. One can only surmise that all slaveholders on occasion stood in need of obtaining slaves by such reciprocal exchange, so that all participated in the expectation of eventual balanced returns.

Slave Domestic Organisation

Slaves resided in small, poorly constructed houses that usually consisted of no more than two rooms and sometimes included a small, attached barn. These houses were located behind or alongside the large and comfortable house of the master. The composition and mode of organisation of slave households is said to have been idiosyncratic and does seem to have differed in numerous ways from citizen households. A summary of the central features of slave domestic organisation will provide a starting point for the discussion of slave-master relationships.

Slave households could be set up with a single woman. The woman's master would then obtain a husband for her; ideally, children would be born soon thereafter. Female children would remain resident with their parents, while sons would be sold or granted to other masters when they reached maturity. In the course of normal developmental processes, a slave household might come to include a core of uxorilocally resident women, their husbands, daughters, and any young unmarried sons.

Such connubial unions of slave men and women may be considered marriage, but the use of this term is subject to strong reservations.[6] Slaves certainly had recognised rights *in personam* over their spouses, but lacked the rights *in rem* characteristic of citizen marriage (see Radcliffe-Brown's discussion of rights *in personam* and rights *in rem* over wives, 1952:32–33). That is, a slave husband had certain expectations of his wife, expectations which she would invariably fulfill. But his rights in the woman did not extend to regulating the conduct of others, particularly of slaveholders and other citizens, towards her. In accordance with this fact, slaves could not expect to win compensation payments for the adultery of their wives. It may be noted that, in contrast, a citizen whose wife is adulterous inevitably obtains satisfactory compensation. Although the male slave's rights in his wife's sexuality were not supported in law, slaves were expected to be faithful to one another. Children born of individuals joined in such a union were considered legitimate, those born of adulterous unions were not. Whereas slave unions lacked the legal supports characterising the unions of the free, they were no doubt regarded as morally binding relationships.

Just as slave men lacked full customary rights in their wives, they also were denied the sorts of rights citizens held in their children. Whereas citizen fathers have rights *in personam* and *in rem* over their children, slave fathers had only limited rights *in personam*, and these rights were unequivocally secondary to those held by their masters. The constraints imposed by servitude on kinsmen are reflected in the proverbial saying, 'just as a dog has no father, a slave has no agnates-affines' (*khyi la aya med yogpo la nyenpun med*). Slaves, of course, did have genealogically recognised kin. However, they were prevented—by the absence of legal support and by the predominant rights of their masters— from exercising the prerogatives normatively considered incumbent on kinsmen and kinswomen. This problem was particularly acute within the family, but it also extended to their inability to offer political or economic support to any relatives in time of trouble. This is one aspect of what has been described as the 'essential kinlessness' of slaves (see Bohannan 1963:180).

The households of Nyinba slaves were thus organised

around women. The marriages of these slave women were most commonly monogamous. Some were initially polygynous and a few remained so throughout the participants' lives, but none were ever polyandrous. Thus, in a number of ways, the domestic arrangements of slaves were completely opposite to those of citizens. The former married uxorilocally, the latter virilocally; the former perpetuated rights and obligations vis-à-vis their masters through daughters, the latter passed down property through sons; the former were predominantly monogamous, the latter normatively polyandrous. The contrasts could not be greater, and they still underlie claims of cultural differences between citizen and ex-slave today.

Cultural Oppositions Between Masters and Slaves

Nyinba citizens believe that slaves were intrinsically different from their masters and definitely inferior. Practices and customs seen as characteristic of slaves are adjudged to be *bibiyan* (Nep. *bipendo*), that is, 'contrary' or 'reversed' and, moreover, are seen as the exact mirror image of normative behaviour. According to citizens, the strongest evidence of the contrariety of slave customs is to be found in the organisation of their households. Citizens find the matrifocality of such households particularly objectionable, but explain that these sorts of practices are part of the historical heritage of the *yogpo* and existed prior to the time of their enslavement. Thus these facts are attributed to the separate ethnic identity of the slaves.

The distinctive features of slave household organisation are just one aspect of the complex of customs and practices associated with slavery. These customs cannot be understood in isolation from other parts of the social system. Indeed, this is implicitly recognised in the native view that slave customs are reversed. That is to say, they are not merely different from or alien to the institutions and values of citizen society, but rather are related to them in a positive and meaningful way.

The analysis of master-slave relations may be developed in

terms of a scheme of congruent oppositions—between high and low, immigrants and settlers, pure and impure, male and female, culture and nature—which has generalised significance in the society. Constraints of space do not permit this scheme to be explicated fully. However, in the context of the concerns of this paper and in light of the significance of females within the slavery system, it is necessary to point out that Nyinba traditions emphasised and built upon an analogy between slaves and women. Both male and female slaves customarily carried out tasks classed as 'women's work': they served food in the homes of their masters, carried wood and water to the homestead, and walked behind their masters carrying loads of grain or trade goods. In homes and at public ceremonies, slaves were seated (as freedmen sit today) in a location normally reserved for women. It may also be noted that the land held in usufruct by slaves is known by the same term as the property held by women (that is, *tragsi*). Furthermore, the procedure followed in purchasing slaves is identical to that followed in a woman's betrothal.

As noted above, in the eyes of Nyinba citizens, 'reversed' practices count as proof of the innate inferiority of slaves. This belief is expressed in terms of racist assertions. Nyinba citizens state that the slaves were physically (*lüba'i*) inferior. They were also said to be of 'a lower line of descent,' of 'inferior blood' or 'tainted ancestry' (*rig mao*). Today's freedmen seem to concur with this judgement. They are proud of any non-slave forbears and speak of potential intermarriage with the citizens as a way of improving their hereditary status (*rig*). Citizens still evince feelings of repugnance toward close physical contact with freedmen. The latter are said to exude an unpleasant—and contagious—body odour and to be unattractive in appearance. Slaves were also thought to be inferior intellectually. Citizens reason that this alone can account for their practice of uxorilocal residence, a custom thought to offend the gods and to be directly responsible for dissolution and decline in so many slave-freedmen households.

The issue of racism as tied to slavery is an interesting one. There may be no necessary connection between the two (see,

for example, DeVos 1966:335) but in certain historical circumstances they have certainly reinforced one another (Finley
1967:10). In the Nyinba case, slavery and racism seem to have
been interdependent, and racial beliefs undoubtedly were an
important concomitant of the system. Racism in this context
may well be related to the resolution of the problem of the
essentially 'marginal' position of the slave (Kopytoff and
Miers 1977; Vaughn 1977). The problem concerns how to
accommodate the slave in a society that denies him the rights
of a full member. Slaves must be included in the society in a
way that both explains and upholds their separateness and
inferiority. Kopytoff and Miers note that in certain African
cases, slave status 'was . . . clearly reinforced by ideas about
the ethnic superiority of the host society' (1977:17).

   In this section I have discussed the cultural assumptions,
distinctions, and categories that underlie the relationships
between masters and slaves. Racist assertions persist to this
day, but the separation between citizens and freedmen is no
longer supported so strongly by socio-cultural realities. Many
of the practices traditionally associated with slavery were
abandoned almost immediately after emancipation by all
but a small fraction of the freedmen. And the only people
who continued to organise their households in the slave
manner were freedmen who remained willingly in the service
of their former masters. A greater understanding of the structural significance, economic consequences, and demographic
concomitants of these customs may be provided by a discussion of the complementarity between slave and master
household composition. In the following section I will discuss
how the two types of households were linked and how certain
deficiencies in personnel in master households may have been
compensated for by slave personnel.

Complementarity and the Relations
Between Masters and Slaves

The homes of Nyinba estate holders are, as stated above,
well-built and spacious. They are appropriately known as

'great houses' (*trongchen*). The far less satisfactory houses of slaves are called 'small houses' (*khangchung*). Members of both great and small households are said to have lived next to one another and also to have shared in one another's lives. The separate families often ate together, particularly in the busy agricultural months. They worked together in the fields, regularly or periodically, depending on individual household circumstances, and their men journeyed together in search of trade opportunities.

The close relationships between masters and slaves were made manifest in the master's references to their 'slave sons and daughters.'[7] This social identification as expressed in the notion of membership in a common family becomes more evident in the rationale given for freely granting slaves for purposes of marriage. As one of my most perceptive informants explained, 'we do not buy and sell our daughters into marriage and similarly we do not purchase or pay for our slaves' spouses.' However, in all other regards, the status distinctions between members of the two families were stringently maintained. Slaves served their masters, never the reverse. It is not surprising to find that slaves addressed their owners—and all citizens—by the terms for 'lord' and 'lady' (*jowo* and *jozhon*). In striking contrast, masters referred to slaves by name (the casual use of names between citizens is considered an insult) or addressed them by consanguineal kin terms appropriate to their age and sex.[8]

This aspect of master-slave relations should be viewed in the context of the intimate linkage of great and small households. Although small households were separate domestic establishments, they were also an integral part of their owner's household in political and economic spheres. Slaves were members —albeit second-rate ones—in the great household. Correspondingly, slaves were identified with their masters' children (in a metaphorical sense); they were addressed as consanguines (again in a metaphorical sense), and their lives were intertwined with the lives of the full members of the great household. The emphasis on status inequality was one counterweight to the otherwise conjoint relationships of masters and slaves. The opposing and yet complementary features of master and slave households reflect an underlying pattern of differentiation coupled with interdependence which characterised the relations between the two groups. The nature of these relations has further implications for the economic correlates of the system of slavery as will be discussed below.

One may note that the masters' attitudes toward their slaves were qualitatively different from attitudes they held toward cattle and other forms of property. In a legal sense, the slaves may have been chattel, but in a moral sense they were also regarded as persons, although vastly inferior persons. The inconsistencies inherent in these mutually contradictory aspects have characteristically plagued the moral and judicial systems of other slaveholding societies (see Genovese 1976:76; Hindess and Hirst 1975:112).

The ownership of slaves had a number of consequences for the slaveholding unit. As noted in an earlier section of this paper, households are the primary organisational units in Nyinba society, and membership in a named household determines the overall place of the individual in that society. Household wealth is a major determinant of social status. Individuals know how much land and cattle each of their neighbours hold and have a rough idea of the wealth of members of other villages. Wealthy people command deference from their poorer counterparts, often hold political office, and thus are able to exercise more power within the community. Slave ownership was pre-eminently a mark of wealth and conferred distinction on all members of a slaveholding household. Today Nyinba are eager to draw attention to the fact that they, their parents or grandparents had slave dependants in the past.

Slaves were thus a source of prestige for their owners. They also formed a servile retinue who could attend to the various lowly chores necessary to personal and household maintenance. However, slaves were more than a means of 'conspicuous consumption' (see, in this regard, Fogel and Engerman 1974) and they were more than a way for their owners to avoid various unpleasant tasks. They provided a readily available supply of labour for their masters' households, labour that compensated for chronic shortages of personnel.

Demographic Consequences of Citizen Household Organisation

As was discussed above, the polyandrous marriage system of citizen households is correlated with a radical sexual imbalance. At the present time, females comprise approximately 40 per cent of the membership of such households and adult females are only 32 per cent of the household population. Consequently, only a third of the average citizen household is qualified by age and sex to participate in the arduous and lengthy tasks associated with women's contributions to agriculture. Moreover, not all women of suitable age are capable of fulfilling their agricultural responsibilities. They may be too ill to work, be hindered by nursing or childcare and other responsibilities. Most Nyinba women who are capable of so doing seem to work very hard during the summer months. Some are overwhelmed by agricultural duties and find it impossible to meet the demands of their work. It is the rare Nyinba household that has an excess of capable, adult personnel. Many clearly experience serious labour shortages. The two Nyinba households with whom I lodged both experienced problems associated with inadequate female labour— with serious economic consequences. In my first place of residence there were ten household members, half of whom were children. There was only one adult female, but she was aided in her domestic tasks by an adolescent daughter. The second household included only one adult female out of a total of eight members (six of whom were male). This woman was in poor health and could not keep up with her responsibilities. In view of their situation, the parents requested that their eldest son marry a hard-working woman as quickly as possible. (He did so in the autumn of 1975). A major problem for both families involved securing sufficient labour for successful agricultural production.

The emphasis on female slaves and female slave labour may be examined in terms of this predicament. Citizen men marry polyandrously.[9] The alternative—multiple marriage or polygynous polyandry—is seen to encourage dissension between siblings and to provide a climate favourable to household partitions. Partition and situations productive of partition are avoided for cogent reasons. Most importantly, partition divides the household wealth, and, as a result, it diminishes household members' stature in the community. Female slave labour could readily rectify temporary or long-term female labour shortages in landholding households. It could also free the women of wealthy households from unpleasant agricultural work for other productive tasks. Wealthy women who need not engage in agricultural work are able, for example, to devote themselves to weaving cloth for their families' use. When masters no longer had need of slaves, they could sell them or grant full or partial rights in their labour to a married daughter's household. Men who partitioned their households and needed their slaves, but could not readily provide their upkeep, could share the slaves' services with their brothers.

Although the prices paid for male slaves may have exceeded those paid for female slaves, all other evidence points to the fact that female slaves were regarded as being of greater consequence to the Nyinba system. This is consistent with the fact that slave children belonged to their mother's master. A male slave was granted freely to the master of his wife, all his labour accruing thereafter to the latter. Female slaves remained in their natal homes, or one could say that masters kept female slaves in their natal homes and usually sold or distributed males in grants to other slaveowners. Also relevant in this regard is the likelihood that the practice of monogamy, with occasional polygyny, accorded with a roughly equivalent sex ratio in slave households. The emphasis on female slave labour, the fact of female-centred slave households and the more equal sex ratio in these small households may be contrasted with the prevailing situation in the masters' own homes. In this way, the structural complementarity of slaves and master households was interrelated with a demographic complementarity which, in turn, had definite consequences for the organisation of slave labour.

Thus it can be argued that this complementarity of personnel provided the major economic benefit of slavery.

The events of emancipation irrevocably altered the traditional base of these relationships. New forms of relationships developed between citizens, former masters and freedmen, depending on the various circumstances of the latter. The types of relationships and the kinds of changes that occurred in freedmen households provide further insights into the significance of small household matrifocality and its role in the system of slavery.

Emancipation and Social Change

Slaves in Nepal were emancipated by governmental decree in 1926. Slaveholders were recompensed for the loss of their property and the Nyinba state that they received the full value at current market prices for each slave. The ex-slaves were thereafter free to choose their own mode of livelihood and were encouraged to reclaim wastelands and develop new landholdings in their own names. Within the Nyinba community, the freedmen pursued a number of options, some more successfully than others.

A certain amount of upheaval and social disorganisation followed upon emancipation. Many freedmen still resident in small households refused to fulfill their traditional service obligations. Masters reacted by evicting their freed slaves and withholding food from them. In the face of this, some of the younger freedmen left the region to seek work in the bazaars of southern Nepal or of India. A number returned after several years away with small stores of cash. It is impossible to offer a reliable estimate of the numbers of individuals who never returned, as their names appear to have been dropped from the genealogies of their surviving kin.

The freedmen who remained in the Nyinba community pursued various options. A number of them settled on and began cultivation of wastelands of doubtful quality on the periphery of their former villages. These freedmen built themselves homes and founded new hamlets affiliated with their ex-masters' village districts. Some have achieved a moderate standard of living, equal to that of citizens of median to lesser wealth. A more fortunate set of individuals managed to gain rights to the properties of citizens who lacked heirs to succeed them. They were aided in this by their wealthy and influential ex-masters. No doubt the latter hoped to secure a living for their former slaves, but they probably also expected that the newly wealthy freedmen would become their clients or followers in village political affairs. Another set of freedmen never truly severed their traditional ties to their former masters. Rather they remained as dependents, resident in small houses, fulfilling many traditional obligations. I will examine the situation of each of these groups in turn.

At the present time there are only twenty-seven extant freedman households. They form 12 per cent of the Nyinba population. Consequently, the following discussion will be based on data that derive from a very small sample of individuals.

Those freedmen who managed to fall heir to vacant properties formerly belonging to citizens are now the economic equals of the typical Nyinba citizen. They have substantial homes, more than adequate landholdings, cattle, sheep, and the like. Particularly noteworthy is their mode of domestic organisation. As the accompanying table shows, their marriages are almost as often polyandrous as they are monogamous.[10] All currently married individuals have chosen virilocal residence. Furthermore, the size and generational composition of their households is roughly equivalent to that of Nyinba citizens. It is important to note that these individuals gave up features of domestic organisation that were associated with slavery as soon as they could afford to do so. Thus the attainment of wealth facilitated this as well as other expressions of status equality.

A second type of contemporary freedman household consists of individuals who have established homes on lands that they themselves brought under cultivation. Some individuals have been more successful at this than others and these households vary with regard to the extent of their landholdings and their total wealth. The poorer households still rely

H

Table 1. *Marital Arrangements, Size and Composition of Citizen and Freedman Households in 1974*

Household and Marital Arrangement	Citizens	Freedmen Heirs to Citizen Households	Landholding Freedmen	Dependent Freedmen
Percent of Marital Unions[a]				
Polyandry[b]	51·1	43	25	0
Monogamy	42·2	57	75	100
Polygyny	6·7	0	0	0
Percent of Postmarital Residential Arrangements				
Virilocal	93	100	77·8	62·5
Uxorilocal	7	0	22·2	37·5
Average Household Size	7·40	8	4·50	3·63
Average Number of Generations Present	2·40	2·75	2·00	1·75
Total Households Surveyed	37	8	6	8

[a] This includes only present-day unions in which spouses of both sexes are present.
[b] Including marriages with several brothers and more than one wife.

on hiring out their labour services to supplement inadequate agricultural yields. Differences in wealth may account for variations in the type of household maintained. The majority of present-day marriages are monogamous, but a full quarter are polyandrous. More than three-fourths of presently married couples reside in the husband's home. Such households are considerably smaller than those of citizens and freedmen with hereditary landholdings, and have slightly lesser generational depth (see Table 1). Oral accounts suggest that such households differ substantially from those characteristic of times of servitude. I shall evaluate possible reasons for these changes below.

The final distinctive type of household includes freedmen still dependent on their former masters. These individuals live in the houses once occupied by their slave forbears, located near the big house to which they are affiliated. They perform agricultural and domestic labour, aid their former masters and present-day patrons in trading endeavours and the like. Nyinba point to these households as being virtually identical to the slave households of the past. However, they do differ slightly from the idealised picture of slave households as sketched above. Most of the married couples reside virilocally; only 37·5 per cent live uxorilocally—the pattern reported as prevalent during the time of servitude. All are monogamous and their households are considerably smaller than those of other freedmen and of citizens. It should be noted that the sex ratio in such households is 107, radically lower than the 146 of citizen landholders. The sex ratio of freedmen on formerly citizen properties is 117 and that of freedmen landholders is 100. The proportion of women in dependent freedmen households may be interpreted in light of the incidence of monogamy and the higher ratio of wives per household than typical of citizens. The relatively low sex ratio among freedmen landholders may be attributed to the large number of female children in two of the households. Of course all these data should be viewed with some caution as they are the product of a very small sample.

It may be assumed that once slaves came into property, especially inherited properties, they felt able to imitate the marital and domestic practices viewed as normative by the dominant society. Now the economic equals of their former masters, they may have wished to avoid all customs associated with their 'marginal' status in Nyinba society. In addition, they may have believed that patrifocal, polyandrous households were better suited to their new circumstances than any other form of household found within the Nyinba system. Polyandry is, as I have stated above, seen as a means of overriding divisiveness among brothers; virilocality is believed to please the gods. Whatever their reasons, once they had property of their own and self-determination, they chose to live as their former masters did. Independent landholders did not completely adopt citizen standards for marriage. They still follow, as alternatives, some of the practices associated with traditional slave households. However, it may be noted that all instances of voluntary uxorilocality were confined to members of parental and grandparental generations. It is likely that as they become more self-sufficient, small landholders will more closely follow the ways of the dominant society.

It is the landless freedmen exclusively who retain practices said to be characteristic of their slave past. This is not surprising inasmuch as their living conditions have not changed in significant respects. It seems that they also believe that their economic situation favours these over other arrangements. Small monogamous households are seen as most suitable to impoverished circumstances and also are favourable to the patron's labour needs.

The Decline of Dependent Relationships

One last issue remains to be discussed. Quite simply stated, this is the question of why so few citizens attempted to reinstitute service-for-support relationships with their former slaves. As noted above, the traditional relationships between masters and slaves were effectively terminated when the latter were evicted from their homes. Only a small number of former slaveholders either chose or were able to institute comparable relationships on a contractual basis with their freedmen. The fact that so few citizens appeared interested in continuing economic relationships with their former slaves raises important questions about their perception of the rationality of the slavery system.

Although most citizens no longer had access to the labour of their former slaves, they did not have to do without the use of outside labour. They had recourse to wage labour from a number of sources—low caste Nepali smiths resident in their own village-districts or from neighbouring Nepalese villages, landless Nepalese and former slaves settled on new lands but not yet financially solvent.[11] Both homes in which I lodged hired outside labourers. The household with eight members and one ailing woman annually hired a smith woman for the entire agricultural season. The household with ten members, including one adolescent and one adult woman, hired women from the neighbouring Nepalese villages on some of the busiest agricultural days of the year. However, they still lacked sufficient labour to cultivate their ample lands to full advantage and harvested barely enough to feed their children. The head of this household told me that he prefers not to hire labour for the entire season because of the expense involved and that he would rather have to make do with a smaller and less successful harvest. Other households are known to hire Nepalese men to help them with the seasonal sheep-herding.

Day wage labour is less expensive than seasonal labour. Day workers are paid only their meals and a few cups of grain. Seasonal labourers—who are usually landless—also expect a food allotment at the end of the harvest, an allotment large enough to tide them through the winter. It is undoubtedly less expensive to provide for one seasonal worker than it is to support an entire household of dependent freedmen. The prestige formerly accorded to slaveholders and today accorded to patrons of dependent freemen is partly based on this fact. Such citizens must be wealthy enough to support a dependent household and they are usually wealthy because of their ample landholdings. I do not know whether wage labour was readily available in the past. It is quite possible that until recently Nepalese villages were less densely populated and included fewer landless individuals.[12] Perhaps, with the increasing availability of wage labour, Nyinba citizens felt less of a need to hold on to their former slaves.

It is equally likely that the citizens had diminishing needs for a permanent source of outside labour at the time of emancipation. There is reason to suppose that in the past the Nyinba community was smaller than today. Each household may have held a slightly larger share of property and was thus more readily able to support slaves. In recent times, even with the slow rate of village growth,[13] the size of landholdings may have declined somewhat. In addition, agricultural yields were more readily supplemented with the proceeds of trade in the past. Recent political circumstances have irrevocably altered the salt-grain trade and seriously curtailed profits for middlemen like the Nyinba (cf. Fürer-Haimendorf 1974, 1975). These are merely suppositions but they are worthy of consideration.

If Nyinba citizens were hard-pressed to support their slaves, then it is quite understandable that they turned to other, cheaper forms of outside labour to replace them. The slaveholders probably derived definite benefits from their slaves in the form of a continually available labour force. They undoubtedly enjoyed being spared various unpleasant tasks and certainly valued the prestige associated with slaveholding. However, at the time of emancipation, control over a permanent labour force was overwhelmingly rejected. I have suggested various reasons, factors involving recent economic and demographic changes, to account for this. Perhaps the system changed for other reasons unknown to me. In any event, the system did change and with it those aspects of slave domestic organisation that seemed to serve the masters so well.

9

Transactions in People: The Chinese Market in Slaves, Servants, and Heirs

JAMES L. WATSON

Until the foundation of the People's Republic in 1949 China had one of the largest and most comprehensive markets for the exchange of human beings in the world. In many parts of China, notably in the south, nearly every peasant household was directly or indirectly affected by the sale of people. A unique feature of the Chinese market was its concentration on children, especially those under the age of ten. Adolescents and younger adults were sometimes bound over to a creditor for a limited time to pay off debts but, in most cases, these people were not exchanged or sold on a permanent basis. The only exceptions were found among the urban elite who bought and sold adult concubines almost as a form of sport. For ordinary peasants the market was directed exclusively at children—male and female—who were sold for cash and were rarely, if ever, returned to their birth parents. In keeping with the highly developed system of commerce and exchange that has characterised Chinese peasant society for over a thousand years, the sale of a child was legalised by a signed receipt that specified the rights of both buyer and seller down to the minutest detail.

Transactions in children were, in most cases, the consequence of extreme poverty, since by selling one child a parent might hope to feed the remaining family members. Male children thus sold had two main uses: first as designated heirs of the buyer, and second as domestic slaves for the owner's household. A purchased heir had most of the rights and privileges of a normal son (subject to the adopting father's pleasure); a slave had minimal rights—he was, in fact, a chattel whose descendants remained the hereditary property of the owner's family. Girls, on the other hand, could be used in several ways in the buyer's household and were not categorised, or 'typed', with the same rigidity as their male counterparts. It was not impossible for a girl to be purchased as a daughter in infancy, exploited like a slave during adolescence, and married to one of her buyer's own sons in adulthood.

The difference in treatment between male and female can be traced to their positions in the Chinese kinship system. The Chinese, especially the southern elite, are fiercely loyal to the patriline and allow very little flexibility for males (Baker 1968; Freedman 1958; Potter 1968; J. Watson 1975b). In contrast to many African patrilineal systems, membership in the Chinese lineage is only conferred at birth or by adoption during infancy (J. Watson 1975a). The role of women in the Chinese patrilineage is much more complicated (M. Wolf 1972). Recent research has shown that, contrary to earlier views, Chinese women are not members of first their fathers' and later their husbands' lineages—they stand outside the male-dominated patrilineage (R. Watson n.d.). This may explain why purchased women are treated with such flexibility: unlike males they do not, indeed could not, represent a threat to the patrilineal system. Women do not inherit and, hence, are not involved with the landed ancestral estates that form the material foci of Chinese lineages. Furthermore, women are not a matter of concern for any unit larger than the household, which means that they can be bought and sold at will. Male children, especially outsiders brought into the kin group, are watched with great care by everyone in the lineage. Innumerable rules, written and unwritten, have been devised to regulate the entry of male heirs into elite Chinese lineages (Liu 1959); in contrast, the few rules that relate to the purchase or sale of women are rarely observed. Thus, while girls are treated with a certain flexibility, a boy will enter his new life as a full heir or a chattel slave. There is no possibility of change in later life.

This essay focuses primarily on people who were purchased as domestic servants and were never accepted as designated heirs or adopted daughters. Formal adoption in China has already been discussed at length in the anthropological literature (see e.g., Freedman 1957; J. Watson 1975a; A. Wolf 1968, 1974). Chinese slavery as a general topic has also received a great deal of attention (e.g., Pulleyblank 1958; Wang 1953; Wilbur 1943); however, with few exceptions, these studies are more concerned with Sinological issues than with the sociology of slavery. The Chinese language materials relevant to this topic are, almost exclusively, products of the Marxist pursuit of an orthodox 'slavery stage' in China's ancient history (e.g., Hsü 1964; Shih 1973). The present study is based on two periods of field research,[1] totalling 29 months, undertaken in Hong Kong's New Territories—a 365-square-mile section of rural China controlled by the British since 1898. Although the colony of Hong Kong is renowned for its cosmopolitan urban centres, significant elements of the traditional peasant culture still survive in the rural hinterland. The New Territories is best known to anthropologists as the home of five major lineages (Baker 1966) which, even today, control the best lands and maintain themselves as elite organisations.

Until the 1920s, these elite lineages harboured a class of hereditary (male) slaves who were purchased as children and raised to be domestic servants. They were owned by wealthy families and their offspring became the inheritable property of the original master's patriline. The same families also bought young girls who served as domestic labourers until their late teens, at which time they were either married out or sold as concubines to another household. This essay is specifically concerned with the purchase and sale of domestic servants in two elite lineages, the *Man* and the *Tang*, settled respectively in the villages of San Tin and Ha Tsuen (populations 4,000 and 2,500). The people of these communities are Cantonese-speaking peasants who have lived in the same localities for nearly 400 years. San Tin and Ha Tsuen are known technically as single-lineage villages because, except for the hereditary slaves and a handful of shopkeepers, every resident male is a direct descendant of the founding ancestor (and, hence, bears the ancestral surname *Man* or *Tang*). Surname exogamy is strictly enforced in this part of China which means that all wives must be brought in from other lineages.

The *Man* and the *Tang* are representative of the rural elite that controlled much of South China prior to the communist land-reform campaigns in the early 1950s. They owned the best agricultural lands, monopolised market-town commerce, and educated enough of their sons to protect themselves from the Imperial bureaucracy. Not everyone in South China was a member of an elite lineage, of course; in the Hong Kong region approximately 40 per cent of the peasantry could claim this status.[2] The remaining 60 per cent had to reach some kind of accommodation with the nearest elite lineage. Most people in the non-elite category lived in satellite villages in the hinterland of the dominant lineages, or as hereditary tenants on lands controlled by the elite (J. Watson 1977). The people of satellite villages are generally 'newcomers' of mixed surname who arrived in the Hong Kong region 200 or 300 years ago, after the *Man* and *Tang*. With few exceptions the domestic servants, male and female, discussed in this essay were found in the villages of the elite. They were symbols of high status which, along with ostentatious dwellings and Imperial degrees, distinguished the regional elite from the common peasantry.

Market Factors: Rights-in-Persons

Before considering the role of slavery in these elite communities I would like to turn to a problem that has wider implications: the market in human beings. Slavery of the type discussed here is best understood in relation to the Chinese peasant's conception of rights in people. Kopytoff and Miers have argued that in parts of Africa the individual constitutes a part of lineage wealth and, as such, can be sold to pay off collective debts. They make a useful and fundamental distinction between the principles of 'belonging to'

and 'belonging in' a kin group (1977:7–11). Briefly summarised, Kopytoff and Miers maintain that lineage members
are both the owners of corporate property (i.e., people) and,
at the same time, part of the group's property—they 'belong
in' the lineage as owners and 'belong to' the lineage as
possessions. This analysis derives from a long history of anthropological writings on 'rights-in-persons' (see e.g., Radcliffe-
Brown 1952:36–48).

In contrast to many Africans, the Chinese draw clear lines
on the basis of sex: all Chinese females 'belong to' the household unit regardless of their status, while males, among the
elite at least, 'belong in' the lineage and, hence, are less likely
to be sold. I intend to show that Chinese women 'belong to'
the males who acquire them through payment of a brideprice or a sale price. Women are, in many ways, treated as the
'property' of the male-dominated household; and, as they do
not have rights of inheritance, they do not 'belong in' the
household or the lineage. For men the picture is far more
complex. Men who are fortunate enough to have been born
into an elite lineage 'belong in' the corporate group. The
Cantonese believe that men thus born are sacrosanct because
they 'belong to' the ancestors; they cannot be sold, even by a
destitute father. Males who are not members of an elite
lineage do not have this protective right of 'belonging in' and
are thereby more subject to sale. These distinctions, admit-
tedly rather abstract, will be clarified in the following para-
graphs.

The sexual difference in 'rights-in-persons' might be traced
to the salience of the patrilineal principle in South China.
Wives and mothers, as outsiders (*ngoi loih yahn*, a Cantonese
term[3] meaning 'those who come from outside'), are never
completely trusted even though they may be respected and
loved by their husbands or sons. Daughters are conceived of
as 'excess baggage' that will marry out eventually and, thus,
their existence is not even noted in the elaborate written
genealogies kept by the larger lineages. It is not a coincidence
that daughters are referred to as 'your precious gold' (*chin
gam*, literally 'thousand gold') in polite conversation; at marriage they are exchanged for an impressive brideprice (see

below) that, in the local view, helps compensate the household for the costs of raising them. Another factor to consider
when discussing the position of women is the high rate of
polygyny among the peasants of South China. In Ha Tsuen
the rate for ordinary farmers was over thirty per cent, meaning that one third of all married men during the past three
generations had two or more wives (R. Watson n.d.). This
figure does not even include the wealthier landlord and merchant families, among whom the rate is much higher. At the
turn of the century it was not uncommon for wealthy men in
San Tin to have four or five wives. The major wife, *daai pou*
('big wife'), had more rights than secondary wives (*sai pou*,
'little wife') primarily because the latter did not go through
the full cycle of expensive and complicated wedding rituals.
During times of extreme crisis, such as famine or flood,
secondary wives and younger daughters were the first to be
sold. Villagers date the downfall of once prominent families,
usually as a consequence of the male head's addiction to
opium, by calculating when the first daughter or secondary
wife disappeared.

Males, on the other hand, were not sold to outsiders—at
least in the elite lineages of South China. I was unable to
discover a single case, or even a rumour, of a family selling a
male child in Ha Tsuen or San Tin—even though I pushed
this line of enquiry over two and a half years of research.
It is possible that a few cases have eluded me but I remain
convinced that elite lineages managed to keep their male
children within the group. In contrast, the non-elite do not
even make a pretence of denying that they were involved
in the sale of male children. I met several elderly women in
satellite villages who admitted, in a flood of tears, that their
husbands had sold one or more of their sons during bad
harvest years. Returning to the distinction raised by Kopytoff
and Miers, in South China the male privilege of 'belonging in'
a lineage, and therefore enjoying relative immunity from
sale, was only a reality among the elite. Women in both elite
and non-elite communities 'belonged to' the domestic unit
and were always subject to sale.

Residents of satellite villages bought only a small fraction of the children offered on the open market; their local economies could not support the extra people. Members of the regional elite, on the other hand, actively bought and sold children according to the needs of their domestic units. The wealthiest men never had to sell their own offspring but they could take on as many extra persons (male slaves, maid servants, secondary wives) as they were able to support—the excess might be sold if the family fortunes took a bad turn. Even a male heir, purchased expressly to carry on a man's line, could be resold or expelled from the household if the buyer later produced his own son. 'Bought sons' (*mai jai*), as they are known colloquially, have no rights of appeal to any higher authority because they 'belong to' the household, they do not 'belong in' the lineage as do all male infants fathered by members in good standing.

Ultimately it is the father who claims the right of lineage membership for his legitimate sons. He does this by presenting the newborn child (*san ding*, lit. 'new male') at a legitimation ritual held in his ancestral hall during the Lunar New Year festival. Every legitimate son is represented by a small lamp placed on the main altar and, in some lineages, the particulars of birth are recorded in a special 'New Male Book', kept to forestall disputes over rights in the ancestral estates. Bought sons are not presented at this ritual; instead the adopting father must go through a separate, and very expensive, recognition banquet during which he is publicly humiliated for defiling the ancestral line. The father who chooses to bring in an outsider as heir must also bribe the elders (males aged 61 and over) to sign an 'adoption banner' which certifies that the new son is accepted as a member of the lineage with rights to inherit his father's share of the ancestral property. However, a 'bought son' can be expelled from the lineage and the household at any time if the adopting father becomes dissatisfied—all he need do is state publicly that he is looking for another son. Legitimate sons might be excluded from the family and even disinherited from the household estate (although this is rare) but their membership in the lineage, and by implication their rights to the ancestral estates, is not subject to their fathers' personal whims. Formal expulsion from the lineage (*chut jok*, lit. 'out of lineage') is a very grave matter and it can only be enacted by a council of elders, usually for flagrant cases of incest.

By their actions, therefore, Chinese villagers make it clear that a legitimate son 'belongs in' the lineage while a bought son is in the precarious position of 'belonging to' the household. This also helps explain why some Chinese peasants readily sell infant sons and others do not. Poverty alone is not the answer; there have always been a handful of destitute families in the *Man* and the *Tang* lineages. Elite lineages do not allow the sale of their legitimate sons to outsiders, no matter how extreme the circumstances might be in individual households. To flout this rule and proceed with such a sale is, in fact, grounds for the formal expulsion of the offending father from the lineage. Adoption within the lineage, known as *gwo gai* (lit. 'to cross and continue', as in a line of descent), is encouraged when a family is too poor to support all of its sons and cash may even exchange hands. But the children thus affected are not called 'bought sons'; they already have full membership in the lineage by virtue of their birth.

In non-elite communities, notably the satellite villages, the lineage may exist, literally, in name only (i.e., as a surname group with little cohesion). The patrilineages in these settlements seldom own property of any significance and they rarely have an ancestral hall in which to place soul tablets or hold rituals. Here the lineage asserts no authority at all. The household is the final, and only, unit of decision making. Under these circumstances there is nothing, not even a myth of superior origin, to prevent a greedy or desperate man from selling his sons on the open market. Inevitably it is the wealthier families of the larger lineages that take on these excess people as heirs or domestic slaves. I am convinced that the gradual transfer of children, male and female, from satellite villages to dominant communities such as San Tin and Ha Tsuen helped sustain the population, and hence the power and prestige, of the regions elite lineages. The implications of this will be explored elsewhere, but it may be of interest to note that the populations of satellite villages surrounding Ha Tsuen and San Tin (over twenty small villages) have, until recently, remained more or less steady—averaging 100 to 200 people—for the past two centuries. The *Man* and the *Tang* lineages have tripled and quadrupled their populations over the same period. Migration and high infant mortality are two primary reasons for the low rate of growth in these satellite villages but the sale of children was no doubt a significant contributing factor as well.

As we are dealing with an androcentric society this discussion, until now, has focussed almost exclusively on the position of males. Women, as outsiders, have no rights of inheritance within the family and they have nothing at all to do with the lineage. Although the subject is far too complicated to cover in any detail here, the high brideprices common in the Hong Kong region, equivalent to two or three years' average income for a factory worker, are the primary means by which males acquire rights over their major wives. Even though Chinese peasants sometimes speak, in jest, of 'buying a daughter-in-law' with the brideprice (*laih gam*, 'wedding gold'), the verbal clues in this case are misleading. In fact, a system of indirect dowry (*gaa jong*, 'marriage adornments'), is practised in most parts of South China; the bride's family ordinarily takes most of the brideprice payment (made in cash) and buys gold jewellery as a dowry for their daughter. Unlike the East African pattern, however, the Chinese brideprice is paid as a lump sum prior to marriage thereby eliminating any ambiguity about the status of the bride: her husband has exclusive rights to her reproductive capabilities and the new household has absolute control over her labour power.

Although there are no formal mechanisms to stop a husband, or father-in-law, from selling a major wife, this is very rare. It only occurred among the most destitute people on the very margin of survival. Secondary wives (*sai pou* 'little wife') are another matter altogether. Ordinarily they are purchased outright from the woman's parents for a modest payment and, in direct contrast to major wives, they are not sent with a dowry. The Cantonese villagers are clear about the status of secondary wives: they are 'bought in' (*mai laih*) not 'brought in' (*cho laih*) like major wives. It is not surprising that secondary wives readily exchanged hands among the wealthy prior to the legal ban on such actions. In San Tin, for instance, a merchant who could not produce an heir with his major wife bought, and then sold, a succession of secondary wives until he finally gave up in old age and acquired a son from an outsider. The fifth and last of these wives was kept in the household to raise the child; she herself was purchased at age 14 from a brothel in Canton (she is still alive at this writing, a sprightly 96 year old). Other categories of 'bought' women will be discussed later in this paper. The essential feature that distinguishes them all from the major wife, 'the tiger of the household', is the absence of a respectable dowry at the time of acquisition. All women 'belong to' the male-dominated household and were therefore subject to sale in times of crisis—but some were more secure than others.

The Market: Buyers, Sellers, and Intermediaries

Prior to the communist victory, the point at which the market in people effectively ended, there were two major sources of saleable children in South China: destitute parents and professional kidnappers. Most children entered the market as a consequence of domestic crises. In the New Territories opium addiction on the part of the father seems to have been a primary cause of family collapse (daughters were sold first, then land, and finally sons). Widows left with young children were another reliable source, especially in non-elite communities where the lineage did not intercede. Except among opium addicts, the decision to sell was not taken lightly. The case cited earlier of an old woman bursting into tears at the mention of the subject is not unusual; the sale of children is an extremely sensitive issue in the communities I have studied. The guilt and remorse felt by the sellers, notably by mothers, is made all the worse by the callousness of village gossip. Cantonese women are fascinated, one might say possessed, by the topic; they never seem to tire of discussing the marriages of local servant girls and the circumstances under which 'bought sons' were acquired.

Kidnapping was no mere sideline for the bandits that plagued South China during the nineteenth and early twentieth centuries, it was their primary *modus operandi*. The sons of the rich were the main targets of the kidnappers since they could be ransomed for huge sums. Ha Tsuen's wealthiest landlord had to pay an undisclosed amount, rumoured to be in excess of ten thousand silver dollars, in the 1920s for his son who had been taken in a bandit raid. The same gangs occasionally kidnapped the infant sons of ordinary peasants in the absence of anything else worth taking. It is significant that bandits always took male children. I have not discovered a single instance of a girl disappearing in this manner. The reason, of course, is that wealthy fathers were unlikely to pay lavish ransoms for their 'excess baggage'. The genealogies of many elite lineages carry a record of kidnapped sons in case they should return and claim their shares in the ancestral estates. This happened among the *Tang* when, in the 1680s, a local boy was captured by bandits and sold as a domestic slave to a merchant. He was traced ten years later and restored to his rightful position in the lineage. An elder brother accomplished this feat by bribing a former gang member and reimbursing the merchant for his expenses (Tang Genealogy n.d.).

Whatever the means by which children entered the market, they were usually sold to an intermediary first. Parents or kidnappers rarely carried out the final transaction themselves, largely because the buyers preferred to have some margin of protection for such a sensitive undertaking. People acquiring a male heir were particularly anxious that the birth parents would never be able to trace the boy at a later date. (In the case cited above, it is doubtful that the kidnapped *Tang* boy would ever have been found if the merchant had acquired him as an heir.) Transactions in girls are less sensitive because there is little at stake; neighbours usually know the origin of most 'bought' women in the village.

Except for a few who serviced the wealthy comprador class

in urban Hong Kong (see Jaschok n.d.), intermediaries were not full-time specialists. The people of San Tin relied on a rice merchant in the nearby market town of Sham Chun. This man was renowned for his honesty, so the village elders claim, and would always back up his transactions with an offer of repayment in kind (i.e., with another child of 'equal quality') or in cash. The merchant was used only for the acquisition of heirs and male slaves. Other intermediaries, notably old women who also acted as marriage matchmakers, handled the traffic in maid servants and adopted daughters. Intermediaries arranged for the delivery and subsequent pick up of the child on an appointed day, in such a manner that the buyer and seller did not meet. The 'market' in children, therefore, was hidden from public view; it consisted of secretive transactions carried out in the shops and teahouses of the larger market towns.

Buyers of children, especially those from elite lineages, demanded signed receipts that absolved them of any responsibility to the sellers. Ordinarily these receipts were what the Chinese referred to as 'white contracts', used for common sales of goods and services. 'Red contracts', used for transactions in land, carried more weight in court but they required the seal of an Imperial Magistrate and were therefore too expensive for the simple exchange of a child (Meijer 1979). In Ha Tsuen the white receipts were called *mai san kai*, which means 'buy body bill'. Model contracts could be copied from household almanacs or handbooks, the most popular being one called *The Complete Set of Domestic Rites* (see Loseby 1936:51–2). The following example (taken from Woods 1937:134) is representative of the contracts used for the purchase of males in the Hong Kong region:

An Absolute Bill of Sale for a Boy Made by x x x, A Native of x x Village: Whereas, on account of daily maintenance being difficult to obtain, I and my spouse agree to sell our own son, aged 8 years, born in [astrological computations follow]. I at first offered him to my relatives but they did not accept. Through the intervention of Lo Shap-yeung, acting as intermediary, a stranger [of another surname] agreed to buy my son and in the presence of the intermediary I was paid the sum of x x taels of silver and a bill of sale was immediately handed over to the buyer. The boy has not been kidnapped or anything of the kind. Should anything be found wrong with him the buyer will not be responsible. The seller and the intermediary will clear up the difficulties. The buyer is at liberty to take the boy home and change his surname, and to rear him for posterity. If accidents befall him hereafter these will be regarded as the will of heaven and no questions will be raised about the boy. To prevent any misunderstandings which might hereafter arise from an oral agreement this bill of sale is made out in writing and handed to the buyer to be retained by him as proof hereof. Signed, in the presence of the intermediary, x x x, May 20th, 1879. [Note: This original translation from the Chinese has been edited by J.L.W.]

Like any other market, the exchange of children in China was subject to fluctuations of supply and demand. Males were always in more demand than females and, hence, were four or five times more expensive. Male slaves, as I have argued elsewhere (J. Watson 1976), were luxuries supported primarily by the rich. Male heirs, on the other hand, were necessities and every man who considered himself even moderately respectable had to have at least one. The high demand for male children in the market might be explained in part by the surprisingly high frequency of heirlessness (defined here as failure to produce sons as indicated by the termination of a line) in elite lineages. For instance, an analysis of the *Man* genealogy shows that 14·5 per cent (N237) out of a total of 1,627 males, over a period of twenty generations, remained heirless (Man Genealogy n.d.). The full count should actually be slightly higher because the genealogy does not distinguish those men who purchased an heir from an outsider. During normal times, therefore, male children were always in demand and, since boys were invariably the last to be sold, they were also in short supply. The problem here is the concept of 'normal times'. If the official history of the New Territories region (prepared by Chinese authorities before the British took control) is to be trusted, famine and bad harvests occurred so often in this part of China that one wonders what 'normal' could possibly have meant (see

Gazetteer 1819). During periods of crisis the market in children was glutted as peasant households struggled for survival.[4] In 1648, four years after the Manchus founded their new dynasty, the area including San Tin and Ha Tsuen suffered a drought so terrible that many people ate corpses and sold their sons for 10 catties (13 pounds) of rice (Gazeteer 1819:365). As late as 1920 a bad harvest in one part of the New Territories caused nearly a thousand infants, mostly girls, to be abandoned. Conditions were so bad that girls were sold for 20 cents, enough to buy a few catties of rice (Blake 1975:39–40). In good years a girl exchanged hands in urban Hong Kong for as much as $65 (1887), although $36–$40 (1879–80) seems to have been more common in the late nineteenth century (Russell 1887:47; Woods 1937:127–9).[5] Wealthy people in San Tin paid up to $200 for 'healthy and whole' male children during the same period.

Male Slavery

Most of the male children who passed through the market described above ended up as designated heirs in the homes of their purchasers. Only the wealthiest families in the region, usually merchants and landlords, could afford to buy adolescent boys and keep them as household servants. The men thus acquired were called *sai man* (Mandarin *hsi min*), a term that means 'little people' or 'minor people' (Baker 1968:155) and is used to distinguish male slaves from other categories of purchased people. In some parts of the New Territories these slaves are also called *ha fu*, a Cantonese term which is difficult to translate but means roughly 'low folk' (Potter 1968:20). Both *ha fu* and *sai man* are highly derogatory terms and are occasionally used as expressions of abuse.

The status of *sai man* was inherited through the male line such that the sons became the property of their father's master. At the death of a master his slaves were divided among the surviving heirs like any other form of property. *Sai man* could not be adopted as the designated heirs of their masters and the members of elite lineages would never permit their daughters to marry a *sai man* under any circumstances. The daughters of slaves were also treated as chattels but they had a better chance to break out of the cycle of servitude than their male siblings. Most of these girls were sold on the open market as domestic servants or were married out as soon as they reached puberty. The category *sai man* is male specific; it is not used for the wives or daughters of slaves. *Sai man* marriages were arranged by the owners, usually as a reward for hard-working or loyal slaves. The wives were either the disabled or retarded castoffs of non-lineage neighbours or the unlucky daughters of other *sai man* purchased specifically for this purpose.

Most of my informants were careful to point out that these unions were not 'marriages' in the usual sense. Unlike ordinary people, slave couples were not bound by a formal ceremony or even a banquet—they simply lived together in a hut provided by the master. The usual practice of surname exogamy was sometimes ignored for slave unions, thereby forcing the couple to live in a state of incest as far as members of the dominant society were concerned. One resident of San Tin pointed out, however, that slaves did not have 'real' surname groups anyway; the original owners gave their *sai man* surnames 'just to tell them apart, slaves had no ancestors'. In the Cantonese view only the uncivilised do not have ancestors, namely barbarians, animals, and slaves.

The duties of *sai man* varied according to the needs of their masters. Yet, in every case I have encountered,[6] the slave's primary role was that of domestic servant in the master's household. *Sai man* were assigned the most difficult and demeaning chores, such as carrying water, gathering cooking fuel, and discarding night soil. In the wealthiest households they served as sedan chair bearers and cord pullers for overhead fans (like Indian *punkah wallahs*). People in Ha Tsuen still reminisce about two old *sai man* who made the rounds of local wine shops and teahouses every evening to carry their drunken master home. A few slaves were lucky enough to be assigned in their youth as study companions for the masters' sons who were preparing for the Imperial examinations (see also Baker 1968:155). The companion's duties included grinding ink, carrying books, cutting paper, and—in one case —serving as whipping boy when the owner's son refused to study. One such companion in Ha Tsuen learned enough on the side to become a trusted accountant-manager with authority over other slaves in the master's household. However, this was an unusual case; most *sai man* spent their entire lives doing menial odd jobs under the direction of the owner's major wife.

All slaves, including the study companions, were restricted to inferior houses clustered near the edge of the village (Potter 1968:20). These dwellings are called *uk jai* ('little houses' or 'huts') and, with their mud brick construction, are easily distinguished from the larger, more elaborate stone houses of ordinary peasants. *Sai man* were not allowed to eat or sleep in the master household. It is clear from my discussions with former owners and their sons that the Cantonese treated their *sai man* as permanently polluting pariahs. It is significant that male slaves often prepared raw foods for the kitchen but they did not cook or serve the finished meals.[7] Female servants, on the other hand, were regularly used as cooks and table maids. Women acquired as domestics also ate and slept in the master household; they were not relegated to the 'little houses' unless, or until, they became *sai man* wives—at which point they ceased cooking for the master and his family.

Although *sai man* were given *de facto* tenancy rights over their 'little houses' as long as they lived, they had no rights of ownership (over people or goods) within the community. Many slaves were granted the use of small vegetable plots but even in these cases they were not expected to be self-sufficient. The bulk of their food, clothing, and bedding came from the master household. Owners were also responsible for the medical and funeral[8] expenses of their *sai man*. In a purely economic sense, therefore, everyone stressed that *sai man* constituted a net loss for the master household. *Sai man* did not generate any surplus; they consumed it. Yet, it cannot be denied that *sai man* worked and thus freed members of the household to engage in other activities. But this is not, in the local view, a very efficient use of resources. All informants maintained that it would have been much cheaper, in the long run, to utilise female servants or to take in more secondary wives for the household head or his sons.

An interesting, perhaps unique, feature of *sai man* slavery is that it did not develop beyond the domestic realm into the areas of agricultural production or manufacturing. Male slaves were, above all else, expensive status symbols that helped distinguish the elite from the ordinary peasantry. The acquisition of hereditary servants was conceived of by their owners in the same context as investments in Imperial titles, stately homes, and ostentatious public rituals. Villagers in the New Territories are conscious, even today, that slave ownership was once equated with gentry status. If an outsider asks 'Did your village have *sai man*?', the answer is invariably phrased in terms of wealth: 'Yes, we had many rich and famous families here', or 'No, we were too poor for such luxuries'. The fact that *sai man* consumed more than they produced does not, in itself, make this form of slavery unique. Finley (1959) and Hopkins (1967) demonstrate that slaves in the ancient world were not all 'instruments of production' in the strict sense. Furthermore, there are many examples in the African literature of domestic slaves who were primarily status symbols. The critical difference, however, is that the African (and the ancient) systems of servitude were more diversified. Wherever 'luxury slavery' appeared it was usually related to broader patterns of exploitation in which slaves also served as primary producers and, in some cases, as administrators or warriors (e.g., Smith 1960). The Chinese pattern outlined here is different in that it was not an outgrowth of, or a secondary development from, other forms of 'productive slavery' in the same society.

Sai Man and the Definition of 'Slavery'

Throughout this paper I have used the term 'slavery' in the context of *sai man* servitude. Previous commentators have defined *sai man* as 'hereditary servants' (Baker 1968:115), 'servile families' (Freedman 1966:9, following Chen 1936:7), and 'subordinate, lower-class client groups' (Potter 1968:20).

In principle there is nothing wrong with these definitions but they do make the task of comparison rather difficult.

Referring to the defining criteria outlined in the Introduction to this volume, I would argue that the *sai man* were clearly and unambiguously 'slaves'. *Sai man* were owned as chattels by specific masters and their labour power was extracted by coercion (i.e., unlike clients they were not paid for their services). They were definitely of a lower hereditary status than ordinary 'free' peasants, both socially and politically. In addition, *sai man* marriages were never given legal recognition and the owners would never grant their slaves the status of kinsmen, even in a symbolic sense. Leach has proposed that it is this absence of kinship between master and dependent that distinguishes chattel slavery from other forms of servitude (1967:23). From a comparative point of view, therefore, it is not an exaggeration to argue that *sai man* slavery is more rigid than the slave systems found in parts of Africa where absorption into the masters' kin group was often the rule (see e.g., Kopytoff and Miers 1977:61–67).

Female Servitude: Adoption, Marriage or Slavery?

Until the communists put an end to it in the late 1940s the Chinese market in people included several categories of women: maid servants, infant daughters-in-law, secondary wives, concubines, and prostitutes. Many girls were purchased by brothel keepers, usually former prostitutes themselves, and trained in the Chinese arts of pleasure (Keswick 1879). The lucky ones were bought by rich patrons and installed as private concubines; in rare cases, a brothel girl might be acquired as a secondary wife. The distinction between concubine (*jip sih*, lit. 'handmaiden in waiting') and secondary wife (*sai pou*, 'little' or 'minor wife') is fuzzy, especially since villagers tend to use the terms to deprecate each other (the secondary wife of one's antagonist is always a *jip sih* no matter what others may call her). As a general rule, however, a secondary wife is acquired to produce sons for the patriline and a concubine is kept for personal pleasure (R. Watson n.d.); it is always up to the father to claim legitimacy for his sons in any case. Women in either category are usually 'bought' (*mai jo la*) and, as such, they are clearly distinguished from the major wife of the household. Earlier I argued that the major wife (*daai pou*, 'big wife') is the only woman in the Chinese family system acquired through a more or less balanced exchange of marriage payments. A brideprice, or purchase price, is paid out for all 'bought' women but this is never matched by a dowry of equal value.

When Chinese discuss the problem of female servitude they usually refer to girls who worked as unpaid domestics in the houses of the wealthy. These children are called *mui jai*, a Cantonese term that literally means 'little younger-sister' but is perhaps best translated as 'maid servant'. Earlier observers (e.g., Loseby 1936; Woods 1937) believed that the Cantonese deliberately used the kinship term *mui* with the diminutive *jai* to confuse outsiders and to cover up an insidious form of slavery. These well-meaning Europeans did not realise that, in the original Cantonese, there is no ambiguity whatsoever in the use of *mui* to designate 'younger sister' in one context and 'maid servant' in another. Both terms are based on the same Chinese ideograph (hence the source of confusion), but in colloquial speech 'younger sister' *mui* is pronounced with a rising tone while 'maid servant' *mui* is distinguished by a high steady tone. The Cantonese never confuse these terms and are extremely careful when using them because a mispronunciation inevitably causes offence.

Mui jai servants were usually purchased when they were just old enough to begin work, thus avoiding the expense and trouble of infant care. In some cases *mui jai* were brought along by wealthy brides (major wives) as part of their dowry. The girls then served as personal body servants of their mistress but the groom's household assumed the burden of support. During the first decade of this century a particularly wealthy woman married into San Tin with two *mui jai* and a young *sai man*. People in the New Territories make a direct connection between *mui jai* and women with bound feet who, because of their stylishly deformed feet (see Levy 1967), are not expected to do domestic labour. Wherever one finds bound feet in South China, a mark of high status, *mui jai* are almost certain to be present as well.

Mui jai were usually married out of their owner's household soon after they reached puberty. In the New Territories they were often sent with a token dowry and were exchanged for a minimal brideprice. Their husbands were invariably of low status but a 'respectable' *mui jai* (i.e., one from an elite household that worried about its reputation) would never be married to a *sai man* slave. There was thus a steady demand for new *mui jai* in wealthy households to replace older maids who had married out. A wealthy woman in San Tin was served by four *mui jai* in succession until it became too difficult to buy new ones in the mid-1950s. *Mui jai* played a particularly interesting role in the marriage customs of Shun Dak, a district made famous by its independent women. Here 'marriage resisters', as they were called, purchased *mui jai* and gave them to their husbands as replacement wives (Topley 1975:82).

Prior to the communist revolution the plight of China's *mui jai* attracted a great deal of attention in European anti-slavery circles (see e.g., Russell 1887, Woods 1937). Yet the many forms of male servitude in China (slavery, debt bondage, hereditary tenancy, etc.) remained almost unknown to the outside world. The reason, of course, is that male servitude was largely confined to the rural areas and was never a significant feature of the urban scene, unlike the *mui jai* system that thrived in Chinese cities. It is also relevant that Chinese merchants took their *mui jai* with them to many parts of the world, notably the European colonies in Southeast Asia. The girls were later imported direct from South China which led to many abuses and a highly visible traffic in human beings (Lasker 1950:53). The British tried to control *mui jai* exploitation in the colonies of Hong Kong and Malaya but they had little success (Purcell 1967:182–83). Female servitude was so well established in the European-controlled treaty ports along the South China coast that foreign merchants, including Indians and Europeans, sometimes bought Chinese *mui jai* for their own households (Mai 1933:323).

Until now I have deliberately avoided using the term 'slave' in the context of female servitude because there was considerable variation in the relationship between 'bought women' and their owners. The fact that they were bought and sold like chattels is not enough, in my view, to categorise these women as slaves (see Introduction to this volume). The *mui jai* are the most difficult to deal with because they were treated much like *sai man* slaves and, yet, a high percentage were allowed to marry out and establish their own families (cynics might argue that, upon marriage, a *mui jai* simply exchanged one form of domestic servitude for another). However, as noted earlier, the critical feature that distinguishes slavery from other categories of servitude in Chinese society is the presence or absence of a kinship link between master and 'bought' dependent. Among the elite of the New Territories *mui jai* were given some of the privileges that a daughter might enjoy, especially as she approached the age of marriage. After marriage a *mui jai* retained ritual ties to her owner's household and, upon the death of her former master or mistress, she is expected to mourn them as her own parents. *Mui jai* are never allowed to forget that they have the status of second-class daughters (ritually reinforced in a hundred different ways) but they are daughters nonetheless. This seems to have been true for *mui jai* in many other parts of the Chinese world as well. Freedman maintained that the *mui jai* of Singapore were 'unpaid skivvies' but not slaves: 'It is not an exaggeration to call the *mui tsai* [*jai*] system a form of female adoption, for, however lowly their status, the girls were allotted a kinship position as daughters or sisters' (Freedman 1957:65).

In some Chinese communities it is clear that maid servants did not fare as well as the New Territories *mui jai*. Arthur Wolf found that many women in Northern Taiwan 'were slaves and were treated like property'; they were not adopted into their masters' families and they did not have the right to marry (1974:147). Citing evidence gathered by E. Ahern, Wolf adds that these Taiwanese women spent their lives as 'servant-slaves' who were 'taken out through the back door and buried like dogs' (i.e., without funerals) when they died

(1974:147). It appears, therefore, that there were many varieties of female servitude in traditional Chinese society. All 'bought women', including *mui jai*, were acquired as chattels without their consent but they were not all slaves.

Closely related to *mui jai* is another category of women purchased in their infancy as future brides of their buyers' sons. In colloquial Cantonese these women are called *san pou jai* ('little daughter-in-law') or *tung yeung sik* ('child nourished bride'); the term *mui jai* is reserved for girls who will eventually marry out. Arthur Wolf has explored this form of marriage in great detail and has found it to be very common on Taiwan (1968, 1974; Wolf and Huang n.d.). The Taiwanese make a clear distinction between the 'servant-slaves' mentioned above, called *ca bo kan* in Hokkien, and *sim pua*, the Hokkien version of little daughter-in-law (A. Wolf 1975:93–99). Child brides were usually brought in during their first year of life and raised as siblings along with their future grooms, but they are not actually married until puberty. In the Hong Kong region these girls are purchased like *mui jai* or *sai man*; they are not acquired through an exchange of daughters between families as often happened on Taiwan. Largely for reasons of status, this type of marriage is rarely found in elite lineages of the New Territories (R. Watson n.d.) but it is more prevalent in the satellite villages nearby. The *Man* and the *Tang* disapprove of these unions because, as one elder put it: 'How can a little daughter-in-law (*san pou jai*) be a proper major wife (*daai pou*) if you buy her like a piglet in the market?'

The infant brides are purchased outright for a small sum that goes to the birth parents, through an intermediary. They arrive at their new homes in tiny red dresses (the customary bridal colour), without a dowry of any kind. Informants claim that this is the surest, and cheapest, way to provide for the marriage of their sons because it avoids the crippling expenses of finding a wife later in life. However, the position of a little daughter-in-law is no more secure than that of a *mui jai*. If for any reason the marriage does not materialise the girl can be resold or exchanged in the nearest market town. In contemporary Hong Kong the stigma attaching to adult women who were married in this manner is at least as great, if not greater, than that suffered by former *mui jai*.

The Legacy of Slavery

Chattel slavery was formally abolished in China during the last decade of Manchu rule (1644–1911) but, like most legal reforms emanating from Peking, this had little effect on ordinary people in the countryside (Meijer 1979; van der Sprenkel 1962:27). The market in children had always been hidden from official view and the new laws only forced the intermediaries to be more secretive. Transactions of the kind described in this paper continued in most parts of China until the communists assumed power in 1949. The sale of girls as domestic servants was eradicated in Hong Kong (and in most Overseas Chinese areas) by the mid-1950s, but a small underground market in male heirs remains. There is evidence that infants are still exchanged for cash on rare occasions in contemporary Hong Kong, even though this is strictly illegal (personal observation and Jaschok n.d.).

The manumission of *sai man* slaves was not an organised political movement of any kind and was not a consequence of pressure from the anti-slavery groups that helped bring an end to *mui jai* servitude in European colonies. In fact, Hong Kong's colonial officials were not even aware that male slavery existed in the New Territories until long after the *sai man* had already been 'liberated' by their owners (Baker 1966:45n). In most parts of South China *sai man* began drifting away from their masters' villages during the first two decades of this century. At that time the Chinese countryside was plagued by social disorder and economic depression; not surprisingly the support of unproductive servants became a burden few households could afford. In San Tin owners simply stopped feeding their *sai man* and told them to make their own way in the world. I have discovered a few cases in the New Territories of *sai man* who remained attached to their former masters into the 1950s, largely because they had no place to go. Potter reports that nineteen households of former *sai man* stayed in the lineage village of Ping Shan; but these families had all stopped working for their original owners and had found other employment (1968:21, 98). Ping Shan is unusual in this regard, however. San Tin had only one family of ex-*sai man* left by the 1970s, while Ha Tsuen and Sheung Shui, the village studied by Baker (1968), had none.

Although the majority of *sai man* moved out of their masters' villages they did not go far. Baker discovered that one group of Sheung Shui slaves had founded a small settlement a few miles away and had cut all ties with their original owners (1968:159). Many ex-*sai man* ended up in the satellite villages surrounding San Tin and Ha Tsuen where they have tried, unsuccessfully, to merge with the local residents. No one is fooled by their stories of wandering ancestors and lost lands. Recently members of a small lineage descending from *sai man* attempted to elevate themselves by building an ancestral hall, the symbol *par excellence* of elite status in South China. Rather than improving their image, however, the costly enterprise backfired on the luckless contributors; they had not realised that the sparkling new hall, inevitably a poor imitation of their original master's, would only subject them to more ridicule. It soon became known as the 'slave hall' and is now a source of great merriment in elite circles.

Descendants of *sai man* in the New Territories obviously have not succeeded in shedding the stigma of their slave origins. In fact, these people have become what might be described as a quasi-ethnic group: they resemble their former masters in almost every respect (language, religion, appearance, etc.) but their questionable background keeps them apart. Until recently this residual category was endogamous, not from choice but of necessity as no one else would consider marriage with slave descendants. Many grandsons of *sai man* now take refuge in Hong Kong's cities where they are easily lost in the crowds. The native peoples of the New Territories, however, will have nothing to do with them.

As mentioned earlier one family of ex-*sai man* remains in San Tin where they own two houses, the result of a benevolent land policy during the early years of colonial rule. Most villagers treat these people like pariahs and exclude them from all social activities not imposed by British authorities (e.g., elections and schools). In the late 1950s the surviving *sai man,* then in his sixties, shocked the *Man* elders by petitioning to change his surname, and that of his children, to *Man*—thereby forming a kinship link with the other villagers. Changing one's surname is not uncommon in Chinese society but it normally occurs in the course of adoption or uxorilocal marriage. After a brief debate the petition was rejected on the grounds that the elders could not risk offending the *Man* ancestors by accepting a *sai man* into the lineage. Today one of the commonest forms of slander in the New Territories is for members of rival lineages to accuse each other of having forefathers so low that they once had to adopt *sai man* to avoid extinction.

San Tin lies just half a mile from the Anglo-Chinese border and, accordingly, the *Man* lineage was not affected by the political and economic changes that swept through China after the communist revolution. There are, of course, hundreds and perhaps thousands of communities in the People's Republic that once harboured slave-owning families. From all accounts (e.g., Vogel 1969; Yang 1959) it is clear that the wealthy landlord class has been stripped of its power and influence. In the 'class struggles' that brought about this reversal the rural elite were frequently criticised for their abuse of slaves and other dependents. Former *sai man* and their descendants, on the other hand, benefited from the inversion of class statuses that followed in the revolution's wake; they found themselves classified as 'landless labourers' (the lowest rural class) and, in theory, local officials were to make every effort to compensate them for the oppression they suffered in the old society. It is difficult to determine whether these compensatory policies have had the desired result. One researcher found that an ex-*sai man* had become a member of the Communist Party (a prestige post in itself) and an important official in his commune. His five sons all graduated from secondary school and the eldest had gone on to university. However, even after 25 years of revolution, the stigma of their slave origin had not dissipated; the sons had difficulty finding wives in their home region and eventually migrated to urban areas.[9] This is particularly unusual because educated men of 'good class background' (i.e., former oppressed groups) are ordinarily showered with offers of marriage from young women who hope to escape the countryside and move to China's cities (Croll 1978; Parish and Whyte 1978). On another commune near Canton ex-*sai man* were still holding the same jobs they had prior to the revolution: unskilled labourer, butcher, and gravedigger.[10] More research needs to be done on this topic before general conclusions are drawn;[11] however, it would appear that the stigma of slave parentage is still a burden for some people in the People's Republic, just as it is in the New Territories.

Conclusions

Although it is difficult to be certain without first-hand research in the areas concerned, what evidence we have suggests that *sai man* slavery existed throughout South China (J. Watson 1976:369–71). The institution has been reported in the provinces of Kwangtung (Woon 1975; Chen 1936), Fukien (Doolittle 1866:211), and Kwangsi (Hsieh and Liu 1939:80). In most cases *sai man* were associated with power-ful, single-lineage villages that dominated the surrounding countryside and owned the best agricultural lands. There were, of course, other forms of Chinese slavery that have not been discussed in this paper.[12] From earliest times the Imperial court maintained a complex system of 'household slavery' to help manage the empire (Eberhard 1962:16–18). One small area even specialised in sending eunuchs to Peking where they were sold as slaves to the Emperor and his entourage (Skinner 1976:352; see also Eitel 1879:307). Less well known are the industrial systems of slavery that survived into the twentieth century by some accounts. Several obser-vers have reported that Chinese coal and tin mines relied heavily on child labour, especially from 'boy slaves' pur-chased by the mine owners (Osgood 1963:135; Lasker 1950: 337). Unfortunately very little is known about these mines.

The Chinese market in people, therefore, was vast and extremely complex. The principles outlined in this paper are only applicable, as far as it is possible to tell, to the southern provinces mentioned above. *Sai man* slavery, I have argued, is best understood in relation to the Southern Chinese peasant's conception of rights-in-persons. People who are not members of the lineage are defined as 'outsiders' and, as such, were subject to all manner of exploitation—including enslavement—once they had been acquired by purchase. 'Bought' males were either adopted as designated heirs in infancy or retained as hereditary slaves by their owners; the patrilineal system was so rigid, among the elite at least, that other possibilities were not tolerated. There was more variation in status for 'bought women' because the Chinese do not worry unduly about the position of women in the male-dominated kinship system. Hence, there are no clear and fast rules about the absorption of women as there are for men.

Women, by definition, are 'outsiders'. Some were purchased outright from market intermediaries while others, notably major wives, were transferred from one household to another through an exchange of marriage payments. Legally, therefore, all women 'belonged to' the males who had acquired them and decisions regarding the disposition of women, including daughters, were confined to the household. Males, on the other hand, 'belonged in' the lineage by right of birth; in elite circles no one had the right to sell his son on the open market. The Cantonese believe, in fact, that all living members of the lineage 'belong to' the ancestors and, accordingly, they are inviolable.

A sexual dichotomy is also evident in the legacy of servitude. The status of slave was inherited through the male line and, not surprisingly, *sai man* became a permanent underclass attached to elite lineages. Even today the descendants of slaves are treated like pariahs in the New Territories. In contrast, there is no hereditary stigma attaching to the descendants of 'bought women'; their sons and grandsons take on the status conferred by the patriline. Adult women who were acquired as *mui jai* or as little daughters-in-law are marked by a personal stigma during their own lifetime but this dies with them and is not passed on to the next generation.

It has been argued that the absence of a kinship link

I

between owner and 'bought' person is what distinguishes slavery from other forms of Chinese servitude. I would argue further that the *sai man* phenomenon was one of the most clearcut and unambiguous systems of chattel slavery on record. In structural terms Chinese slaves were not part of a 'slavery-to-kinship continuum' that characterised most 'indigenous' systems of African slavery (Kopytoff and Miers 1977: 24). All evidence suggests that African kinship groups had, in comparison to the Chinese, a far greater capacity to incorporate outsiders—including slaves—as full or potential members (e.g., Goody 1976; Tuden and Plotnicov 1970:13). In elite Chinese lineages, by contrast, the only way for an outsider to be absorbed into the corporate kin group is through adoption and this can only be arranged for infants, at great personal expense to the adopting father.

Demographically, slavery was never as significant in Chinese society as it was in Africa, or in the New World. *Sai man* constituted, by generous estimate, no more than 2 per cent of the population in the Hong Kong region at the turn of the century; there is little reason to think that other parts of South China were substantially different. It would be a mistake, however, to conclude from these figures that slavery was simply an aberration in an otherwise 'free' peasant society. Male slaves and their offspring were part of a vast market in human beings that affected millions of households throughout the Chinese empire. *Sai man* differed from other categories of 'bought' people primarily in the hereditary nature of their servitude.

10

Thai Institutions of Slavery

ANDREW TURTON

Institutions of slavery have been very widespread over many centuries both in South East Asian states, including all Thai states and their neighbours, and in many 'stateless' societies with which Thai states had relations. It has been claimed that the Thai system of slavery was 'un des types locaux les plus représentatifs' (Lingat 1931:2). It was also a local manifestation and transformation of the Hindu laws on slavery, though Siamese laws on slavery are held to be closer to the Mon-Burmese laws than to the Hindu (Lingat 1931:25). In this survey I have attempted wherever possible to correct certain emphases made, often for good reason, in earlier accounts. For instance, an attempt is needed to treat the full range of types of slavery. Robert Lingat's monumental work *L'esclavage privé dans le vieux droit Siamois* of 1931 (the most important source in a non-Thai language, and not yet translated into English) deals almost entirely with purchased, privately owned slaves, largely or entirely omitting slaves acquired through trade, capture, donation, birth, juridical sentence etc. This is due to his treating only the 1805 recension of laws on slavery, by which time all forms of slavery were beginning to be assimilated to the category of redeemable slaves by purchase. Other writers too, by focusing on slavery in the nineteenth century, when most of the legally unfree population were redeemable 'debt slaves', have implied or asserted that Thai institutions of slavery were not really slavery; or were quite *sui generis,* or were exceptionally benign and voluntary; or have so stressed the extent to which

they merged into other social conditions, statuses and forms
of labour that some of the distinctions and specificity of the
various institutions of slavery may have been lost. There is
also a need to try to view slavery not only in legal and
political terms, but also rather more in economic, social and
ideological terms.

In an essay of this length I can make no claim to have
exhausted all potential sources. The largest readily available
body of data is the laws on slavery; it is less easy to try to
establish customary ideas and practices and the real conditions and functions of slavery. There is also considerable
difficulty in achieving a satisfactory degree of both specificity
and generality in dealing with the subject due to the scattered and fragmentary nature of sources and to the historical
depth and spread of Thai institutions of slavery. 'The Thai
were mentioned as slaves or prisoners of war in Cham epigraphy in the eleventh century. They appeared again, in the
twelfth century, on the bas-reliefs of Angkor Wat, represented
as warriors or mercenaries in Khmer armies' (Charnvit 1976:
34). There were institutions of slavery in the Thai kingdoms
of Sukhothai (1250–1438 A.D.), Ayuthaya (1350–1767 A.D.) and
in the Bangkok period (1767 to the final abolition in the early
twentieth century). There were also slaves in the Thai (Lao
and Shan) Kingdoms of Lannathai, Lan Chang, Vieng Chang,
Luang Prabang and others. Basically I shall be dealing with
the Kingdom of Siam, as it was known to the West, and
especially from the later Ayuthaya period (seventeenth and
eighteenth centuries) and the early Bangkok period, with
occasional references outside this framework. It has to be
borne in mind that there were undoubtedly variations and
fluctuations in the relative size, importance and functions of
slavery, and of the different institutions of slavery, over the
centuries; and also a secular change towards uniformity and
mitigation from the eighteenth century, until eventual abolition by the early twentieth century.

The pre-capitalist states (Ayuthaya and early Bangkok) are
characterised by the *sakdina* system, which is often loosely
referred to as 'Thai feudalism', though a theoretical debate as
to the appropriateness of the concepts 'feudal mode of pro-

duction' and 'asiatic mode of production' continues un-
resolved (See e.g. Chit 1974; Chaianan 1976; Elliott 1977).
At the head of the society was an absolute monarch whose
status was supported by a specifically Thai transformation of
Hindu and Buddhist ideology (Tambiah 1976). The political-
territorial system has been termed a 'galactic polity', a 'concept of territory as a variable sphere of influence that
diminishes as royal power radiates from a center...' (Tambiah 1976:122). Territories close to the centre were governed
by royalty and aristocracy (*cao*) and nobility (*khunnang, nai*),
all of whom, in theory, held non-hereditary offices from the
king. Tributary princedoms and states on the periphery tended
to use the hereditary principle to a greater extent. The
entire population was allotted social ranks in a numerical-
hierarchical system known as *sakdina* (lit. power/rank/
prestige in or over fields). To simplify, those holding *sakdina*
of 400 and over, up to 100,000, were appointed directly by
the king and formed the small ruling stratum. Perhaps no
more than 2,000 persons had *sakdina* 400 or higher in the
Ayuthaya period out of an estimated two million population
(Chaianan 1976). Most of the population were freemen-
commoners with *sakdina* 25 (for an adult married male).
Adult male slaves (*that*—from Sanskrit *dasa*—or *kha*) and
beggars and destitute persons had *sakdina* 5.

While recallable grants of land could be made to the ruling
stratum, and while landed estates existed, like manorial
enclaves (especially those of the king, of certain monasteries,
and of well-established aristocrats), all land (and human life)
was strictly speaking the property of the king. A legal category of 'patrons' (*nai*) were entitled to a certain number of
freeman 'clients' (*phrai*) according to *sakdina* rank (especially
over 400), title and office. The unpaid labour of these clients
was requisitioned by their personal patrons for periods of
from three to six months each year either for personal service
(*phrai som*) or for public (royal) works (*phrai luang*). A further
category (*phrai suai*), often more distantly located, contributed highly valued goods in lieu of service. By and large,
members of the ruling stratum were also the owners of slaves.

The absence of private property, in the full sense, in land;

the relative autonomy and unity of production in agriculture and manufacture of rural village communities; the relative lack of development of cities, which were above all political and religious centres, as centres of trade and commerce, and especially of manufacturing for trade and commerce; even the limited involvement of the ruling stratum in irrigation works; the power and ideological status of the monarchy: all these factors contribute to the plausibility of the application of the 'asiatic mode of production' concept. At the very least they serve here as an initial orientation, and contrast with other pre-capitalist social formations. It will become clear that at no time are we dealing with a 'slave mode of production'. Slave labour, quite apart from its relatively inferior size, at no time forms the basis of production; there are no labour processes exclusive to slaves; slaves are 'legally/ideologically inferior subject[s] who [are] added to an existing set of relations' (Hindess and Hirst 1975:140).

War Slaves

Perry Anderson (1974:28) has characterised the expansion of states in classical (European) antiquity thus: 'Plunder, tribute and slaves were the central objects of aggrandisement, both means and ends to colonial expansion.' This was a 'lateral' path of expansion, geographical conquest rather than economic advance. This might well also serve for classical Thai states for which frequent warfare was above all a means of competing not so much for territory as such but for increase in population and no doubt for the maintenance and replacement of a population constantly ravaged by malaria, smallpox, famine, flood and drought, and not least by the depredations of other states' wars and raids. Indeed the abduction or failure to return slaves and freemen clients might well be a *casus belli* between states (Charnvit 1976:103). That it was a capital offence to sell a slave to a foreigner (outside the state) also emphasises the need to retain labour power within the system. The same applied to social units within the state: some of the most elaborated sections of laws on slavery deal with abduction of slaves and return of runaway slaves.

Simon de La Loubère (1969:90) writes of warfare in late seventeenth-century Ayuthaya: 'They busie themselves only in making slaves. If the Peguins (sic), for example, do on one side invade the lands of Siam, the Siamese will at another place enter the Lands of Pegu, and both Parties will carry away whole Villages into Captivity.' Wales generalises in similar vein that: 'expeditions that were little more than slave raids were the regular occupation of the dry season' (1934:64). The very word for 'enemy' (*kha soek*, lit. 'slave fight') suggests that adversaries were regarded as potential slaves. Chronicles record the number of captives taken, *that chaloei* (*chaloei* is a Khmer word for war captive). These sometimes numbered many tens of thousands, as in wars against the Khmer empire in the fourteenth century. Six thousand *families* were taken from the Vientiane region of Laos after the Siamese capture of Vientiane in 1826 by an army of some 20,000 (Le Boulanger 1931). In 1462 King Tilok of the Lannathai Kingdom (Chiengmai) conquered eleven Shan principalities (*muang*) and carried off 12,328 people who were relocated in three towns and several frontier posts 'where their descendants have lived until our days' says the chronicle (Notton 1926–32, Vol. 3:135). Care is taken to record quite small gains: in three successive annual campaigns against Sukothai (1513–1515) Lannathai acquired respectively '40 prisoners', '20 prisoners and some Karen tribespeople' (many others dying of smallpox), '2 elephants and 80 prisoners'. It must be borne in mind that we are dealing with political entities whose effective labour forces were numbered in thousands, at most a few hundred thousands.

Little distinction was made between captured 'soldiers' or 'civilians': 'the Siamese equally carry off the peasantry of the open country of both sexes' (Crawfurd 1915:145). Strictly speaking, such captives were only non-Siamese (Mon, Khmer, Burmese, Vietnamese, Malay) though they included people from other Thai states (Shan, Lao, Lannathai, etc.), and there were possible abuses, as when the army might gather in Siamese war refugees (Lingat 1931:49–50). This human booty was immediately the property of the king, or prince of a tributary state. Rewards (rank, money, slaves, etc.) might be given for the capture of prisoners, sometimes according to the rank of the prisoner. Most captives remained in the possession of the king as royal slaves (*that luang*). A proportion might be given to nobles according to the rank of the recipient. Gifts of slaves might also be made to a political superior and between princes (Notton 1926–32, Vol. 3:138). War slaves were thus a form of currency in political transactions.

The numbers of such slaves would fluctuate considerably according to political and military circumstances. It is possible that slavery by capture in war was the earliest form of slavery and that at times, perhaps for long periods, war slaves predominated among all kinds of slaves. By 1805, and following losses in the wars against the Burmese and the rise in debt slavery, they had declined in relative importance, though the campaigns against Vientiane in the 1820s showed that their numbers could increase spectacularly. Bowring estimated that during the reign of Rama III (1824–1851) there were 46,000 war slaves including 20,000 Lao, probably mostly from Vientiane (1857:190).

War slaves might be used for any private or public work, as could other slaves. Some were donated as temple slaves. Others 'were frequently employed in performing the most contemptible of tasks, cutting grass for the royal elephants' (Wales 1934:61) and in agricultural production and public works: 'At the Siamese capital [Bangkok in 1821] we daily saw great numbers of these unfortunate persons [war captives] employed in sowing, ditching and other severe labour' (Crawfurd 1915:145). An important use of war slaves was in military service (army and navy) for the king, as members of royal bodyguards and on campaigns.

Treatment of war slaves, perhaps especially first-generation slaves, may have been harsher than other classes of slaves. Wales claimed that 'no regard was paid to the sufferings of the persons thus transported' (1934:63). Lingat refers to frequent mistreatment and Crawfurd considered that war captives were better treated by the Burmese than the Siamese, despite his judgement that in war the Burmese were 'cruel and ferocious to the last degree'; and none were condemned to work in chains as in Siam (Crawfurd 1830, Vol. 1:422;

Vol. 2:134–135). However, many were allowed to settle and farm near Bangkok, forming ethnically distinct communities, some of which persist despite considerable cultural assimilation to this day.

Slave Trade

Slave labour also entered the system through trade by land and sea. A legal phrase refers to slaves bought 'on board a junk' indicating that the seller was not permanently resident so no contract of sale could be enforced (Lingat 1931:113). Slaves acquired through external trade would almost certainly be non-redeemable, though there are some references to ransom being paid. The trade appears to have existed throughout mainland South East Asia and there would seem to be no major ethnic group which did not have some members participating in the trade as dealers and purchasers. The main victims were members of those hill-dwelling minority peoples generically known to the Thai as *kha*, the basic Thai word glossed here as 'slave' (together with *that* cf. Sanskrit *dasa*). The effect of the trade was a net drain on the populations of the hills (some writers suggest large-scale depopulation) to the benefit of the lowland states, a classic instance of the global relation between a mode of production in which slaves played an important part and other modes of production 'at a lower level of technical and social development and unable to resist the depredations of its slave traders' (Hindess and Hirst 1975:145). However, the traders included members of some of the minority group themselves (e.g. Karen), and the victims included members of lowland states (e.g. Shan). Although slave raids were probably mainly inter-ethnic, traders were evidently not always averse to dealing in people of their own ethnic group.

In the north the 'Chiengmai Shans' were said to be the chief purchasers, buying especially children who were cheaper. It is clear that there was also a considerable onward sale of slaves into Siamese territory proper. The trade continued until late in the nineteenth century; Colquhoun (1885:53–4) refers to 'the slave-dealers, who still [1879] drive a flourishing trade among the independent tribes'. The scale and value of the trade evidently fluctuated with other forms of commodity exchange. Early in the nineteenth century there was a decline in the slave trade owing to an increase in price of cattle from 2½ to 10–12 rupees 'though it is said there are still nearly 300 persons sold annually into the Siamese territory' (Sao Saimong 1965:78). It seems likely that hill people were valued highly as against other peoples, for their 'uprightness' and no doubt because escape was less likely. For instance in Phnom Penh in the late nineteenth century 'tribesmen' were valued at 800 francs compared with Cambodians at 500 and 'Annamites' at 200 francs (Colquhoun 1885:54). In the northern Thai trade there was a differential evaluation of the labour of women as between many hill people and the lowland Thai which was likely to benefit the latter. The slave trade was also linked with other forms of trade, including the accumulation of forest produce: 'black cattle and buffaloes are received [by the Karen] in barter for slaves and stick-lack from the Siamese Shans' (Sao Saimong 1965:78).

Although slaves from the hill minorities were culturally even more distinct from their owners than were most of the slaves acquired through warfare, there would seem to have been a similar tendency towards cultural assimilation of such slaves. Colquhoun, who regarded 'kidnapping for sale' as leading to a 'by far more iniquitous and remorseless state of slavery' nonetheless cites Garnier that such slaves were: '... treated with the greatest kindness. They live so intimately and familiarly with their masters, that but for their long hair and different physiognomy, they could not otherwise be recognised by a visitor' (Colquhoun 1885:54).

Temple Slaves

The institution of slaves serving Buddhist monasteries, temples and reliquaries existed in Thai states from earliest times (*kha phra*, slave of monk, or of Buddha). They are the category of 'donated' slaves in the list of seven types derived from the Hindu Laws of Manu (see Bühler 1969). That many were by origin war captives or persons convicted of serious crimes (Wales 1934) and that all temple slaves were normally exempt from *corvée*, suggests that they were non-redeemable, hereditary slaves. Yet they had a status and rights somewhat distinct from other slaves; for instance, there seem to be no references to such slaves being sold by their corporate owners. Some people may have voluntarily offered themselves as temple slaves, whether out of piety, poverty, or seeking refuge from the law.

There are numerous references in chronicles and epigraphy to grants of land and slaves by kings and princes to existing Buddhist institutions or in order to found new ones. For instance the Crystal Sands Chronicle (Wyatt 1975; see also Notton 1926–32; Charnvit 1976; La Loubère 1969) refers to monasteries with 'large amounts of lands and monastery slaves'; to the endowment of slaves and land as meritorious acts by kings; to the registration of temples and their lands and slaves; to petitions from monasteries for title deeds to land cultivated by slaves. Such grants might also be made by other wealthy people, and not necessarily to monasteries under royal patronage: a stone inscription of 1523 A.D. from Wat Phan Tao, Chiengmai (now in the Chiengmai National Museum) refers to a man and wife (without titles) who '. . . gladly donated paddy fields (valued at) 60,000 cowries, slaves . . .' to the monastery.

The institution of temple slavery had important economic, political and ideological functions. It enabled new settlements and clusters of manpower to be established (Charnvit 1976) which was ever a political and economic priority for the state; endowments of land included forest land on which the slaves had the arduous task of creating rice fields from scratch (Wyatt 1975:158). Charnvit refers to the 'shrewd understanding of the political importance of the Buddhist religion' of King Trailok (ruled 1448–88), who 'devoted much attention to building an effective politico-religious base' in order to obtain the support and co-operation of the people through the Buddhist *sangha* 'the informal leadership of rural society' at that time (1976:135).

The actual conditions of temple slaves varied between those who were obliged to give all their produce to the temple, by which they were maintained as on a manorial estate, and those who were obliged to 'present tithes of all they produce for the use and maintenance of the pagoda and its priests' (Colquhoun 1885:101–2). In addition to producing food the slaves were required to build, rebuild and maintain temples and other structures. In these tasks they are likely to have been assisted by the *corvée* labour of freemen and voluntary 'meritorious' labour. They might be required to defend the temple in time of war and even travel abroad, perhaps conducting some trade, on behalf of the temple. The Crystal Sands Chronicle records a cutting from a sacred Bodhi tree being shipped from Ceylon to southern Thailand 'aboard a *sampan*, using monastery slaves' (Wyatt 1975:127–128).

There are references to the misuse of temple slaves for public works, such use being condemned except in time of war (Notton 1926–32, Vol. 1:42) which was not perhaps an infrequent exception. In general though, texts and commentaries imply that the lot of temple slaves was a relatively light form of servitude (Colquhoun 1885:101–2) and even that many preferred the status to a more 'free' one (Charnvit 1976:42).

> The king died, and his ashes were divided up and put into reliquaries in various monasteries, and his relatives were divided up to maintain the reliquaries as monastery slaves in those places, and they all put themselves at His Majesty's mercy, [asking that] if they had children and grandchildren, these would be presented as slaves to the king without fail (Wyatt 1975:108).

Wyatt comments that:

> The implication is that the status of monastery slave was felt to be desirable, no doubt as it exempted individuals from compulsory labour [and military] service and tied them permanently to monasteries near their homes (1975:108 n.3).

As always, royal strategies of allocating and balancing different forms of labour and their ownership and control required continual supervision and revision. In late Ayuthaya, censuses were taken to check on illegal residence in temples and according to Charnvit rulers usually had ways of limiting the numbers of *kha phra* (1976:42).

Other slaves, not of the status of *kha phra* (temple slaves) would of course be employed in the work of maintaining religious buildings and serving their occupants. La Loubère (1969:59) speaks of novices of good family who 'have one or more slaves to wait upon them.' Young boys, and some adults, are to this day given to temples as unpaid servants (in northern Thai *khayom*). This customary practice is not entirely dissimilar in effect from earlier forms of committing children to a servile condition, though it is now usually seen as having meritorious and educational functions, sometimes as a religious apprenticeship, and as a means of alleviating the poverty of donor families.

Judicial Slaves

A person might become a slave for judicial reasons in a number of ways which could lead to either a redeemable or non-redeemable status. It is clear that condemnation to servile status, and consequent 'hard labour' for the life of the offender and possibly descendants, could be a punishment in itself: 'As soon as sentenced the prisoner is manacled and turned over to some Prince or noble, whose slave he becomes, and he is placed under a task master who proceeds to get all the work out of him possible' (Child 1892:136). Hallett (1890) refers to the sentencing of monks guilty of fornication or adultery to slave status and condemnation with all his descendants to cutting grass for royal elephants. Colquhoun (1885: 54) likewise refers to 'slaves by judicial confiscation' for theft other crimes.

Sentence to pay heavy cash fines for criminal offences could also lead to a convicted person becoming the debt slave of a third party who paid the fine. The category of slaves for judicial cause also included insolvent debtors and persons unable to pay compensation to the plaintiff in civil cases, for instance, an adulterer might become the debt slave of the woman's husband. Furthermore it was possible for someone with the right of alienation of persons, whether slave or free (e.g. wife), to sell such a person into slavery as a punishment. This could result in either the change of ownership of an existing slave, or the subjection to servile status of a free person, for instance a wife guilty of adultery unless the male adulterer had already paid compensation.

Debt Slaves

From the early nineteenth century all slaves were progressively assimilated to a legal category of slaves by purchase. The term used is 'slaves purchased with property' (property = *khao khong*; lit. rice and possessions) though it is clear that cash transactions were usual; another term is *that nam ngoen* (money slaves). The generic legal term is *that thai*. The term *thai* (not to be confused with the ethnic term which has a different spelling and tone) introduces a difficulty. It has the meaning 'redeem'; whereas the common word 'to sell' (*khai*) was used in slave transactions, the common word 'to buy' (*su*) was not: 'Thai words for buying slaves are interesting. It was not *su that* (buy a slave) but *chuai thai* (help to redeem). The reason for using the term "help" was that one helped the poor by lending money to him" (Akin 1969:110). So the person who becomes the initial owner of a slave has 'helped to redeem' him. Subsquent purchases of the same slave, as we shall see, might mean either change of ownership or enfranchisement. Another complication is that the owner is referred to interchangeably as master or creditor, whereas the slave might be paying off a debt incurred by him in the first place with the owner, or by him with another person now paid off by the owner; or the slave might be paying off a debt incurred, with either the owner or another person, by the person selling the slave. A further complication is that 'purchased' slaves (*that thai*) fall into two main categories which are usually glossed (as by Wales) 'redeemable' (*that thai khai faak*, lit. slave redeemed, or, 'purchased', and sold on trust) and 'non-redeemable' (*that thai khat kha*, lit. slave redeemed or purchased at an absolute price—*kha* here = price, a different spelling and tone from the word for slave). These two categories have also been translated respectively as 'fiduciary' and 'definitive' (Lingat 1931), and as 'temporary' (which as we shall see is inappropriate) and 'absolute' (Smith 1880). I shall be discussing the distinctions between 'redeemable' and 'non-redeemable' status more fully in the following section. Here I wish to discuss within the wider context of slavery the question of 'debt slaves' or 'debt bondsmen' for whom no distinct legal category exists.

People becoming *that thai* by reason of debt might become either redeemable or non-redeemable *that*. However it is undoubtedly the case that during the first half of the nineteenth century the overwhelming majority of the population having the legal status *that* were redeemable and were *that* by reason of 'indebtedness'. The number and proportion of such *that* were apparently increasing during the nineteenth century. Now in the interpretation of Thai institutions of slavery something of a consensus or even ideal type has emerged, which I would argue may obscure as much as it clarifies. One might characterise this view, which is probably not held in full by any one commentator, as follows: 'Slavery' is an inappropriate term to represent the Thai institutions of *that* (either all or especially that of redeemable 'debt bondsmen' who in any case constituted almost all *that*). People in this category sold *themselves*, and sold themselves *willingly*. Debt slaves were redeemable and redeemability led to redemption. Such bondage was 'attractive'. Distinctions between such persons and freemen clients were slight and/or a continuum of types of labour control is more apparent.

Akin Rabibhadana (1969:109), echoing Sir John Bowring and others, writes:

> The necessity to use the word 'slave' for *that* is very unfortunate. The ideas associated with the word 'slave' in the Western World are quite different from the ideas associated with the word *that*. . . . To carry over the idea of Western slavery and apply it to *that* is to misunderstand *that* completely. The only way to understand *that* is in the context of Thai social organisation.

Certainly *that* have to be understood in the context of Thai social organisation, but such an argument tends to minimise both the variety and the comparability of forms of slavery in both the Thai and 'Western' (and other) worlds. It also tends to exclude the application of *theoretical* 'ideas' of slavery. The most fundamental of such concepts, such as that 'slavery' is 'a form of bondage in which human beings are a form of property' (Hindess and Hirst 1975:113) would seem to be widely applicable to most forms of the Thai institution of *that*. In so far as the view quoted above reflects the preponderance of redeemable slaves for debt in the nineteenth century, it tends to distort the picture of slavery in earlier centuries. Finally it should be borne in mind that neither apologies nor condemnations are in order here, and that a pure type of chattel slavery never existed (Finley 1973:67; Hindess and Hirst 1975:112).

> . . .[I]n King Mongkut's time [1851–1868] slavery was not a system whereby one or more human beings were subjugated by another. It was, strangely enough, the right of free men to sell themselves into bondage which, in most cases, was exercised with the object of extricating these persons from financial difficulties (Ingram 1971:61; citing an unpublished paper by Seni Pramoj and Kukrit Pramoj).

In the first place it is not so much 'subjugation' as ownership of persons and their labour power that we are concerned with, though the Thai root terms for 'lord' and 'owner' *cao* are identical (see Chit Phumisak 1976). The observation by Hindess and Hirst (1975:113) is relevant here: 'The slave is neither a subject nor a subordinate, he is a form of property; the master is not his lord, he is his *owner*'. Secondly this 'right of free men' was restricted by severe punishments for people who tried to sell themselves fraudulently when not in dire necessity (Lingat 1931). Thirdly 'selling oneself' was far from being the general case. The status of redeemable slave required a 'seller' or 'guarantor' other than the slave himself. A person in debt could himself initiate the transaction and sell himself, with a kinsman, friend or creditor acting as guarantor, but in a great many cases (perhaps most, though it would be hard to establish) the person in 'financial difficulties' would himself be the seller and guarantor while the object of the transaction, the *that*, would be a third party whom the seller/debtor had the right to dispose of in this way.

Lingat lists the categories of persons who might be so used to satisfy a creditor by a debtor. An existing slave might be used, but more frequently a wife or close junior kin. From the category of wives, custom, but not law according to Lingat, excluded a senior wife or one who had brought a dowry to the marriage. Unmarried children could be sold, while still resident, including adopted children, together with grandchildren, younger siblings, and siblings' children. Until the nineteenth century the consent of the person sold was not required by law.

Nor were persons sold to discharge debt necessarily redeemable. Bowring, observing that over four-fifths of nonredeemable slaves fled when they could, comments that they included especially young girls sold by their parents. Such slaves would have been sold outright, i.e. for the full price, by their parents or elders. Similarly if an indebted person sold himself for the full price and without guarantor his status would be that of non-redeemable *that*. Another form of social indebtedness, to a patron who fed a person in time of dearth and famine, led to non-redeemable slavery; if the beneficiary was a redeemable slave his status was thereby automatically changed to non-redeemable (Lingat 1931).

Redeemable slaves for debt were by no means necessarily redeemed. Thompson (1941) for example, considered that few redeemed themselves (or were redeemed by others). Moreover 'redemption' could mean purchase by another owner, which while perhaps sometimes leading to improved conditions, did not necessarily mean enfranchisement. In the Ayuthaya period, children of redeemable slaves were not redeemable.

That the *that* for debt was not always, even commonly, the indebted person, already challenges arguments for the 'attractions of bondage':

It appears probable that more people were attracted to some form of bondage by the security and protection it provided,

than were driven to it by dire economic necessity. . . . Only
by noting the *attractions* of bondage can we explain the situation which puzzles Hallett; namely that debt slavery could be
so prevalent when a labourer's wages are such as to enable
him to subsist on a fourth of his wages (Ingram 1971:61,
italics in original).

The two main reasons why Thai freemen became *that* for
'debt' are usually given as heavy taxation and gambling
to which Colquhoun added 'indolent improvidence'. Such
prejudiced terms, part of the 'myth of the lazy native', were
not infrequently used by Westerners in the nineteenth
century, anxious that there should be a 'free' labour market.
The possibilities for regular waged labour in the nineteenth
century, of the sort referred to by Hallett, must have been
relatively few however. Some writers also refer to the availability of (potential) agricultural land and use rights in it for
those prepared to work it. Yet there was not complete freedom
of movement of *phrai*; such a relatively long-term solution
would scarcely be a valid option for someone already deeply
in debt; or indeed the indebted person might well already be
working the land. It should also be borne in mind that land
was not available as collateral since the possessor did not
have full rights of ownership.

The use of *persons* as collateral, the mortgaging of persons,
emerges clearly in the third form of 'debt slavery' in which
fewest rights were transferred. This is the form known as
that thai mai dai chai (lit. slave bought but not used), also
referred to as 'interest bearing slave' (Smith 1880) and 'pro
forma security' slave (Cruickshank 1975). This type of *that*
(typically a wife) was pledged as security for the capital
of the loan and had the legal status of *that*, but remained
at home while the debtor/husband paid interest in cash.
Interestingly it seems that, at least in the Bangkok period, the
creditor had no right to foreclose and take possession, but on
the other hand the contract enabled the creditor to demand
double the amount of interest overdue, which would be quite
likely to force the debtor to make a non-redeemable slave of
the person thus pledged.

It has been argued that slaves 'are very much part of the

total system's continuum of labour control and patron-client relationships,' (Cruickshank 1975:330) and that a more appropriate model of stratification in Thai society would place *that* and freemen clients (*phrai*) at the same level, above destitute persons and beggars, i.e. persons without patrons, owners or guarantors. Lingat writes, with a little more nuance, that 'Les esclaves ne forment pas au Siam une classe distincte ...'; they are at the bottom of the hierarchy more because of their presumed indigence than because of their servile condition. 'Leur servitude est moins un état qu'un lien établi, d'autorité privé, entre leurs maitres et eux, un lien plus fort, mais de même nature que celui qui unit le débiteur au créancier' (Lingat 1931:227). Once again such views may make us forget the different statuses of *that* in periods before the nineteenth century (temple slaves, war captives and other state slaves) and those obtained, even in the nineteenth century, in the slave trade proper. More seriously they tend to conflate the different status, rights, wealth and treatment *within* the social and legal categories *that* and *phrai*. Here Akin Rabibhadana's notion of 'interpenetration' of *phrai* and *that* is more apt (1975:106; 1969:124 diagram). Some *phrai* might be poor and harshly worked, while other free commoners of the same legal status (*sakdina* 25 or over) might be relatively wealthy, able to pay composition and other taxes with no difficulty and even possibly to own slaves, which a slave could or would not be able to. Whatever his circumstances a *that* had the same *maximum sakdina* of 5 in common with destitute persons and beggars, who indeed might well only be 'free' at the price of having sold wife and/or children into slavery. Moreover just as the social *prestige* of a *phrai* might vary according to the social *rank* of his master, so 'it was unthinkable that the *that* of a *somdet chaophraya* or a *chaofa* [prince] would rank lower than the *phrai* of a minor official' (Akin 1975:106).

Redeemable and Non-Redeemable Slaves

Certain features of the status of redeemable (fiduciary) and non-redeemable (definitive) *that* are common to both types

and will be considered together before distinguishing differences in the rights and obligations of seller, buyer and slave
in each case. In this section I draw very heavily on Lingat's
translation of nineteenth century laws and commentaries on
these and occasionally earlier forms. It cannot help therefore
but be a summary and largely a reflection of the legal/
theoretical position.

The transaction of obtaining a slave by purchase was based
on a legal notion of the value of a person. The entire population was given such a value according to social rank in the
sakdina system, sex, age and marital status. Some collections
of customary law start with an exposition of these 'values of
people' expressed in money terms. They were used in civil
and criminal law for the settlement of grievances. In theory,
and put simply, if a buyer paid the full 'value', *or more,* he
acquired the most absolute rights legally possible over the
person bought; if he paid less than the full value then he
acquired fewer rights, to some extent in proportion to the
amount paid. The question of personal value and market
price is considered further in a later section.

In general the transaction is seen as one between a seller
and a buyer, the future owner; the object of the sale had no
legal right to consent to the sale (though this was progressively changed in the nineteenth century). A form of written
contract (*kromathan*) was usual from the seventeenth century
but was not necessary for establishing legal slave status.
It was a private contract, recording date, names of the parties
involved and witnesses, the price paid and the signature or
mark of the seller only, a kind of 'unilateral promise' as
Lingat puts it. It did not guarantee that the slave was the
legally disposable property of the seller unless made before a
judge (e.g. when the subject of the transaction had committed
an offence leading to enslavement or change of owner).
Problems of fictitious documents (e.g. made to escape *corvée*
obligations) are evident in the laws, and for a while after the
fall of Ayuthaya (1767) when there were many ownerless
slaves, all slave sales were made before a judge or provincial
governor; later on, only in doubtful cases. However there
were serious punishments for the person even unwittingly

selling the slave of another, a form of theft. Such a person could be beaten, fined, made a slave of the king (condemned to cut grass for royal elephants or work in royal rice mills) and his wife and children became slaves of the buyer.

The buyer had no rights until the full agreed sum had been paid; there was no buying of slaves on credit as with other commodities. Once the sum had been paid the seller had to deliver within three days. If he then claimed not to have the slave the buyer could demand no less than three tenths of the sum for each month of delay: an indication not only of the serious view the legislator took of deceit (and perhaps its possible occurrence), but also of the economic value of the slave to the buyer. Once sold the seller must not trouble the buyer without due cause. For instance if a father were to seek to remove his children once they had been definitively sold he was guilty of theft. There were no restrictions on the type of labour the slave might be required to perform, and either a redeemable or non-redeemable slave might be allowed to work on their own account and deliver an agreed sum to their owner. The uses to which slave labour was put are considered in detail in a later section. No owner had the right to kill, or so mistreat as to cause the death of a slave. Causing the death of a slave could lead to the owner being tried for homicide.

Male slaves had the right to marry, without the consent of his owner, either a slave or a free woman. Female slaves required their owners' consent. Female slaves could marry a free man, who would normally redeem her, but she then had a status between a second (free) wife and a slave wife. This is one of the very few indications of anything like a 'freedman' status. In earlier times and in other Thai kingdoms the intermarriage of slave and free may have been illegal or a breach of custom. A text from the Lannathai kingdom states that it is 'taboo' (*khut*) for a freeman to marry a slave wife (MS. cited in Turton 1976).

Slaves were able to possess individual property and to transmit it by inheritance. A male slave had rights against his owner in the case of adultery between his wife and her/their owner. If the owner was guilty the male and female slaves were freed, or if the wife chose to remain with the owner, the husband was freed and obtained his 'price' from the owner. The owner had rights over the persons of slaves and their labour, and all goods accumulated during their service which reverted to him at the death of a slave, but not over goods held by the slave before purchase. A slave could not enter into contracts without the owner's consent. As to access to law, slaves had the same rights and obligations as free men, with the exception that slaves (along with a large number of other categories of persons) could not act as witnesses, nor could slaves bring any action against their owners. They could be represented at law by their owner, as a client (*phrai*) of a patron (*nai*). The laws of compensation applied to all slaves; interestingly for the lowest freeman of *sakdina* 5 the compensation was half as much again as that for a slave of the same age (Wales 1934). The childbearing slave wife of a freeman was accorded a *sakdina* grade one eighth that of her husband, compared with half for a major wife and one quarter for a minor wife.

A non-redeemable slave was one who had been sold outright, definitively (*khat kha*), for a *minimum* of the full personal value. Non-redeemable slaves had no subsequent guarantor and their names were struck off the official rolls (*hang wao*) registering population for *corvée*. The only continuing relationship between buyer and seller imposed obligations on the seller to restore the full capital sum to the buyer within one month of sale if the slave ran away or contracted serious illness, or within three years if the slave committed an act of banditry, theft or assault against the buyer.

The owner had almost absolute rights except notably that of causing the death of the slave. He could, for instance, send his slave to receive physical punishment to which he the owner had been condemned. The owner could resell at any time for the highest price. There were only two circumstances, both effectively removing the slave from civil society, under which the owner was obliged to enfranchise a non-redeemable slave: prior to ordination as a Buddhist monk, which in any case the owner had to agree to (see below), and on capture as a prisoner of war (unless sent on the king's orders). If a female slave was married by her owner she was not enfranchised, as a redeemable slave might be, but gained a slightly higher status and provided the union was not sterile (i.e. she had reproduced the household's slave-labour force) she was enfranchised on the death of the owner. The children of such a marriage, but not the wife, might inherit, but a smaller share than the children of their owner/father's free wives.

A redeemable slave was one who had been sold for less than (theoretically not more than half) the full personal value. It was a kind of mortgage transaction. Prior to the 1805 laws (which this section is so largely bound to reflect) there appears to have been a time limit on redemption, at the end of which the slave might be regarded as definitively sold. Until redemption (which might never be realised) the non-redeemable slave is 'entrusted' (*faak*) to the 'buyer'. The person of the slave represents the original capital sum 'loaned'; the slave is referred to as *ruan bia* (lit. home of the cowries, or cash). The slave's labour represents interest paid on the principal, but never pays off the principal.

The most outstanding characteristic of this form is not so much the amount (certainly not type) of labour required of the slave, though this was expected to bear some relation to the size of the capital sum, as the continuing relationship between seller/guarantor, slave, and buyer/owner. Although the rights to labour, the potentially limitless interest paid on the capital sum, were little restricted in law, the owner's rights in the person of the slave were limited in a number of ways; but at the same time the owner also had a number of possible additional claims on the slave and/or guarantor. For instance the owner was entitled to a variety of cash compensations and damages which could be added to the original price, making the eventual redemption price higher, and so perhaps redemption less likely, and also increasing the owner's right to labour. A redeemable slave could not only be physically punished by the owner (though more circumspectly) but unlike a non-redeemable slave he could also be required to pay cash reparations. The owner could further be compensated for the loss of labour to him during the pregnancy and childbirth of a female slave and for the costs of raising children up to the age of seven.

There appears to have been no minimum time before which the seller could redeem. In a law of 1795 the buyer was obliged to accept the redemption price within one month of offer, or the slave could be redeemed on payment of the price to the royal treasury. On the other hand the seller was obliged to redeem if the buyer no longer wished to keep the slave, though if the seller were unable to redeem (or find another buyer) the owner could not acquire definitive ownership. Nor could the owner resell definitively. The seller was obliged to repay or replace at any time if the slave died, fled or was lost, unless the buyer could be held responsible. If the slave died, however, only one quarter of the value had to be restored 'out of compassion for the survivors'.

Limitations of sexual rights in the person of a redeemable slave included a reduction in value by half if the owner constrained a female slave to marry, and by one quarter for lesser sexual offences. Although the slave could not bring a legal action against the owner, the guarantor could. A redeemable slave had to be enfranchised if sent to war and actually fought; or if made a war captive (unless sent on king's orders); prior to ordination (if the owner permitted it); and if married by the owner. A redeemable slave was not released on the death of either seller or buyer but would be inherited by both sides.

The phrase 'half-free, half-slave' was sometimes used of redeemable slaves in law. During the Auythaya period this could mean in practice six months labour for the owner and six months *corvée* labour for the king. In the later Ayuthaya period this was altered to four months labour for each of king and owner, and four months on his own account, to pay for their subsistence while working for the king. Such was the advantage, in terms of the right of the slave to the fruits of his labour, of being 'half-free'. By the end of the nineteenth century the *corvée* requirement had been considerably reduced.

Kinship and Marriage

A number of references have already been made to kinship and marriage in the context of slavery, in particular the right of a married freeman to sell or 'mortgage' wives and close junior lineal and collateral kin of both sexes. In 1805 siblings, grandchildren, nephews and nieces were declared independent (*issara*) of the power of their elder kinsmen and by 1868 a free wife, but not a slave wife, could not be alienated without her consent. King Mongkut reportedly disapproved of old laws which treated 'women like buffaloes and only men as human beings'.

In earlier times it is likely that marriages between freemen and slaves were customarily disapproved. Normally the slave spouse would be redeemed on marriage to a free person but legal provision is made for mixed marriages. Such marriages were likely to be polygamous marriages with the slave wife occupying a status lower than that of minor wives (or 'wives of affection') and of course below senior wife and wife of royal gift. If a freeman sold his wife she remained his wife but the children of the marriage became the property of the owner, with the provision that the patron of the freeman husband was entitled to the *corvée* labour of a proportion of the offspring. After 1805 the freeman husband of a slave wife could redeem his children for half value or receive one child in two. Theoretically if a male slave were to marry a free woman the offspring would follow the status of the woman. If slaves of different owners married, the children would likewise belong to the slave mother's owner, 'like calf of cattle' says the law, with the proviso that if the slave father's owner had arranged (contributed to) the marriage he was entitled to one child in three. If two married slaves of different owners divorced, the children again followed the mother, but the slave husband's owner was entitled to one male child (or one female if there were no males). Variations might occur according to whether the children had been raised in the owner's household or not; the principle being that of compensation for loss of labour and for the maintenance of young children before they reached productive age. However in general it would seem likely that when slaves of different owners married, one owner, usually that of the woman, would buy the slave of the other. In theory the owner of married non-redeemable slaves could sell one and retain the other, or sell both to different owners, especially if the sale were a punishment. All children of slave parents, or a slave mother, were termed *luuk that* (child[ren] of slave[s]) and in the Ayuthaya period were hereditary non-redeemable slaves. Provisions for the allocation of slave children show very clearly not only concern to provide for clear-cut ownership of these forms of productive property, but also the value of the reproductive labour of slaves, reproducing simultaneously both the slave-owning society and the slave-labour force.

It is clear that the institution of slavery could definitively split up families, husband from wife, and children from father or both parents, by the initial act of enslavement or by subsequent sale. It also reinforced the matrifocal tendency, found also in some other societies with institutions of slavery, and which in Thai society is also found outside the institution of slavery, combined with more extensive matrilocal or even matrilineal tendencies within a broadly bilateral system of kinship. The Thai bilateral kinship system in turn afforded possibilities both for the relative ease of entry or committal into slavery by persons of both sexes and for the relative ease of assimilation of slaves into new communities or into owners' households without the additional hindrance or stigma which might be found in unilineal systems.

Numbers and Value of Slaves

Figures for the proportion of the population with the status of *that* are either non-existent or disputed for every period of Thai history. Even approximate orders of magnitude for the total or relative size of the slave population are difficult to assess, let alone the proportions of different types of slave.

In the state of Sukhothai (1250–1438) we are told that 'a substantial portion of the population were slaves' (Griswold and Prasert 1975:72). One of two senior town officers named in a royal edict was an 'Officer of Slave Affairs' (*ca kha*).

Van Vliet (1975:88) writes of seventeenth-century Ayuthaya that slaves 'make up a large part of Siamese wealth, splendour and fame.' Pallegoix estimated that in the mid-nineteenth century one quarter to one third of a population of some six million (of whom some two million Siamese proper) were slaves, the majority redeemable debt slaves (1854:8, 235, 298). The proportions may have been far higher in the capital city. Later in the nineteenth century Hallett cites 'Mr. Alabaster . . . confidential adviser to the king . . . that nine tenths of the non-Chinese inhabitants of Bangkok were slaves' (1890:447). Between 45 and 60 per cent of the population of Bangkok were Chinese for most of the nineteenth century (Skinner 1957:83).

Most references to numbers of slaves are to particular captures of war slaves (numbered as we have seen from several tens to several tens of thousands) and particular endowments of monasteries (usually numbered in several tens of *families* each). Slaves are mentioned as part of dowries; for instance the wife of King Mangrai (reigned 1259–1317) is recorded as bringing 500 slave families (perhaps between 2,000 and 3,000 people) as part of her dowry (Notton 1926–32, Vol. 3:48). Colquhoun (1885:257) reports the numbers of slaves, totalling many thousands, owned by the aristocracy and nobility of the small Lannathai kingdom of Chiengmai in the nineteenth century as follows:

Title	No. of slaves	(No. of elephants)
tsobua	1,500	(150+)
chao hona	1,000	(100)
kyoukoopone	800	(135)
other *chao*	70–100 each	(5–20)
puniahs (minor officials)	15–20 each	

Some idea of the scale of ownership can be inferred from the size of armies, bodyguards and retinues of royalty, aristocracy and nobility composed sometimes entirely of slaves. To give one example there were very large complements of rowers (male and female) of the boats of the aristocracy etc.

Seventeenth century observers report processions of up to 400 boats with complements of from 16 to 80 rowers each, depending on the rank of the owners (Van Vliet 1975; Tachard 1686; La Loubère 1969). Travel on land by sedan chair or elephant required considerable manpower, allowing for relief crews. Apart from transport itself, travelling retinues were large. La Loubère records that the king's bodyguard contained 500 men; his retinue when travelling was always 200 to 300 persons, with a 'Train of 15–20,000 on days of ceremony'.

The exchange value of slaves, as we have seen, was reckoned on the basis of a personal value allotted to slaves as to all freemen on the basis of social rank, age and sex, what Lingat and Wales called *wergeld* (or weregild), or in the context of slaves 'legal price', 'legal redemption price'. In the nineteenth century the tariff was as follows (Lingat 1931:79–80; figures in brackets from Tej Bunnag 1977:77):[1]

Male		Female	
Child to 3 months	6 ticals	Child to 3 months	4 ticals
26–40 years	56	21–30 years	48 (40)
91–100	4 (3)	91–100	3 (4)

There was no market place, nor a free market in slaves, except perhaps for the slave trade proper, the capture for sale of ethnic minorities. It would seem that there were no legal taxes on the ownership and exchange of slaves. However, the sale of both *phrai* (Akin 1969) and non-redeemable *that* (Lingat 1931) for profit existed. In the nineteenth century a freer market seems to have developed with the 'market price' of slaves well in excess of the legal tariff. In Indochina 'The French found that local chiefs when asked the worth of merchandise in their villages always added that of slaves, whose value fluctuated like that of other things, according to the law of supply and demand' (Colquhoun 1885:54 citing De Carné). Crawfurd (1915:138) wrote that:

An extraordinary advance in latter times in the price of slaves would seem to imply an important change in the frame of society. About 50 ticals [i.e. about the legal tariff] was in former periods the price of a good slave, but at present [1821] the average is about three times this amount. This implies an increased demand for labour . . .

Pallegoix, a little later, reports the prices of male slaves: aged twelve to sixteen years, 40–60 ticals, adults, 80–160 ticals. Later still Smith reports prices of 219 ticals for an adult male, 180 ticals for an adult female slave in Bangkok.

In northern Thailand women tended to be valued more highly than men: 'The average price for a woman, provided she is under forty-five years of age, being about £6·4; while that of a man, the inferior animal, is about £4' (Colquhoun 1885:257). Hallett gives the prices of adult males as 54 (British Indian) rupees, women 72 rupees: 'Among the warlike races of the hills the opposite rules, the value of the male being greater than that of the female, but in the Shan State (including Chiengmai) where the woman does most of the work, the woman is decidedly as a worker worth more than the man' (1890:131). But that this higher valuation of women did not always apply in the north is shown in an early table of 'The value of people' in a collection of northern Thai customary law in which slaves are compared with freeman (Sommai 1975a:1):

	Freemen		Slaves	
	Male	Female	Male	Female
Child	4 *baht*	3	3	2
Youth	5	10	10	7
Adult	34	25	30	20

The 'external' slave trade appears to have been conducted by barter for example in trade with the Karen (to whom the Thai traded cattle) a young male slave was valued at 7 bullocks, a young woman 8–10 bullocks (when the best bullock was valued at five shillings). One can see why if the internal rates were 54 rupees (men) and 72 rupees (women) trade declined when the value of cattle (in Chiengmai) rose from 2½ to 10–12 rupees.

Socio-Economic Location of Slaves

Slaves were involved in almost every branch of social production and reproduction as members of a subordinate stratum which included free peasants, labourers, craftsmen and servants performing equivalent functions. That is to say that neither by their legal or social status, nor by their relation to the ownership of means of production did slaves as a whole constitute a distinct socio-economic class. Nor were there 'labour processes specific to slavery' (Hindess and Hirst 1975: 140). There were two occupations in which I can find no reference to slaves. One is mining, which was doubtless performed in a number of small-scale operations by tribute paying freemen (*phrai suai*). The second is administration. It would seem that no use was made of slaves in state offices, which would be a kind of contradiction in terms since officials had *sakdina* rank above that of slave and freeman client. It may not have been impossible for an enfranchised slave to receive office. Certain slaves may have had a limited technical authority within hierarchically organised productive tasks, but they did not themselves own slaves.

The question of whether slaves were employed in agricultural production is of some interest. Bowring, exceptionally, states that 'The slavery to which they are subjected is not that of field labour' (1857:455), but the evidence for most periods shows that some slaves were engaged in agricultural production. The economic value of slaves in agriculture is indicated by the legal right of an owner to delay the redemption of a slave until ploughing and harvesting were completed (Lingat 1931). By agricultural production I here include the development of paddy fields and production of rice especially, but also other crops, the production of livestock, and such craft production as was necessary for the reproduction of the peasant household, or estate. These and other slaves would also contribute to agricultural production through the construction of irrigation works, whether on local or state initiative and control.

Slave production in agriculture took several forms. First, some were employed on the many estates of royalty, aristocracy and nobility, and of particular monasteries; these might either be constrained to deliver the whole product or a tithe. Secondly, some were engaged in production on land granted by their owner, or developed by themselves, delivering a rent in cash or kind. Thirdly, some were engaged in more autonomous production, perhaps delivering occasional tribute rent and always available for recall or for such services as their owner might require (Colquhoun 1885:257). Such slaves, producing their own instruments of production and having effective possession and control of the instruments and processes of production, might be regarded as a distinct category, perhaps resembling the Spartan helots, 'legally unfree bondsmen tied to the land' (Hindess and Hirst 1975:140), but they were always *ultimately* alienable chattels.

Slaves were employed in craft production, working in metals, wood, fibres, stone, brickmaking etc. Such production would contribute both to the private sector, for domestic consumption and perhaps limited commerce, and to the public sector for military and religious purposes and for royal trade. The co-option of craft skills would seem to have severely fettered the forces of production: '...there is no Person in this Country that dare distinguish himself in any Art [sc. crafts etc.] for fear of being forced to work gratis all his life for the service of his Prince' (La Loubère 1969:69). Thompson too refers to *hereditary* craftsmen and artisans: 'skilled craftsmen were drafted into perpetual service for which they received a miserly wage' and which 'stifled initiative' (1941:677).

War, probably the principal occupation of the state, served both to maintain and develop the resources of the state, and to contribute to the reproduction of both the slave population and the political system. Slaves were employed not only as fighting soldiers and bodyguards but also as artisans, and in the construction of fortifications, canals and roads for military purposes; and in those tasks which must have occupied the greater part of labour mobilised for war, in the commissariat and in transport, as bearers, carters, drovers, caring for elephants and horses etc. Slaves of all types might be mobilised for war and, for the king's military purposes short of war, private slaves could be drafted, as part of the royal ceremonial bodyguard. Slaves appear also to have served to maintain internal order as members of a civil police force (Graham 1924, Vol. 1:330–331).

In the sphere of exchange, slaves were used in a number of functions. They constructed the canals and roads used in commerce and themselves constituted a means of transport. They were commodities received in exchange together with other commodities (e.g. forest produce) from outside the social formation, and they were commodities for sale or hire, to their owners' profit, within the system. They were a form of currency in political transactions.

Slaves were engaged in religious works to a considerable extent. They could be used as objects of 'sacrifice' (*dana*) in a Buddhist sense, that is to say donated to monasteries as labour or even ordained as members of the Buddhist *sangha* to 'make merit' for their owners (in which case they were enfranchised). Their labour contributed chiefly to the construction of religious buildings and to agricultural production for the maintenance of the non-labouring population of monasteries.

One of the most signal uses of slaves was in a wide range of personal and domestic services, as 'family slaves' (cf. Engels 1972:121) and it is likely that all owners of slaves employed some in this way. The term slave is not infrequently doubled with that of 'house person' or domestic (*kha khon ruan*); in the 'stateless' Thai minorities of Indochina such slavery (*con huon*) was the only form (Dang Nghiem Van 1972:183). I have already referred to the huge personal retinues of the ruling stratum. 'No Magnificence appears like a great number of men devoted to serve you' (La Loubère 1969:42). Even in the carrying of sedan chairs 'the dignity herein consists in the number' (of bearers). The ceremonial importance of retainers, slaves and clients, for both prestige and the maintenance of the etiquette of official rank and status, cannot be stressed enough. Every emblem of rank and office (sword, betel boxes, cushions, fans etc.) would be carried wherever the dignitary moved. Consider the labour requirements implied in this list of perquisites of office granted by the king: 'The Prince lodges them, which is no great matter, and gives them some moveables, as Box of Gold or Silver for Betel, some Arms, and a Balon [boat], some Beasts, as Elephant, Horse and Buffalo, some Services, Slaves and in fine some Arable Land' (La Loubère 1969:81). One is reminded of Duby's observations (1973:107–8, 260) on the 'consumption economy' of early feudal Europe in which the 'needs' of the aristocracy were above all for 'le sacrifice et la parure'.

Other domestic work would of course include preparation of food (rice milling, cooking), care of children, and small-scale craft production. The person of the slave could also serve as a legal substitute for *corvée*. Of particular importance is the use of female slaves for sexual and reproductive 'services', as concubines and slave wives, thus serving both for domestic 'consumption' and use, and for the reproduction and increase of the slave-labour force of the household. The whole question of women and slavery needs further research. We have seen that even in a 'free' state women were regarded, in law at least if not in popular custom, as the alienable property of the husband or other closely bilaterally related elder male kinsman. It is also of interest that slavery was a means to mobilise female labour which might otherwise not be so directly available. For in the *corvée* system it was above all the labour of men that was directly mobilised, the women's role being largely to maintain the household and its corvéable males during the months of compulsory service each year. We have seen that female slaves were valued not much lower than men, and sometimes more highly. There is no evidence that the slave population contained a preponderance of men.

A further aspect of female slavery is that of prostitution. Even in the seventeenth century La Loubère (1969:85) refers to a titled official as 'that infamous fellow who buys Women and Maids to prostitute them . . .' and Hallett claims that 'the prostitutes are all slaves' sold by their kinsmen (1890:452). Even when not sold directly into prostitution the relative lack of customary and legal protection for female slaves, especially non-redeemable, must have made them vulnerable to sexual exploitation. To this day young girls and women are

K

sold into prostitution by their parents, or sell themselves, with varying degrees of 'willingness', with or without an informal 'guarantor', and more or less 'definitively', but always now without such specific limited forms of legal protection as were available under legal slavery.

So we can see that slave labour was used in almost all tasks, but more especially in the less productive, in a way which contributed above all to the conspicuous consumption of the ruling stratum, serving to develop the fetters rather than the forces of production. It is possible that more of the labour of slaves contributed to this sphere of consumption than the *corvée* labour of freemen clients (*phrai*). In some households at least, and possibly in some tasks, slave labour may have been locally preponderant. Nonetheless the total slave population was not only always considerably smaller than the freeman client population, but no labour process was exclusive to slaves. Though neither freemen nor slaves had full ownership of the most important means of production, especially land, slaves by and large had even less effective possession or control over the means of production, let alone the product of their labour.

Geographically slaves were concentrated in and around the political, urban centres, for they were overwhelmingly owned proportionate to social rank, and high-ranking aristocrats and office-holding nobility would themselves tend to be concentrated in the political centres. Slaves were also located, as we have seen, in outlying districts and the rural hinterlands of cities. But in towns and cities slaves may have formed a higher proportion of the total labour force.

If slave labour (and the *corvée* labour of freemen) was not the most productive form of labour from a material point of view—it did not contribute markedly to the development of trade and exchange, or to the development of productive forces, in the capital city—its *political* importance was crucial, as we have seen in a number of instances. At the same time it may have posed problems, in some periods, for the balance of political and economic forces within the state. Ownership of slaves was possibly a way in which a wealthy patron could increase his private labour force outside, so to speak, the formal allocation of clients by rank and office. It seems clear too that despite the owner having to 'maintain' slaves, they were not economically inefficient for their owners, even in a material sense and bearing in mind the emphasis on prestige production and conspicuous consumption (Watson 1976). Pallegoix (1854:234) refers to slaves being 'the principal wealth of rich families'; Lasker (1950:56) citing Alberti, to the Siamese elite being 'wealthy above all because of the herds of slaves they owned'. The king was constantly concerned to increase the numbers of royal *phrai* as against those allotted to officials and this appears also to be the case with slaves. Van Vliet (1975:88) writes of King Ramesuan (reigned 1369–1370, 1388–1395) that: 'He demanded that all subject lands and cities under [his] crown list their slaves. . . . If someone possessed more slaves than he reported, those unreported slaves were given to the king.'

In Colquhoun's judgement (1885:191), redolent of the capitalist ethic, 'Slavery is a canker which saps the manhood out of a people, encourages them in indolence, prevents them from enriching themselves and the State.' In reality the slaves may actually have enriched their private owners, and this was one of the several reasons for the abolition of legal slavery by King Chulalongkorn.

> This humanitarian reform [1874] had noticeable political implications. As 'slaves' were saleable commodities, the princes and the nobility were in fact going to be be progressively deprived of their capital and income. This in turn affected their power because hitherto they had been able to use their wealth to acquire both political and military support. The monarchy, on the other hand, benefitted from the reform for, while 'slaves' had either to work for the government for eight days of the year [by the late nineteenth century] or pay a commutation tax of 1 baht 50 stangs, free men either had to work for three months of the year or pay the government 18 baht (Tej Bunnag 1977:57).

There was at first considerable resistance to the proposed abolition in Siam, as in Indochina (Ingram 1971; Steinberg 1971). But it may also be the case that the introduction of

K*

legislation abolishing slavery (in any case gradually accomplished), or its success, were in part due to the fact that the slave-owning elite had new needs for cash rather than personal services, that new forms of consumption and display were emerging and that large retinues of slaves became less economical (Sharp and Hanks 1978:260 note 7). Also new forms of production, and use of capital were emerging, and in some cases land development, sale and rental became more profitable (van der Heide 1906).

Further discussion of the causes, processes and consequences of the abolition of slavery lie outside the scope of this paper. It may be mentioned however that the movement towards abolition, which received its main impetus in 1874, was not completed in the provinces until 1915. Many features of dependent, involuntary or forced labour continued, some to the present, though they may stem as much from the tradition of the *corvée* system as from slavery. According to Lasker the Act of 1900 'concerning the pay of the common people's service' prohibited the use of forced labour except by the central government and when wage labour was unobtainable. The labour of judicial prisoners continued to be used, for example in the building of the new city of Nakorn Pathom (Tej Bunnag 1977). And in the same year as the final Act abolishing slavery (1905) the Act concerning military conscription was introduced. Lingat refers to a law of 1899 (still in force when he wrote in 1931) concerning a kind of indentured labour, or sale of labour in advance. It became a criminal offence, with penalties of up to three years' imprisonment, to break such a labour contract. This form of labour bears a slight resemblance to that of fiduciary slave; the crucial difference being that both the capital and interest of the 'loan' (wages in advance) were paid off, and within a fixed period. Analogous forms of private labour hire exist to this day, and the unpaid labour of peasants is still occasionally requisitioned for public works by official authority, a practice not without its abuses. Nor is 'wage slavery' a term of mere rhetorical content, as Lasker (1950:103–4) wrote:

... this tendency for the spirit of outmoded labor attitudes to survive the formal suppression of the institutions from which they sprang, was reinforced in Siam ... by the barbarity of the new labor relations imported from without under the auspices of modern commercial enterprise.

Treatment of Slaves and the Ideology of Slavery

There is a broad consensus that Thai institutions of slavery were 'benign', both relative to the treatment of slaves in other social formations, and other forms of labour in Thai social formations. However, the evidence is not lacking in contradictions, and since the issue has a bearing on the ideology of slavery, both that of slave owners and that contained in the analysis of the institution, it is worth reviewing some of the arguments.

First there are those arguments which, in a humanitarian spirit, suggest that the absence of physical mistreatment and oppression blurs the distinction between slave and free. Such arguments not only minimise the fact that slavery entailed distinct legal statuses of unfree persons, but, more importantly from a theoretical perspective, ignore the degree of exploitation of labour of such unfree persons. There is no necessary reason why a slave who has no legal or effective control over the means of production or the products of his labour should not otherwise be treated 'benignly'.

Secondly there are arguments that the laws and decrees of rulers provided for the protection and well-being of slaves. We have seen that many did indeed. There are also numerous references to the characteristics of the good ruler which include the obligation to 'love his freemen and slaves' (cf. Sommai 1975b:5). Certain caveats need to be entered. The legal sources are more numerous and precise than accounts of actual practice. The existence of laws providing for the punishment of owners who sexually abuse, wound or kill slaves suggests that such occurrences took place, and perhaps precisely because the slave could in so many respects be treated as an object of property. Occasional excesses are reported. According to Van Vliet, King Naret (reigned 1590–1605) executed 1,600 rowers of royal boats for one boat crew's having made an error in landing, and in twenty years of rule ordered the death (other than in warfare) of 80,000 subjects, including slaves. This, though, appears to be as exceptional as King Trailok (reigned 1448–1488) who 'used labourers as workers with daily wages, and not as slaves as most Siamese kings have done and still do' (Van Vliet 1975:64, 83). Seni Pramoj (1967), a lawyer by training, refers, as evidence in mitigation, to the law forbidding the hunting of people to capture and sell as slaves, but we know for certain that this occurred.

The very numerous laws concerning the flight and recovery of runaway slaves suggest that flight from slavery was a common occurrence. It is by no means certain that war captives would not try to escape if they could. A Thai term for Achilles tendon is *en roi wai*, which literally means 'tendon thread rattan', a reference to the wounding and hobbling of prisoners in a far-from-benign manner. The emphasis on redeemable slaves in the nineteenth century may again distort the broader picture, but even then, we are told, four-fifths of non-redeemable slaves escaped when they could (Bowring 1857). When slavery was abolished in British Burma there was a steady stream of runaway slaves from the Shan states (Sao Saimong 1965).

Another argument is based on the reported unwillingness of many slaves to be freed when the laws were changed to require enfranchisement (Akin 1969 citing Anuman Rajadhon 1956). If indeed by that time some kinds of slavery had become uneconomical this may have been appreciated by the slaves. In any case the slaves, if young enough to make a new start, might well not have seen a better opportunity, or a less harsh or dependent one. It also does not argue that people were still willing to enter into slavery and the 'attractions of bondage'. It is worth noting too that the promise of freedom from slavery to people in non-subject territories appears to have been used occasionally as a strategy in South East Asian politics (Steinberg 1971). Seni Pramoj suggests that the absence of slave revolts argues for lack of oppression. In the Lao states, where a large proportion of slaves were of ethnic minorities, some such revolts did occur (Chit 1976). Perhaps more pertinent is that there were many other forms of protest and popular resistance, including flight.

Some writers imply that benignity can be established by comparison with persons in other dependent or servile conditions. A well-known remark by Pallegoix that slaves, though beaten, cursed and ill-fed, were in general treated with humanity and often better than servants in nineteenth-century France, is usually taken as evidence of good treatment, on the implicit assumption that servants in nineteenth-century France were well treated. Such arguments once again ignore the 'interpenetration' of effective status of legally free and unfree persons and corresponding differences in treatment. A law of 1647 exhorted patrons not to use royal clients (*phrai luang*) as if they were slaves. It is not a very convincing argument either way that *that* were no worse off than *phrai*, as La Loubère (1969:77) wrily observed:

> The Master has all power of the Slave, except that of killing him: And tho' some may report, that slaves are severely beaten there, (which is very probable in a country where free persons are so rigidly bastinado'd) yet the Slavery there is so gentile (sic), or, if you will, the Liberty so abject, that it is become a Proverb, that the Siameses (sic) sell it to eat of a Fruit, which they call Durions [durian].

The mitigating effect of Buddhist ideas and practices is often adduced as an argument for leniency in the Thai institutions of slavery. It is surely the case that Buddhism, as well as other customary ideas and practices, had a mitigating effect on possible abuses of persons, slave and free, and that these are reflected to some extent in laws and reforms, in a way comparable to the effect of Christianity on medieval European slavery (Duby 1968). The Burmese case provides a challenging comparison, which cannot be developed here. For in Burma, also a Theravada Buddhist country, temple slaves were regarded as impure, and there were restrictions on intermarriage and even commensality with such slaves (Crawfurd 1830:397). Lasker observed that 'the most miserable among them [slaves in Burma], according to all accounts, were the pagoda slaves' (1950:52).

One of the rights denied to a (male) slave was that of entering the Buddhist *sangha* as monk or novice. It may well not be possible to know what effect this prohibition may have had in the psychology and consciousness of slaves and free-men, but it is important as being perhaps the only indication that a slave was regarded not merely as an inferior, unfree human subject, but even to some extent as less than fully human. This said, it was possible for an owner, or his kinsmen at his death, to enfranchise a slave or child of a slave as a pious act in order to sponsor his ordination as a free person. This, Lingat says, 'seems to have been fairly frequent'. But the issue was clearly complex and problematic: an interesting section of customary law deals with 'the ordination of slaves' at length, several pages and by far the longest section in the whole collection (Sommai 1975a). To some extent this law protected the slave, for he might not be ordained if his owner intended to re-enslave him on leaving the monastery. The decision whether to accept the slave as a candidate for ordina-tion (and therefore prior enfranchisement) rested with the monks, who were bound not to ordain a slave proposed in a hurry, or whose owner or kinsmen could not be traced (unless authorized by a prince). If the monks, for whatever reasons, did not permit ordination this meant that the slave's *buppa-chakam* (merit for ordination) was not 'pure' and that he had not freed himself *spiritually* from the condition of slave (*phon thatpawa*).

With this one possible exception, there seems to have been none of the 'desocialisation' or 'depersonalisation' of the slave reported in Africa (Meillassoux 1975), not even in a ritual manner. Thus even members of other ethnic groups could be culturally assimilated, while they might retain a certain ethnic distinctness. Lingat claims that slavery was accepted without shame, though according to Wales (1934: 60–61) while there was 'no shame attaching to the status of private slave' the royal slaves were 'deeply despised'.

Certainly a notable feature of the Thai case is that there seems to have been no stigma imposed on an enfranchised slave. Furthermore, with the exception of the status of enfranchised slave wife referred to earlier, there was never anything approaching a 'freedman' status. Yet at least one term of abusive reference to a person as a slave exists, *khii kha* (lit. excrement slave, slave rubbish). And the terms of at least one form of judicial oath implies that slavery was a state devoutly to be eschewed: '... may I (if I bear false witness) after death migrate into the body of a slave, and suffer all the hardships and pain attending the worst state of such a being ...' (Bowring 1857:180).

On the other hand, the category 'slave' is widely found in even current linguistic usage, part of a persistent and pervasive culture of subordination. There are a number of first-person pronouns used, especially by women and in speaking to seniors, which derive from the root word *kha*, or slave. Village congregations refer to themselves as *phuu kha thanglai* (all of us your slaves) in addressing superhuman entities, divinities and spirits. Even senior officials are 'slaves of the king' (*kha luang*, a popular term for provincial governors). In the Ayuthaya period senior officials could be beaten, disgraced, and subsequently reinstated. The king himself is the 'slave of the Buddha' when he addresses the Enlightened and Compassionate One. As Ingram (1971:13) says, in a sense 'all people were chattels of the king', the 'lord of life'.

Conclusions

In conclusion I shall recapitulate some of the distinctive features of Thai institutions of slavery. Slaves originated from both outside and inside the social formation: from outside, from other states and hill peoples, by trading, raiding and warfare; and from inside chiefly through indebtedness and juridical confiscation. The origin of slaves had little bearing on the uses of their labour, nor did outside origin lead to a marked or permanent 'outsider' status. Both outsiders and insiders reproduced themselves as a slave labour force. The possibility of enfranchisement was however far more likely for those originating from inside, especially slaves for debt, though not all these were redeemable. After enfranchisement there was virtually nothing approximating a 'freedman' status.

Slaves possessed considerable personal rights, though these varied over time and according to legal status, with hereditary, non-redeemable slaves having fewest rights. Redeemable slaves were by no means always eventually enfranchised, and though they had a 'guarantor' who could uphold their rights against abuses by their owner, this did not necessarily provide them with as much protection as that for a freeman client from his patron. In one respect (male) slaves were regarded as less than fully human in that they could not, as slaves, be ordained in the Buddhist *sangha*. If some slaves enjoyed relatively extensive personal freedoms, they were part of a society in which 'free' subjects were relatively dependent and subordinate.

Slave labour at no times formed the principal basis of production and there were no labour processes specific to slaves. Thai social formations were not therefore characterised by a slave mode of production. Slaves were engaged in almost all forms of production and services, with the notable exceptions of mining and administration. They were above all a means of augmenting the labour power of freeman clients, alongside whom they often worked. Institutions of slavery appear to have directly mobilised the labour of women and children more effectively than the legal patron-client system. Slaves may have contributed more, proportionately, to the sphere of consumption than freeman client labour, especially as domestic servants and retainers.

Similarities in the economic location of slaves and freeman clients, even some similarities in their rights as persons, should not however be allowed to blur the distinction between the freeman client who owed a fixed amount of labour power to his master, and the slave whose labour power had been sold outright to an owner or mortgaged indefinitely. Nonetheless economic and status differentiations existed among slaves of the same legal category, as among freeman clients. Although legally and ideologically a lowest stratum, slaves may be regarded as having had a social existence in practice alongside freeman clients (Akin 1969, 1975; Cruickshank 1975; Miers and Kopytoff 1977).

Slaves were a form of property and of *private* property.

Slavery was arguably the most important form of private property in a society where, in theory at least, all land and persons and offices were the property of the king who could recall and reallot them at will. What is more, the remarkably complex body of laws on slavery was developed and superintended by the state. Though authorising and guaranteeing this form of private property, the state, in the person of the king, was able to control the development and distribution of slave labour in a number of ways. Many slaves were owned directly by the king, who could also mobilise privately owned slaves for war, and also redeemable slaves for *corvée* labour. Royal control was also exercised through the monopoly in land, through the distribution of prisoners of war, by restricting the passage into slavery of freeman clients, and by periodic checks on abuses (e.g. registrations of monastery slaves). In the nineteenth century there was an increase in privately owned slaves and informal clientage. The nineteenth century reforms and eventual abolition of slavery can be seen in this context as moves in the centuries-old strategy of balancing royal and private power (Akin 1975; Tej Bunnag 1977).

Finally, institutions of slavery had a distinct political and ideological importance. Slavery, originating in violence, was a means of subordinating otherwise non-subject peoples for whom the existing ideological constraints had no force. Slaves were eminently available to be distributed, in new settlements and as monastery slaves for instance, in ways which shored up or expanded the politico-religious base of the monarchy (Charnvit 1976). Slaves obtained by trade, in warfare or juridically, provided an ever-renewable source of labour which the monarch could distribute in new political transactions with the aristocracy and nobility who formed his bureaucracy, thus allowing an extra dimension of flexibility over and above his control of client labour. Although undoubtedly more research is needed into the distribution of slaves among owners and their precise economic location (including possibly at lower social levels), it was predominantly the same ruling class of aristocrats and nobles, patrons with legal entitlement to the labour of clients for private and public uses, that appears to have owned slaves. Slaves thus constituted an apparently crucial extra amount of labour for the reproduction of this political class, its mode of consumption and prestige production.

This broad sociological survey has perhaps been over bold in ranging rather widely in time and space, but the historical work has scarcely yet been done which would allow a full theoretical consideration of slavery for one limited period or conjuncture in a specific Thai social formation. It is hoped that it may have served to establish both the specificity of the varied and complex forms of slavery in historical Thai societies, and at the same time that there is a basis for comparison and that 'slavery' is not an entirely inappropriate term in the consideration of Thai institutions of *that*.

11

Slaves, Aristocrats and Export of Sago in Sarawak

H. S. MORRIS

The problem to be considered in this paper is that of a ranking system rather than that of the position of slaves and
aristocrats among the Coastal Melanau of Sarawak. It is not
specifically about slavery which is, I shall argue, only one
part, and perhaps in the final analysis, not an essential part of
a wider system of power relationships.

The Coastal Melanau inhabit an area stretching from the
delta district of the Rejang River along the north-west coast
of Borneo as far as Bintulu. They also have close cultural,
linguistic and social connections with groups in the interior
who claim historical links with the Coastal Melanau, but
whose languages, though clearly related, are not intelligible
to the latter. One group merges so gradually into the next
that it becomes difficult to decide what connection, linguistic,
social or cultural, the last group has with the first.

In the census of the population of Sarawak made in
1960 the Melanau people, who were arbitrarily defined as
the coastal dwelling groups, numbered 44,000, of whom
about 10,000 were still 'pagan'. Most of the others were
Muslim, though a small number had become Roman Catholic
Christians (Jones 1960).

The coastal area is a low-lying swampy plain extending
from three to twenty miles inland, often below sea level,
made up of poor peat soil, covered by dense tropical rain-
forest. The soil does not easily allow the inhabitants to grow

rice by shifting cultivation, the characteristic mode of farming of people in the interior districts. The area is traversed
by meandering rivers, all flowing roughly north-west into the
South China Sea. These rivers are tidal for long distances
upstream, and during the north-east monsoon, from November to March, they are likely to overflow their banks and
flood the surrounding land. Swamp rice (*padi paya*), a strain
of dry rice that tolerates wet soil but not flooding, can be
grown on the river banks which are slightly raised, and which
are therefore drier than the adjacent land. The rice grown in
such conditions is an uncertain crop and is frequently ruined
before it can be harvested. It cannot be relied on as a staple.
The only food plant that flourishes in this environment is the
sago palm (*metroxylon sagus*) and for many centuries the
people living in these swampy forests, even those outside the
Melanau districts, have cultivated the palm. From it they
produce a flour for subsistence and export. Certain essential
commodities such as salt, iron, copper, and stone are not
found in the swamp area, and without them the Melanau
cannot be self-sufficient. To obtain these commodities they
exported sago and forest products—rattan, gums and resins,
beeswax, camphor, birds' feathers and timber. The exchange
of sago and forest products for goods from Brunei and
Pontianak on the coasts of north-west and western Borneo
and from Indonesia, Malaya, Siam, Indo-China, and China
itself has for several centuries been a characteristic feature of
the economies of the Melanau people and also of many of
the inland shifting cultivators as well. The environment in
which the Melanau live made this export and import trade
indispensable, whereas for the shifting cultivators of the
interior it was not essential; the goods acquired by the trade
were either better than those they could make for themselves
or carried greater prestige. The trade, which for the shifting
cultivators as much as for the Melanau often required long
periods away from home, was possible only because the
forests produced commodities that more civilised communities overseas or on the coasts were willing to buy, but for
which they were not willing on the whole to undertake long
or dangerous expeditions. Expeditions to the coast or over-

seas were facilitated for the shifting cultivators and the
Coastal Melanau alike by their economic and social systems
which made it possible for a certain number of men to be set
free for relatively long periods from the task of growing
staple food crops.

A broad band of stratified societies extended from the
Coastal Melanau district on the north-west of Borneo across
the island, and in these societies trade was organised by the
aristocrats. To the north and the south of this band of hierarchically ordered societies were other types of social systems
with more egalitarian structures. Many of them, the Iban of
Sarawak for example, also took part in the trade for manu-
factured goods from the coast; but in these societies men
were set free for the trading expeditions in other ways and
the trade was not organised by aristocrats. In all these
societies, if the men did not use the free time for trading
expeditions they used it for obtaining extra subsistence by
hunting and gathering in the forests, fishing in the rivers, or
in warfare.

The sago palm is grown by the Melanau in small, individually owned plantations. It is a perennial plant, and a plantation once established does not need to be renewed. When a
stem is felled a sucker is allowed to grow up and form a new
trunk which matures in about fifteen years. The palm at
maturity need not be immediately felled, and consequently
in an old plantation cropping can take place the whole year
round. All that is required to keep it in order is the occasional
clearing of weeds; and a plantation in full production and
within convenient distance of a village is an important item
of capital property. In contrast with the cultivation of rice,
the growth and production of sago continues throughout the
year. The men fell the palms and float them to the village;
and after cutting up the trunk and reducing it to pith, they
hand it over, in the traditional system, to the women for
producing flour. This flour is then washed and baked into an
edible biscuit for domestic consumption or export. The men
are then free for a short period, until more palms are needed,
to hunt and gather and fish. These periods, though long
enough for short local trading expeditions up or down river,

did not allow them time to organise or go on long overseas expeditions. It is significant that in the Melanau villages for which there is information, aristocrats and slaves each numbered approximately ten per cent of the total population. Most slaves in practice, though not necessarily in theory, were owned by aristocrats, some of whom were thus set free from the tasks of organising economic production and the problems of defence at a period when almost every village lived in a state of hostility and in which raiding was endemic. It was not until after the conquest of the district in 1861 by the Rajah of Sarawak that peaceful conditions were established in the 1870s and 1880s.

Traditional Melanau Social Structure

Traditionally a Melanau village consisted of two or three long-houses. These were massive wooden fortresses built on piles, often thirty feet high, which were usually situated at the confluence of a strategically important stream with the main river. Each village was politically independent within its own territory, and was, as mentioned in the last section, frequently on terms of active hostility with its Melanau neighbours and the people up-river, most of the latter from the beginning of the nineteenth century being Iban invaders from western Sarawak. Investment of labour and capital in a Melanau longhouse was so great that it was seldom moved or completely rebuilt. When peaceful conditions were established under Brooke rule, the houses were gradually abandoned and their inhabitants built separate dwellings along the banks of the rivers.

Although physically a single structure, a longhouse was made up of separately built apartments, each owned and inhabited ideally by one married couple and perhaps one married child, often but not invariably the youngest. Frequently, especially towards the end of the nineteenth century when the longhouses were being abandoned, the individual apartments were overcrowded and might hold as many as fifteen to twenty people, some of whom slept on the verandah that ran in front of all the apartments. Much of the village life and ceremonial took place on this verandah, and when small separate houses came to replace the longhouses a great deal of the culture, especially the performance of communal ceremonies, fell into disuse because no new central meeting house took the place of the verandah.

The political control of the villages was in the hands of a small group of aristocratic elders whose families ideally owned the central apartments, and who were said to be the descendants of the village founders. On each side of this central core were apartments owned by freemen, and at each end of the house were the apartments of the slaves. An elaborate set of customary rules (*adet*) regulated the behaviour of the ranks to one another and of most other aspects of social life. The *adet*, one of the community's most valued possessions, was in the custody of the aristocratic elders. No single elder was superior to the others, though he might have special knowledge that fitted him for particular tasks. For example, a man with unusual abilities in war might be put in charge of raids, and another with knowledge of rituals might assume leadership on special occasions. But leadership of this kind was not formalised into permanent office, and there were no political chiefs who ruled villages as a personal right (Morris 1953). Occasionally a man with charismatic qualities might rise to pre-eminence during his lifetime and maintain a loose alliance of villages. He might even challenge the claims of the representatives of the Sultan of Brunei who had settled at the mouths of the rivers to control the sago trade, and who asserted suzerainty over the whole river's length. Such men, however, were never able to establish permanent kingdoms and their rule invariably broke up at their deaths, if not before.

Each household in a longhouse was economically independent. Its members were responsible for its subsistence, whether in the form of sago, rice or products obtained from hunting, gathering or fishing. There was, generally speaking, little specialised division of labour and a household could normally supply its own needs and look after the ritual health of its members.

Traditionally, Melanau society made use of three distinct

criteria in organising social life. The first was that of local grouping; the second was that of kinship; and the third was that of hereditary rank. A Melanau thought of himself in each of these social dimensions. He was closely identified with a particular locality, especially a village, whose inhabitants were thought to be, and often were, unique in matters of dialect and custom. As an individual, a man or woman was the focal point of a kindred with whom he or she shared a wide range of social and economic interests, regulated by principles of bilateral descent. Lastly he had by virtue of birth a rank status. In any context the behaviour of one man towards another was largely determined by the fact that the two men were neighbours or strangers, kinsmen or not, of equal or unequal rank. In addition, behaviour was also regulated by facts of age and sex, and was, further constrained by the concept of *adet*. This word is most usefully translated as *order*. *Adet*, together with the cognate Malay term *adat*, is often limited to the concept of customary law, but it also governs an individual's ritual as much as his social behaviour.

The Rank System

At birth a Melanau acquired not only a place in a village and a circle of kinsmen, but he was also placed in a theoretically unalterable rank category, *basa'*, which in theory was that of his father. Three main categories were recognised which can roughly be translated into English as aristocrats (*menteri*), freemen, (*bumi*), and slaves (*dipen*) (Morris 1953, 1967). The preferred marriage was with a second cousin of any kind, provided it was not across a rank boundary. However, although each *basa'* was ideally an endogamous category, marriages between individuals of different ranks were in fact not uncommon. Relationships between the ranks were formally laid down in the *adet* and a breach of rank rules was an act of disrespect (*tulah*), and incurred civil and supernatural penalties.

This ideal formulation of their rank system by the Melanau would have led to consequences that were not in fact found.

Each *basa'* was ideally a caste-like endogamous group, and theoretically a man could not move up or down from the position into which he was born; but in a small-scale society of the kind found among the Melanau, where politically independent villages seldom contained more than six or seven hundred people, such a rigid system would probably have been unworkable had there not been considerable flexibility in interpreting the rules of rank.

In Melanau villages the numbers of slaves and aristocrats, as we have already noted, were roughly equal; and the fact that most of the slaves were owned by aristocrats meant that some of the latter, at any rate, could be set free from the agricultural tasks that tied them down to a narrow routine. This fact, as we saw earlier, allowed the organisation of large-scale trading expeditions overseas; but, as we also saw, some of the inland peoples without a stratified social structure participated equally in overseas trade; and it would not be hard to visualise a state of affairs in which the Melanau exchanged the same goods with the coastal centres such as Brunei or Pontianak by a series of step-by-step transactions, as did the tribes of New Guinea or Australia. Short periods, which ordinary men were able to spend away from the tasks of sago production, and which were enough for small ventures, would have been sufficient for such an exchange system. It is probably useless to speculate on how ranking originated among the Melanau; but given the fact that it existed in the form that it did, it is easy to see how it persisted with little change until the foundation of Singapore in 1819 created a market for sago flour, not the biscuit that had hitherto been exported. This new demand was first met by Malay merchants from Brunei and Kuching and later by Chinese entrepreneurs, but not by the Melanau aristocrats, who gradually withdrew from the sago trade and were left with the functions of warfare, and later only with the function of administering the customary law, the *adet*.

In daily life a man's rank was publicly and importantly manifested on occasions such as those of birth, marriage, and death, when the ritual, the insignia, and the words used were all regulated by the ranks of the participants. Ideally a man's status was also shown by the position of his apartment in the longhouse, by the amount and kinds of property he owned, and by his being a member or not of the group of governing elders. In addition the rank of a man or woman was thought to be plain for all to see in his manners. Those of high rank were expected to speak with care and in a modulated voice. Deference to rank was due from everybody. In a canoe, high position and age occupied the centre places, and slaves and youths the bow and stern. In collecting a party of guests or workers by boat an aristocrat was expected to leave the canoe, mount the ladder to the house and sit down in the apartment of a man of high rank before inviting him to accompany the party. He could invite a man of middle rank by getting out of the boat, but it was not necessary for him to enter the apartment, whereas a slave or freed slave would be summoned by shouting from the boat.

A traveller to Sarawak in 1863, a Mr. Boyle, made the following observations of a Melanau group on the river Rejang, but which still applied both to the Rejang and the Coastal Melanau in 1948:

> The condition of the slave in Borneo is by no means deplorable. We always found a difficulty in distinguishing the servile population of a household from the free born population, and the honours and distinction open to the latter class are likewise accessible to the former. The Kennowit chieftain, Joke, ... was born a slave, and remains so, I believe, to this moment; nevertheless he has been elected to preside over a considerable clan and is followed in the field by a hundred free warriors. And although the case of the slave in the possession of high power and distinction is necessarily rare, personal merit and bravery will carry a Dayak of any origin to the highest positions in a community so democratic. These observations do not apply to marriage, in which a taint of servile blood, though incurred generations back, will outweigh the highest personal qualities (Boyle 1865:99).

Two very tangible, and a number of more intangible, factors underwrote aristocratic power. Although any man or woman in Melanau society might own sago land, the largest holdings belonged to the aristocrats; and that was still so in 1948, even after sixty years of relative freedom from raiding under the rule of Rajahs of Sarawak. In 1860 it was only the aristocrats who could mobilise work parties and guards to work in safety in the sago plantations. An ordinary man might go into the jungle, the sago gardens, or on a trading expedition with a few friends or relatives, but the risk of death from enemies was high. Every year, too, the aristocrats organised the planting and cultivation of rice by the village in one large field in which each household was allotted a strip. In short, the aristocrats traditionally controlled land and military power; they were also the custodians of the *adet* and sat in judgement on all cases of breach of the *adet*, cases that might cover either social or ritual offences. For some offences the penalty might be death or exile, the latter being tantamount to a death sentence. Disrespect (*tulah*) for rank or age was only one of a variety of offences that were *palei* or forbidden by the *adet*, and which were thought to endanger the proper order of the social and symbolic worlds. Even when an offence was thought to endanger only the offender and his punishment was left to automatic supernatural sanction, the aristocrats, as guardians of the *adet*, were nevertheless concerned because a relatively harmless sexual misdemeanour with a cousin, for example, might, by another reading of the offenders' genealogies, be seen as a more seriously incestuous offence involving persons of different generations, thus endangering not just themselves, but also the community as a whole.

Changes in Rank

My argument so far has been that a Melanau village was a hierarchy of power in which, because of the structural arrangements, because of endemic warfare, and because of the overriding need for external trade, those at the top, a small group of aristocrats (*menteri*), effectively controlled the system. But against this has to be set the fact that we are dealing with small communities, between 500 and 1,000 people, and that the field for recruiting talent to run the society was necessarily small. In these circumstances for the society to work at all, given the ideologically rigid social structure, there had in practice to be considerable flexibility that allowed talent to be recruited to the places where it was useful, and dead wood to be discarded from positions of influence. The mechanisms for doing this were of course the hundreds of small daily actions in which people interacted and displayed their talents, but the results, the shifts in status, the movements up and down the ranking system, can be seen on formal occasions when rank, reference to which in normal life was considered to be bad manners, was unambiguously displayed. Of these occasions, the most important was the marriage of a man's daughter. Theoretically she took his rank, and this fact was shown in the bride wealth and the symbolic gifts which the groom's family formally presented to the bride's father at the wedding. The negotiation of these gifts and their reception, as well as the bringing and presentation of them by the groom's party, were the responsibility of members of the aristocratic families of the village. These occasions on which the ranking system was, so to speak, on public display, and the next generation was being allocated its position in the system, were thought to be so important that pretty well every wedding in a village, from that of a slave upwards, had an aristocrat in charge of the arrangements.

What I have just said means that the aristocrats were in fact able to control public recognition of changes in status. A man who for example had military skills or who had acquired land or influence in other ways, and who frequented the company of the governing clique of aristocrats, and whom they consulted, could with their consent claim bride wealth for his daughter appropriate to a higher rank than his own. He could do this because marriages across the rank barriers and the tracing of connections to former holders of the symbols of the desired rank was permissible through either male or female forebears. This kind of flexibility had always been possible, and, had the ideal of strict endogamy within the rank categories always been observed, would have had no practical consequences in changing an individual's status. It was therefore not very difficult for almost anybody in the society to claim the bride wealth of any rank for his daughter if the aristocrats in charge of the wedding agreed. On the other hand, if it was the groom who wanted to acquire a higher rank than that given him by birth, there was an institutionalised mechanism for doing it by presenting extra bride wealth before the bride wealth proper was given. The amount was adjusted to the rank being bought. Again it was the aristocrats in charge of the wedding who had to agree to the use of this institution (*tebuih basa'*). This phrase is usually translated as 'redeeming the rank'. A cognitive word in Malay is defined in one of the standard dictionaries as 'redeem or ransom, especially of getting things out of pawn and acquiring debt slaves by handing over the amount of the debt to the creditor' (Wilkinson 1959).

At this point more needs to be said about the rank system itself, which has so far been described as a three-tiered structure. The reality was more complex; among the aristocrats were three grades: the top, the middle and the low, each of which was marked by the right to use a particular type of weapon to symbolise the status of their daughters at their weddings and for the parents to receive a fixed weight of brassware as bride wealth. The low status aristocrats were usually the children of mixed rank marriages. Similarly, there were two grades of freeman; the true freemen who could be *commanded* by nobody to perform services for aristocrats, and the 'tied' freemen or (*bumi giga'*) who were, translating the Melanau strictly, those who could be called upon by a former owner to perform services. These 'tied' freemen were freed slaves. Similarly the rank *dipen*, which I have translated as slave, was also divided into a number of grades which were shown by the symbols and the weight of brass presented at the wedding of a man's daughter. A slave, like anybody else was entitled to redeem rank at a wedding, or in this case, at other times. The system of redeeming rank (*tebuih basa'*) was organised in steps (*tirih*). The full redemption of a slave from the lowest group to the status of a 'tied' freeman took seven steps. Each one was measured by a fixed weight of brassware. The slave could and usually did take fewer than seven steps at a time, and therefore still remained a slave (*dipen*). In the same way, but this time only at a wedding, a freeman could redeem his rank and become a lower aristocrat by taking fifteen steps. In short, this mechanism brought the essential element of flexibility into the conceptually rigid system. In some ways it is the most interesting aspect of the whole system; for in a sense everybody in the community below the aristocrats was placed on a ladder in degrees of servitude, thus concentrating effective power in the hands of the few men and women who eventually found their way to the top of the system of honours. The question now remains—how far can one usefully call those at the bottom 'slaves'?

Slavery among the Melanau

Information about slavery in this society is very patchy indeed. The institution was not formally abolished until 1928, but it had been severely discouraged by the Rajah's administrative officers since the conquest of the district in 1861. District-office court records begin about 1870 and continued until approximately 1910. There are a number of disputes about rank recorded, including some involving slaves; so we know something of the system in its later stages. In 1948 there were still many elderly people who knew a great deal about it; and the observances of rank at weddings were still fully practised. In other respects the system was in decay, except that the elders who ran the village were all still nominally aristocratic in rank. With patience it was possible to discover the rank of every person in a village.

The status of slave, however, needs yet further consideration. Who were the slaves and how were they recruited? In the late nineteenth century most were debt slaves, often men or women whose economic circumstances made it easier for them to go voluntarily into the protection of a powerful individual. Children who were left orphan were usually taken into slavery. By that time the economic functions of the aristocrats had been almost completely eroded and the economy had largely become dependent on the sale of a cash crop. Before 1861 no doubt slaves were more often acquired as prisoners of war, but there is virtually no information on how many they may have been or how frequently they were captured. Most slaves, of course, were born slaves. The children of a slave and a free person were alternately slave and free.

There were two categories of slave: house slave and field slave. The closer translation of the Melanau terms is 'inside' and 'outside' slaves. The house slaves lived in the owner's household and helped in domestic tasks and accompanied aristocrats as servants and companions wherever they went. The outside slaves lived in a household of their own and were entitled to their own strip of land in the communal rice field. Like inside slaves they might even own sago gardens in their own right. But they were subject of course to all the demands made by the owner, and certain of the later recorded cases were those in which aristocratic owners claimed ownership of a slave's sago garden by virtue of owning the slave.

Already the more important rights and duties inherent in the status of slave have been set out. He was in a sense owned by a master because he could be transferred from one master to another. When an aristocratic woman was married, one of the items of bride wealth presented to her by the groom was a female slave. A slave's right to work for his own advantage was restricted: the lower his degree of redemption the less right in practice he had to work for himself. A field slave had taken almost all the five steps necessary to redeeming his rank and was entitled to set up his own household, whereas a house slave might be only two and a half steps up the scale, and therefore had less opportunity to work for himself. No slave had the right to regulate his own marriage or that of his child. In a society where everybody needed a kinsman to be answerable for his actions and his safety, a slave was a person jurally without a family, especially if he were a prisoner of war. His owner stood in *loco parentis*. As a father the owner arranged all matters concerning the slave's marriage and of the children: in return he received the bride wealth. As the slave had no 'social kinsmen' the master did not distribute any of the bride wealth to the slave or any to the slave's biological kin, though he usually made a few *ex gratia* gifts.

When a slave redeemed his rank and became a tied free-man, although he was still in some degree in a servile relation-ship to his ex-master, he was independent in arranging his own marriage and those of his children. In most respects, then, the status of slave was not that a chattel slave, except possibly in the matter of being transferred either by the owner's marriage or by inheritance on the death of a master, when the slaves were divided in equal numbers among the children. However a slave did take on one aspect of being a 'thing' in certain ritual contexts.

One of the most highly regarded stories in all Melanau villages is the history of Tugau, a legendary chieftain who appears at the head of most aristocratic genealogies, and who in his lifetime, perhaps four or five centuries ago, built up a large empire of allies which seriously rivalled that of the Sultan of Brunei. In the story Tugau met his death when he and his followers were building a new longhouse. The main post was so large that it could not be erected. Tugau there-fore ordered the daughter of one of his slaves to be placed in the pit below the post and killed as it came down on her. This gave the post life (*nyawa*), and it was successfully raised; but the father of the girl seized Tugau's own spear and killed him before being speared himself.

The status of a slave as a ritual commodity, which in the last resort can be destroyed, is also illustrated by stories told of the erection of *klideng*. These are elaborately carved secondary burial posts that were hollowed out and erected to hold the bones of eminent chiefs, such as Tugau himself. To give the post 'life' a male slave was crushed below it, and to give the dead chief a personal attendant in the after world a girl was tied to the top of the post and allowed to die of hunger and thirst. To go with the dead chief, always sup-posing he had died a natural death, she also had to die naturally, for those who died violently went to a different part of the land of the dead. Occasions such as these, in which a slave was treated as a chattel, were exceptional. The norm was that described by Mr. Boyle, the traveller in

1863, when he said: 'We always found a difficulty in distinguishing the servile population of a household from the freeborn population' (Boyle 1865). It is not possible to say how
many slaves there were in 1863. The figure of 10 per cent of
the population who were called slaves in 1948 was made up
of people whom the rest of the community said were un-
redeemed slaves or whose fathers had been so. Work on
similar societies such as the Kayan and the Kenyah in the
interior, where the system still exists in a covert form, has
produced comparable percentages (Rousseau 1974).

Conclusions

The problem considered in this paper, then, can be summarised quite shortly. The environment in which the Melanau
lived made it necessary for the inhabitants to acquire goods
from outside the area. This was done by a system of trade in
which sago biscuit, a food in a durable form, and a variety of
jungle products were exchanged for the necessary imports.
The economy was a mixture of settled agriculture and hunting and gathering which released men and women from the
daily routine for only short periods. The trade was organised
so that small-scale individual exchanges were confined to a
small locality, in contrast with large-scale overseas expeditions, in which a fairly large number of men might be absent
from the villages for long periods. Among the Melanau, as
also among the Kayan and the Kenyah in the interior, these
expeditions were organised by the aristocrats; but it seems
unlikely that either the environment or the economic organisation of agriculture and trading was a determining factor in
producing a class of aristocrats in control of the system of
production and exchange, whose decisions were ideally a
collective group responsibility backed by the political and
ideological organisation of the society. Nor is it likely that
such factors can easily explain the existence of slaves and the
varying degrees of servitude among the non-aristocratic
population; for all the same data as are found among the
ranked societies of the Melanau, the Kayan, and the Kenyah
concerning agriculture, hunting and gathering, exchange,

and enslaved war captives, can also be found among neighbouring, but egalitarian societies, such as the Iban.

In the relatively small longhouse villages of the Melanau, even though the structure of the society and the system of ranking were defined in rigid and absolute terms, in practice it was neither feasible nor safe to run the society in an inflexible way. The people at the bottom of the hierarchy could, it is true, be exchanged or destroyed like other goods, but to do so was unusual. Given the fact that the Melanau, in contrast with the Iban, had an ideology of hierarchy, then many of the special features of the society become comprehensible; even the development, ideally at any rate, of the absolute authority of the aristocrat at one extreme, and the absolute social nullity of the sacrificed slave at the other, was mediated by elaborate rules which allowed those in between to improve their status. But as every Melanau also knew, the *adet*, the ideal, could not always be observed in practice. Whenever an accommodation of the ideal to the practical was made somebody would say: 'To speak the *adet* is sufficient'; in other words, as long as the ideal was symbolically observed the system was not in danger.

Contributors

BURTON BENEDICT is Professor of Anthropology, University of California at Berkeley.

MAURICE BLOCH is Reader in Anthropology, London School of Economics, University of London.

PHILIP BURNHAM is Lecturer in Anthropology, University College London.

LIONEL CAPLAN is Reader in Anthropology with reference to South Asia, School of Oriental and African Studies University of London.

JACK GOODY is William Wyse Professor of Social Anthropology, University of Cambridge.

NANCY LEVINE is Lecturer in Anthropology, University of California at Los Angeles.

H. S. MORRIS is Reader in Anthropology, London School of Economics, University of London.

GILL SHEPHERD has taught at the University of Sussex and is currently completing her Ph.D. thesis at the London School of Economics.

ANDREW TURTON is Lecturer in Anthropology with reference to South East Asia, School of Oriental and African Studies, University of London.

JAMES L. WATSON is Lecturer in Asian Anthropology and Head, Contemporary China Institute, School of Oriental and African Studies, University of London.

Notes

Chapter One

1. This argument applies only to *male* slaves. Female slaves were more socially mobile in these Asian closed systems. In China and in South Asia, for example, free men could take slave women as mates (or secondary wives) and their children might be legally 'free'. However, this does not mean that the systems were 'open'; male slaves were never allowed to marry 'up and in', and the female slaves thus elevated did not reproduce themselves as a class of slaves.

2. The African market may have been more complicated than it first appears. In a comprehensive survey of the Atlantic slave trade, Bean found that males brought higher prices on the open market than females. For example, males on the African side cost 129·3 per cent of the average female price and in the Americas the average male brought 113·7 per cent of female prices (Bean 1975:132). It might be argued that these price structures were dictated primarily by the high demand for male labourers in the Americas prior to the abolition of trans-Atlantic slave trading. This factor may have overshadowed the local demand for female captives in some internal African economies, a situation that could only act as a further stimulus to the raiding activities outlined in chapters 3, 4, and 5 of this book. Both males and females were thus in high demand in the African slave markets.

Significantly, Bean's study covers the years 1650–1775, while the Atlantic trade itself closed down in the period between 1774 and 1808 (Genovese 1969:97). From this time on, the New World plantation owners were dependent on slave women for the reproduction of their work forces and it is likely that the internal price structures changed accordingly (cf. Hindess and Hirst 1975:143). Genovese argues that the Africans who were settled in the Southern United States constituted the only plantation slave class in the Americas that successfully reproduced itself (1969:98).

Chapter Two

1. According to Dr. Samuel W. Cartwright, negroes were particularly subject to a disease called *Drapetomania*, which caused them to run away (Stampp 1964:112).

2. See J. R. Goody, Gonja Fieldnotes (1964) J2672.

3. 'Slaves were never natives of Taleland but hapless strangers ... found wandering in the country'. 'It is said that a man usually bought a male slave if he lacked a son to help him with his farming and to support him in his old age' (Fortes 1949:25).

4. Evidence of the large numbers of slaves in some African states is provided by the contributors to *Slavery in Africa* (eds. Suzanne Miers and Igor Kopytoff, 1977). This book appeared after I had written this essay, so I have made no attempt to incorporate or assess the data presented there. The introduction is mainly concerned with the status of the slave in African societies, whereas I have tried to deal with the wider and more slippery problem of the position of slavery, and specifically African slavery, in the history of human society. This problem directs one's attention to the question of production and reproduction rather than to status, important as the latter undoubtedly is.

5. Hopkins regards his discussion as amending two other common assumptions about traditional societies, namely, the existence of 'levelling' mechanisms and of cohesiveness due to shared values. Differentiation, he insists, exists. Of course he is right, but the remarks he quotes refer primarily to stateless societies. In any case levelling factors and ideas of shared values also play an important part in contemporary states such as Russia and the U.K. Why discount their presence in Africa?

6. The subject of slavery is surrounded by deeply held opinions and it is doubtful if those colleagues with whom I have discussed the matter will find it any easier to agree with my views than they do with each other's. But I would nonetheless record my indebtedness for discussions held, lectures heard, comments received, remarks made, to Richard Rathbone, Eugene Genovese, Robert Fogel, Edmund Leach, John Lonsdale, Claude Meillassoux and most especially to Moses Finley, to whom I offer this essay on the occasion of his retirement from the Chair of Ancient History at the University of Cambridge.

Chapter Three

1. My field research among the Gbaya and Fulbe peoples of Cameroon was carried out during twenty-one months between 1968 and 1970 and again for short periods totalling four months in 1973 and 1974. Financial support for this work was provided by the University of California at Los Angeles, the Wenner-Gren Foundation, and the Hayter Fund of University College London.

2. I wish to thank Eldridge Mohammadou for giving me access to the text of an oral history of Ngaoundere (*Taariha Ngawndere*) which he has recorded.

3. Relevant parallels for the pre-*jihad* Wolarbe social organisation include the Wodaabe of late nineteenth-century Bornu (Stenning 1959:73–76) and the Jafun of the Adamawa Plateau in Cameroon after the turn of the century (Dupire 1970:241–244).

4. Although superficially the two terms *diimaajo* and *dimo* might appear to share the same root, they in fact have nothing in common.

5. Ruxton (1916:73, 351–352), in his standard text on Maliki law, notes that the 'law strictly prohibits the enslaving of any Muhammadan'. On the other hand, he further points out that although the freeing of a slave who has become Muslim is a source of special blessing, a slave who converts is not *ipso facto* free. Froelich (1954:18) cites the case of certain formerly pagan peoples such as the Langui, a Bata group, who accompanied the Fulbe of Ngaoundere on their conquests as auxiliaries. Having converted to Islam, they eventually passed from slave to free status. But, Froelich (1954:19) also notes that slave masters might sell young slave children, an indication that second-generation slave status in itself did not exempt a slave from sale.

6. As will be apparent from the preceding comments, I would reject Lacroix's contention (1952:32; see also Goldstein 1908) that the Fulbe of the Adamawa states made little economic use of their cattle other than as a store of prestige. Most contemporary observers of the precolonial Fulbe states reported that cattle were extensively used for tribute and for exchanges for slaves. The situation was different among nomadic Fulani pastoralists, but they are not relevant to the present topic.

7. See also Rapport de M. de Brazza à M. le Sous-Secrétaire d'Etat aux Colonies, Gaza, 23 April 1892: Section Outre-Mer des Archives Nationales, Paris, Dossier Gabon-Congo III 13 (henceforth referred to as Arch. 1).

8. Arch. 1 *op. cit.* and Rapport de Mission Ponel 1892–93: Section Outre-Mer des Archives Nationales, Paris, Dossier Gabon-Congo III 14 (henceforth referred to as Arch. 2).

9. An amusing anecdote about an altercation over gambling (Flegel 1885: 19) indicates, however, that the ruler did manage to exercise some indirect authority in the Gbaya region.

10. Arch. 1 and Arch. 2, *op. cit.*

11. Arch. 1 and Arch. 2, *op. cit.* See also Rapport général sur l'expedition de 1896, A. Goujon à M. de Brazza à Libreville, Nola 23 December 1896: Section Outre-Mer des Archives Nationales, Paris, Dossier Gabon-Congo IV 13 (henceforth referred to as Arch. 3). And also Rapport de Mission Pedrizet 1897: Section Outre-Mer des Archives Nationales, Paris, Dossier Gabon-Congo III 18 (henceforth referred to as Arch. 4). And also Trois Itineraires entre la Haute-Sangha, le Haut Logone et Lai, Lt. Lancrenon (*sic*, cf. Lacrenon), April 1906: Section Outre-Mer, Dépôt d'Archives d'Aix-en-Provence, Dossier 2 D 33 (henceforth referred to as Arch. 5).

12. Arch. 1 and Arch. 4, *op. cit.*

13. Arch. 1 and Arch. 2, *op. cit.*

14. Arch. 1 and Arch. 4, *op. cit.*

15. Arch. 2, *op. cit.*

16. Arch. 1, Arch. 2, Arch. 3, and Arch. 4, *op. cit.* See also CCCCF Dossier: Rapport No. 5 de M. l'Administrateur Danvin sur les incidents de la 4CF, Affaires Gaboriaud et Denizart, no date (circa 1901–1902): Section Outre-Mer

des Archives Nationales, Paris, AEF Concessions Carton XXX (hereafter referred to as Arch. 6).

17. Arch. 1 and Arch. 6, *op. cit.*
18. Arch. 3, *op. cit.*
19. Arch. 3, *op. cit.*
20. Arch. 3, *op. cit.*
21. Arch. 1, *op. cit.*

Chapter Four

I am grateful to the SSRC who supported my original research on Comorians, to International Voluntary Service who enabled me to return to the Comoros in 1977 and to Peter Loizos, whose support has been both financial and moral. I am also grateful to Maurice Bloch for fruitful discussion of the material presented here when the original draft was being written, and to Brad Martin for translating parts of Mkelle's manuscript for me.

1. The Comoros were under the suzerainty of Kilwa in the twelfth century (Strandes 1961:85).
2. I owe this interpretation of Merina-Sakalave relations to Maurice Bloch.
3. Hafkin (1973:53) quotes from a fascinating series of letters written in the 1870s and exchanged by Mozambique Swahili and Comorian slave traders. They were seized in a Portuguese anti-slaving raid.
4. Some of these slaves were being traded by the Sakalave to the Merina, who used them for commercial agriculture (Alpers 1975:257, n.73).
5. R. F. Morton drew my attention to this reference.
6. For age grades among the Swahili see Wijeyewardene (1961:241–250). Kikuyu and Kamba age grades are described in Middleton and Kershaw (1965:32–35, 74–75). Giriama, Digo and Duruma age grades are briefly mentioned in Prins (1952:74–76).
7. Gluckman's analysis of the succession of chiefs among the matrilineal Bemba reveals striking parallels with the Ngazija sultans (Gluckman 1963: 84ff.).
8. The Comoro Islands made a Unilateral Declaration of Independence from France in July 1975 and the new socialist President, Ali Soilih, banned competitive marriages in 1976 along with various other customs which institutionalised hierarchy. He was ousted and killed in 1978 by a faction which announced a return to the old forms. It will be interesting to see whether, after a two-year pause, the population restores them intact.

Chapter Five

1. I wish to acknowledge the valuable comments and criticisms of an earlier version of this paper by G. Berg, R. Kent and B. W. Williams.

Chapter Six

1. Fieldwork was carried out in Mauritius between July 1955 and October 1957 under a grant from the Colonial Social Science Research Council (U.K.). Fieldwork was carried out in Seychelles for six months in 1960 under a grant from the Department of Technical Co-operation (U.K.) and for five months in 1975 with the assistance of a Humanities Research Fellowship from the University of California, Berkeley. Grateful acknowledgement is made for this assistance. In Mauritius my work was principally among Indo-Mauritians. In Seychelles it was chiefly among Creoles. Consequently statements about Indians derive mainly from Mauritius and statements about Creoles from Seychelles.

2. This subject is discussed in some detail in Tinker (1974:39–60). He also furnishes a map of the main districts of recruitment in India (*Ibid.* 40).

Chapter Seven

1. Audrey Hayley, Janet Bujra, Pat Caplan ad J. L. Watson kindly read and commented on an earlier version of this paper, while members of a seminar for South Asian specialists at Sussex University and of another for postgraduates in South Asian history at the School of Oriental and African Studies also gave me the benefit of their criticisms.

2. Dumont himself does not discuss the implications of slavery in South Asia in his major work *Homo Hierarchicus* (1966). Elsewhere (1967:189–191) he suggests that it was 'little developed' in ancient India.

3. It is, of course, perfectly possible that some of these tribal groups may themselves have had indigenous forms of slavery. These certainly existed in Assam to the east (see Fürer-Haimendorf 1967).

4. Buchanan throws some doubt on how widespread was the care of old slaves. He claims that many resorted to 'beggary'—but this statement would certainly have applied only to the larger population centres in Kathmandu Valley (1819:235).

5. The fact that the great majority of slaves were of lower caste than their masters probably precluded their involvement in cooking. None of the sources I have seen specifically mentions that this was a duty normally expected of household slaves; but then none indicates that it was expressly forbidden them.

6. As we might expect, there were a plethora of terms for 'slave' in multilingual India. The ancient Sanskrit texts most commonly use *dasa* to denote such a person, although originally it may have meant simply 'conquered people', and later implied forms of servitude other than slavery as well (see Chanana 1959).

7. Chanana, in a reference to ancient slavery, suggests that the 'social integration of the Indian freed slave was immediate and complete' (1960: 113).

8. Miers and Kopytoff also suggest that the essential characteristic of

African slavery is that the slaves are 'strangers in a new setting', although by this they appear to mean both persons from within the same ethnic community (but a different kin group) as well as those belonging to different communities altogether (1977:15, 17, 32, 40).

9. Chattopadhyay points to the obvious difficulty posed, on the one hand, by the need for purchasers to know the caste of their household slaves, and, on the other, the inability of slave-traders to provide such information (1977:36). Until more detailed historical data emerges, we might assume either that the great majority of transactions in slaves for household duties took place directly between individuals already known to one another, and without the intercession of traders, or, that where the latter were involved, the fiction of the slave's ritual purity was upheld, whatever the reality of the situation.

Chapter Eight

1. The data on which this chapter is based derive from fieldwork carried out in Nepal from May 1973 through June 1975. I would like to express my gratitude to the National Science Foundation and National Institute of Mental Health (USA) for funding this research. I also want to thank Tshewang Bahadur Lama of Humla who clarified several points that arose during the writing of this paper, and Tahir Ali who read and commented on various drafts.

2. See the discussion of systems of social stratification in culturally Tibetan communities presented by Fürer-Haimendorf (1964, 1975), Goldstein (1975), and Jest (1975).

3. It should be noted that indebtedness is cited as a primary cause of slavery throughout Nepal (cf. Fürer-Haimendorf 1966:23, 1975:150; Regmi 1971:117–118).

4. For a discussion of the implications of the slave's position as chattel, see Finley (1968:307).

5. Kinsmen of the buyer and seller may have been invited to witness the sale. Afterwards all individuals present partook of the barley beer, thus confirming that the contract was sealed.

6. Some writers have considered such circumstances as evidence of the impossibility of slave marriage (e.g. DeTocqueville, cited in Gutman 1976: xxi; Sio 1965:294). Others have focused on the moral ties between husbands and wives or on the recognition of the existence of these ties by the community irrespective of the legal disabilities suffered by slaves in all aspects of their lives (see, for example, Genovese 1976:125 and Gutman 1976:270 on slave marriage in the American South).

7. It is not uncommon for slaveholders to treat slaves as equivalent in certain regards to their children. Both slaves and children owed obligations to the household head cum father and both had the right to be maintained by him (Genovese 1976:73–75, 133; Tlou 1977:385). However, slaves lacked

the legal prerogatives of full household membership and remained as jural minors, and thus like children (and also like women), their entire lives.

8. It should be noted that members of one Nyinba clan address and refer to their eldest father as 'lord' (*jowo*). Local citizens state that they typically addressed slaves by the terms: 'youngest father' (*au*); 'youngest mother' (*mazhig*); 'eldest brother' (*azho*); 'eldest sister' (*azhi*), and so on. The use of only consanguineal terms precludes the suggestion of affinal connections between masters and slaves.

9. Genealogies suggest that polyandry was normative over the past two centuries as well.

10. The incidence of monogamy among these individuals may be related to their high rate of household partition. A discussion of this latter issue would extend beyond the scope of this paper.

11. Villagers from Limi, a community that is four days' journey northwest, often spend the winter in Nyinba villages. The women weave and men make sheepskin coats. But due to the time of year, the women contribute minimally to agricultural efforts. I do not know how common this seasonal migration was in the past.

12. Nepal has a high rate of population growth, with dramatic population increases in many villages (for a discussion of population growth among the Gurung, see Macfarlane 1976).

13. At the present time at least, the rate of growth in the Nyinba population seems to be far lower than that reported for Nepal as a whole. Nor does village size seem to have increased substantially in the last four generations (cf. Levine 1977).

Chapter Nine

1. The first period of research (1969–70) was supported by the Foreign Area Fellowship Program, SSRC-ACLS (USA) and by the Center for Chinese Studies, University of California at Berkeley. The second period (1977–78) was made possible by grants from the School of Oriental and African Studies, the Social Science Research Council (UK), and the Joint Committee on Contemporary and Republican China, SSRC-ACLS (USA).

2. In this paper the term 'elite' is used in a restricted sense, referring to people who were members of dominant, landowning lineages. There were, of course, wealthy as well as poor families in 'elite' lineages, but everyone benefited from the power vested in the corporate group. The distinction between 'elite' and 'non-elite' is well understood by people in the New Territories; it is reflected in the local dialect by the dichotomous terms *daai jok* ('big lineages') and *sai ga* ('little families').

3. All Chinese terms are given in the local Cantonese dialect, Yale Romanisation system, modified to exclude tone indicators.

4. In particularly bad years the market was so flooded that destitute mothers often gave their daughters to passing strangers rather than see them die (see e.g., Clementi 1929:49).

5. These prices are in Mexican silver dollars, a standard currency in late-Imperial China.

6. Involving 176 cases in twelve elite communities.

7. Unlike Indians, the Chinese are not generally fussy about the status of their cooks and they have few qualms about sharing meals with outsiders. However, Cantonese villagers in the New Territories refuse to eat with two categories of people (assuming they are identified as such): former *sai man* and funeral specialists. The latter are men who handle corpses and dig graves.

8. *Sai man* had inexpensive and very abbreviated funerals with a minimum of ritual. This shows that the slaves were so powerless they were not even feared as ghosts. Normally the Cantonese are preoccupied with proper funeral rituals to ensure that the deceased do not return to settle old scores (see e.g., Potter 1974). Most *sai man* were buried without coffins, an unthinkable fate for ordinary peasants.

9. Interviews in Hong Kong by Dr. John Burns; informant was a recent émigré from Toishan District, Kwangtung Province.

10. Interviews of Chinese émigré in Hong Kong by Professors William Parish and Martin K. Whyte.

11. During my own visit to a village near Canton (Hua County) in 1978 local residents reacted with great discomfort whenever I raised the question of *sai man* slavery. Judging from the ancestral halls in the area, this community was once the stronghold of an elite lineage.

12. I regret that I am unable to include a discussion of James P. McGough's recent work on Chinese servitude; his paper, a detailed critique of Watson (1976), arrived after this book was in press: see 'Slavery and Servitude in Traditional China', paper presented at the Annual Meeting of the American Anthropological Association, November 1978.

Chapter Ten

1. Lingat (1931:61, n. 1) gives the following table of comparison:
1,200,000 cowries (*bia*) = 12 *tamlung* = 48 ticals (or *baht*)
1,400,000 „ „ = 14 „ = 56 „ „
and
1 tical = 15 grams of silver at the legal rate.
But according to Griswold and Prasert (1975:72) the silver/cowrie exchange rate varied enormously from time to time.

L

Bibliography

Chapter One

Bean, Richard N. (1975) *The British Trans-Atlantic Slave Trade, 1650–1775*. New York: Arno Press.

Bloch, Maurice (ed.) (1975) *Marxist Analyses and Social Anthropology*. London: Malaby.

Bohannon, Paul (1963) *Social Anthropology*. New York: Holt, Rinehart and Winston.

David, Paul A., Herbert Gutman, *et. al.* (1976) *Reckoning with Slavery: A Critical Study in the Quantitative History of American Negro Slavery*. New York: Oxford University Press.

Davis, David B. (1966) *The Problem of Slavery in Western Culture*. Ithaca: Cornell University Press.

Elkins, Stanley M. (1959) *Slavery: A Problem in American Institutional and Intellectual Life*. New York: Grosset and Dunlap.

Evans-Pritchard, E. E. (1940) *The Nuer*. Oxford: Clarendon.

Finley, Moses I. (1959) Was Greek Civilization Based on Slave Labour? *Historia* 8:145–164.

—— (1968) Slavery. *International Encyclopedia of the Social Sciences* 14:307–313.

—— (1976) A Peculiar Institution? *Times Literary Supplement*, 2 July 1976, 3877:819–821.

Fogel, Robert W. and Stanley L. Engerman (1974) *Time on the Cross: The Economics of American Negro Slavery*. Boston: Little, Brown and Co.

Fortes, Meyer (1949) *The Web of Kinship among the Tallensi*. Oxford: Clarendon.

Genovese, Eugene D. (1969) The American Slave Systems in World Perspective, in his *The World the Slaveholders Made*. New York: Vintage Books.

—— (1975) *Roll, Jordan, Roll: The World the Slaves Made*. New York: Vintage Books.

Godelier, Maurice (1977) *Perspectives in Marxist Anthropoloy*. (Trans. by Robert Brain). Cambridge: Cambridge University Press.

Goody, Jack (1971) *Technology, Tradition, and the State in Africa*. Oxford: Oxford University Press.

Gutman, Herbert G. (1975) *Slavery and the Numbers Game: A Critique of 'Time on the Cross'.* Urbana: University of Illinois Press.

—— (1976) *The Black Family in Slavery and Freedom, 1750–1925.* New York: Pantheon Books.

Haskell, Thomas L. (1975) The True and Tragical History of 'Time on the Cross'. *New York Review of Books,* 2 Oct. 1975, 22(15):33–39.

Hindess, Barry and Paul Q. Hirst (1975) *Pre-Capitalist Modes of Production.* London: Routledge and Kegan Paul.

Hopkins, Keith (1967) Slavery in Classical Antiquity, in *Caste and Race: Comparative Approaches* (eds.) Anthony de Reuck and Julie Knight. London: Churchill.

Lasker, Bruno (1950) *Human Bondage in Southeast Asia.* Chapel Hill: University of North Carolina Press.

Leach, Edmund R. (1967) Caste, Class and Slavery: The Taxonomic Problem, in *Caste and Race: Comparative Approaches* (eds.) Anthony de Reuck and Julie Knight. London: Churchill.

Meillassoux, Claude (1975) (ed.) *L'Esclavage en Afrique précoloniale.* Paris: Maspero.

—— (1978) Correspondence (on slavery). *Economy and Society* 7:321–331.

Meirs, Suzanne and Igor Kopytoff (eds.) (1977) *Slavery in Africa: Historical and Anthropological Perspectives.* Madison: University of Wisconsin Press.

Mendelsohn, Isaac (1949) *Slavery in the Ancient Near East.* New York: Oxford University Press.

Nadel, S. F. (1942) *A Black Byzantium.* London: Oxford University Press.

Nieboer, H. J. (1910) *Slavery as an Industrial System: Ethnological Researches* (2nd ed.) The Hague: Martinus Nijhoff.

Radcliffe-Brown, A. R. (1952) *Structure and Function in Primitive Society.* New York: Free Press.

Smith, M. G. (1960) *Government in Zazzau.* London: Oxford University Press.

Tuden, Arthur (1970) Slavery and Stratification among the Ila of Central Africa, in *Social Stratification in Africa* (eds.) Arthur Tuden and Leonard Plotnicov. New York: Free Press.

Tuden, Arthur and Leonard Plotnicov (1970) Introduction, in *Social Stratification in Africa* (eds.) A. Tuden and L. Plotnicov. New York: Free Press.

Walton, Gary M. (ed.) (1975) A Symposium on 'Time on the Cross'. *Explorations in Economic History* 12 (fall).

Watson, James L. (1976) Chattel Slavery in Chinese Peasant Society: A Comparative Analysis. *Ethnology* 15:361–375.

Wilbur, C. Martin (1943) *Slavery in China During the Former Han Dynasty.* Chicago Field Museum of Natural History, Anthropological Series, vol. 34.

Chapter Two

Adams, R. McC. (1966) *The Evolution of Urban Society*. London.

Baer, G. (1967) Slavery in Nineteenth-Century Egypt. *J. African Hist.* 8:417–441.

Baks, C. J. C. *et al.* (1966) Slavery as a System of Production in Tribal Societies. *Bijdragen tot de Taal-, Land- en Volkenkunde* 122:90–109.

Bateson, G. (1958) *Naven*. Stanford (1st edition Cambridge, 1936).

Bazin, J. (1974) War and Slavery in Segu. *Economy and Society* 3:107–144.

—— (1975) Guerre et servitude à Segou, in C. Meillassoux (ed.) *L'Esclavage en Afrique précoloniale*. Paris.

Bennett, N. R. (1960) Christian and Negro Slavery in Eighteenth-Century North Africa. *J. African Hist.* 1:65–82.

Binger, L. G. (1892) *Du Niger au Golfe de Guinée*. Paris.

Braimah, J. A. and Goody, J. R. (1967) *Salaga: the Struggle for Power*. London.

Childe, V. G. (1954) Early Forms of Society, in *A History of Technology*, C. Singer, E. J. Holmyard and A. R. Hall, eds. *Vol. 1*. Oxford.

Coquéry-Vidrovitch, C. (1969) Recherches sur un mode de production africain. *Le Pensée* 144:61–78.

Curtin, P. D. (1969) *The Atlantic Slave Trade: A Census*. Madison, Wisconsin.

Davidson, B. (1970) *Black Mother*. London.

Dieng, A. A. (1974) Classes sociales et mode de production esclavagiste en Afrique de l'Ouest. *Cahiers du Centre d'Etudes et de Recherches Marxistes*. Paris.

Domar, E. D. (1970) The Causes of Slavery or Serfdom: a Hypothesis. *J. Economic Hist.* 30:18–32.

Doutté, E. (1909) *Magie et religion dans l'Afrique du Nord*. Paris.

Driver, G. R. and Miles, J. C. (1952) *The Babylonian Laws, Vols. 1 & 2*. Oxford.

Dupuis, J. (1824) *Journal of a Residence in Ashantee*. London.

Fage, J. (1969a) *A History of West Africa*. Cambridge.

—— (1969b) Slavery and the Slave-trade in the Context of West African History. *J. African Hist.* 10:393–404.

Finley, M. I. (1968) Slavery. *International Encyclopedia of the Social Sciences* 14:307–313. New York.

—— (1973) *The Ancient Economy*. London.

Fisher, A. G. B. and Fisher, H. J. (1970) *Slavery and Muslim Society in Africa*. London.

Fortes, M. (1949) *The Web of Kinship among the Tallensi*. London.

Goody, J. R. (1956) *The Social Organisation of the LoWiili*. London.

Held, G. J. (1957) *The Papuas of Waropen*. The Hague.

Hindess, B. and Hirst, P. (1975) *Pre-capitalist Modes of Production*. London.

Hobhouse, L. T., Wheeler, G. C. and Ginsberg, M. (1930) *The Material and Social Institutions of the Simpler Peoples*. London.

Hopkins, A. G. (1973) *An Economic History of West Africa*. London.

Ibn Batuta (1969) *Voyages d'Ibn Batuta* (transl. Defremery and Sanguinetti). Paris.

Jewitt, J. R. (1898) (1815) *The Adventures of John Jewitt*. London.

Kinnier Wilson, J. V. (1972) *The Nimrod Wine Lists: A Study of Administration at the Assyrian Capital in the Eighth Century, B.C.* British School of Archaeology in Iraq.

Köbben, A. J. P. (1967) Why Exceptions? The Logic of Cross-cultural Analysis. *Current Anthropology* 8:3–34.

Kramer, S. N. (1956) *From the Tablets of Sumer*. Indian Hills, Colorado.

Landsberger, B. (1955) *Materialen zum Sumerischen Lexicon, Vol XII*. Rome.

—— (1969) *Materialen zum Sumerischen Lexicon, Vol. III*. Rome.

Last, M. (1967) *The Sokoto Caliphate*. London.

Law, R. C. C. (1967) The Garamantes and Trans-Saharan Enterprise in Classical Times. *J. African Hist.* 8:181–200.

Lovejoy, P. E. (1978) Plantations in the Economy of the Sokoto Caliphate. *J. African Hist.* 19:341–368.

MacLeod, W. C. (1925) Debtor and Chattel Slavery in Aboriginal North America. *American Anthropologist* 27:370–80.

—— (1928) Economic Aspects of Indigenous American Slavery. *American Anthropologist* 39:632–50.

Malamat, A. (1971) Mari. *The Biblical Archaeologist* 34:2–22.

Meakin, J. E. B. (1902) *The Moors*. London.

Meillassoux, C. (ed.) (1975) *L'Esclavage en Afrique précoloniale*. Paris.

Miers, S. and Kopytoff, I. (eds.) (1977) *Slavery in Africa: Historical and Anthropological Perspectives*. Madison, Wisconsin.

Miller, J. (1969) *The Spice Trade of the Roman Empire*. Oxford.

Murdock, G. P. (1966) Ethnographic Atlas: a Summary. *Ethnology* 6:109–236.

Nieboer, H. J. (1900) *Slavery as an Industrial System*. The Hague.

Oppenheim, A. L. (1964) *Ancient Mesopotamia: A Portrait of a Dead Civilization*. Chicago.

Prins, A. H. J. (1961) *The Swahili-Speaking Peoples of Zanzibar and the East African Coast* (Ethnographic Survey of Africa, International African Institute). London.

Rodney, W. M. (1970) *A History of the Upper Guinea Coast 1545–1800*. Oxford.

Ruyle, E. E. (1973) Slavery, Surplus, and Stratification on the Northwest Coast: the Ethnoenergetics of an Incipient Stratification System. *Current Anthropology* 14:603–631.

Ryder, A. F. C. (1969) *Benin and the Europeans 1485–1897*. London.

Shabayni, S. (1967) *An Account of Timbuctoo and Housa*. London (reprint).

Siegel, B. J. (1945) Some Methodological Considerations for a Comparative Study of Slavery. *American Anthropologist* 47:357–392.

Stampp, K. M. (1964) (1956) *The Peculiar Institution: Negro Slavery in the American South*. London.

Strathern, A. (1971) *The Rope of Moka*. Cambridge.

Terray, E. (1974) Long-distance Trade and the Formation of the State. *Economy and Society* 3:315–45.

—— (1975) La captivité dans le royaume abron du Gyaman, in *L'Esclavage en Afrique précoloniale* (ed.) C. Meillassoux.

Vicedom, G. F. and Tischner, H. (1943–48) *Die Mbowamb*, 3 vols. Hamburg.

Chapter Three

Abdoullaye, Hamadjoda and Eldridge Mohammadou (1972) *Les Yillaga de la Benoue: Ray ou Rey-Bouba*. Yaounde: Ministère de l'Information et de la Culture.

Abubakar, Sa'ad (1972) The Establishment of Fulbe Authority in the Upper Benue Basin, 1809–47. *Savanna* 1:67–80.

Althusser, Louis and Etienne Balibar (1970) *Reading Capital*. London: NLB.

Anon. (1893) Congo Français. *Bulletin du Comité de l'Afrique Française* 4:6.

—— (1895) Dans la Haute Sangha: La Mission Clozel. *Bulletin du Comité de l'Afrique Française* 5:133–135.

Barth, Heinrich (1857) *Travels and Discoveries in North and Central Africa*. 5 vols. London: Longman, Brown, Green, Longmans & Roberts.

Brussaux, E. (1908) Notes sur la Race Baya. *Bulletins et Mémoires de la Société d'Anthropologie de Paris*, Série V, 9:80–102.

Burnham, Philip (in press) Notes on Gbaya History, in *Contribution de la recherche ethnologique à l'histoire des civilisations du Cameroun* (ed.) Claude Tardits. Paris: CNRS.

Büttner, Thea (1967) On the Social-Economic Structure of Adamawa in the Nineteenth Century. Slavery or Serfdom?, in *African Studies* (ed.) Walter Markov. Leipzig: Karl Marx Universitat.

Charreau, P. (1905) Un coin du Congo. *Mémoires de la Société Nationale des Sciences Naturelles et Mathematiques de Cherbourg* 35:1–212.

Coquery-Vidrovitch, Catherine (1972) *Le Congo au temps des grandes compagnies concessionaries: 1898–1930*. Paris: Mouton & Co.

—— (1975) Research on an African Mode of Production. *Critique of Anthropology* 4 & 5: 38–71.

Dupire, Marguerite (1970) *Organisation sociale des Peul*. Paris: Plon.

Fisher, Allan and Humphrey Fisher (1970) *Slavery and Muslim Society in Africa*. London: C. Hurst & Co.

Flegel, Eduard (1883) Reise nach Adamawa. *Petermanns Mitteilungen* 29:241–249.

—— (1885) *Lose Blätter aus dem Tagebuche meiner Haussa-Freunde* ... Hamburg: L. Friederichsen & Co.

Friedman, Jonathan (1976) Marxist Theory and Systems of Total Reproduction. *Critique of Anthropology* 2(7) 3–16.

Froelich, J. C. (1954) Le commandement et l'organisation sociale chez les Foulbe de l'Adamawa. *Etudes Camerounaises* 45–46.

Goldstein, F. (1908) Viehthesaurierung in Haussa Fulbien und in Adamaua. *Globus* 93:373–376.

Goody, Jack (1971) *Technology, Tradition, and the State in Africa*. London: Oxford University Press for International African Institute.

Harttmann, Hermann (1927) Ethnographische Studie über die Baja. *Zeitschrift für Ethnologie* 59:1–61.

Hill, Polly (1976) From Slavery to Freedom: the Case of Farm Slavery in Nigerian Hausaland. *Comparative Studies in Society and History* 18:395–426.

Kopytoff, Igor and Suzanne Miers (1977) Introduction, in *Slavery in Africa* (eds.) S. Miers and I. Kopytoff. Madison: University of Wisconsin Press.

Lacroix, P. F. (1952) Matériaux pour servir à l'histoire des Peul de l'Adamawa. *Etudes Camerounaises* 37–38:3–62.

Lenfant, Commandant (1909) *La découverte des grandes sources du centre de l'Afrique*. Paris. Hachette.

Loefler, Capitaine (1907) Les régions comprises entre la Haute-Sanga, le Chari et le Cameroun. *Bulletin du Comité de l'Afrique Française* 9:224–240.

Meillassoux, Claude (1971) Introduction, in *The Development of Indigenous Trade and Markets in West Africa* (ed.) C. Meillassoux. London: Oxford University Press for the International African Institute.

—— (1975) Introduction, in *L'Esclavage en Afrique précoloniale* (ed.) C. Meillassoux. Paris: Maspero.

Miers, Suzanne and Igor Kopytoff (eds.) (1977) *Slavery in Africa*. Madison: University of Wisconsin Press.

Mizon, L. (1895) Itinéraire de la source de la Benoué au confluent des rivières Kadei et Mambéré. *Bulletin de la Société de Géographie* (de Paris). Série 7, 16:342:369.

Mohammadou, Eldridge (in press) L'Implantation des Foulbe dans l'Adamawa, in *Contribution de la recherche ethnologique à l'histoire des civilisations du Cameroun* (ed.) Claude Tardits. Paris: CNRS.

Passarge, Siegfried (1895) *Adamaua*. Berlin: Dietrich Reimer.

Ponel, Edouard (1896) La Haute Sangha. *Bulletin de la Société de Géographie* (de Paris) Série 7:17:188–211.

Robinson, C. H. (1896) *Hausaland*. London.

Ruxton, F. H. (1916) *Maliki Law*. London: Luzac & Co.

Stenning, Derrick (1959) *Savannah Nomads*. London: Oxford University Press for the International African Institute.

Strümpell, Kurt (1912) Die Geschichte Adamauas. *Mitteilungen der Geogr. Gesell. in Hamburg*. 26:46–107.

Terray, Emmanuel (1975) La captivité dans le royaume Abron du Gyaman, in *L'Esclavage en Afrique précoloniale* (ed.) C. Meillassoux. Paris: Maspero.

Tessmann, Gunter (1934) *Die Baja: Teil I: Materielle und seelische Kultur.* Stuttgart: Strecker und Schröder.

—— (1937) *Die Baja: Teil II: Geistige Kultur.* Stuttgart: Strecker und Schröder.

Chapter Four

Information on slaves, where not drawn from published sources as indicated, is from my own fieldnotes. Comorians of both free and slave descent discussed slavery with me when I was in Kenya and Ngazija.

Alpers, Edward A. (1967) *The East African Slave Trade.* Historical Association of Tanzania, paper 3. Nairobi: East African Publishing House.

—— (1969) Trade, State and Society among the Yao in the Nineteenth Century. *Journal of African History* 10.3:405–420.

—— (1975) *Ivory and Slaves in East and Central Africa.* London: Heinemann.

Beachey, R. W. (1976) *The Slave Trade of Eastern Africa.* London: Rex Collings.

Boteler, Thomas (1835) *Narrative of a Voyage of Discovery to Africa and Arabia Performed by His Majesty's Ships Leven and Barracouta from 1821 to 1826.* vol. II. London: Richard Bentley.

Christie, James (1876) *Cholera Epidemics in East Africa.* London: Macmillan and Co.

Cooper, Frederick (1977) *Plantation Slavery on the East Coast of Africa.* New Haven and London: Yale University Press.

Coupland, Reginald (1938) *East Africa and its Invaders.* Oxford: Clarendon Press.

Decary, Raymond (1960) *L'Ile Nosy Bé de Madagascar.* Paris: Éditions Maritimes et D'Outre-Mer.

Faurec, Urbain (1941) *L'Archipel aux Sultans Batailleurs.* Tananarive: Éditions Musée de Tananarive.

Fischer, François (1949) *Grammaire-Dictionnaire Comorien.* Strasbourg: Societe d'Édition de la Basse-Alsace.

Fontoynont and Raomandahy (1937) *La Grande Comore.* Tananarive: Imprimerie Moderne de L'Emyrne.

Fort, Jacques n.d. Note sur le Magnahouli. Paris: BDPA (roneo).

Freeman-Grenville, G. S. P. (1965) *The French at Kilwa Island.* Oxford: Clarendon Press.

Gevrey, Alfred (1870) *Essai sur les Comores.* Pondicherry: Saligny.

Gluckman, Max (1963) *Order and Rebellion in Tribal Africa.* London: Cohen and West.

Grandidier, A. and G. (eds.) (1903) *Collection des ouvrages anciens concernant Madagascar.* I, 1500–1613 Paris: Comité de Madagascar.

—— (1904) *Ibid.,* II, 1613–1640.

—— (1905) *Ibid.,* III, 1640–1716.

Hafkin, Nancy J. (1973) Trade, Society and Politics in Northern Mozambique c. 1753–1913. Boston: Unpublished Ph.D. Dissertation, Boston University.

Harries, Lyndon (ed.) (1977) *The Swahili Chronicle of Ngazija by Said Bakari bin Sultan Ahmed.* Bloomington: African Studies Program, Indiana University.

Lienhardt, Peter (1959) The Mosque College of Lamu and its Social Background. *Tanganyika Notes and Records.* 53:228–242, October.

Livingstone, David (1865) *Narrative of an Expedition to the Zambezi and its Tributaries.* London: Murray.

Martin, Bradford G. (1971) Notes on some Members of the Learned Classes of Zanzibar and East Africa in the Nineteenth Century. *African Historical Studies* 4(3): 525–545.

—— (1976) *Muslim Brotherhoods in Nineteenth-Century Africa.* Cambridge: Cambridge University Press.

Meillassoux, Claude (1975) (ed.) *L'Esclavage en Afrique Précoloniale.* Paris: Maspéro.

—— (1978) Correspondence (on slavery). *Economy and Society* 7:321–331.

Middleton, John and Greet Kershaw (1965) *The Kikuyu and Kamba of Kenya.* Ethnographic Survey of Africa, East Central Africa, Part V. London: International African Institute.

Mkelle, Burhan b. Mohammed (c. 1930) *Ta'rikh jaziratina al-Qumr al-Kubra* ('A history of our island of Grande Comore') m.s. in possession of Mohammed b. Burhan Mkelle, Dar-es-Salaam.

Morton, Roger F. (1976) Slaves Fugitives and Freedmen on the Kenya Coast 1873–1907. Unpublished Ph.D. Dissertation, Syracuse University.

Nicholls, C. S. (1971) *The Swahili Coast: Politics Diplomacy and Trade on the East African Littoral 1798–1856.* St. Antony's College, Oxford, Publications no. 2. London: Allen and Unwin.

Prins, A. H. J. (1952) *The Coastal Tribes of the North-Eastern Bantu.* Ethnographic Survey of Africa, East Central Africa, Part III. London: International African Institute.

Robineau, Claude (1966) *Societé et économie d'Anjouan.* Paris: O.R.S.T.O.M.

Russell, Mrs. Charles E. (1935) *General Rigby, Zanzibar and the Slave Trade, with Journals Dispatches etc.* London: Allen and Unwin.

Shepherd, Gillian M. (1977) Two Marriage Forms in the Comoro Islands: an Investigation. *Africa* 47(4):344–359.

Strandes, Justus (1961) *The Portuguese Period in East Africa,* translated from German by J. F. Wallwork and edited with notes by J. S. Kirkman from the original edition (Berlin 1899). Nairobi: East African Publishing House.

Sulivan, George L. (1873) *Dhow Chasing in Zanzibar Waters.* London: Sampson Low, Marston, Low and Searle.

Vérin, Pierre (1972) *Histoire ancienne du Nord-Ouest de Madagascar.* Taloha 5. Tananarive: Université de Madagascar.

Viallard, Paule (1971) Les antiquités de la Grande Comore. *Civilisation du*

326   Bibliography

Sud-Ouest: archéologie, anthropologie sociale et art de Madagascar. Taloha 4. Tananarive: Université de Madagascar.

Villiers, Alan (1940) *Sons of Sindbad.* London: Hodder and Stoughton.

Wijeyewardene, G. E. T. (1961) Some Aspects of Village Solidarity in Ki-Swahili Speaking Coastal Communities of Kenya and Tanganyika. Unpublished Ph.D. Thesis, University of Cambridge.

Chapter Five

Bloch, Maurice (1971a) *Placing the Dead: Tombs, Ancestral Villages, and Kinship Organisation in Madagascar.* London and New York: Seminar Press.

—— (1971b) The Implications of Marriage Rules and Descent Categories for Merina Social Structure. *American Anthropologist* 73:164–178.

—— (1975) Property and the End of Affinity, in *Marxist Analyses and Social Anthropology* (ed.) Maurice Bloch. London: Malaby Press, A.S.A. Studies, no. 2.

—— (1977) The Disconnection between Rank and Power as a Process, in *The Evolution of Social Systems* (ed.) J. Friedman and M. J. Rowlands.

de Copalle, (1970) *Voyage à la capitale du roi Radama 1825–1826* reprinted from the *Bulletin* of the Académie Malgache in Documents Anciens sur Madagascar I Association Malgache Archéologie.

Coulaud, D. (1973) *Les Zafimaniry: un groupe ethnique de Madagascar à la poursuite de la forêt.* Tananarive: Fanotam-Boky Malagasy.

Curtin, P. D. (1969) *The Atlantic Slave Trade: A Census.* Madison: University of Wisconsin Press.

Dez, J. (1965) Les taux ruraux coutumiers à Madagascar, in *Etudes de droit Africain et de droit Malgache* (ed.) J. Poirier. Paris: Etudes Malgaches 16 Cuzas.

Dumaine de la Josserie, J. P. (1810) Voyage fait au pays d'Aucaye dans l'île de Madagascar en 1790, in *Annales des Voyages de la géographie et de l'histoire* (ed.) Malte Brun, Vol. XI.

Ellis, W. (1838) *History of Madagascar.* London: Fisher.

—— (1858) *Three Visits to Madagascar.* London: John Murray.

Filliot, J. M. (1974) *La traite des esclaves vers les Mascareignes au 18ième Siècle.* Paris: O.R.S.T.O.M.

Hayes, E. H. (1923) *David Jones: Dauntless Pioneer.* London: Teachers and Taught.

Kopytoff, Igor and Suzanne Miers (1977) African 'Slavery' as an Institution of Marginality, in *Slavery in Africa: Historical and Anthropological Perspectives* (eds.) S. Miers and I. Kopytoff. Madison: University of Wisconsin Press.

Meillassoux, C. (ed.) (1975) *L'Esclavage en Afrique précoloniale.* Paris: Maspero.

Razafindratovo, J. (1971) Hiérarchie et tradition chez les Tsimahafotsy (Imerina). Unpublished Thesis, Paris.

Sibree, J. (1924) *Fifty Years in Madagascar*. London: Allen & Unwin.

Terray, E. (1975) La captivité dans le royaume Abron du Gyaman, in *L'Esclavage en Afrique précoloniale* (ed.) C. Meillassoux. Paris: Maspero.

—— (1977) De l'exploitation. *Dialectiques* 21:134–143.

Verin, P. (1964) Les Zafimaniry et leur art. Un groupe forestier continuateur d'une tradition esthétique malgache méconnue. *Revue de Madagascar*, no. 27.

Wurtz, J. (1970) Evolution des structures foncières entre 1900 et 1968 à Ambohiboanjo (Madagascar). *Etudes rurales* nos. 37, 38, 39.

Chapter Six

Alpers, E. A. (1975) *Ivory and Slaves: Changing Pattern of International Trade in East Central Africa to the Later Nineteenth Century*. Berkeley, Los Angeles: Univ. of California Press.

Baker, P. (1972) *Kreol: A Description of Mauritian Creole*. London: C. Hurst.

Banks, L. (1840) *The Seychelles*. Mauritius.

Barnwell, P. J. (1942) Jean Joseph Lebrun, in *Dictionary of Mauritian Biography* 7: 212.

Barnwell, P. J. & Toussaint, Auguste (1949) *A Short History of Mauritius*. London, New York, Toronto: Longmans Green.

Beidelman, T. O. (1959) *A Comparative Analysis of the Jajmani System*. New York: J. J. Augustin.

Benedict, B. (1958) Education without Opportunity: Education, Economics and Communalism in Mauritius. *Human Relations* 12: 315–329.

—— (1961) *Indians in a Plural Society: A Report on Mauritius*. London. H.M.S.O.

—— (1965) *Mauritius: The Problems of a Plural Society*. London: Pall Mall.

—— (1967) Caste in Mauritius, in *Caste in Overseas Indian Communities* (ed.) B. M. Schwartz. San Francisco: Chandler.

—— (1970) *People of the Seychelles*. 3rd ed. London: H.M.S.O.

Beyts, H. N. D. (1861) Report on his Mission to India. Port Louis.

Billiard, A. (1822) *Voyage aux colonies orientales*. Paris: La librairie francaise de l'advocat.

Darwin, C. (1933) *Charles Darwin's Diary of the Voyage of H.M.S. Beagle* (ed.) Nora Barlow. Cambridge: Univ. Press.

Delaplace, P. F. & Pivault, P. J. M. (1932) *Le P. Jacques-Desiré Laval: apôtre de l'ile Maurice*. Paris: Gabriel Beauchesne.

Ehrlich, A. S. (1971) History, Ecology, and Demography in the British Caribbean: an Analysis of East Indian Ethnicity. *Southwestern Journal of Anthropology* 27: 166–180.

Epstein, S. (1967) Productive Efficiency and Customary Systems of Rewards in Rural South India, in *Themes in Economic Anthropology* (A. S. A. Monogr. 6) (ed.) R. Firth. London: Tavistock.

Filliot, J. M. (1974) *La traite des esclaves vers les Mascareignes au xviiie siécle*. Paris: Orstom.

Goody, J. (1976). *Production and Reproduction: A Comparative Study of the Domestic Domain.* Cambridge: Univ. Press.

Gordon, Sir A. H. (1894) *Mauritius: Records of Private and Public Life (1871–1874).* 2 vols. Edinburgh: R. & R. Clark.

Graham, G. S. (1967) *Great Britain in the Indian ocean: A Study of Maritime Enterprise 1810–1850.* Oxford: Clarendon Press.

Grant, C. (1801) *The History of Mauritius or the Isle of France and the Neighboring Islands from Their First Discovery to the Present Time.* London: W. Bulmer.

—— (1886) *Letters from Mauritius in the Eighteenth Century.* Mauritius.

Gutman, H. G. (1976) *The Black Family in Slavery and Freedom, 1750–1925.* New York: Pantheon.

Hazarresingh, K. (1950) *A History of Indians in Mauritius.* Mauritius: General Printing and Stationery.

Hugon, T. *Notes on Immigration 1857–58.* Ms. report to H. E. The Governor. Mauritius.

Howell, B. M. (1950) Mauritius 1832–1849: A Study of a Sugar Colony. Unpublished Thesis, University of London.

Jayawardena, C. (1968) Migration and Social Change: a Survey of Indian Communities Overseas. *The Geographical Review* 58: 426–449.

Kuczynski, R. R. (1949) *Demographic Survey of the British Colonial Empire,* vol. II. London, New York, Toronto: Oxford Univ. Press.

Lionnet, G. (1972) *The Seychelles.* Newton Abbot: David and Charles.

Milbert, M. J. (1812) *Voyage pittoresque à l'île de France, au Cap de Bonne Esperance et à l'île de Teneriffe.* 2 vols. & atlas. Paris: A. Nepveu.

Nevadomsky, J. J. (1977) The Changing Family Structure of the East Indians in Rural Trinidad. Unpublished Thesis, University of California, Berkeley.

Noble, C. F. (1793) *Some Remarks Made at Mauritius Called by the French Isle de France: and at the Island Bourbon.* London: G. Bigg.

Owen, W. F. W. (1833) *Narrative of Voyages to Explore the Shores of Africa, Arabia, and Madagascar; Performed in H.M. Ships Leven and Barracouta.* 2 vols. London: Richard Bentley.

Précis Showing the Different Phrases Through which Immigration to Mauritius from the East Indies Has Passed Before it Assumed its Present Form. (1905) Port Louis: Mauritius Archives.

Report on Liberated Africans in the Seychelles Islands (No. 108 of 1881.) Seychelles.

Report of the Slave Trade (1829) B. P. P. XXV (292). London.

Reports: The Past and Present State of Her Majesty's Colonial Possessions. Part I. West Indies and Mauritius (1863). B. P. P. XXXVII. London.

Royal Society of Arts and Sciences of Mauritius, Extracts from the Transactions (1932) Port Louis: La typographie moderne.

Schapera, I. (1962) Should Anthropologists be Historians? *The Journal of the Royal Anthropological Institute* 92: 143–156.

Seychelles Archives Vols. B 33, B 85, C/AM/16.

Smith, R. T. (1956) *The Negro Family in British Guiana: Family Structure and Social Status in the Villages.* London: Routledge & Kegan Paul.

—— (1962) *British Guyana.* London: Oxford Univ. Press.

Stack, C. B. (1974) *All Our Kin: Strategies for Survival in a Black Community.* New York: Harper & Row.

Tinker, H. (1974) *A New System of Slavery: The Export of Indian Labour Overseas 1830–1920.* London: Oxford Univ. Press.

Toussaint, A. (1972) *Histoire des îles Mascareignes.* Paris: Berger-Levrault.

Unienville, M. C. A. M. d'. (1838) *Statistique de l'île Maurice et ses dependences.* 3 vols. Paris: Gustave Barba.

Webb, A. W. T. (1966) *The Story of Seychelles.* 3rd ed. Seychelles.

Chapter Seven

Adam, Leonard (1949–50) Criminal Law and Procedure in Nepal a Century Ago: Notes left by Brian H. Hodgson. *The Far Eastern Quarterly* 9: 146–168.

Adam, William (1840) *The Law and Custom of Slavery in British India.* Boston: Weeks, Jordan and Co.

Adhikari, Krishna Kant (1976) Criminal Cases and their Punishments before and during the Period of Jang Bahadur. *Contributions to Nepalese Studies* 3:105–116.

Banaji, D. R. (1933) *Slavery in British India.* Bombay: D. B. Taraporevala Sons.

Basham, Arthur L. (1963) *The Wonder that was India.* Calcutta: Orient Longmans.

Borgström, Bengt-Erik (1976) *The Patron and the Pancha: Village Values and Panchayat Democracy in Nepal.* Stockholm: Department of Social Anthropology, University of Stockholm.

Buchanan, Francis Hamilton (1807) *A Journey from Madras through the Countries of Mysore, Canara, and Malabar.* London: T. Cadell and W. Davies.

—— (1819) *An Account of the Kingdom of Nepal, and of the Territories Annexed to this Dominion by the House of Gorkha.* Edinburgh: Constable.

Bujra, Janet M. (1978) Female Solidarity and the Sexual Division of Labour. Introduction to *Women United, Women Divided: Cross-Cultural Perspectives on Female Solidarity* (eds.) A. Patricia Caplan and Janet M. Bujra. London: Tavistock.

Caplan, A. Patricia (1972) *Priests and Cobblers: a Study of Social Change in a Hindu Village in Western Nepal.* San Francisco: Chandler.

—— (1975) *Choice and Constraint in a Swahili Community: Property, Hierarchy and Cognatic Descent on the East African Coast.* London: Oxford University Press.

Caplan, Lionel (1970) *Land and Social Change in East Nepal: A Study of Hindu-Tribal Relations.* London: Routledge and Kegan Paul.

—— (1975) *Administration and Politics in a Nepalese Town: The Study of a District Capital and its Environs.* London: Oxford University Press.

Cavenagh, Capt. Orfeur (1851) *Rough Notes on the State of Nepal, its Government, Army and Resources.* Calcutta: W. Palmer.

Chanana, Dev Raj (1959) The Sudra, the Dasa, and Manu. *The Indian Journal of Social Work* 20:201:208.

—— (1960) *Slavery in Ancient India: as Depicted in Pali and Sanskrit Texts.* New Delhi: People's Publishing House.

Chattopadhyay, A. Kumar (1977) *Slavery in the Bengal Presidency: 1772–1843.* London Golden Eagle Publishing House.

Cooper, Frederick (1977) *Plantation Slavery on the East Coast of Africa.* New Haven: Yale University Press.

Dumont, Louis (1966) *Homo Hierarchicus: The Caste System and its Implications.* London: Weidenfeld and Nicolson.

—— (1967) Discussion: Classical and American Slavery Compared, in *Caste and Race: Comparative Approaches* (eds.) Anthony de Reuck and Julie Knight. London: Churchill.

Elkins, Stanley M. (1967) Slavery and its Aftermath in the Western Hemisphere, in *Caste and Race: Comparative Approaches* (eds.) Anthony de Reuck and Julie Knight. London: Churchill.

—— (1976) *Slavery: a Problem in American Institutional and Intellectual Life* (Third Revised Edition). Chicago: University of Chicago Press.

Fallers, Lloyd, A. (1973) *Inequality: Social Stratification Reconsidered.* Chicago: University of Chicago Press.

Finley, Moses I. (1968) Slavery. *International Encyclopedia of the Social Sciences* 14:307–313.

Fürer-Haimendorf, Christoph von (1966) Unity and Diversity in the Chetri Caste of Nepal, in *Caste and Kin in Nepal, India and Ceylon* (ed.) Christoph von Fürer-Haimendorf. Bombay: Asia.

—— (1967) *Morals and Merit: A Study of Values and Social Controls in South Asian Societies.* London: Weidenfeld and Nicolson.

Harper, Edward B. (1968) Social Consequences of an 'Unsuccessful' Low Caste Movement, in *Social Mobility in the Caste System in India* (ed.) James Silverberg. The Hague: Mouton.

Hjelje, Benedicte (1967) *Slavery and Agricultural Bondage in South India in the Nineteenth Century.* Copenhagen: The Scandinavian Institute of Asian Studies.

Hodgson, Brian H. n.d. *Judicial Systems of Nepal* (Unpublished Notes in the India Office Library), Vol. IV, 6.

Hopkins, Keith (1967) Slavery in Classical Antiquity, in *Caste and Race: Comparative Approaches* (eds.) Anthony de Reuck and Julie Knight. London: Churchill.

Indian Law Commissioners (ILC) (1841) *Report Relating to Slavery in the East Indies.* London: Parliamentary Papers.

Jain, M. S. (1972) *Emergence of a New Aristocracy in Nepal (1837–1858).* Agra: Shri Ram Mehra.

Kennion, R. L. (1925) Abolition of Slavery in Nepal. *Nineteeth Century* 98:381–389.

Khare, R. S. (1976) *The Hindu Hearth and Home*. New Delhi: Vikas.

Kirkpatrick, Colonel William (1811) *An Account of the Kingdom of Nepaul, Being the Substance of Observations Made during a Mission to that Country in the Year 1793*. London: William Miller.

Kumar, Dharma (1965) *Land and Caste in South India*. Cambridge: Cambridge University Press.

Landon, Perceval (1928) *Nepal* (Vol. II). London: Constable.

Lane, Ann. J. (ed.) (1971) *The Debate over Slavery: Stanley Elkins and his Critics*. Urbana: University of Illinois.

Leach, Edmund R. (1967) Caste, Class and Slavery: The Taxonomic Problem, in *Caste and Race: Comparative Approaches* (eds.) Anthony de Reuck and Julie Knight. London: Churchill.

Lévi, Sylvain (1905) *Le Népal: étude historique d'un royaume Hindou*. Paris. Ernest Leroux.

Macdonald, Alexander W. (1975) The Hierarchy of the Lower Jāt, in *Essays on the Ethnology of Nepal and South Asia*. Kathmandu: Ratna Pusta Bhandar.

Miers, Suzanne and Igor Kopytoff (1977) African 'Slavery' as an Institution of Marginality. Introduction to *Slavery in Africa: Historical and Anthropological Perspectives* (eds.) Suzanne Miers and Igor Kopytoff. Madison: The University of Wisconsin Press.

Nadel, S. Fred (1942) *A Black Byzantium*. London: Oxford University Press.

Nieboer, H. J. (1900) *Slavery as an Industrial System: Ethnological Researches*. The Hague: Martinus Nijhoff.

Passin, Harold (1967) Discussion: Characterization of Caste and Class Systems, in *Caste and Race: Comparative Approaches* (eds.) Anthony de Reuck and Julie Knight. London: Churchill.

Prindle, Peter H. (1974) Socio-Economic Relationships in a Brahmin Village in East Nepal. Unpublished Ph.D. Thesis, Washington State University.

Rana, Chandra Shumshere (1925) *Appeal to the People of Nepal for the Emancipation of Slaves and Abolition of Slavery in the Country*. Kathmandu: Subba Rama Mani.

Regmi, Mahesh Chandra (1969) Documents on Slavery. *Regmi Research Series* 1:44–45.

—— (1971) *A Study in Nepali Economic History, 1768–1846*. New Delhi: Manjusri.

Saletore, Bhasker Anand (1934) *Social and Political Life in the Vijayanagara Empire*. (Vol. II) Madras: B. G. Paul.

Sanwal, Rami D. (1976) *Social Stratification in Rural Kumaon*. Delhi: Oxford University Press.

Sarup, V. L. (1921) Some Aspects of Slavery. *Journal of the Punjab Historical Society* 8:174–184.

Sharma, P. R. (1977) Caste, Social Mobility and Sanskritization: a Study of Nepal's Old Legal Code. *Kailash* 4:277–299.

Siegel, Bernard J. (1945) Some Methodological Considerations for a Comparative Study of Slavery. *American Anthropologist* 47:357–392.

Simon, Kathleen (1929) *Slavery*. London: Hodder and Stoughton.

Srivastava, Ram P. (1966) Tribe-Caste Mobility in India and the Case of Kumaon Bhotias, in *Caste and Kin in Nepal, India and Ceylon* (ed.) Christoph von Fürer-Haimendorf. Bombay: Asia.

Turner, Ralph L. (1931) *A Comparative and Etymological Dictionary of the Nepali Language*. London: Routledge and Kegan Paul.

Watson, James L. (1976) Chattel Slavery in Chinese Peasant Society: a Comparative Analysis. *Ethnology* 15:361–375.

Wright, Daniel (ed.) (1877) *History of Nepal*. Cambridge: Cambridge University Press.

Chapter Eight

Bohannan, Paul (1963) *Social Anthropology*. New York: Holt, Rinehart and Winston.

DeVos, George (1966) Essential Elements of Caste: Psychological Determinants in Structural Theory, in *Japan's Invisible Race* (eds.) George DeVos and Hiroshi Wagatsuma. Berkeley: University of California Press.

Finley, Moses I. (1967) Review of Davis, The Problem of Slavery in Western Culture. *New York Review of Books* 8 (Jan. 26): 6–10.

—— (1968) Slavery. *International Encyclopedia of the Social Sciences* 14:307–313.

Fogel, Robert W. and Stanley L. Engerman (1974) *Time On The Cross: The Economics of American Negro Slavery*. Boston: Little, Brown and Co.

Fürer-Haimendorf, Christoph von (1964) *The Sherpas of Nepal*. Berkeley: University of California Press.

—— (1966) Unity and Diversity in the Chetri Caste of Nepal, in *Caste and Kin in Nepal, India and Ceylon* (ed.) C. von Fürer-Haimendorf. London: Asia Publishing House.

—— (1974) The Changing Fortunes of Nepal's High Altitude Dwellers, in *Contributions to the Anthropology of Nepal* (ed.) C. von Fürer-Haimendorf. Warminster, England: Aris and Phillips.

—— (1975) *Himalayan Traders*. London: John Murray.

Genovese, Eugene D. (1976) *Roll, Jordan, Roll*. New York: Random House.

Goldstein, Melvyn C. (1975) Report on Limi Panchayat, Humla District, Karnali Zone. *Contributions to Nepalese Studies* 2:89–101.

Gutman, Herbert G. (1976) *The Black Family In Slavery and Freedom, 1750–1925*. New York: Pantheon Books.

Hindess, Barry and Paul Q. Hirst (1975) *Pre-Capitalist Modes of Production*. London: Routledge and Kegan Paul.

Jest, Corneille (1975) *Dolpo. Communautés de langue Tibetaine du Nepal*. Paris: Editions du C.N.R.S.

Kopytoff, Igor and Suzanne Miers (1977) Introduction, in *Slavery in Africa* (eds.) S. Miers and I. Kopytoff. Madison: University of Wisconsin Press.

Levine, Nancy E. (1977) The Nyinba. Population and Social Structure in a Polyandrous Society. Unpublished Ph.D. Dissertation, University of Rochester.

Macfarlane, Alan (1976) *Resources and Population. A Study of the Gurungs of Nepal.* Cambridge: University of Cambridge Press.

Netting, Robert McC. (1972) Of Men and Meadows: Strategies of Alpine Land Use. *Anthropological Quarterly* 45:132–144.

Radcliffe-Brown, A. R. (1952) *Structure and Function in Primitive Society.* Glencoe: Free Press.

Regmi, Mahesh C. (1971) *A Study in Nepali Economic History, 1768–1846.* New Delhi: Manjusri Publishing House.

Rhoades, Robert E. and Stephen I. Thompson (1975) Adaptive Strategies in Alpine Environments: Beyond Ecological Particularism. *American Ethnologist* 2:535–551.

Sio, Arnold, A. (1965) Interpretations of Slavery. *Comparative Studies in Society and History* 7:289–308.

Tlou, Thomas (1977) Servility and Political Control: Botlhanka Among the BaTawana of Northwestern Botswana, in *Slavery in Africa* (eds.) S. Miers and I. Kopytoff. Madison: University of Wisconsin Press.

Vansina, Jan (1965) *Oral Tradition.* Chicago: Aldine.

Vaughn, James H. (1977) *Mafakur*: A Limbic Institution of the Margi, in *Slavery in Africa* (eds.) S. Miers and I. Kopytoff. Madison: University of Wisconsin Press.

Chapter Nine

Baker, Hugh D. R. (1966) The Five Great Clans of the New Territories. *Journal of the Hong Kong Branch of the Royal Asiatic Society* 6:25–47.

—— (1968) *A Chinese Lineage Village: Sheung Shui.* Stanford: Stanford University Press.

Blake, C. Fredric (1975) Negotiating Ethnolinguistic Symbols in a Chinese Market Town. Unpublished Ph.D. Thesis, University of Illinois. University Microfilms no. 75–24, 263.

Chen Han-seng (1936) *Agrarian Problems in Southernmost China.* Shanghai: Kelly and Walsh.

Clementi, C. (1929) Dispatch on Mui-tsai, no. 18, in *Hong Kong Papers Relative to the Mui-tsai Question.* London: H.M.S.O., Cmd. 3424.

Croll, Elizabeth (1978) The Negotiation of Marriage in the People's Republic of China. Unpublished Ph.D. Thesis, School of Oriental and African Studies, University of London.

Doolittle, Justus (1866) *Social Life of the Chinese, Vol. II.* London: Sampson Low and Sons.

Eberhard, Wolfram (1962) *Social Mobility in Traditional China.* Leiden: E. J. Brill.

Eitel, E. J. (1879) Report on Chinese Slavery, in *Mui Tsai in Hong Kong and Malaya* (ed.) W. W. Woods. London: H.M.S.O., Colonial no. 125.

Finley, Moses I. (1959) Was Greek Civilisation Based on Slave Labour? *Historia* 8:145–164.

Freedman, Maurice (1957) *Chinese Family and Marriage in Singapore.* Colonial Research Studies, no. 20. London.

—— (1958) *Lineage Organization in Southeastern China.* London: Athlone Press.

—— (1966) *Chinese Lineage and Society: Fukien and Kwangtung.* London: Athlone Press.

Gazetteer (1819) *Hsin-an Hsien-chih* (Hsin-an County Gazetteer). Taipei: Ch'eng-wen Reprint Series.

Goody, Jack (1976) *Production and Reproduction: A Comparative Study of the Domestic Domain.* Cambridge: Cambridge University Press.

Hopkins, Keith (1967) Slavery in Classical Antiquity, in *Caste and Race: Comparative Approaches* (eds.) Anthony de Reuck and Julie Knight. London: J. & A. Churchill, Ltd.

Hsieh Yu-lin and Liu Tuan-sheng (1939) Agricultural Labourers in Kwangsi, in *Agrarian China* (ed.) Institute of Pacific Affairs. London: George Allen and Unwin.

Hsü Lun (1964) *Shen-ma shih nu-li chih-tu.* (What is the Institution of Slavery?) Shanghai: People's Publisher.

Jaschok, Maria n.d. *Mui Jai* Slavery and Upper Class Women in Hong Kong. Manuscript, School of Oriental and African Studies, London.

Keswick, W. (1879) Conditions of Prostitution in Hong Kong, in *Hongkong Report of the Commissioners to Inquire into the Working of 'The Contagious Diseases Ordinance, 1867'.* Hong Kong: Government Printers.

Kopytoff, Igor and Suzanne Miers (1977) African 'Slavery' as an Institution of Marginality, in *Slavery in Africa: Historical and Anthropological Perspectives* (eds.) S. Miers and I. Kopytoff. Madison: University of Wisconsin Press.

Lasker, Bruno (1950) *Human Bondage is Southeast Asia.* Chapel Hill: University of North Carolina Press.

Leach, Edmund (1967) Caste, Class and Slavery: The Taxonomic Problem, in *Caste and Race: Comparative Approaches* (eds.) Anthony de Reuck and Julie Knight. London: J. & A. Churchill, Ltd.

Levy, Howard S. (1967) *Chinese Footbinding: The History of a Curious Erotic Custom.* New York: Bell Publishing Co.

Liu Hui-chen Wang (1959) *The Traditional Chinese Clan Rules.* Association for Asian Studies Monograph no. 7. Locust Valley, New York: J. J. Augustin, Inc.

Loseby, F. H. (ed.) (1936) *Mui-tsai in Hong Kong: Report of the Committee Appointed by the Governor.* London: H.M.S.O., Cmd. 5121.

Mai Mei-sheng (1933) *Fan-tui hsü pi shih-lieh.* (Short History of the Opposition to Female Slavery.) Hong Kong: Fuk Hing Publishers.

Man Genealogy n.d. Handwritten Genealogy (in Chinese) of the *Man* Lineage at San Tin, New Territories. Photographed by J. L. Watson, 187 pp.

Meijer, Marinus J. (1979) Slavery at the End of the Ch'ing Dynasty, in *China's Legal Tradition* (eds.) J. A. Cohen, F. M. Ch'en and R. Edwards. Princeton: Princeton University Press.

Osgood, Cornelius (1963) *Village Life in Old China: A Community Study of Kao Yao, Yunnan*. New York: Ronald Press.

Parish, William and Martin K. Whyte (1978) *Village and Family in Contemporary China*. Chicago: University of Chicago Press.

Potter, Jack M. (1968) *Capitalism and the Chinese Peasant: Social and Economic Change in a Hong Kong Village*. Berkeley: University of California Press.

—— (1974) Cantonese Shamanism, in *Religion and Ritual in Chinese Society* (ed.) Arthur P. Wolf. Stanford: Stanford University Press.

Pulleyblank, E. G. (1958) The Origins and Nature of Chattel Slavery in China. *Journal of the Economic and Social History of the Orient* 1:185–220.

Purcell, Victor (1967) *The Chinese in Malaya*. London: Oxford University Press.

Radcliffe-Brown, A. R. (1952) *Structure and Function in Primitive Society*. New York: Free Press.

Russell, J. (1887) Report on Child Adoption and Domestic Service among Hongkong Chinese, in *Mui-tsai in Hong Kong* (ed.) F. H. Loseby. London: H.M.S.O., Cmd. 5121.

Shih Hsing (1973) *Nu-li she-hui*. (Slave Society.) Shanghai: People's Publisher.

Skinner, G. William (1976) Mobility Strategies in Late Imperial China: A Regional Analysis, in *Regional Analysis, Vol. 1: Economic Systems* (ed.) Carol A. Smith. New York: Academic Press.

Smith, M. G. (1960) *Government in Zazzau*. New York: Oxford University Press.

Tang Genealogy n.d. Handwritten Genealogy (in Chinese) of the *Tang* Lineage at Ha Tsuen, New Territories. Photographed by R. S. Watson, 374 pp.

Topley, Marjorie (1975) Marriage Resistance in Rural Kwangtung, in *Women in Chinese Society* (eds.) Margery Wolf and Roxane Witke. Stanford: Stanford University Press.

Tuden, Arthur and Leonard Plotnicov (eds.) (1970) *Social Stratification in Africa*. New York: Free Press.

van der Sprenkel, Sybille (1962) *Legal Institutions in Manchu China*. London: Athlone Press.

Vogel, Ezra F. (1969) *Canton Under Communism: Programs and Politics in a Provincial Capital, 1949–1968*. Cambridge: Harvard University Press.

Wang Yi-t'ung (1953) Slavery and other Comparable Social Groups during the Northern Dynasties. *Harvard Journal of Asiastic Studies* 16:293–364.

Watson, James L. (1975a) Agnates and Outsiders: Adoption in a Chinese Lineage. *Man* (N.S.) 10:293–306.

—— (1975b) *Emigration and the Chinese Lineage.* Berkeley: University of California Press.

—— (1976) Chattel Slavery in Chinese Peasant Society: A Comparative Analysis. *Ethnology* 15:361–375.

—— (1977) Hereditary Tenancy and Corporate Landlordism in Traditional China: A Case Study. *Modern Asian Studies* 11:161–182.

Watson, Rubie S. n.d. Marriage and Affinity in a Chinese Lineage. Field Report no. 2 (manuscript), London School of Economics.

Wilbur, C. Martin (1943) *Slavery in China During the Former Han Dynasty.* Chicago Field Museum of Natural History, Anthropological Series, vol. 34.

Wolf, Arthur P. (1968) Adopt a Daughter-in-law, Marry a Sister: A Chinese Solution to the Problem of the Incest Taboo. *American Anthropologist* 70:864–874.

—— (1974) Marriage and Adoption in Northern Taiwan, in *Social Organization and the Applications of Anthropology: Essays in Honor of Lauriston Sharp* (ed.) Robert J. Smith. Ithaca: Cornell University Press.

—— (1975) The Women of Hai-shan: A Demographic Portrait, in *Women in Chinese Society* (eds.) Margery Wolf and Roxane Witke. Stanford: Stanford University Press.

Wolf, Arthur P. and Huang Chieh-shen n.d. *Marriage and Adoption in China, 1845–1945.* Stanford: Stanford University Press (in press).

Wolf, Margery (1972) *Women and the Family in Rural Taiwan.* Stanford: Stanford University Press.

Woods, W. W. (ed.) (1937) *Mui Tsai in Hong Kong and Malaya: Report of Commission.* London: H.M.S.O., Colonial no. 125.

Woon Yuen-fong (1975) Social Organization of South China: The Case of the Kwaan Lineage of Hoi-p'ing. Unpublished Ph.D. Thesis, University of British Columbia.

Yang, C. K. (1959) *A Chinese Village in Early Communist Transition.* Cambridge: M.I.T. Press.

Chapter Ten

Akin Rabibhadana (1969) *The Organization of Thai Society in the Early Bangkok Period 1782–1873.* Cornell University Southeast Asia Program Data Paper No. 74. Ithaca: Cornell University.

—— (1975) Clientship and Class Structure in the Early Bangkok Period, in *Change and Persistence in Thai Society* (eds.) G. William Skinner and A. Thomas Kirsch. Ithaca: Cornell University Press.

Anderson, Perry (1974) *Passages from Antiquity to Feudalism.* London: New Left Books.

Anuman Rajadhon (1956) *ruang loek that nai ratchakan ha.* (The Abolition of Slavery in the Fifth Reign.) Bangkok.

Bowring, John (1857) *The Kingdom and People of Siam, with a Narrative of the Mission to that Country in 1855.* London: John W. Parker.

Bühler, Georg (transl.) (1969) *The Laws of Manu.* New York: Dover.

Chaianan Samutwanit (1976) *sakdina kap phatanakan khong sangkhom thai.* (*sakdina* and the Development of Thai Society). Bangkok: H. J. K. Nam Akson Printers.

Charnvit Kasetsiri (1976) *The Rise of Ayudhya: A History of Siam in the Fourteenth and Fifteenth Centuries.* Kuala Lumpur: Oxford University Press.

Child, Jacob T. (1892) *The Pearl of Asia: Reminiscences of the Court of a Supreme Monarch, or Five Years in Siam.* Chicago: Donahue, Henneberg.

Chit Phumisak (1974) *chomna sakdina thai.* (The True Face of Thai Feudalism.) Bangkok: chomrom nangsue saengtawan.

—— (1976) *khwampenma khong kham syam, thai, lao, khom; lae laksana thang sangkhom khong chu chon chat.* (History of the Words Siam, Thai, Lao, and Khmer . . .) Bangkok: Social Science Association of Thailand.

Colquhoun, Archibald Ross (1885) *Amongst the Shan.* London: Field and Tuer.

Crawfurd, John (1830) *Journal of an Embassy from the Governor-General of India to the Courts of Siam and Cochin-China, Exhibiting a View of the Actual State of those Kingdoms.* 2 Vols. London: Henry Colburn and Richard Bentley.

—— (1915) *The Crawfurd Papers: A Collection of Official Records Relating to the Mission of Dr. Crawfurd sent to Siam by the Government of India in the Year 1821.* Bangkok: National Library.

Cruikshank, R. B. (1975) Slavery in Nineteenth-Century Siam. *Journal of the Siam Society* 63 (pt. 2):315–333.

Dang Nghiem Van (1972) An Outline of the Thai of Viet Nam. *Vietnamese Studies* 32:143–196.

Duby, Georges (1968) *Rural Economy and Country Life in the Medieval West.* London: Edward Arnold.

—— (1973) *Guerriers et paysans: viie–xiie siècle: premier essor de l'économie Européenne.* Paris: Gallimard.

Elliott, David L. (1977) *Thailand: Origins of Military Rule.* London: Zed Press.

Engels, Frederick (1972) *The Origin of the Family, Private Property and the State.* London: Lawrence and Wishart.

Finley, Moses I. (1973) *The Ancient Economy.* London: Chatto and Windus.

Graham, Walter A. (1924) *Siam: A Handbook of Practical, Commercial and Political Information.* 2 Vols. London: Alexander Maring.

Griswold, A. B. and Prasert na Nagara (1975) On Kingship and Society at Sukhodaya, in *Change and Persistence in Thai Society* (eds.) G. William Skinner and A. Thomas Kirsch. Ithaca: Cornell University Press.

Hallett, Holt S. (1890) *A Thousand Miles on an Elephant in the Shan States.* Edinburgh: Blackwood.

Heide, J. Homan van der (1906) The Economical Development of Siam During the Last Half Century. *Journal of the Siam Society* 3 (1):74–109.

Hindess, Barry and Paul Q. Hirst (1975) *Pre-Capitalist Modes of Production.* London: Routledge and Kegan Paul.

Ingram, James C. (1971) *Economic Change in Thailand 1850–1970.* Stanford: Stanford University Press.

La Loubère, Simon de (1969) *The Kingdom of Siam.* Kuala Lumpur: Oxford University Press. (Reprint of 1693 *A New Historical Relation of the Kingdom of Siam.* 2 Vols., transl. from the French. London: T. Horne.)

Lasker, Bruno (1950) *Human Bondage in Southeast Asia.* Chapel Hill: University of North Carolina Press.

Le Boulanger, Paul (1931) *Histoire du Laos Français.* Paris: Plon. (Reprinted 1969, Farnborough: Gregg International.

Lingat, Robert (1931) *L'esclavage privé dans le vieux droit Siamois (avec une traduction des anciennes lois siamoises sur l'esclavage).* Paris: Domat-Montchrestien.

Meillassoux, Claude (ed.) (1975) *L'esclavage en Afrique précoloniale.* Paris: Maspéro.

Miers, Suzanne and Igor Kopytoff (eds.) (1977) *Slavery in Africa.* Madison: University of Wisconsin Press.

Notton, Camille (ed. and transl.) (1926–1932) *Annales du Siam.* 3 Vols. Paris: Charles-Lavauzelle (Vols. 1 & 2), Paul Geuthner (Vol. 3).

Pallegoix, Jean Baptiste (1854) *Description du royaume Thai ou Siam.* 2 Vols. Paris: La Mission de Siam. (Reprinted 1969, Farnborough: Gregg International.)

Sao Saimong Mangrai (1965) *The Shan States and the British Annexation.* Cornell University Southeast Asia Program Data Paper No. 57. Ithaca: Cornell University.

Seni Pramoj (1967) *kotmai samai ayuthaya.* (Law in the Ayuthaya Period.) Bangkok: khana kammakan cat ngan anusorn ayuthaya.

Sharp, Lauriston and Lucien M. Hanks (1978) *Bang Chan: Social History of a Rural Community in Thailand.* Ithaca: Cornell University Press.

Skinner, G. William (1957) *Chinese Society in Thailand: an Analytical History.* Ithaca: Cornell University Press.

Smith, Samuel J. (transl.) (1880) *Siamese Domestic Institutions: Old and New Laws on Slavery.* Bangkok: S. J. Smith.

Smyth, Herbert Warington (1898) *Five Years in Siam.* 2 Vols. London: John Murray.

Sommai Premchit (ed. and transl.) (1975a) *kotmai lanna: phak pariwat lamdap thi 3.* (Lanna Custom Law: Transliteration Series 3.) Chiengmai: Faculty of Social Sciences, Chiengmai University.

—— (1975b) *mangraisat: phak pariwat lamdap thi 1.* (Mangrai Custom Law: Transliteration Series 1.) Chiengmai: Faculty of Social Sciences, Chiengmai University.

Steinberg, David J. (ed.) (1971) *In Search of Southeast Asia: A Modern History*. London: Pall Mall Press.

Tachard, Guy (1686) *Voyage de Siam des pères Jésuites envoyez par le Roy aux Indes et à la Chine*. Paris.

Tambiah, Stanley J. (1976) *World Conqueror and World Renouncer: A Study of Buddhism and Polity in Thailand against a Historical Background*. Cambridge: Cambridge University Press.

Tej Bunnag (1977) *The Provincial Administration of Siam 1892–1915: The Ministry of Interior under Prince Damrong Rajanubhab*. Kuala Lumpur: Oxford University Press.

Thompson, Virginia (1941) *Thailand: The New Siam*. New York: Macmillan.

Turton, Andrew (1976) Northern Thai Peasant Society: a case study of Political and Jural Structures at the Village Level and their Twentieth-Century Transformations. Unpublished Ph.D. Dissertation. University of London.

Van Vliet, Jeremias (1975) *The Short History of the Kings of Siam*. (ed.) David K. Wyatt. Bangkok: Siam Society.

Wales, H. G. Quaritch (1934) *Ancient Siamese Government and Administration*. London: Quaritch.

Watson, James L. (1976) Chattel Slavery in Chinese Peasant Society: A Comparative Analysis. *Ethnology* 15:361–375.

Wyatt, David K. (ed. and transl.) (1975) *The Crystal Sands: The Chronicles of Nagara Sri Dharmaraja*. Cornell University Southeast Asia Program Data Paper No. 98. Ithaca: Cornell University.

Chapter Eleven

Boyle, Frederick (1865) *Adventures among the Dayaks of Borneo*. London: Hurst & Blackett.

Jones, L. W. (1960) *Sarawak: Report on the Census of Population taken on 15th June, 1960*. Kuching.

Morris, H. S. (1953) *Report on a Melanau Sago Producing Community in Sarawak*. London: H.M.S.O.

—— (1967) Shamanism among the Oya Melanau, in *Social Organisation: Essays Presented to Raymond Firth* (ed.) Maurice Freedman. London: Frank Cass.

Rousseau, J. (1974) The Social Organisation of the Baluy Kayan. Unpublished Ph.D. Thesis, University of Cambridge.

Wilkinson, R. J. (1959) *A Malay-English Dictionary*. London: Macmillan.

Index